The Essential Catholic Survival Guide

THE STAFF OF
CATHOLIC ANSWERS

The Essential Catholic Survival Guide

*Answers to
Tough Questions
About the Faith*

CATHOLIC ANSWERS
SAN DIEGO
2005

Published by Catholic Answers, Inc.
P.O. Box 199000
San Diego, CA 92159-9000
(888) 291-8000 (orders)
(619) 387-0042 (fax)
www.catholic.com (web)

NIHIL OBSTAT: I have concluded that the materials presented in this work are free of doctrinal or moral errors.

Bernadeane Carr, STL, Censor Librorum, August 10, 2004

IMPRIMATUR: In accord with 1983 CIC 827 permission to publish this work is hereby granted.

+Robert H. Brom, Bishop of San Diego, August 10, 2004

Cover by Devin Schadt, Davenport, Iowa

Printed in the United States of America
ISBN 1-888992-81-6

Contents

- What is the doctrine of infallibility, and does it apply only to the pope?
- What mandate did Christ give that indicates papal infallibility?
- How can objections to papal infallibility be answered?
- Don't the numerous "bad popes" show that the papacy is not protected by infallibility?

Scripture and Tradition

- What are the differences between Catholic and Protestant views of Scripture and its authority?
- What arguments support each view?
- What does the Bible say about its own authority?
- What does the Catholic Church mean by Tradition?
- Why do Fundamentalists argue with this understanding of Tradition?

- What is *sola scriptura*?
- How do Protestants explain their belief in biblical inspiration, and why it is the sole rule of faith?
- How do Catholics prove that the Bible is inspired?
- Is Protestant reasoning for belief in biblical inspiration adequate?

- What is the first thing you should ask a missionary at your door?
- What Bible verses will he likely bring up in response, and why don't these verses answer the question?
- What is the Bible's role in Christian faith?
- How do the writings of the early Church Fathers de-

monstrate the need for the Catholic Church's teaching authority?

- What do Catholics and Protestants believe about development of doctrine and public revelation?
- What does the Catholic Church teach about further development of doctrine, and what examples support this understanding?
- Why wasn't Church doctrine defined clearly in the beginning, so that confusion could be avoided later?
- Why do Fundamentalists believe that Catholic "development of doctrine" is actually the accumulation of pagan beliefs and rites?

- What two philosophies do translators use?
- What are the advantages and disadvantages of the resulting translations?
- How does a Catholic find a balance between the two types of translation philosophies?
- What are examples of different Bible translations, and how would each be classified by translation philosophy?
- Which translation is best for serious Bible study?
- Does Catholic Answers recommend a translation?

Mary and the Saints

- Can the saints hear us when we pray to them?
- Doesn't prayer to the saints violate the sole mediatorship of Christ?
- Isn't prayer to the saints considered contact with the dead?

- How can the saints, mere human beings, hear the prayers of millions of Catholics, in many different countries, praying in many different languages, all at the same time?
- Why would anyone want the saints, rather than Jesus, to pray for him?

- How does contemporary understanding of worship distort its meaning?
- What are the different types of honor?
- How is the honor we give to living people (public officials, parents, etc.) related to the honor given to the saints?
- What biblical form of honor is most important in honoring the saints?

- Aren't Catholics practicing idolatry with images of Christ and the saints, not to mention the statues in their churches?
- What is the difference between a religious use of images and the worship of images?
- Why do Catholics and Protestants number the Ten Commandments differently?
- What does the Catholic Church teach about idolatry?

- Why do non-Catholics dislike the mingling of spirit and matter, the sacramental aspect of Catholicism?
- Why do relics of the saints present the biggest problem for non-Catholics?
- Aren't most relics frauds?
- Does the Bible support veneration of relics?
- What did the early Christians say about relics?

Sacraments

- Does the Catholic Church teach that Christ is re-crucified at every Mass? Didn't Christ die "once for all"?
- Which Old Testament passage predicted that Christ would offer a true sacrifice to God using the elements of bread and wine?
- In the Old Testament, a repeated blood sacrifice was necessary for remission of sins. How can the bloodless sacrifice of the Catholic Mass be effective?

- Why is the Holy Eucharist the most important sacrament?
- How should a Catholic prepare for reception of Communion?
- Can non-Catholics ever receive Communion? What about non-Christians?
- How should one receive Communion?

- Where is this sacrament in the Bible?
- What gifts does the anointing of the sick provide?
- What did the early Church Fathers say about the practice of anointing the sick?
- Is there any value to suffering?

- Why do Fundamentalists claim that addressing priests as "father" is an unbiblical practice?
- Do the Old and New Testaments agree about the use of the term *father*?
- What did Jesus mean when he said, "Call no man your father on earth"?
- What biblical passage clearly points to the spiritual fatherhood of priests?

• Don't indulgences duplicate or even negate the work of Christ?
• How do you gain an indulgence?

Salvation

• What are the two kinds of grace?
• Is it possible to commit spiritual suicide?
• Does sanctifying grace actually cleanse the soul, or is the soul simply covered in the cloak of Christ's righteousness?
• How do Catholic and Protestant views of justification and sanctification differ?
• Can you lose sanctification?

• Do Catholics believe that they must be "born again" to be saved?
• Does the Bible use the phrase "born again"?
• What did the early Christians say about the connection between baptism and being "born again"?
• What are the effects of baptism?
• What did Martin Luther and John Calvin say about baptism?

• What do many Protestants believe about salvation?
• Is this view of salvation found in the Bible?
• What crucial aspect of redemption do Protestants fail to understand?
• What does the Catholic Church teach about salvation?
• How should a Catholic respond when asked if he is saved?

Last Things

Morality and Science

Anti-Catholicism

- Why do Catholics tell their sins to a priest instead of directly to God?

- Why do some people believe that Catholicism is a pagan religion, and which books promote this idea?
- How does a round Communion wafer become evidence of paganism?
- What is the pagan-influence fallacy, and how can it be combated?
- Are the claims that Catholicism is pagan difficult to refute?

- Was there only one Inquisition, or did several inquisitions take place?
- Fundamentalists write about the "scandal" of the Inquisition. What sources do they use for information?
- Is it true that more people died under the Inquisition than in any war or plague?
- Who were the Catharists, and are Fundamentalists right to identify with them?
- What really happened during the Inquisition, and why?

- What is the video *Catholicism: Crisis of Faith* about, and who is its producer?
- Why is this product packaged as a Catholic video?
- Isn't a real Catholic priest interviewed in this video?
- What deceptions and fallacies are found in *Catholicism: Crisis of Faith*?

Non-Catholic Groups

• What is heresy, and how is it different from other sins against the faith?
• What three conditions must be present for someone to be considered a heretic?
• What heresies plagued the early Christians, and what did these heresies teach?
• Why is Protestantism considered a heresy?

• What caused the division between Eastern and Western Christendom?
• When did the schism between the East and West occur?
• Why did the Eastern Orthodox church fragment into many different churches?
• Was the *Filioque* disagreement a main cause of the division?
• What do the Orthodox churches believe about the pope's role within the Church?

• How did Fundamentalism originate, and where did the name come from?
• What are the five essential doctrines of Fundamentalism?
• How do Fundamentalists recognize their belief in Christ's divinity, and how is this different from the Catholic understanding?
• What are the distinguishing marks of Fundamentalism?

- What are some sample openings Witnesses may use when engaging potential converts?
- How are Witnesses instructed to respond to "conversation stoppers" such as "I'm busy" or "I have my own religion"?
- How do they respond to people who say they are not interested in the Jehovah's Witnesses?
- What lessons can Catholics learn from Jehovah's Witnesses?

- What two magazines are published by Jehovah's Witnesses?
- Why was the Bible translation committee kept secret, and why are there no author bylines in Jehovah's Witness magazines?
- What articles are found in these magazines?
- What "techniques" do these publications use to attack the Catholic Church?

- Is the Watch Tower Society reliable?
- Can you trust the New World translation of the Bible?
- Is God's name "Jehovah"?
- Do humans possess an immortal soul?
- Is hell real or not?

- Are Jesus and Michael the archangel really the same person?
- Is Jesus a creature or the Creator?
- Is the Holy Spirit a force?
- Was Christ bodily resurrected?
- Is heaven just for the "anointed class"?

Practical Apologetics

- What are the best ways to deal with different religious opinions?
- "I don't want to be divisive in my dealings with others, can't I focus on the areas where we all agree?"

- What are the most essential books a Catholic apologist should have on his bookshelf?
- Where can one get copies of these works?
- Are some works more useful than others?
- Which Bible does Catholic Answers recommend?

- Why is a strong prayer life essential to Catholics (as well as to others)?
- Why does the Catholic Church teach formulaic prayers?
- What are some fundamental Catholic prayers?
- Why do Catholics pray to Mary, the angels, and the saints?

- Is *sola scriptura* valid?
- What scriptural evidence supports the doctrine of faith and works?
- Where is the Trinity mentioned in the Bible?
- Are Christ's divinity and the Real Presence in the Eucharist both supported by Scripture?
- Did Catholics make up the papacy, purgatory, honoring Mary, and praying to the saints?

I

Peter and the Papacy

There is ample evidence in the New Testament that Peter was first in authority among the apostles. Whenever they were named, Peter headed the list (Matt. 10:1–4; Mark 3:16–19; Luke 6:14–16; Acts 1:13); sometimes the apostles were referred to as "Peter and those who were with him" (Luke 9:32). Peter was the one who generally spoke for the apostles (Matt. 18:21; Mark 8:29; Luke 12:41; John 6:68–69), and he figured in many of the most dramatic scenes (Matt. 14:28–32; 17:24–27; Mark 10:23–28). On Pentecost it was Peter who first preached to the crowds (Acts 2:14–40), and he worked the first healing in the Church age (Acts 3:1–7). It is Peter's faith that will strengthen his brethren (Luke 22:31–32) and Peter is given Christ's flock to shepherd (John 21:15–17). An angel was sent to announce the resurrection to Peter (Mark 16:5–7), and the risen Christ first appeared to Peter (Luke 24:34). He headed the meeting that elected Matthias to replace Judas (Acts 1:13–26), and he received the first converts (Acts 2:37–41). He inflicted the first punishment (Acts 5:1–11), and excommunicated the first heretic (Acts 8:18–24). He led the first council in Jerusalem (Acts 15), and announced the first dogmatic decision (Acts 15:7–11). It was to Peter that the revelation came that Gentiles were to be baptized and accepted as Christians (Acts 10:46–48).

Peter the Rock

Peter's preeminent position among the apostles was symbolized at the very beginning of his relationship with Christ. At their first meeting, Christ told Simon that his name would thereafter be Peter, which translates as "Rock" (John 1:42). The startling thing was that—aside from the single time that Abraham is called a "rock" (Hebrew: *tsur;* Aramaic: *kepha*) in Isaiah 51:1–2—in the Old Testament only God was called a rock. The word *rock* was not used as a proper name in the ancient world. If you were to turn to a companion and say, "From now on, your name is Asparagus," people would wonder: Why Asparagus? What is the meaning of it? What does it signify? Indeed, why call Simon the fisherman "Rock"? Christ was not given to meaningless gestures, and neither were the Jews as a whole when it came to names. Giving a new name meant that the status of the person was changed, as when Abram's name was changed to Abraham (Gen. 17:5), Jacob's to Israel (Gen. 32:28), Eliakim's to Joakim (2 Kgs. 23:34), or the names of the four Hebrew youths—Daniel, Hananiah, Mishael, and Azariah to Belteshazzar, Shadrach, Meshach, and Abednego (Dan. 1:6–7). But no Jew had ever been called "Rock." The Jews would give other names taken from nature, such as Deborah ("bee") and Rachel ("ewe"), but never "Rock." In the New Testament, James and John were nicknamed Boanerges, meaning "Sons of Thunder," by Christ, but that was never regularly used in place of their original names, and it certainly was not given as a new name. But in the case of Simon-bar-Jonah, his new name Kephas (Greek: *Petros*) definitely replaced the old.

Look at the Scene

Not only was there significance in Simon being given a new and unusual name, but the place where Jesus solemnly conferred it upon Peter was also important. It happened "when Jesus came into the district of Caesarea Philippi" (Matt. 16:13), a city that Philip the Tetrarch built and named in honor of Caesar Augustus, who had died in A.D. 14. The city lay near cascades in the Jordan River and near a gigantic wall of rock, a wall about 200 feet high and 500 feet long, which is part of the southern foothills of Mount Hermon. The city no longer exists, but its ruins are near the small Arab town of Banias; and at the base of the rock wall may be found what is left of one of the springs that fed the Jordan. It was here that Jesus pointed to Simon and said, "You are Peter" (Matt. 16:18).

The significance of the event must have been clear to the other apostles. As devout Jews, they knew at once that the location was meant to emphasize the importance of what was being done. None complained of Simon being singled out for this honor, and in the rest of the New Testament he is called by his new name, while James and John remain just James and John, not Boanerges.

Promises to Peter

When he first saw Simon, "Jesus looked at him, and said, 'So you are Simon the son of John? You shall be called Cephas' (which means Peter)" (John 1:42). The word *cephas* is merely the transliteration of the Aramaic *kepha* into Greek. Later, after Peter and the other disciples had been with Christ for some time, they went to Caesarea Philippi, where Peter made his profession of faith: "You are the Christ, the Son of the living God" (Matt. 16:16). Jesus told him that this truth was specially revealed to him, and then he solemnly reiterated: "And I tell you, you are Peter" (Matt. 16:18). To this was added the promise that the Church would be founded, in some way, on Peter (cf. Matt. 16:18).

Then two important things were told to the apostle. "Whatever you bind on earth shall be bound in heaven, and whatever you loose on earth shall be loosed in heaven" (Matt. 16:19). Here Peter was singled out for the authority that provides for the forgiveness of sins and the making of disciplinary rules. Later the apostles as a whole would be given similar power (cf. Matt.18:18), but here Peter received it in a special sense.

Peter alone was promised something else also: "I will give you the keys of the kingdom of heaven" (Matt. 16:19). In ancient times, keys were the hallmark of authority. A walled city might have one great gate, and that gate had one great lock, worked by one great key. To be given the key to the city—an honor that exists even today, though its import is lost—meant to be given free access to and authority over the city. The city to which Peter was given the keys was the heavenly city itself. This symbolism for authority is used elsewhere in the Bible (cf. Is. 22:22; Rev. 1:18).

Finally, after the Resurrection, Jesus appeared to his disciples and asked Peter three times, "Do you love me?" (cf. John 21:15-17). In repentance for his threefold denial, Peter gave a threefold affirmation of love. Then Christ, the Good Shepherd (cf. John 10:11, 14), gave Peter the authority he earlier had promised: "Feed my sheep" (John 21:17). This specifically included the other apostles, since Jesus asked Peter, "Do you love me more than these?" (John 21:15), the word *these* referring to the other apostles who were present (cf. John 21:2). Thus was completed the prediction made just before Jesus and his followers went for the last time to the Mount of Olives.

Immediately before his denials were predicted, Peter was told, "Simon, Simon, behold, Satan demanded to have you, that he might sift you like wheat, but I have prayed for you that your faith may not fail; and when you have turned again [after the denials], strengthen your brethren" (Luke 22:31-32). It was Peter whom Christ prayed would have faith that would not fail and that would be a guide for the others. His prayer, being perfectly efficacious, was sure to be fulfilled.

Who Is the Rock?

Now take a closer look at the key verse: "You are Peter, and on this rock I will build my Church" (Matt. 16:18). Disputes about this passage have always been related to the meaning of the term *rock*. To whom, or to what, does it refer? Since Simon's new name of Peter itself means "rock," the sentence could be rewritten as: "You are Rock, and on this rock I will build my Church." The play on words seems obvious, but commentators who wish to avoid what follows from this—namely the establishment of the papacy—have suggested that the word *rock* could not refer to Peter but must refer to his profession of faith or to Christ. From the grammatical point of view, the phrase "this rock" must relate back to the closest noun. Peter's profession of faith ("You are the Christ, the Son of the living God") is two verses earlier, while his name, a proper noun, is in the immediately preceding clause.

As an analogy, consider this artificial sentence: "I have a car and a truck, and it is blue." Which is blue? The truck, because that is the noun closest to the pronoun *it*. This is all the more clear if the reference to the car is two sentences earlier, as the reference to Peter's profession is two sentences earlier than the term *rock*.

Another Alternative

The previous argument also settles the question of whether the word refers to Christ himself, since he is mentioned within the profession of faith. The fact that he is elsewhere, by a different metaphor, called the cornerstone (Eph. 2:20; 1 Pet. 2:4–8) does not disprove that here Peter is the foundation. Christ is naturally the principal and, since he will be returning to heaven, the invisible foundation of the Church that he will establish. But Peter is named by him as the secondary and—because he and his successors will remain on earth—the visible foundation. Peter can be a foundation only because Christ is the cornerstone.

In fact, the New Testament contains five *different* metaphors for the foundation of the Church (cf. Matt. 16:18; 1 Cor. 3:11; Eph. 2:20; 1 Pet. 2:4; Rev. 21:14). One cannot take a single metaphor from a single passage and use it to twist the plain meaning of other passages. Rather, one must respect and harmonize the different passages, for the Church can be described as having different foundations since the word *foundation* can be used in different senses.

Look at the Aramaic

Opponents of the Catholic interpretation of Matthew 16:18 some-times argue that in the Greek text the name of the apostle is *Pet-ros*, while "rock" is rendered as *petra*. They claim that the former refers to a small stone, while the latter refers to a massive rock. So, if Peter was meant to be the massive rock, why isn't his name Petra?

Note that Christ did not speak to the disciples in Greek. He spoke Aramaic, the common language of Palestine at that time. In that language the word for rock is *kepha*, which is what Jesus called Peter in everyday speech. (Note that in John 1:42 he was told, "You will be called *Cephas*.") What Jesus said in Matthew 16:18 was: "You are *Kepha*, and upon this *kepha* I will build my Church."

When Matthew's Gospel was translated from the original Ara-maic to Greek, there arose a problem that did not confront the evangelist when he first composed his account of Christ's life. In Aramaic the word *kepha* has the same ending whether it refers to a rock or is used as a man's name. In Greek, though, the word for "rock," *petra*, is feminine in gender. The translator could use it for the second appearance of *kepha* in the sentence, but not for the first because it would be inappropriate to give a man a feminine name. So he put a masculine ending on it, and hence Peter became Petros.

Furthermore, the premise of the argument against Peter being the rock is simply false. In first-century Greek the words *petros* and *petra* were synonyms. They had previously possessed the meanings of "small stone" and "large rock" in some early Greek poetry, but by the first century this distinction was gone, as Protestant Bible scholars admit (see D. A. Carson's remarks on this passage in *The Expositor's Bible Commentary*, Zondervan, 8:368).

Some of the effect of Christ's play on words was lost when his statement was translated from the Aramaic into Greek, but that was the best that could be done in Greek. In English, like Aramaic, there is no problem with endings; so an English rendition could read: "You are Rock, and upon this rock I will build my church."

Consider another point: If "the rock" really did refer to Christ as some claim, based on 1 Corinthians 10:4 ("and the Rock was Christ," though the rock there was a literal, physical rock), then why did Matthew leave the passage as it was? In the original Aramaic—and in the English, which is a closer parallel to it than is the Greek—the passage is clear enough. Matthew must have realized that his readers would conclude the obvious.

If he meant Christ to be understood as the rock, why didn't he say so? Why did he take a chance and leave it up to Paul to write a clarifying text? This presumes, of course, that 1 Corinthians was written after Matthew's Gospel. If it came first, it could not have been written to clarify it.

The reason, of course, is that Matthew knew full well that what the sentence seemed to say was just what it really was saying. It was Simon, weak as he was, who was chosen to become the rock and thus the first link in the chain of the papacy.

2

Peter the Rock

One of the points I try to emphasize when giving a seminar is that you can begin to be an effective apologist right away; you don't have to wait until you become a theological whiz. Just work with what you know, even if it's only one fact.

I illustrate this from my own experience, and you can use this technique the next time you have verses thrown at you by an anti-Catholic.

Some years ago, before I took a real interest in reading the Bible, I tried to avoid missionaries who came to the door. I had been burned too often. Why open the door, or why prolong the conversation (if they caught me outside the house), when I had nothing to say?

Sure, I had a Bible. I used it perhaps the way you use yours today: to catch dust that otherwise would gather on the top shelf of the bookcase. It was one of those "family" Bibles, crammed with beautiful color plates and so heavy that my son didn't outweigh it until he was five.

As I said, I had a Bible, but I didn't turn to it much, so I had little to say about the Bible when missionaries cornered me. I didn't know which verses I should refer to when explaining the Catholic position.

For a layman, I suppose I was reasonably well informed about my faith—at least I never doubted it or ceased to practice it—but my own reading had not equipped me for verbal duels.

Then, one day, I came across a nugget of information that sent a shock wave through the next missionary who rang the bell and that proved to me that becoming skilled in apologetics isn't really all that difficult. Here's what happened.

When I answered the door, the lone missionary introduced himself as a Seventh-day Adventist. He asked if he could "share" with me some insights from the Bible. I told him to go ahead.

He flipped from one page to another, quoting this verse and that, trying to demonstrate the errors of the Church of Rome and the manifest truth of his own denomination's position.

Not Much to Say

Some of the verses I had encountered before. I wasn't entirely illiterate with respect to the Bible, but many verses were new to me. Whether familiar or not, the verses elicited no response from me, because I didn't know enough about the Bible to respond effectively.

Finally the missionary got to Matthew 16:18: "You are Peter, and on this rock I will build my Church."

"Hold it right there!" I said. "I know that verse. That's where Jesus appointed Simon the earthly head of the Church. That's where he appointed him the first pope." I paused and smiled broadly, knowing what the missionary would say in response.

I knew he usually didn't get any defense of the Catholic position at all as he went door to door, but sometimes a Catholic would speak up as I had. He had a reply, and I knew what it would be, and I was ready for it.

"I understand your thinking," he said, "but you Catholics misunderstand this verse because you don't know any Greek. That's the trouble with your Church and with your scholars. You people don't know the language in which the New Testament was written. To understand Matthew 16:18, we have to get behind the English to the Greek."

"Is that so?" I said, leading him on. I pretended to be ignorant of the trap being laid for me.

"Yes," he said. "In Greek, the word for rock is *petra*, which means a large, massive stone. The word used for Simon's new name is different; it's *petros*, which means a little stone, a pebble."

In reality, what the missionary was telling me at this point was false. As Greek scholars—even non-Catholic ones—admit, the words *petros* and *petra* were synonyms in first-century Greek. They meant "small stone" and "large rock" in some ancient Greek poetry, centuries before the time of Christ, but that distinction had disappeared from the language by the time Matthew's Gospel was rendered in Greek. The difference in meaning can be found only in Attic Greek, but the New Testament was written in Koine Greek—an entirely different dialect. In Koine Greek, both *petros* and *petra* simply meant "rock." If Jesus had wanted to call Simon a small stone, the Greek *lithos* would have been used. The missionary's argument didn't work and showed a faulty knowledge of Greek. (For an Evangelical Protestant Greek scholar's admission of this, see D. A. Carson, *The Expositor's Bible Commentary* [Grand Rapids: Zondervan, 1984], Frank E. Gaebelein, ed., 8:368).

"You Catholics," the missionary continued, "because you don't know Greek, imagine that Jesus was equating Simon and the rock. Actually, of course, it was just the opposite. He was contrasting them. On the one side, the rock on which the Church would be built, Jesus himself; on the other, this mere pebble. Jesus was really saying that he himself would be the foundation, and he was emphasizing that Simon wasn't remotely qualified to be it."

Case closed, he thought.

It was the missionary's turn to pause and smile broadly. He had followed the training he had been given. He had been told that a rare Catholic might have heard of Matthew 16:18 and might argue that it proved the establishment of the papacy. He knew what he was supposed to say to prove otherwise, and he had said it.

"Well," I replied, beginning to use that nugget of information I had come across, "I agree with you that we must get behind the English to the Greek." He smiled some more and nodded. "But I'm sure you'll agree with me that we must get behind the Greek to the Aramaic."

"The what?" he asked.

"The Aramaic," I said. "As you know, Aramaic was the language Jesus and the apostles and all the Jews in Palestine spoke. It was the common language of the place."

"I thought Greek was."

"No," I answered. "Many, if not most of them, knew Greek, of course, because Greek was the *lingua franca* of the Mediterranean world. It was the language of culture and commerce; and most of the books of the New Testament were written in it, because they were written not just for Christians in Palestine but also for Christians in places such as Rome, Alexandria, and Antioch, places where Aramaic wasn't the spoken language.

"I say most of the New Testament was written in Greek, but not all. Many hold that Matthew was written in Aramaic—we know this from records kept by Eusebius of Caesarea—but it was translated into Greek early on, perhaps by Matthew himself. In any case the Aramaic original is lost (as are all the originals of the New Testament books), so all we have today is the Greek."

I stopped for a moment and looked at the missionary. He seemed a bit uncomfortable, perhaps doubting that I was a Catholic because I seemed to know what I was talking about. I continued.

Aramaic in the New Testament

"We know that Jesus spoke Aramaic because some of his words are preserved for us in the Gospels. Look at Matthew 27:46, where he says from the cross, '*Eli, Eli, lama sabachthani?*' That isn't Greek; it's Aramaic, and it means, 'My God, my God, why have you forsaken me?'

"What's more," I said, "in Paul's epistles—four times in Galatians and four times in 1 Corinthians—we have the Aramaic form of Simon's new name preserved for us. In our English Bibles it comes out as *Cephas*. That isn't Greek. That's a transliteration of the Aramaic word *kepha* (rendered as *kephas* in its Hellenistic form).

"And what does *kepha* mean? It means a rock, the same as *petra*. (It doesn't mean a little stone or a pebble.) What Jesus said to Simon in Matthew 16:18 was this: 'You are *Kepha*, and on this *kepha* I will build my Church.'

"When you understand what the Aramaic says, you see that Jesus was equating Simon and the rock; he wasn't contrasting them. We see this vividly in some modern English translations, which render the verse this way: 'You are Rock, and upon this rock I will build my church.' In French one word, *pierre*, has always been used for both Simon's new name and the rock."

For a few moments the missionary seemed stumped. It was obvious he had never heard such a rejoinder. His brow was knit in thought as he tried to come up with a counter. Then it occurred to him.

"Wait a second," he said. "If *kepha* means the same as *petra*, why don't we read in the Greek, 'You are *Petra*, and on this *petra* I will build my Church'? Why, for Simon's new name, does Matthew use a Greek word, *petros*, which means something quite different from *petra*?"

"Because he had no choice," I said. "Greek and Aramaic have different grammatical structures. In Aramaic you can use *kepha* in both places in Matthew 16:18. In Greek you encounter a problem arising from the fact that nouns take differing gender endings.

"You have masculine, feminine, and neuter nouns. The Greek word *petra* is feminine. You can use it in the second half of Matthew 16:18 without any trouble. But you can't use it as Simon's new name, because you can't give a man a feminine name—at least back then you couldn't. You have to change the ending of the noun to make it masculine. When you do that, you get *Petros*, which was an already-existing word meaning 'rock.'

"I admit that's an imperfect rendering of the Aramaic; you lose part of the play on words. In English, where we have *Peter* and *rock*, you lose all of it. But that's the best you can do in Greek."

Beyond the grammatical evidence, the structure of the narrative does not allow for a downplaying of Peter's role in the Church. Look at the way Matthew 16:15–19 is structured. After Peter gives a confession about the identity of Jesus, the Lord does the same in return for Peter. Jesus does not say, "Blessed are you, Simon Bar-Jona! For flesh and blood has not revealed this to you, but my Father who is in heaven. And I tell you, you are an insignificant pebble and on this rock I will build my Church. . . . I will give you the keys of the kingdom of heaven." Jesus is giving Peter a threefold blessing, including the gift of the keys to the kingdom, not undermining his authority. To say that Jesus is downplaying Peter flies in the face of the context. Jesus is installing Peter as a form of chief steward or prime minister under the King of Kings by giving him the keys to the kingdom. As can be seen in Isaiah 22:22, kings in the Old Testament appointed a chief steward to serve under them in a position of great authority to rule over the inhabitants of the kingdom. Jesus quotes almost verbatim from this passage in Isaiah, and so it is clear what he has in mind. He is raising Peter up as a father figure to the household of faith (cf. Is. 22:21), to lead them and guide the flock (cf. John 21:15–17). This authority of the prime minister under the king was passed on from one man to another down through the ages by the giving of the keys, which were worn on the shoulder as a sign of authority. Likewise, the authority of Peter has been passed down for 2,000 years by means of the papacy.

My Turn to Pause

I stopped and smiled. The missionary smiled back uncomfortably but said nothing. We exchanged smiles for about thirty seconds. Then he looked at his watch, noticed how time had flown, and excused himself. I never saw him again.

So what came of this encounter? Two things—one for me, one for him.

I began to develop a sense of confidence. I began to see that I could defend my faith if I engaged in a little homework. The more homework, the better the defense.

I realized that any literate Catholic—including you—could do the same. You don't have to suspect that your faith might be untrue when you can't come up with an answer to a pointed question.

Once you develop a sense of confidence, you can say to yourself, "I may not know the answer to that, but I know I could find the answer if I hit the books. The answer is there, if only I spend the time to look for it."

And what about the missionary? Did he go away with anything? I think so. I think he went away with a doubt regarding his understanding (or lack thereof) of Catholics and the Catholic faith. I hope his doubt has since matured into a sense that maybe, just maybe, Catholics have something to say on behalf of their religion and that he should look more carefully into the faith he once so confidently opposed.

—Karl Keating

3

Was Peter in Rome?

Like other Protestants, Fundamentalists say Christ never appointed Peter as the earthly head of the Church for the simple reason that the Church has no earthly head and was never meant to have one. Christ is the Church's only foundation, in any possible sense of that term.

The papacy, they say, arose out of fifth- or sixth-century politics, both secular and ecclesiastical; it has no connection with the New Testament. It has not been established by Christ, even though supposed "successors" to Peter (and their defenders) claim it was. At best the papacy is a ruse; at worst, a work of the devil. In any case, it is an institution designed to give the Catholic Church an authority it doesn't have.

A key premise of their argument is the assertion that Peter was never in Rome. It follows that if Peter was never in Rome, he could not have been Rome's first bishop and so could not have had any successors in that office. How can Catholics talk about the divine origin of the papacy, Fundamentalists argue, when their claim about Peter's whereabouts is wrong?

How to Understand the Argument

At first glance, it might seem that the question of whether Peter went to Rome and died there is inconsequential. And in a way it is. After all, his being in Rome would not itself prove the existence of the papacy. In fact, it would be a false inference to say he must have been the first pope since he was in Rome and later popes ruled from Rome. With that logic, Paul would have been the first pope, too, since he was an apostle and went to Rome.

On the other hand, if Peter never made it to the capital, he still could have been the first pope, since one of his successors could have been the first holder of that office to settle in Rome. After all, if the papacy exists, it was established by Christ during his lifetime, long before Peter is said to have reached Rome. There must have been a period of some years in which the papacy did not yet have its connection to Rome.

So, if the apostle got there only much later, that might have something to say about who his legitimate successors would be (and it does, since the man elected bishop of Rome is automatically the new pope on the notion that Peter was the first bishop of Rome and the pope is merely Peter's successor), but it would say nothing about the status of the papal office. It would not establish that the papacy was instituted by Christ in the first place.

No, somehow the question, while interesting historically, isn't crucial to the real issue: whether the papacy was founded by Christ. Still, most anti-Catholic organizations take up the matter and go to considerable trouble to "prove" Peter could not have been in Rome. Why? Because they think they can get mileage out of it.

"Here's a point on which we can point to the lies of Catholic claims," they say. "Catholics trace the papacy to Peter, and they say he was martyred in Rome after heading the Church there. If we could show he never went to Rome, that would undermine —psychologically if not logically—their assertion that Peter was the first pope. If people conclude the Catholic Church is wrong on this historical point, they'll conclude it's wrong on the larger one, the supposed existence of the papacy." Such is the reasoning of some leading anti-Catholics.

The Charges in Brief

The case is stated perhaps most succinctly, even if not so bluntly, by Loraine Boettner in his best-known book, *Roman Catholicism*: "The remarkable thing, however, about Peter's alleged bishopric in Rome is that the New Testament has not one word to say about it. The word Rome occurs only nine times in the Bible [actually, ten times in the Old Testament and ten times in the New], and never is Peter mentioned in connection with it. There is no allusion to Rome in either of his epistles. Paul's journey to the city is recorded in great detail (Acts 27 and 28). There is in fact no New Testament evidence, nor any historical proof of any kind, that Peter ever was in Rome. All rests on legend" (117).

Well, what about it? Admittedly, the Bible nowhere explicitly says Peter was in Rome; but, on the other hand, it doesn't say he wasn't. Just as the New Testament never says, "Peter then went to Rome," it never says, "Peter did not go to Rome." In fact, very little is said about where he, or any of the apostles other than Paul, went in the years after the Ascension. For the most part, we have to rely on books other than the New Testament for information about what happened to the apostles, Peter included, in later years. Boettner is wrong to dismiss these early historical documents as conveyors of mere "legend." They are genuine historical evidence, as every professional historian recognizes.

What the Bible Says

Boettner is also wrong when he claims "there is no allusion to Rome in either of [Peter's] epistles." There is, in the greeting at the end of the first epistle: "The Church here in Babylon, united with you by God's election, sends you her greeting, and so does my son, Mark" (1 Pet. 5:13, Knox). Babylon is a code word for Rome. It is used that way multiple times in works like the *Sibylline Oracles* (5:159f), the *Apocalypse of Baruch* (2:1), and *4 Esdras* (3:1). Eusebius Pamphilius, in *The Chronicle*, composed about A.D. 303, noted, "It is said that Peter's first epistle, in which he makes mention of Mark, was composed at Rome itself; and that he himself indicates this, referring to the city figuratively as Babylon."

Consider now the other New Testament citations: "Another angel, a second, followed, saying, 'Fallen, fallen is Babylon the great, she who made all nations drink the wine of her impure passion' " (Rev. 14:8). "The great city was split into three parts, and the cities of the nations fell, and God remembered great Babylon, to make her drain the cup of the fury of his wrath" (Rev. 16:19). "And on her forehead was written a name of mystery: 'Babylon the great, mother of harlots and of earth's abominations' " (Rev. 17:5). "And he called out with a mighty voice, 'Fallen, fallen is Babylon the great' " (Rev. 18:2). "They will stand far off, in fear of her torment, and say, 'Alas! alas! thou great city, thou mighty city, Babylon! In one hour has thy judgment come' " (Rev. 18:10). "So shall Babylon the great city be thrown down with violence" (Rev. 18:21).

These references can't be to the one-time capital of the Babylonian empire. That Babylon had been reduced to an inconsequential village by the march of years, military defeat, and political subjugation; it was no longer a "great city." It played no important part in the recent history of the ancient world. From the New Testament perspective, the only candidates for the "great city" mentioned in Revelation are Rome and Jerusalem.

"But there is no good reason for saying that 'Babylon' means 'Rome,' " insists Boettner. But there is, and the good reason is persecution. The authorities knew that Peter was a leader of the Church, and the Church, under Roman law, was considered organized atheism. (The worship of any gods other than the Roman was considered atheism.) Peter would do himself, not to mention those with him, no service by advertising his presence in the capital—after all, mail service from Rome was then even worse than it is today, and letters were routinely read by Roman officials. Peter was a wanted man, as were all Christian leaders. Why encourage a manhunt? We also know that the apostles sometimes referred to cities under symbolic names (cf. Rev. 11:8).

In any event, let us be generous and admit that it is easy for an opponent of Catholicism to think, in good faith, that Peter was never in Rome, at least if he bases his conclusion on the Bible alone. But restricting his inquiry to the Bible is something he should not do; external evidence has to be considered, too.

Early Christian Testimony

William A. Jurgens in his three-volume set *The Faith of the Early Fathers*, a masterly compendium that cites at length everything from the *Didache* to John Damascene, includes thirty references to this question, divided, in the index, about evenly between the statements that "Peter came to Rome and died there" and that "Peter established his See at Rome and made the bishop of Rome his successor in the primacy." A few examples must suffice, but they and other early references demonstrate that there can be no question that the universal—and very early—position (one hesitates to use the word *tradition*, since some people read that as "legend") was that Peter certainly did end up in the capital of the empire.

A Very Early Reference

Tertullian, in *The Demurrer against the Heretics* (A.D. 200), noted of Rome, "How happy is that church . . . where Peter endured a passion like that of the Lord, where Paul was crowned in a death like John's [referring to John the Baptist, both he and Paul being beheaded]." Fundamentalists admit that Paul died in Rome, so the implication from Tertullian is that Peter also must have been there. It was commonly accepted, from the very first, that both Peter and Paul were martyred at Rome, probably in the Neronian persecution in the 60s.

In the same book, Tertullian wrote that "this is the way in which the apostolic churches transmit their lists: like the church of the Smyrnaeans, which records that Polycarp was placed there by John; like the church of the Romans, where Clement was ordained by Peter." This Clement, known as Clement of Rome, later would be the fourth pope. (Note that Tertullian didn't say Peter consecrated Clement as pope, which would have been impossible since a pope doesn't consecrate his own successor; he merely ordained Clement as priest.) Clement wrote his *Letter to the Corinthians* perhaps before the year 70, just a few years after Peter and Paul were killed; in it he made reference to Peter ending his life where Paul ended his.

In his *Letter to the Romans* (A.D. 110), Ignatius of Antioch remarked that he could not command the Roman Christians the way Peter and Paul once did, such a comment making sense only if Peter had been a leader, if not the leader, of the church in Rome.

Irenaeus, in *Against Heresies* (A.D. 190), said that Matthew wrote his Gospel "while Peter and Paul were evangelizing in Rome and laying the foundation of the Church." A few lines later he notes that Linus was named as Peter's successor, that is, the second pope, and that next in line were Anacletus (also known as Cletus), and then Clement of Rome.

Clement of Alexandria wrote at the turn of the third century. A fragment of his work *Sketches* is preserved in Eusebius of Caesarea's *Ecclesiastical History*, the first history of the Church. Clement wrote, "When Peter preached the word publicly at Rome, and declared the gospel by the Spirit, many who were present requested that Mark, who had been for a long time his follower and who remembered his sayings, should write down what had been proclaimed."

Lactantius, in a treatise called *The Death of the Persecutors*, written around 318, noted that "when Nero was already reigning (Nero reigned from 54–68), Peter came to Rome, where, in virtue of the performance of certain miracles that he worked by that power of God that had been given to him, he converted many to righteousness and established a firm and steadfast temple to God."

These citations could be multiplied. (Refer to Jurgens's books or to the Catholic Answers tract *Peter's Roman Residency*.) No ancient writer claimed Peter ended his life anywhere other than in Rome. On the question of Peter's whereabouts, they are in agreement, and their cumulative testimony carries enormous weight.

What Archaeology Proved

There is much archaeological evidence that Peter was at Rome, but Boettner, like other Fundamentalist apologists, must dismiss it, claiming that "exhaustive research by archaeologists has been made down through the centuries to find some inscription in the catacombs and other ruins of ancient places in Rome that would indicate Peter at least visited Rome. But the only things found which gave any promise at all were some bones of uncertain origin" (118).

Boettner saw *Roman Catholicism* through the presses in 1962. His original book and the revisions to it since then have failed to mention the results of the excavations under the high altar of St. Peter's Basilica, excavations that had been underway for decades but were undertaken in earnest after World War II. What Boettner casually dismissed as "some bones of uncertain origin" were the contents of a tomb on Vatican Hill that was covered with early inscriptions attesting to the fact that Peter's remains were inside.

After the original release of Boettner's book, evidence had mounted to the point that Pope Paul VI was able to announce officially something that had been discussed in archaeological literature and religious publications for years: that the actual tomb of the first pope had been identified conclusively, that his remains were apparently present, and that in the vicinity of his tomb were inscriptions identifying the place as Peter's burial site, meaning early Christians knew that the prince of the apostles was there. The story of how all this was determined, with scientific accuracy, is too long to recount here. It is discussed in detail in John Evangelist Walsh's book *The Bones of St. Peter*. It is enough to say that the historical and scientific evidence is such that no one willing to look at the facts objectively can doubt that Peter was in Rome. To deny that fact is to let prejudice override reason.

4

Papal Infallibility

The Catholic Church's teaching on papal infallibility is one that is generally misunderstood by those outside the Church. In particular, Fundamentalists and other "Bible Christians" often confuse the charism of papal infallibility with "impeccability." They imagine that Catholics believe the pope cannot sin. Others, who avoid this elementary blunder, think the pope relies on some sort of amulet or magical incantation when an infallible definition is due.

Given these common misapprehensions regarding the basic tenets of papal infallibility, it is necessary to explain exactly what infallibility is *not*. Infallibility is not the absence of sin, nor is it a charism that belongs only to the pope. Indeed, infallibility also belongs to the body of bishops as a whole, when, in doctrinal unity with the pope, they solemnly teach a doctrine as true. We have this from Jesus himself, who promised the apostles and their successors (the bishops, the magisterium of the Church): "He who hears you hears me" (Luke 10:16), and "Whatever you bind on earth shall be bound in heaven" (Matt. 18:18).

Vatican II's Explanation

Vatican II explained the doctrine of infallibility as follows: "Although the individual bishops do not enjoy the prerogative of infallibility, they can nevertheless proclaim Christ's doctrine infallibly. This is so, even when they are dispersed around the world, provided that while maintaining the bond of unity among themselves and with Peter's successor, and while teaching authentically on a matter of faith or morals, they concur in a single viewpoint as the one that must be held conclusively. This authority is even more clearly verified when, gathered together in an ecumenical council, they are teachers and judges of faith and morals for the universal Church. Their definitions must then be adhered to with the submission of faith" (*Lumen Gentium* 25).

Infallibility belongs in a special way to the pope as head of the bishops (cf. Matt. 16:17–19; John 21:15–17). As Vatican II remarked, it is a charism the pope "enjoys in virtue of his office, when, as the supreme shepherd and teacher of all the faithful, who confirms his brethren in their faith (cf. Luke 22:32), he proclaims by a definitive act some doctrine of faith or morals. Therefore his definitions, of themselves, and not from the consent of the Church, are justly held irreformable, for they are pronounced with the assistance of the Holy Spirit, an assistance promised to him in blessed Peter" (LG 25).

The infallibility of the pope is not a doctrine that suddenly appeared in Church teaching; rather, it was implicit in the early Church. It is only our understanding of infallibility that has developed and been more clearly understood over time. In fact, the doctrine of infallibility is implicit in these Petrine texts: John 21:15–17 ("Feed my sheep"), Luke 22:32 ("I have prayed for you that your faith may not fail"), and Matthew 16:18 ("You are Peter").

Based on Christ's Mandate

Christ instructed the Church to preach everything he taught (Matt. 28:19–20) and promised the protection of the Holy Spirit to "guide you into all the truth" (John 16:13). That mandate and that promise guarantee that the Church will never fall away from his teachings (cf. Matt. 16:18; 1 Tim. 3:15), even if individual Catholics might.

As Christians began to more clearly understand the teaching authority of the Church and the primacy of the pope, they developed a clearer understanding of the pope's infallibility. This development of the faithful's understanding has its clear beginnings in the early Church. For example, Cyprian of Carthage, writing about 256, put the question this way: "Would the heretics dare to come to the very seat of Peter whence apostolic faith is derived and whither no errors can come?" (*Letters* 59 [55], 14). In the fifth century, Augustine succinctly captured the ancient attitude when he remarked, "Rome has spoken; the case is concluded" (*Sermons* 131, 10).

Some Clarifications

An infallible pronouncement—whether made by the pope alone or by an ecumenical council—is usually made only when some doctrine has been called into question. Most doctrines have never been doubted by the large majority of Catholics.

Pick up a catechism and look at the great number of doctrines, most of which have never been formally defined. But many points have been defined, and not just by the pope alone. There are, in fact, many major topics on which it would be impossible for a pope to make an infallible definition without duplicating one or more infallible pronouncements from ecumenical councils or the ordinary magisterium (teaching authority) of the Church.

At least the outline, if not the references, of the preceding paragraphs should be familiar to literate Catholics, to whom this subject should appear straightforward. It is a different story with "Bible Christians." For them, papal infallibility often seems a muddle because their idea of what it encompasses is often incorrect.

Some ask how popes can be infallible if some of them lived scandalously. This objection, of course, illustrates the common confusion between infallibility and impeccability. There is no guarantee that popes won't sin or give bad example. (The truly remarkable thing is the great degree of sanctity found in the papacy throughout history; the "bad popes" stand out precisely because they are so rare.)

Other people wonder how infallibility could exist if some popes disagreed with others. This, too, shows an inaccurate understanding of infallibility, which applies only to solemn, official teachings on faith and morals, not to disciplinary decisions or even to unofficial comments on faith and morals. A pope's private theological opinions are not infallible. Only what he solemnly defines is considered to be infallible teaching.

Even Fundamentalists and Evangelicals who do not have these common misunderstandings often think that infallibility means that popes are given some special grace that allows them to teach positively whatever truths need to be known. But that is not quite correct, either. Infallibility is not a substitute for theological study on the part of the pope.

What infallibility does do is prevent a pope from solemnly and formally teaching as "truth" something that is, in fact, error. It does not help him know what is true, nor does it "inspire" him to teach what is true. He has to learn the truth the way we all do —through study—though, to be sure, he has certain advantages because of his position.

Peter Not Infallible?

As a biblical example of papal fallibility, Fundamentalists like to point to Peter's conduct at Antioch, where he refused to eat with Gentile Christians in order not to offend certain Jews from Palestine (cf. Gal. 2:11–16). For this Paul rebuked him. Did this demonstrate that papal infallibility was non-existent? Not at all. Peter's actions had to do with matters of discipline, not with issues of faith or morals.

Furthermore, the problem was Peter's actions, not his teaching. Paul acknowledged that Peter very well knew the correct teaching (Gal. 2:12–13). The problem was that he wasn't living up to his own teaching. Thus, in this instance, Peter was not doing any teaching; much less was he solemnly defining a matter of faith or morals.

Fundamentalists must also acknowledge that Peter did have

some kind of infallibility—they cannot deny that he wrote two infallible epistles of the New Testament while under protection against writing error. So, if his behavior at Antioch was not incompatible with this kind of infallibility, neither is bad behavior contrary to papal infallibility in general.

Turning to history, critics of the Church cite certain "errors of the popes." Their argument is really reduced to three cases: those of Popes Liberius, Vigilius, and Honorius. All opponents of papal infallibility turn to these three cases, because they are the only ones that do not collapse as soon as they are mentioned. There is no point in giving the details here—any good history of the Church will supply the facts—but it is enough to note that none of the cases meet the requirements outlined by the description of papal infallibility given at Vatican I (cf. *Pastor Aeternus* 4).

Their "Favorite Case"

According to Fundamentalist commentators, their best case lies with Pope Honorius. They say that he specifically taught Monothelitism, a heresy that held that Christ had only one will (a divine one), not two wills (a divine one and a human one) as all orthodox Christians hold.

But that's not at all what Honorius did. Even a quick review of the records shows that he simply decided not to make a decision at all. As Ronald Knox explained, "To the best of his human wisdom, he thought the controversy ought to be left unsettled, for the greater peace of the Church. In fact, he was an inopportunist. We, wise after the event, say that he was wrong. But nobody, I think, has ever claimed that the pope is infallible in *not* defining a doctrine."

Knox wrote to Arnold Lunn (a future convert who would become a great apologist for the faith—their correspondence is found in the book *Difficulties*): "Has it ever occurred to you how few are the alleged 'failures of infallibility'? I mean, if somebody propounded in your presence the thesis that all the kings of England have been impeccable, you would not find yourself murmuring, 'Oh, well, people said rather unpleasant things about Jane Shore . . . and the best historians seem to think that Charles II spent too much of his time with Nell Gwynn,' Here have these popes been, fulminating anathema after anathema for centuries—certain in all human probability to contradict themselves or one another over again. Instead of which you get this measly crop of two or three alleged failures!" While Knox's observation does not establish the truth of papal infallibility, it does show that the historical argument against infallibility is weak.

The rejection of papal infallibility by "Bible Christians" stems from their view of the Church. They do not think that Christ established a visible Church, which means that they do not believe in a hierarchy of bishops headed by the pope.

This is no place to give an elaborate demonstration of the establishment of a visible Church. But it is simple enough to point out that the New Testament shows the apostles setting up, after their Master's instructions, a visible organization, and every Christian writer in the early centuries—in fact, nearly all Christians until the Reformation—fully recognized that Christ set up an ongoing organization.

One example of this ancient belief comes to us from Ignatius of Antioch. In his second-century letter to the church in Smyrna, he wrote, "Wherever the bishop appears, let the people be there; just as wherever Jesus Christ is, there is the Catholic Church" (*Letter to the Smyrnaeans* 8, 1 [A.D. 110]).

If Christ did set up such an organization, he must have provided for its continuation, for its easy identification (that is, it had to be visible so it could be found), and—since he would be gone from earth—for some method by which it could preserve his teachings intact.

All this was accomplished through the apostolic succession of bishops. The preservation of the Christian message, in its fullness, was guaranteed through the gift of infallibility of the Church as a whole but mainly through its Christ-appointed leaders: the bishops (as a whole) and the pope (as an individual).

It is the Holy Spirit who prevents the pope from officially teaching error, and this charism follows necessarily from the existence of the Church itself. If, as Christ promised, the Church will be shielded from the gates of hell, then it must be protected from fundamentally falling into error and thus away from Christ. It must prove itself to be a perfectly steady guide in matters pertaining to salvation.

Of course, infallibility does not include a guarantee that any particular pope won't "neglect" to teach the truth, or that he will be sinless, or that mere disciplinary decisions will be intelligently made. It would be nice if he were omniscient or impeccable, but his not being so will fail to bring about the destruction of the Church.

But he must be able to teach rightly, since instruction for the sake of salvation is a primary function of the Church. For men to be saved, they must know what is to be believed. They must have a perfectly steady rock to build upon and to trust as the source of solemn Christian teaching. And that's why papal infallibility exists.

Since Christ said that the gates of hell would not prevail against his Church (cf. Matt. 16:18), this means that his Church can never pass out of existence. But if the Church ever apostatized by teaching heresy, then it would cease to exist. It would cease to be Jesus' Church. Thus the Church *cannot* teach heresy; anything it solemnly defines for the faithful to believe is true. This same reality is reflected in the apostle Paul's statement that the Church is "the pillar and bulwark of the truth" (1 Tim. 3:15). If the Church is the foundation of religious truth in this world, then it is God's own spokesman. As Christ told his disciples: "He who hears you hears me, and he who rejects you rejects me, and he who rejects me rejects him who sent me" (Luke 10:16).

5

Scripture and Tradition

Protestants claim that the Bible is the only rule of faith, meaning that it contains all the material one needs for theology and that this material is sufficiently clear that one does not need apostolic Tradition or the Church's magisterium (teaching authority) to help one understand it. In the Protestant view, the whole of Christian truth is found within the Bible's pages. Anything extraneous to the Bible is simply non-authoritative, unnecessary, or wrong—and may well hinder one in coming to God.

Catholics, on the other hand, recognize that this view is not endorsed in the Bible; in fact, it is repudiated in Scripture. The true "rule of faith"—as expressed in the Bible itself—is Scripture plus apostolic Tradition, as manifested in the living teaching authority of the Catholic Church, to which were entrusted the oral teachings of Jesus and the apostles, along with the authority to interpret Scripture correctly.

In the Second Vatican Council's document on divine revelation, *Dei Verbum* (Latin: "The Word of God"), the relationship between Tradition and Scripture is explained: "Hence there exists a close connection and communication between sacred Tradition and sacred Scripture. For both of them, flowing from the same divine wellspring, in a certain way merge into a unity and tend toward the same end. For sacred Scripture is the word of God inasmuch as it is consigned to writing under the inspiration of the divine Spirit. To the successors of the apostles, sacred Tradition hands on in its full purity God's word, which was entrusted to the apostles by Christ the Lord and the Holy Spirit.

"Thus, by the light of the Spirit of truth, these successors can in their preaching preserve this word of God faithfully, explain it, and make it more widely known. Consequently it is not from

Sacred Scripture alone that the Church draws her certainty about everything that has been revealed. Therefore both Sacred Tradition and Sacred Scripture are to be accepted and venerated with the same devotion and reverence" (DV 9).

But Evangelical and Fundamentalist Protestants, who place their confidence in Martin Luther's theory of *sola scriptura* (Latin: "Scripture alone"), will usually argue for their position by citing a couple of key verses. The first is this: "These are written that you may believe that Jesus is the Christ, the Son of God, and that believing you may have life in his name" (John 20:31). The other is this: "All scripture is inspired by God and profitable for teaching, for reproof, for correction, and for training in righteousness, that the man of God may be complete, equipped for every good work" (2 Tim. 3:16–17). According to these Protestants, these verses demonstrate the reality of *sola scriptura* (the "Bible only" theory).

Not so, reply Catholics. First, the verse from John refers to the things written in that book. (Read it with John 20:30, the verse immediately before it to see the context of the statement in question.) If this verse proved anything, it would not prove the theory of *sola scriptura* but that the Gospel of John is sufficient.

Second, the verse from John's Gospel tells us only that the Bible was composed so we can be helped to believe Jesus is the Messiah. It does not say the Bible is all we need for salvation, much less that the Bible is all we need for theology; nor does it say the Bible is even necessary to believe in Christ. After all, the earliest Christians had no New Testament to which they could appeal; they learned from oral, rather than written, instruction. Until relatively recent times, the Bible was inaccessible to most people, either because they could not read or because the printing press had not been invented. All these people learned from oral instruction, passed down, generation to generation, by the Church.

Much the same can be said about 2 Timothy 3:16–17. To say that all inspired writing is "profitable" is one thing; to say that only inspired writing need be followed is something else. Besides, there is a telling argument against claims of Evangelical and Fundamentalist Protestants. John Henry Newman explained it in an 1884 essay entitled "Inspiration in its Relation to Revelation."

Newman's Argument

He wrote: "It is quite evident that this passage furnishes no argument whatever that the sacred Scripture, without Tradition, is the sole rule of faith; for, although sacred Scripture is profitable for these four ends, still it is not said to be sufficient. The Apostle [Paul] requires the aid of Tradition (cf. 2 Thess. 2:15). Moreover, the Apostle here refers to the scriptures that Timothy was taught in his infancy.

"Now, a good part of the New Testament was not written in his boyhood: Some of the Catholic epistles were not written even when Paul wrote this, and none of the books of the New Testament were then placed on the canon of the Scripture books. He refers, then, to the scriptures of the Old Testament, and, if the argument from this passage proved anything, it would prove too much, viz., that the scriptures of the New Testament were not necessary for a rule of faith."

Furthermore, Protestants typically read 2 Timothy 3:16–17 out of context. When read in the context of the surrounding passages, one discovers that Paul's reference to Scripture is only part of his exhortation that Timothy take as his guide Tradition and Scripture. The two verses immediately before it state: "But as for you, continue in what you have learned and have firmly believed, knowing from whom you learned it, and how from childhood you have been acquainted with the sacred writings which are able to instruct you for salvation through faith in Christ Jesus" (2 Tim. 3:14–15).

Paul tells Timothy to continue in what he has learned for two reasons: first, because he knows from whom he has learned it —Paul himself—and second, because he has been educated in Scripture. The first of these is a direct appeal to apostolic Tradition, the oral teaching that the apostle Paul had given Timothy.

So Protestants must take 2 Timothy 3:16–17 out of context to arrive at the theory of *sola scriptura*. But when the passage is read in context, it becomes clear that it is teaching the importance of apostolic Tradition!

The Bible denies that it is sufficient as the complete rule of faith. Paul says that much Christian teaching is to be found in Tradition, which is handed down by word of mouth (cf. 2 Tim. 2:2). He instructs us to "stand firm and hold to the traditions which you were taught by us, either by word of mouth or by letter" (2 Thess. 2:15).

This oral teaching was accepted by Christians, just as they accepted the written teaching that came to them later. Jesus told his disciples: "He who hears you hears me, and he who rejects you rejects me" (Luke 10:16). The Church, in the persons of the apostles, was given the authority to teach by Christ; the Church would be his representative. He commissioned them, saying, "Go therefore and make disciples of all nations" (Matt. 28:19).

And how was this to be done? By preaching, by oral instruction: "So faith comes from what is heard, and what is heard comes by the preaching of Christ" (Rom. 10:17). The Church would always be the living teacher. It is a mistake to limit "Christ's word" to the written word only or to suggest that all his teachings were reduced to writing. The Bible nowhere supports either notion.

Further, it is clear that the oral teaching of Christ would last until the end of time. " 'But the word of the Lord abides for ever.' That word is the good news which was preached to you" (1 Pet. 1:25). Note that the word has been "preached"—that is, communicated orally. This would endure. It would not be supplanted by a written record like the Bible (supplemented, yes, but not supplanted), and would continue to have its own authority.

This is made clear when the apostle Paul tells Timothy: "What you have heard from me before many witnesses entrust to faithful men who will be able to teach others also" (2 Tim. 2:2). Here we see the first few links in the chain of apostolic Tradition that has been passed down intact from the apostles to our own day. Paul instructed Timothy to pass on the oral teachings (Tradition) that he had received from the apostle. He was to give these to men who would be able to teach others, thus perpetuating the chain. Paul gave this instruction not long before his death (cf. 2 Tim. 4:6–8) as a reminder to Timothy of how he should conduct his ministry.

What Is Tradition?

In this discussion it is important to keep in mind what the Catholic Church means by *Tradition*. The term does not refer to legends or mythological accounts, nor does it encompass transitory customs or practices that may change, as circumstances warrant, such as styles of priestly dress, particular forms of devotion to saints, or even liturgical rubrics. Sacred or apostolic Tradition consists of the teachings that the apostles passed on orally through their preaching. These teachings largely (perhaps entirely) overlap with those contained in Scripture, but the mode of their transmission is different.

They have been handed down and entrusted to the Church. It is necessary that Christians believe in and follow this Tradition as well as the Bible (cf. Luke 10:16). The truth of the faith has been given primarily to the leaders of the Church (cf. Eph. 3:5), who, with Christ, form the foundation of the Church (cf. Eph. 2:20). The Church has been guided by the Holy Spirit, who protects this teaching from corruption (cf. John 14:25–26; 16:13).

Handing on the Faith

Paul illustrated what Tradition is: "For I delivered to you as of first importance what I also received, that Christ died for our sins in accordance with the scriptures. . . . Whether then it was I or they, so we preach and so you believed" (1 Cor. 15:3, 11). The apostle praised those who followed Tradition: "I commend you because you remember me in everything and maintain the traditions even as I have delivered them to you" (1 Cor. 11:2).

The first Christians "devoted themselves to the apostles' teaching" (Acts 2:42) long before there was a New Testament. From the very beginning, the fullness of Christian teaching was found in the Church as the living embodiment of Christ, not in a book. The teaching Church, with its oral, apostolic Tradition, was authoritative. Paul himself gives a quotation from Jesus that was handed down orally to him: "It is more blessed to give than to receive" (Acts 20:35).

This saying is not recorded in the Gospels and must have been passed on to Paul. Indeed, even the Gospels themselves are oral Tradition that has been written down (cf. Luke 1:1–4). What's more, Paul does not quote Jesus only. He also quotes from early Christian hymns, as in Ephesians 5:14. These and other things have been given to Christians "through the Lord Jesus" (1 Thess. 4:2).

Fundamentalists note that Jesus said, "And why do you transgress the commandment of God for the sake of your tradition?" (Matt. 15:3). Paul warned, "See to it that no one makes a prey of you by philosophy and empty deceit, according to human tradition, according to the elemental spirits of the universe, and not according to Christ" (Col. 2:8). But these verses merely condemn erroneous human traditions, not truths that were handed down orally and entrusted to the Church by the apostles. These latter truths are part of what is known as apostolic Tradition, which is to be distinguished from human traditions or customs.

"Commandments of Men"

Consider Matthew 15:6–9, which Fundamentalists and Evangelicals often use to defend their position: "So, for the sake of your tradition, you have made void the word of God. You hypocrites! Well did Isaiah prophesy of you, when he said: 'This people honors me with their lips, but their heart is far from me; in vain do they worship me, teaching as doctrines the precepts of men.'"

Look closely at what Jesus said. He was not condemning all traditions. He condemned only those that made God's word void. In this case, it was a matter of the Pharisees feigning the dedication of their goods to the temple so they could avoid using them to support their aged parents. By doing this, they dodged the commandment to "honor your father and your mother" (Ex. 20:12).

Elsewhere, Jesus instructed his followers to abide by traditions that are not contrary to God's commandments. "The scribes and the Pharisees sit on Moses' seat; so practice and observe whatever they tell you, but not what they do; for they preach, but do not practice" (Matt. 23:2–3).

What Fundamentalists and Evangelicals often do, unfortunately, is see the word *tradition* in Matthew 15:3 or Colossians 2:8 or elsewhere and conclude that anything termed a "tradition" is to be rejected. They forget that the term is used in a different sense, as in 1 Corinthians 11:2 and 2 Thessalonians 2:15, to describe what should be believed. Jesus did not condemn all traditions; he condemned only erroneous traditions, whether doctrines or practices, that undermined Christian truths. The rest, as the apostles taught, were to be obeyed. Paul commanded the Thessalonians to adhere to all the traditions he had given them, whether oral or written.

The Indefectible Church

The task is to determine what constitutes authentic tradition. How can we know which traditions are apostolic and which are merely human? The answer is the same as how we know which books of Scripture are apostolic and which are merely human—by listening to the magisterium or teaching authority of Christ's Church. Without the Catholic Church's teaching authority, we would not know with certainty which purported books of Scripture are authentic. If the Church revealed to us the canon of Scripture, it can also reveal to us the "canon of Tradition" by establishing which traditions have been passed down from the apostles. After all, Christ promised that the gates of hell would not prevail against the Church (cf. Matt. 16:18) and the New Testament itself declares the Church to be "the pillar and bulwark of the truth" (1 Tim. 3:15).

6

Proving Inspiration

The Protestant Reformers said that the Bible is the sole authoritative source of religious truth whose proper understanding must be found by looking only at the words of the text itself. This is the Protestant teaching of *sola scriptura* (Latin: by Scripture alone). According to this teaching, no outside authority may mandate an interpretation, because no outside authority, such as the Church, has been established by Christ as an arbiter to determine which of the conflicting interpretations is correct.

There is perhaps no greater frustration in dealing with Evangelical and Fundamentalist Protestants than trying to pin them down on why the Bible should be taken as a rule of faith at all, let alone the sole rule. It reduces to the question of why Fundamentalists accept the Bible as inspired, since the Bible can be taken as a rule of faith only if it is *first* held to be inspired and, thus, inerrant.

Now, this is a problem that doesn't keep many nominal Christians awake at night. Most have never even given it any serious thought. To the extent that they believe in the Bible, they do so because they operate in a milieu that is, if post-Christian in many ways, still steeped in Christian presuppositions and ways of thought.

A lukewarm Christian who would not give the slightest credence to the Qur'an would think twice about casting aspersions on the Bible. It has a certain official status for him, even if he cannot explain why. You might say that he accepts the Bible as inspired (whatever that may mean to him) for some "cultural" reason, but that is hardly an adequate reason, since on such a basis that would mean the Qur'an rightly would be considered inspired in a Muslim country.

"It Inspires Me"

Some Fundamentalists say they believe the Bible is inspired because it is "inspirational," but that is an ambiguous term. On the one hand, if used in the strict theological sense, it clearly begs the question, which is: How do we know the Bible is inspired, that is, "written" by God, using human authors as instruments? But if "inspirational" means nothing more than "inspiring" or "moving," then someone might decide that the works of Shakespeare are inspired. Furthermore, parts of the Bible, including several whole books of the Old Testament, cannot at all be called "inspirational" in this sense. One bears no disrespect in admitting that some parts of the Bible are as dry as military statistics— indeed, some parts *are* military statistics—and offer little to move the emotions.

Witness of the Bible

What about the Bible's own claim to inspiration? There are not many places where such a claim is made even elliptically, and most books in the Old and New Testaments make no such claim at all. In fact, no New Testament writer explicitly claims that he himself is writing at the direct behest of God, with the exception of John, the author of Revelation.

Besides, even if every biblical book began with the phrase "The following is an inspired book," this would prove nothing. A book of false scriptures can easily assert that it is inspired, and many do. The mere claim of inspiration is insufficient to establish that something is *bona fide*.

These tests failing, most Fundamentalists fall back on the notion that "the Holy Spirit tells me the Bible is inspired," an exercise in subjectivism akin to their claim that the Holy Spirit guides them in interpreting the text. For example, the anonymous author of *How Can I Understand the Bible?*, a booklet distributed by the

Evangelical organization "Radio Bible Class," lists twelve rules for Bible study. The first is "Seek the help of the Holy Spirit. The Spirit has been given to illumine the scriptures and make them alive to you as you study them. Yield to his enlightenment."

If one takes this to mean that anyone asking for a proper interpretation will receive one from God—and that is exactly how most Fundamentalists understand the assistance of the Holy Spirit to work—then the multiplicity of interpretations, even among Fundamentalists, should give people a gnawing suspicion that the Holy Spirit has not been doing his job very well.

No Rational Basis

Most Fundamentalists do not say in so many words that the Holy Spirit has spoken to them directly to assure them of the inspiration of the Bible. Rather, in reading the Bible they say that they are "convicted" that it is the word of God, they get a positive "feeling" that it is inspired, and that's that. But this reduces their acceptance of the Bible to the influence of their culture, habit, or any number of other emotional or psychological factors.

No matter how it is examined, the Fundamentalist position is not one that is rigorously reasoned out. It is a rare Fundamentalist who, even for sake of argument, first approaches the Bible as though it is not inspired and then later, upon reading it, syllogistically concludes that it must be. In fact, Fundamentalists begin with the *fact* of inspiration—just as they take the other doctrines of Fundamentalism as premises, not as conclusions—and *then* they find passages in the Bible that seem to support inspiration. They finally "conclude," with obviously circular reasoning, that the Bible confirms its inspiration, which they knew all along.

The man who wrestles with the Fundamentalist approach to inspiration is eventually unsatisfied, because he knows that the Fundamentalist has no sound basis for his belief. So where does one find a reasonable proof for the inspiration of Scripture? Look no further than the Catholic Church. Ultimately, the Catholic position is the only one that proves conclusively the divine inspiration of Scripture, the only one that can satisfy a person intellectually.

The Catholic method of proving the Bible to be inspired is this: The Bible is initially approached as any other ancient work. It is not, at first, presumed to be inspired. From textual criticism we are able to conclude that we have a text the accuracy of which is more certain than the accuracy of any other ancient work.

An Accurate Text

Sir Frederic Kenyon, in *The Story of the Bible*, notes that "for all the works of classical antiquity we have to depend on manuscripts written long after their original composition. The author who is the best case in this respect is Virgil, yet the earliest manuscript of Virgil that we now possess was written some 350 years after his death. For all other classical writers, the interval between the date of the author and the earliest extant manuscript of his works is much greater. For Livy it is about 500 years, for Horace 900, for most of Plato 1,300, for Euripides 1,600." Yet no one seriously disputes that we have accurate copies of the works of these writers. However, in the case of the New Testament we have parts of manuscripts dating from the first and early second centuries, only a few decades after the works were penned.

Not only are the biblical manuscripts that we have *older* than those for classical authors, we have in sheer numbers far more manuscripts from which to work. Some are whole books of the Bible, others fragments of just a few words, but there are literally thousands of manuscripts in Hebrew, Greek, Latin, Coptic, Syriac, and other languages. This means that we can be sure we have an authentic text, and we can work from it with confidence.

The Bible As Historical Truth

Next we take a look at what the Bible, considered merely as a history, tells us, focusing particularly on the New Testament and more specifically the Gospels. We examine the account contained therein of Jesus' life, death, and resurrection.

Using what is in the Gospels themselves and what we find in extra-biblical writings from the early centuries, together with what we know of human nature (and what we can otherwise, from natural reason alone, know of divine nature), we conclude that either Jesus was just what he claimed to be—God—or he was crazy. (The one thing we know he could not have been was merely a good man who was not God, since no merely good man would make the claims he made.)

We are able to eliminate the possibility of his being a madman not just from what he said but from what his followers did after his death. Many critics of the Gospel accounts of the Resurrection claim that Christ did not truly rise, that his followers took his body from the tomb and then proclaimed him risen from the dead. According to these critics, the Resurrection was nothing more than a hoax. Devising a hoax to glorify a friend and mentor is one thing, but you do not find people dying for a hoax, at least not one from which they derive no benefit. Certainly if Christ had not risen his disciples would not have died horrible deaths affirming the reality and truth of the Resurrection. The result of this line of reasoning is that we must conclude that Jesus indeed rose from the dead. Consequently, his claims concerning himself—including his claim to be God—have credibility. He meant what he said and did what he said he would do.

Further, Christ said he would found a Church. Both the Bible (still taken as *merely a historical* book, not yet as an inspired one) and other ancient works attest to the fact that Christ established a Church with the rudiments of what we see in the Catholic Church today—papacy, hierarchy, priesthood, sacraments, and teaching authority.

We have thus taken the material purely historically and concluded that Jesus founded the Catholic Church. Because of his Resurrection we have reason to take seriously his claims concerning this Church, including its authority to teach in his name.

This Catholic Church tells us the Bible is inspired, and we can take the Church's word for it precisely because the Church is infallible. Only after having been told by a properly constituted authority—that is, one established by God to assure us of the truth concerning matters of faith—that the Bible is inspired can we reasonably begin to use it as an inspired book.

A Spiral Argument

Note that this is not a circular argument. We are not basing the inspiration of the Bible on the Church's infallibility and the Church's infallibility on the word of an inspired Bible. That indeed would be a circular argument! What we have is really a spiral argument. On the first level we argue to the reliability of the Bible insofar as it is history. From that we conclude that an infallible Church was founded. And then we take the word of that infallible Church that the Bible is inspired. This is not a circular argument because the final conclusion (the Bible is inspired) is not simply a restatement of its initial finding (the Bible is historically reliable), and its initial finding (the Bible is historically reliable) is in no way based on the final conclusion (the Bible is inspired). What we have demonstrated is that without the existence of the Church, we could never know whether the Bible is inspired.

Inadequate Reasons

The point is that Fundamentalists are quite right in believing the Bible to be inspired, but their reasons for so believing are inadequate. In reality this conviction can be based only on an authority established by God to tell us the Bible is inspired, and that authority is the Church.

And this is where a more serious problem comes to light. It seems to some that it makes little difference why one believes in the Bible's inspiration, just so long as one believes in it. But the basis for one's belief in its inspiration directly affects how one proceeds to interpret the Bible. The Catholic believes in inspiration because, to put it bluntly, the Church tells him so and that same Church has the authority to interpret the inspired text. Fundamentalists believe in inspiration, though on weak grounds, but they have no interpreting authority other than themselves.

Cardinal Newman put it this way in an essay on inspiration first published in 1884: "Surely then, if the revelations and lessons in Scripture are addressed to us personally and practically, the presence among us of a formal judge and standing expositor of its words is imperative. It is antecedently unreasonable to suppose that a book so complex, so unsystematic, in parts so obscure, the outcome of so many minds, times, and places, should be given us from above without the safeguard of some authority; as if it could possibly from the nature of the case, interpret itself. Its inspiration does but guarantee its truth, not its interpretation. How are private readers satisfactorily to distinguish what is didactic and what is historical, what is fact and what is vision, what is allegorical and what is literal, what is [idiomatic] and what is grammatical, what is enunciated formally and what occurs, what is only of temporary and what is of lasting obligations. Such is our natural anticipation, and it is only too exactly justified in the events of the last three centuries, in the many countries where private judgment on the text of Scripture has prevailed. The gift of inspiration requires as its complement the gift of infallibility."

The advantages of the Catholic approach are two: First, the inspiration is really proved, not just "felt." Second, the main fact behind the proof—the reality of an infallible, teaching Church—leads one naturally to an answer to the problem that troubled the Ethiopian eunuch (cf. Acts 8:30–31): How is one to know which interpretations are correct? The same Church that authenticates the Bible, that attests to its inspiration, is the authority established by Christ to interpret his word.

7

"What's Your Authority?"

In Catholic Answers' seminars, we emphasize that you should *always* demand that a missionary who comes to your door first establish his authority for what he is going to tell you, and only then proceed to discuss the particular issues he has in mind.

By *authority*, we don't mean his personal or academic credentials. We mean his authority to claim that he can rightly interpret the Bible. The missionary (unless he is a Mormon, of course, in which case his authority is the *Book of Mormon*) will always claim to fall back on the authority of Scripture. "Scripture says this," or "Scripture proves that," he will tell you.

So before you turn to the verses he brings up, and thus to the topic he brings up, demand that he demonstrate a few things.

First, ask him to prove from the Bible that the Bible is the only rule of faith (if he's an Evangelical or Fundamentalist Protestant, he holds to the Reformation theory of *sola scriptura*—the Bible alone).

Second, have him tell you how he knows which books belong in the Bible in the first place.

And third, require that he prove to you both that he has the authority to interpret the Bible for you (remember that his doctrines will almost always be drawn from *interpretations* of the sacred text rather than the words themselves) and that his interpretations will always be accurate.

Imagine the conversation goes something like this:

"Good afternoon, neighbor. May I share a few words of Christian truth with you?"

"Sure," you say. "Where do you get this truth?"

"From the Bible, of course."

"That's your authority? The Bible?"

"Yes. It's the only authority for Christians."

"Can you prove that from the Bible?"

"What do you mean?"

"I mean I don't believe the Bible claims to be the sole rule of faith. I mean that the doctrine of *sola scriptura* is itself unbiblical. Please show me where the Bible claims such a status for itself."

A Sufficient Rule of Faith?

At this point the missionary will probably bring up one of several verses. The passage most commonly brought up by Evangelicals and Fundamentalists is 2 Timothy 3:16–17. In the King James Version, the verse reads this way: "All Scripture is given by inspiration of God and is profitable for doctrine, for reproof, for correction, for instruction in righteousness; that the man of God may be perfect, thoroughly furnished unto all good works."

Many claim that 2 Timothy 3:16–17 claims Scripture is sufficient as a rule of faith. But an examination of the verse in context shows that it doesn't claim that at all. It claims only that Scripture is "profitable" (Greek: *ōphelimos*), that is, helpful. Many things can be profitable for moving one toward a goal without being sufficient in getting one to the goal. Notice that the passage nowhere even hints that Scripture is "sufficient"—which is, of course, exactly what Protestants think the passage means.

Point out that the context of 2 Timothy 3:16–17 is Paul laying down a guideline for Timothy to make use of Scripture and Tradition in his ministry as a bishop. Paul says, "But as for you, continue in what you have learned and have firmly believed, knowing from whom you learned it and how from childhood you have been acquainted with the sacred writings which are able to instruct you for salvation through faith in Christ Jesus. All scripture is inspired by God [Greek: *theopneustos*, "God-breathed"] and profitable for teaching, for reproof, for correction, and for training in righteousness, that the man of God may be complete, equipped for every good work" (2 Tim. 3:14–17). In verse 14, Timothy is initially exhorted to hold to the oral teachings—the Tradition —that he received from the apostle Paul. This echoes Paul's reminder of the value of oral Tradition in 1:13–14: "Follow the pattern of the sound words which you have *heard* from me, in the faith and love which are in Christ Jesus; guard the truth that has been entrusted to you by the Holy Spirit who dwells within us;" "what you have *heard* from me before many witnesses entrust to faithful men who will be able to teach others also" (2:2). Here Paul refers exclusively to *oral* teaching and reminds Timothy to follow that as the "pattern" for his own teaching. Only after this is Scripture mentioned as "profitable" for Timothy's ministry.

The few other verses that might be brought up to "prove" the sufficiency of Scripture can be handled the same way. Not one uses the word *sufficient*—each one implies profitability or usefulness, and many are given at the same time as an exhortation to hold fast to the *oral teaching* of our Lord and the apostles. The thing to keep in mind is that nowhere does the Bible say, "Scripture alone is sufficient," and nowhere does the Bible imply it.

Understanding the Bible's Role

After you have demonstrated that the verses the missionary brings up simply don't prove this point, continue the discussion this way:

"If you recognize Scripture for what it is, you'll see that it wasn't intended to be an instructional tool for converts. In fact, not one book of the Bible was written for non-believers. The Old Testament books were written for Jews, the New Testament books for people who already were Christians.

"The Bible is not a catechism or a full-scale theological treatise. Just look at the twenty-seven books of the New Testament. You won't find one that spells out the elements of the faith the way catechisms do or even the way the ancient creeds did. Those twenty-seven books were written for the most part (excepting, for example, the Gospels and the general epistles such as James and 1 and 2 Peter) as provisional documents addressed to particular audiences for particular purposes.

"Most of the epistles," you continue, "were written to local churches that were experiencing moral and/or doctrinal problems. Paul and most of the other New Testament writers sent letters to these local churches in order to rectify these problems. There was no attempt on the part of the writers to impart a vast body of basic doctrinal instruction to non-believers, nor even to simply summarize everything for the believers who received the letters."

"I don't agree with any of that," replies the missionary. "The New Testament is the basis of the Christian faith."

"But how can it be," you respond, "since the Christian faith existed and flourished for years *before* the first book of the New Testament was written? The books of the New Testament were composed decades after Christ ascended into heaven, and it took centuries for there to be general agreement among Christians about which books comprised the New Testament.

"And that brings up another point. How do you know what constitutes the New Testament canon? How do you know for certain that these twenty-seven books here in your New Testament are in fact inspired and should be in the New Testament? And how do you know for certain that some inspired books haven't been left out of the canon?"

Who Decided?

"Well, the early Christians agreed on the twenty-seven books of the New Testament," answers the missionary. "The Holy Spirit led them to this agreement."

"Sure the Holy Spirit did, but only over a pretty long period of time, and a study of early Christian history shows that there was a considerable disagreement among Christians until the issue of the canon was finally settled. Some early Christians said the book of Revelation didn't belong in the canon. Others said Pope

Clement's letter to the Corinthians (written circa A.D. 80) and *The Shepherd*, an early second-century allegory written by a Christian writer named Hermas, *did* belong in the New Testament. How do you handle that?"

"We know by examining the contents of the books. Some books —like 1 Corinthians and Revelation—obviously belong. Others —like Clement's letter to the Corinthians—obviously don't."

"But is it really so obvious? Tell me, what is so obvious in Philemon to indicate that it is inspired? And what is so obviously unorthodox in *The Shepherd* or the *Didache* or Clement's letter or any of the other first- and second-century Christian writings? You've never even seen the autographs (originals) of the twenty-seven books in the New Testament. Nobody today has. The earliest copies of those books we possess are centuries newer than the originals. Like it or not, you have to take the say-so of the Catholic Church that in fact those copies are accurate, as well as her decision that those twenty-seven books are the inspired canonical New Testament Scriptures. You *do* accept her testimony as trustworthy, or else your Protestant Bible would not have those twenty-seven books. See what I mean?"

Look to the Fathers

If you happen to have the writings of the early Church Fathers, this would be a good time to read from them. The writings are, at least in the case of the apostolic Fathers, rather short, and you can demonstrate that many of these writings seem every bit as orthodox as the New Testament writings themselves. Then read aloud the book of Philemon or 3 John or some other short canonical book.

"Tell me: What's in these books that so obviously makes them inspired? If you didn't know that Philemon was written by Paul or that 3 John was written by John, would you give either a second reading? Would you automatically assume that they belong in the Bible as canonical Scripture? It's not disrespectful to say that they don't have much doctrinal content in them—and that's not surprising, since they're too short to contain substantial doctrinal discussions. One can imagine the Christian Church surviving well enough without either.

"Neither book claims inspiration for itself. If there is, as a matter of fact, more solid Christian doctrine in other, non-canonical writings (that is, if they contain more Christian truths and no religious errors), then how can you say that it's obvious which books are inspired and which are not?"

Here the missionary will fumble around awhile, perhaps repeating his earlier statements. Then you say:

"Look, the fact is that the only reason you and I have the New Testament canon is because of the trustworthy teaching authority of the Catholic Church. As Augustine put it, 'I would not believe in the Gospels were it not for the authority of the Catholic Church.' Any Christian accepting the authority of the New Testament does so, whether or not he admits it, because he has implicit trust that the Catholic Church made the right decision in determining the canon.

"The fact is that the Holy Spirit guided the Catholic Church over time to recognize and determine the canon of the New and Old Testaments in A.D. 382 at the synod of Rome, under Pope Damasus I. This decision was ratified again at the councils of Hippo (393) and Carthage (397 and 419). You, my friend, accept exactly the same books of the New Testament that Pope Damasus decreed were canonical, and no others.

"Furthermore, the reason you accept the books you do is that they were in the Bible someone gave you when you first became a Christian. You accept them because they were handed on to you. This means you accept the canon of the New Testament that you do because of Tradition, because Tradition is simply what is handed on to us from those who were in the faith before us. So your knowledge of the exact books that belong in the Bible, such as Philemon and 3 John, rests on Tradition rather than on Scripture itself!

"The question you have to ask yourself is this: Where did we get the Bible? Until you can give a satisfactory answer, you aren't in much of a position to rely on the authority of Scripture or to claim that you can be certain that you know how to accurately interpret it.

"After you answer that question—and there's really only one answer that can be given—you have some other important questions to ask: If the Bible, which we received from the Catholic Church, is our sole rule of faith, who's to do the interpreting? Why are there so many conflicting understandings among Evangelicals and Fundamentalists even on central doctrines that pertain to salvation?"

"We Agree on the Essentials"

"Well, that I can answer easily enough," responds the missionary. "Evangelicals and Fundamentalists agree on the essentials, but we disagree on secondary matters."

"Is that so? Where in Scripture do we find some doctrines listed as essential, others as 'secondary'? The answer is: nowhere. Evangelicals and Fundamentalists disagree on central issues such as baptismal regeneration and the necessity of baptism (is it merely a sign to other Christians, or does it have a real role in the process of justification?), whether or not one can forfeit salvation (some Protestants say that's impossible to do, others say it is possible). You *all* claim to be 'Bible-only Christians,' but which group is right?"

8

Can Dogma Develop?

The opening verse of the book of Hebrews tells us that "in many and various ways God spoke of old to our fathers by the prophets." This was done fragmentarily, under various figures and symbols. Man was not given religious truth as though from a Scholastic theologian, nicely laid out and fully indexed. Doctrines had to be thought out, lived out in the liturgical life of the Church, even pieced together by the Fathers and ecumenical councils. In this way, the Church has gained an ever-deepening understanding of the deposit of faith that had been "once for all delivered" (Jude 3) to it by Christ and the apostles.

Protestants—especially Fundamentalists and Evangelicals—admit that much. They recognize that there was a real development in doctrine: There was an initial message, much clouded at the fall, and then a progressively fuller explanation of God's teachings as Israel was prepared for the Messiah, until the apostles were instructed by the Messiah himself. Jesus told the apostles that in the Old Testament "many prophets and righteous men longed to see what you see, and did not see it, and to hear what you hear, and did not hear it" (Matt. 13:17).

Hold Fast to What You Were Taught

Christians have always understood that at the close of the apostolic age—with the death of the last surviving apostle, John, perhaps around A.D. 100—public revelation ceased (cf. *Catechism of the Catholic Church* 66–67, 73). Christ fulfilled the Old Testament law (cf. Matt. 5:17) and is the ultimate teacher of humanity: "You

have one teacher, the Messiah" (Matt. 23:10). The apostles recognized that their task was to pass on, intact, the faith given to
them by the Master: "And what you have heard from me before
many witnesses entrust to faithful men who will be able to teach
others also" (2 Tim. 2:2); "But as for you, continue in what you
have learned and have firmly believed, knowing from whom you
learned it" (2 Tim. 3:14).

However, this closure to public revelation doesn't mean that
there isn't progress in the understanding of what has been entrusted to the Church. Anyone interested in Christianity will ask,
"What does this doctrine imply? How does it relate to that doctrine?"

Vatican II on Development

In answering these questions, the Church facilitates the development or maturing of doctrines. The Blessed Virgin Mary models
this process of coming to an ever deeper understanding of God's
revelation: "But Mary kept all these things, pondering them in her
heart" (Luke 2:19). It's important to understand that the Church
does not, indeed *cannot*, change the doctrines God has given it,
nor can it "invent" new ones and add them to the deposit of faith
that has been "once for all delivered to the saints." New beliefs
are not invented, but obscurities and misunderstandings regarding
the deposit of faith are cleared up.

Vatican II explained, "The tradition that comes from the apostles develops in the Church with the help of the Holy Spirit. For
there is a growth in the understanding of the realities and the
words that have been handed down. This happens through the
contemplation and study made by believers, who treasure these
things in their hearts, through a penetrating understanding of the
spiritual realities that they experience, and through the preaching
of those who have received through episcopal succession the sure
gift of truth. For, as the centuries succeed one another, the Church
constantly moves forward toward the fullness of divine truth until
the words of God reach their complete fulfillment in her" (*Dei
Verbum* 8).

As we read Scripture, we see in it doctrines we already hold, each of us having been instructed in the faith before ever picking up the sacred text. This is a necessary process, as Scripture indicates. Peter explained, "There are some things in them [Paul's letters] hard to understand, which the ignorant and unstable twist to their own destruction, as they do the other scriptures" (2 Pet. 3:16). Those who are ignorant of orthodox Christian doctrine because they have never been taught it, or who are unstable in their adherence to the orthodox doctrine they have been taught, can twist Paul's writings and the rest of Scripture to their own destruction. Therefore, it is important that we read Scripture within the framework of the Church's constant tradition, as handed down from the apostles in the Catholic Church.

However, when we read Scripture in the light of the apostles' authentic teachings, we sometimes forget that some central doctrines (such as the Trinity and the hypostatic union) were not always understood or as clearly expounded in the Church's early days the way they are now. Understanding grew and deepened over time. As an example, consider the Holy Spirit's divinity. In Scripture, references to it seem to jump out at us. But if we imagine ourselves as ancient pagans or as present-day non-Christians reading the Bible for the first time, we realize that, for them, the Holy Spirit's status as a divine person is not as clearly present in Scripture, since they are less likely to notice details pointing to it. If we think of ourselves as having no recourse to apostolic Tradition and the Church's teaching authority that the Holy Spirit guides into all truth (cf. John 14:25–26; 16:13), we can appreciate how easy it must have been for the early heresies concerning the Trinity and Holy Spirit to arise.

Another example is the early heresy known as Monothelitism. This heresy, which Catholics, Eastern Orthodox, and Protestants reject, claimed that Christ had only one will—the divine—and that he had no human will. This error sprang up because people had not yet clearly perceived that, since Christ is fully God, he must have a divine will, and, since he is fully man, he must have a human will. If he lacks one or the other will, then he would either not be fully God or not be fully man. Thus Christ must have two wills, one divine and one human. But because the issue had never been raised before, this teaching had not yet been discerned as a necessary inference from the fact that Christ is fully God and fully man—two teachings that had been understood for ages.

Transubstantiation (the teaching that during Mass, at the moment of consecration, the substance of the bread and wine becomes, through a miraculous change wrought by God's grace, the substance of the body and blood, soul and divinity of Jesus Christ, though the *appearances* of bread and wine remain) is another example of a doctrine that had always been believed by the Church but whose exact meaning was understood more clearly over time. In the sixth chapter of John's Gospel, the Eucharist is promised by Jesus. If this chapter is read in conjunction with the accounts of the Last Supper, it is easy to see why the first Christians knew that the bread and wine are transubstantiated into Christ's actual body and blood. The Bible clearly says this change happens (cf. 1 Cor. 10:16–17; 11:23–29), but it is silent about *how* it happens.

The technical theological term "transubstantiation" was not formally adopted by the Catholic Church until the Fourth Lateran Council, in 1215. This was not the addition of a new doctrine but the Church's way of defining what it had *always* taught on this subject in terms that would be so exact as to exclude all the incorrect explanations proposed over the years to explain what happens at the moment of consecration. Because people gave a lot of thought to the meaning and implications of Christ's Real Presence in the Eucharist, because they tried their best to draw true inferences from this true doctrine, and because not all of them were adept at that, disputes arose, and a formal definition by the Church became necessary.

No Necessity to Define

As these and many other cases demonstrate, doctrinal questions can remain in a not yet fully defined state for years. The Church has never felt the need to formally define what there has been no particular pressure to define. This strikes many, particularly non-Catholics, as strange. Why weren't things cleared up in, say, A.D. 100, so folks could know what's what? Why didn't Rome issue a laundry list of definitions in the early days and let it go at that? Why wasn't an end-run made around all these troubles that plagued Christianity precisely because things were unclear? The remote reason is that God has had his own timetable and set of reasons (to which we aren't privy) for keeping it. The same could be said about Old Testament prophets: Why didn't they understand the fullness of the doctrine of the Trinity all at once? Or the identity of the Messiah? Or the fullness of Christian teaching? Partly because God had not revealed it all yet, and partly because their understanding of the implications of the doctrines they had needed to grow clearer over time.

This need to discern more clearly what is contained in the deposit of faith given to the Church by the apostles points us to the related subjects of infallibility and inspiration. The pope and the bishops (when teaching in union with him) have the charism of infallibility when defining matters of faith or morals, but infallibility works only negatively. Through the intervention of the Holy Spirit, the pope and bishops are prevented from teaching what is untrue, but they are not forced or told by the Holy Spirit to teach what is true. To put it another way, the pope and the bishops are not inspired the way the authors of Scripture or the prophets were. To make a new definition, to clear up some dogmatic confusion, they first have to use human reason, operating on what is known to date, to be able to teach more precisely what is to be held as true. They cannot teach what they do not know, and they learn things the same way we do. They have no access to prophetic shortcuts—they must delve by study into the riches of the words God has already given us.

Borrowing from Paganism?

Fundamentalists assert that what Catholics label as development is nothing more than a centuries-old accumulation of pagan beliefs and rites. The Catholic Church has not really refined the original deposit of faith, they claim. Instead, it has added to it from the outside. In its hurry to increase membership, particularly in the early centuries, the Church let in nearly anybody. When existing inducements were not enough, it adopted pagan ways to encourage pagans to convert. Each time the Church did this, it moved away from authentic Christianity.

Consider Christmas. Strict Fundamentalists do not observe it, and not only because the name of the feast is inescapably "Christ's Mass." Some say they disapprove of it because there is no proof Christ was born on December 25. Others argue he couldn't have been born in winter because the shepherds, who were in the fields with their sheep, never put sheep into fields during that season (a plausible, though in this case, erroneous assumption). Others, noting the Bible is silent about the feast of Christmas, say that should settle the matter. But these are all secondary considerations.

The real reasons many Fundamentalists oppose the celebration of Christmas are, first, that the feast of Christmas was established by the Catholic Church (which is bad enough) and, next, that the Church provided celebrating the birth of Christ as an alternative to celebrating a pagan holiday occurring at the same time.

The Fundamentalist objections notwithstanding, Scripture sanctions this practice. The Jewish Feast of Tabernacles was on the same day as a Canaanite vintage festival that it supplanted, much as Christmas coincided with the festival of *Sol Invictus* that non-Christians were celebrating. This is the same principle that Protestant churches use when they replace the celebration of Halloween with "Reformation Day" or "harvest festival" celebrations. It is an attempt to provide a wholesome alternative celebration to a popular but unwholesome one. Anti-Catholics who accuse Christmas of having "pagan origins" fail to recognize that it is precisely *anti-pagan* in origin.

Paul's Command about Tradition

More significant than Fundamentalists' rejection of the development of human traditions—such as when Christ's birth is celebrated—is their rejection of apostolic Tradition. Human traditions may be good or bad, but they do not have the weight that apostolic Tradition does. The latter, since it conveys God's revelation to us, is essential to the proper development of doctrine.

Catholics know that public revelation ended with the last apostle's death. But the part of revelation that was not written down —the part outside the Bible, the apostles' inspired oral teaching (1 Thess. 2:13) and their binding interpretations of Old Testament Scripture that forms the basis of sacred Tradition—is a part of revelation Catholics also accept. Catholics follow Paul's command: "So then, brethren, stand firm and hold to the traditions which you were taught by us, either by word of mouth or by letter" (2 Thess. 2:15; cf. 1 Cor. 11:2).

9

Bible Translations Guide

At Catholic Answers we are often asked which Bible version a person should choose. This is an important question about which Catholics need to be informed. Some have been given very little help about how to pick a Bible translation, but keeping in mind a few tips will make the decision much easier.

There are two general philosophies that translators use when they do their work: formal or complete equivalence and dynamic equivalence. Formal equivalence translations try to give as literal a translation of the original text as possible. Translators using this philosophy try to stick close to the originals, even preserving much of the original word order.

Literal translations are an excellent resource for serious Bible study. Sometimes the meaning of a verse depends on subtle cues in the text; these cues are preserved only by literal translations.

The disadvantage of literal translations is that they are harder to read because more Hebrew and Greek style intrudes into the English text. Compare the following renderings of Leviticus 18:6–10 from the New American Standard Bible (a literal translation) and the New International Version (a dynamic translation):

The NAS reads: "None of you shall approach any blood relative of his to uncover nakedness. . . . You shall not uncover the nakedness of your father's wife; it is your father's nakedness. The nakedness of your sister, either your father's daughter or your mother's daughter, whether born at home or born outside, their nakedness you shall not uncover. The nakedness of your son's daughter or your daughter's daughter, their nakedness you shall not uncover; for their nakedness is yours."

The NIV reads: "No one is to approach any close relative to have sexual relations. . . . Do not have sexual relations with your father's wife; that would dishonor your father. Do not have sexual relations with your sister, either your father's daughter or your mother's daughter, whether she was born in the same home or elsewhere. Do not have sexual relations with your son's daughter or your daughter's daughter; that would dishonor you."

Because literal translations can be difficult to read, many have produced more readable Bibles using the dynamic equivalence philosophy. According to this view, it does not matter whether the grammar and word order of the original is preserved in English so long as the meaning of the text is preserved. This frees up the translator to use better English style and word choice, producing more readable translations. In the above example, the dynamic equivalence translators were free to use the more readable expression "have sexual relations with" instead of being forced to reproduce the Hebrew idiom "uncover the nakedness of."

The disadvantage of dynamic translation is that there is a price to pay for readability. Dynamic translations lose precision because they omit subtle cues to the meaning of a passage that only literal translations preserve. They also run a greater risk of reading the translators' doctrinal views into the text because of the greater liberty in how to render it.

For example, dynamic Protestant translations, such as the NIV, tend to translate the Greek word *ergon* and its derivatives as "work" when it reinforces Protestant doctrine but as something else (such as "deeds" or "doing") when it would serve Catholic doctrine.

The NIV renders Romans 4:2 as: "If, in fact, Abraham was justified by works (*ergōn*), he had something to boast about—but not before God." This passage is used to support the Protestant doctrine of salvation by faith alone. But the NIV translates the *erg-* derivatives in Romans 2:6–7 differently: "God 'will give to each person according to what he has done (*erga*).' To those who by persistence in doing (*ergou*) good seek glory, honor and immortality, he will give eternal life."

If the *erg-* derivatives were translated consistently as "work," then it would be clear that the passage says God will judge "every person according to his works" and will give eternal life to

those who seek immortality "by persistence in working good"—
statements that support the Catholic view of salvation.

Even when there is no doctrinal agenda involved, it is difficult
to do word studies in dynamic translations because of inconsistency in how words are rendered. Beyond this, the intent of the
sacred author can be obscured.

Finding a Balance

Both literal and dynamic equivalence philosophies can be carried
to extremes. One translation that carries literalism to a ludicrous
extreme is the Concordant Version, which was translated by a man
who had studied Greek and Hebrew for only a short time. He
made a one-to-one rendering in which each word in the ancient
originals was translated by one (and only one) word in English.
This led to numerous absurdities. For example, compare how the
Concordant Version of Genesis 1:20 compares with the NIV:

Concordant Version: "And saying is God, 'Roaming is the water with the roaming, living soul, and the flyer is flying over the
earth on the face of the atmosphere of the heavens.'"

NIV: "And God said, 'Let the water teem with living creatures,
and let birds fly above the earth across the expanse of the sky.'"

At the other extreme are absurdly dynamic translations, such
as the Cotton-Patch Version. This was translated from Greek in
the 1960s by Clarence Jordan, who decided not only to replace
ancient ways of speaking with modern ones (like most dynamic
translations) but to replace items of ancient culture with items of
modern ones.

Compare the NIV rendering of Matthew 9:16–17 with what is
found in the CPV:

NIV: "No one sews a patch of unshrunk cloth on an old garment, for the patch will pull away from the garment, making the
tear worse. Neither do men pour new wine into old wineskins. If
they do, the skins will burst, the wine will run out and the wine-

skins will be ruined. No, they pour new wine into new wineskins, and both are preserved."

CPV: "Nobody ever uses new, unshrunk material to patch a dress that's been washed. For in shrinking, it will pull the old material and make a tear. Nor do people put new tubes in old, bald tires. If they do, the tires will blow out, and the tubes will be ruined and the tires will be torn up. But they put new tubes in new tires and both give good mileage."

Between the extremes of the Concordant Version and the Cotton-Patch Version is a spectrum of respectable translations that strike different balances between literal and dynamic equivalence.

Toward the literal end of the spectrum are translations such as the King James Version, the New King James Version, the New American Standard, and the Douay-Rheims Version.

Next come slightly less literal translations, such as the Revised Standard Version and the Confraternity Version.

Then there are mostly dynamic translations such as the New International Version and the New American Bible.

And finally, toward the very dynamic end of the spectrum are translations such as the New Jerusalem Bible, the New English Bible, the Revised English Bible, the Contemporary English Version, and the "Good News Bible," whose translation is called Today's English Version.

One translation that is hard to place on the spectrum is the New Revised Standard Version. The basic text of the NRSV is rendered literally, following the RSV, but it uses "gender inclusive language," which tries to translate the original text into a modern "gender neutral" cultural equivalent. When you read the NRSV you will often encounter "friends," "beloved," and "brothers and sisters," and then see a footnote stating "Gk brothers." The NRSV also shows a preference for using "God" and "Christ" when the original text says "he."

There is also a host of minor versions, most of which are dynamic equivalence translations. These include well-known ones (such as the Moffatt, Philips, and Knox translations) and also unique, specialty versions such as the Jewish New Testament (translated by David Stern), which renders New Testament names and expressions with the Hebrew, Aramaic, or Yiddish equivalents.

Finally, there are paraphrases, which are not translations based on the original languages but are paraphrased versions of English translations. These tend toward the extreme dynamic end of the spectrum. The best known is the Living Bible, also known as "the Book."

The basic question you need to ask when selecting a Bible version is the purpose you are pursuing. If you simply want a Bible for ordinary reading, a moderate or dynamic version would suffice. This would enable you to read more of the text quickly and comprehend its basic meaning, though it would not give you the details of its meaning, and you would have to watch out more for the translators' doctrinal views coloring the text.

What Is the Best Bible?

If you intend to do serious Bible study, a literal translation is what you want. This will enable you to catch more of the detailed implications of the text but at the price of readability. You have to worry less about the translators' views coloring the text, though even very literal translations are not free from this entirely.

A second question you will need to ask yourself is whether you want an old or a modern translation. Older versions, such as the King James and the Douay-Rheims, can sound more dignified, authoritative, and inspiring. But they are much harder to read and understand because English has changed in the almost 400 years since they were done.

One down side to using certain modern translations is that they do not use the traditional renderings of certain passages and phrases, and the reader may find this annoying. The "Good News Bible" or TEV is especially known for non-traditional renderings. For example, "the abomination of desolation" referred to in the book of Daniel and the Gospels is called "the awful horror," and the ark of the covenant is known as "the covenant box."

Some Protestants will tell you that the only acceptable version of the Bible is the King James. This position is known as King James-onlyism. Its advocates often make jokes such as "If the King James Version was good enough for the apostle Paul, it is good enough for me," or "My King James Version corrects your Greek text."

They commonly claim that the King James is based on the only perfect set of manuscripts we have (a false claim—there is no perfect set of manuscripts, and the ones used for the KJV were compiled by a Catholic, Erasmus), that it is the only translation that avoids modern liberal renderings, and that its translators were extremely saintly and scholarly men. Since the King James is also known as "the Authorized Version," its advocates sometimes argue that it is the only version to ever have been "authorized." To this one may point out that it was only authorized in the Anglican church, which now uses other translations. For a still-in-print critique of King James-onlyism, see D. A. Carson, *The King James Version Debate: A Plea for Realism* (Grand Rapids: Baker, 1979).

As amusing as King James-onlyism may sound, some people take it very seriously. There is even a Catholic equivalent, which we might call "Douay-Rheims-onlyism." The Douay-Rheims version, which predates the King James by a few years (the complete KJV was published in 1611; the complete Douay-Rheims came in 1609), was the standard Bible for English-speaking Catholics until the twentieth century.

What many advocates of both King James-onlyism and Douay-Rheims-onlyism do not know is that neither Bible is the original issued in the 1600s. Over the last three centuries, numerous minor changes (spelling and grammar, for example) have been made in the King James, with the result that most versions of the KJV currently on the market are significantly different from the original. This has led one publisher to recently re-issue the 1611 King James Version.

The Douay-Rheims currently on the market is also not the original 1609 version. It is technically called the "Douay-Challoner" version because it is a revision of the Douay-Rheims done in the mid-eighteenth century by Bishop Richard Challoner. He also consulted early Greek and Hebrew manuscripts, meaning that the Douay Bible currently on the market is not simply a translation of the Vulgate (which many of its advocates do not realize).

For most the question of whether to use an old or a modern translation is not so pointed, and once a decision has been reached on this question it is possible to select a particular Bible version with relative ease.

We recommend staying away from translations with unconventional renderings, such as the TEV, and suggest using the Revised Standard Version: Catholic Edition. This is a Church-approved version of the RSV that has a few, minor changes in the New Testament. It has been reissued by Ignatius Press under the title *The Ignatius Bible* (available from Catholic Answers).

In the end, there may not be a need to select only one translation of the Bible to use. There is no reason that a Catholic cannot collect several versions of the Bible, aware of the strengths and weaknesses of each. It is often possible to get a better sense of what is being said in a passage by comparing several different translations.

So, which Bible is the best? Perhaps the best answer is this: The one you'll read.

10

Praying to the Saints

The historical Christian practice of asking our departed brothers and sisters in Christ—the saints—for their intercession has come under attack in the last few hundred years. Though the practice dates to the earliest days of Christianity and is shared by Catholics, Eastern Orthodox, other Eastern Christians, and even some Anglicans—meaning that all-told it is shared by more than three-quarters of the Christians on earth—it still comes under heavy attack from many within the Protestant movement that started in the sixteenth century.

Can They Hear Us?

One charge made against it is that the saints in heaven cannot even hear our prayers, making it useless to ask for their intercession. However, this is not true. As Scripture indicates, those in heaven are aware of the prayers of those on earth. This can be seen, for example, in Revelation 5:8, where John depicts the saints in heaven offering our prayers to God under the form of "golden bowls full of incense, which are the prayers of the saints." But if the saints in heaven are offering our prayers to God, then they must be aware of our prayers. They are aware of our petitions and present them to God by interceding for us.

Some might try to argue that in this passage the prayers being offered were not addressed to the saints in heaven but directly to God. Yet this argument would only strengthen the fact that those in heaven can hear our prayers, for then the saints would be aware of our prayers even when they are not directed to them!

In any event, it is clear from Revelation 5:8 that the saints in heaven do actively intercede for us. We are explicitly told by John that the incense they offer to God is the prayers of the saints. Prayers are not physical things and cannot be physically offered to God. Thus the saints in heaven are offering our prayers to God mentally. In other words, they are interceding.

One Mediator

Another charge commonly leveled against asking the saints for their intercession is that this violates the sole mediatorship of Christ, which Paul discusses: "For there is one God, and there is one mediator between God and men, the man Christ Jesus" (1 Tim. 2:5).

But asking a person to pray for you in no way violates Christ's mediatorship, as can be seen from considering the way in which Christ is a mediator. First, Christ is a unique mediator between man and God because he is the only person who is both God and man. He is the only bridge between the two, the only God-man. But that role as mediator is not compromised in the least by the fact that others intercede for us. Furthermore, Christ is a unique mediator between God and man because he is the mediator of the New Covenant (cf. Heb. 9:15; 12:24), just as Moses was the mediator (Greek: *mesitās*) of the Old Covenant (cf. Gal. 3:19–20).

The intercession of fellow Christians—which is what the saints in heaven are—also clearly does not interfere with Christ's unique mediatorship, because in the four verses immediately preceding 1 Timothy 2:5, Paul *says* that Christians should intercede: "First of all, then, I urge that supplications, prayers, intercessions, and thanksgivings be made for all men, for kings and all who are in high positions, that we may lead a quiet and peaceable life, godly and respectful in every way. This is good, and it is acceptable in the sight of God our Savior, who desires all men to be saved and to come to the knowledge of the truth" (1 Tim. 2:1–4). Clearly, then, intercessory prayer offered by Christians on behalf of others is something "good and pleasing to God," not something infringing on Christ's role as mediator.

"No Contact with the Dead"

Sometimes Fundamentalists object to asking our fellow Christians in heaven to pray for us by declaring that God has forbidden contact with the dead in passages such as Deuteronomy 18:10–11. In fact, he has not, because he has at times given it—for example, when he had Moses and Elijah appear with Christ to the disciples at the transfiguration (Matt. 17:3). What God has forbidden is necromantic practice of conjuring up spirits. "There shall not be found among you any one who burns his son or his daughter as an offering, any one who practices divination, a soothsayer, or an augur, or a sorcerer, or a charmer, or a medium, or a wizard, or a necromancer. . . . For these nations, which you are about to dispossess, give heed to soothsayers and to diviners; but as for you, the Lord your God has not allowed you so to do. The Lord your God will raise up for you a prophet like me from among you, from your brethren—him you shall heed" (Deut. 18:10–11, 14–15).

God thus indicates that one is not to conjure the dead for purposes of gaining information; one is to look to God's prophets instead. Thus one is not to hold a seance. But anyone with an ounce of common sense can discern the vast qualitative difference between holding a seance to have the dead speak through you and a son humbly saying at his mother's grave, "Mom, please pray to Jesus for me. I'm having a real problem right now." The difference between the two is the difference between night and day. One is an occult practice bent on getting secret information, while the other is a humble request for a loved one to pray to God on one's behalf.

Overlooking the Obvious

Some objections to the concept of prayer to the saints betray restricted notions of heaven. One comes from anti-Catholic Loraine Boettner:

"How, then, can a human being such as Mary hear the prayers of millions of Roman Catholics, in many different countries, praying in many different languages, all at the same time?

"Let any priest or layman try to converse with only three people at the same time and see how impossible that is for a human being. . . . The objections against prayers to Mary apply equally against prayers to the saints. For they too are only creatures, infinitely less than God, able to be at only one place at a time and to do only one thing at a time.

"How, then, can they listen to and answer thousands upon thousands of petitions made simultaneously in many different lands and in many different languages? Many such petitions are expressed, not orally, but only mentally, silently. How can Mary and the saints, without being like God, be present everywhere and know the secrets of all hearts?" (*Roman Catholicism*, 142–3).

If being in heaven were like being in the next room, then of course these objections would be valid. A mortal, unglorified person in the next room would indeed suffer the restrictions imposed by the way space and time work in our universe. But the saints are not in the next room, and they are not subject to the time/space limitations of this life.

This does not imply that the saints in heaven must therefore be omniscient, as God is, for it is only through God's willing it that they can communicate with others in heaven or with us. And Boettner's argument about petitions arriving in different languages is even further off the mark. Does anyone really think that in heaven the saints are restricted to the King's English? After all, it is God himself who gives the gift of tongues and the interpretation of tongues. Surely those saints in Revelation understand the prayers they are shown to be offering to God.

The problem here is one of what might be called a primitive or even childish view of heaven. It is certainly not one on which enough intellectual rigor has been exercised. A good introduction to the real implications of the afterlife may be found in Frank Sheed's book *Theology and Sanity*, which argues that sanity depends on an accurate appreciation of reality, and that includes an accurate appreciation of what heaven is really like. And once that is known, the place of prayer to the saints follows.

"Directly to Jesus"

Some may grant that the previous objections to asking the saints for their intercession do not work and may even grant that the practice is permissible in theory, yet they may question it on other grounds, asking why one would *want* to ask the saints to pray for one. "Why not pray directly to Jesus?" they ask.

The answer is: *Of course* one should pray directly to Jesus! But that does not mean it is not also a good thing to ask others to pray for one as well. Ultimately, the "go-directly-to-Jesus" objection boomerangs back on the one who makes it: Why should we ask any Christian, in heaven or on earth, to pray for us when we can ask Jesus directly? If the mere fact that we can go straight to Jesus proved that we should ask no Christian in heaven to pray for us, then it would also prove that we should ask no Christian on earth to pray for us.

Praying for each other is simply part of what Christians do. As we saw in 1 Timothy 2:1–4, Paul strongly encouraged Christians to intercede for many different things, and that passage is by no means unique in his writings. Elsewhere Paul directly asks others to pray for him (Rom. 15:30–32; Eph. 6:18–20; Col. 4:3; 1 Thess. 5:25; 2 Thess. 3:1), and he assured them that he was praying for them as well (2 Thess. 1:11). Most fundamentally, Jesus himself required us to pray for others, and not only for those who asked us to do so (cf. Matt. 5:44).

Since the practice of asking others to pray for us is so highly recommended in Scripture, it cannot be regarded as superfluous on the grounds that one can go directly to Jesus. The New Testament would not recommend it if there were not benefits coming from it. One such benefit is that the faith and devotion of the saints can support our own weaknesses and supply what is lacking in our own faith and devotion. Jesus regularly supplied for one person based on another person's faith (e.g., Matt. 8:13; 15:28; 17:15–18; Mark 9:17–29; Luke 8:49–55). And it goes without saying that those in heaven, being free of the body and the distractions of this life, have even greater confidence and devotion to God than anyone on earth.

Also, God answers in particular the prayers of the righteous. James declares: "The prayer of a righteous man has great power in its effects. Elijah was a man of like nature with ourselves and he prayed fervently that it might not rain, and for three years and six months it did not rain on the earth. Then he prayed again and the heaven gave rain, and the earth brought forth its fruit" (Jas. 5:16–18). Yet those Christians in heaven are more righteous than anyone on earth, since they have been made perfect to stand in God's presence (cf. Heb. 12:22–23), meaning their prayers would be even more efficacious.

Having others praying for us thus is a *good* thing, not something to be despised or set aside. Of course, we should pray directly to Christ with every pressing need we have (cf. John 14:13–14). That's something the Catholic Church strongly encourages. In fact, the prayers of the Mass, the central act of Catholic worship, are directed to God and Jesus, not the saints. But this does not mean that we should not also ask our fellow Christians, including those in heaven, to pray with us.

In addition to our prayers directly to God and Jesus (which are absolutely essential to Christian life), there are abundant reasons to ask our fellow Christians in heaven to pray for us. The Bible indicates that they are aware of our prayers, that they intercede for us, and that their prayers are effective (or else they would not be offered). It is only narrow-mindedness that suggests we should refrain from asking our fellow Christians in heaven to do what we already know them to be anxious and capable of doing.

In Heaven and on Earth

The Bible directs us to invoke those in heaven and ask them to pray with us. Thus in Psalm 103, we pray, "Bless the Lord, O you his angels, you mighty ones who do his word, hearkening to the voice of his word! Bless the Lord, all his hosts, his ministers that do his will!" (Ps. 103:20–21). And in Psalm 148 we pray, "Praise the Lord! Praise the Lord from the heavens, praise him in the heights! Praise him, all his angels, praise him, all his host!" (Ps. 148:1–2).

Not only do those in heaven pray with us, but they also pray for us. In the book of Revelation, we read: "[An] angel came and stood at the altar [in heaven] with a golden censer; and he was given much incense to mingle with the prayers of all the saints upon the golden altar before the throne; and the smoke of the incense rose with the prayers of the saints from the hand of the angel before God" (Rev. 8:3–4).

And those in heaven who offer to God our prayers aren't just angels but humans as well. John sees that "the twenty-four elders [the leaders of the people of God in heaven] fell down before the Lamb, each holding a harp, and with golden bowls full of incense, which are the prayers of the saints" (Rev. 5:8). The simple fact is as this passage shows: The saints in heaven offer to God the prayers of the saints on earth.

Saint Worship

The word *worship* has undergone a change in meaning in English. It comes from the Old English *weorthscipe*, which means "the condition of being worthy of honor, respect, or dignity." To worship in the older, larger sense is to ascribe honor, worth, or excellence to someone, whether a sage, a magistrate, or God.

For many centuries, the term *worship* simply meant showing respect or honor, and an example of this usage survives in contemporary English. British subjects refer to their magistrates as "Your Worship," although Americans would say "Your Honor." This doesn't mean that British subjects worship their magistrates as gods. (In fact, they may even despise a particular magistrate they are addressing.) It means that they are giving them the honor appropriate to their office, not the honor appropriate to God.

Outside of this example, however, the English term *worship* has been narrowed in scope to indicate only that supreme form of honor, reverence, and respect that is due to God. This change in usage is quite recent. In fact, one can still find books that use *worship* in the older, broader sense. This can lead to confusion when people who are familiar with only the use of words in their own day and their own circles encounter material written in other times and other places.

In Scripture, the term *worship* was similarly broad in meaning, but in the early Christian centuries, theologians began to differentiate between different types of honor in order to make clearer which is due to God and which is not.

As the terminology of Christian theology developed, the Greek term *latria* came to be used to refer to the honor that is due to God alone, and the term *dulia* came to refer to the honor that is due to human beings, especially those who lived and died in

God's friendship—in other words, the saints. Scripture indicates that honor is due to these individuals (cf. Matt. 10:41). A special term was coined to refer to the special honor given to the Virgin Mary, who bore Jesus—God in the flesh—in her womb. This term, *hyperdulia* (*huper* [more than] + *dulia* = "beyond dulia"), indicates that the honor due to her as Christ's own Mother is more than the *dulia* given to other saints. It is greater in degree, but still of the same kind. However, since Mary is a finite creature, the honor due to her is fundamentally different in kind from the *latria* owed to the infinite Creator.

All of these terms—*latria*, *dulia*, and *hyperdulia*—used to be lumped under the one English word *worship*. Sometimes when one reads old books discussing how particular persons are to be honored, they will qualify the word *worship* by referring to "the worship of *latria*" or "the worship of *dulia*." To contemporaries and those not familiar with the history of these terms, however, this is too confusing.

Another attempt to make clear the difference between the honor due to God and that due to humans has been to use the words *adore* and *adoration* to describe the total, consuming reverence due to God, and the terms *venerate*, *veneration*, and *honor* to refer to the respect due to humans. Thus, Catholics sometimes say, "We *adore* God but we *honor* his saints."

Unfortunately, many non-Catholics have been so schooled in hostility toward the Church that they appear unable or unwilling to recognize these distinctions. They confidently (often arrogantly) assert that Catholics "worship" Mary and the saints, and, in so doing, commit idolatry. This is patently false, of course, but the education in anti-Catholic prejudice is so strong that one must patiently explain that Catholics *do not* worship anyone but God —at least given the contemporary use of the term. The Church is very clear about the fact that *latria*, adoration—what contemporary English speakers call "worship"—is to be given *only* to God.

Though one should know it from one's own background, it often may be best to simply point out that Catholics do not worship anyone but God and omit discussing the history of the term.

Many non-Catholics might be more perplexed than enlightened by hearing the history of the word *worship*. Familiar only with *their group's* use of the term, they may misperceive a history lesson as rationalization and end up even more adamant in their declarations that the term is applicable only to God. They may even go further. Wanting to attack the veneration of the saints, they may declare that *only* God should be honored.

Both of these declarations are in direct contradiction to the language and precepts of the Bible. The term *worship* was used in the same way in the Bible that it used to be used in English. It could cover both the adoration given to God alone and the honor that is to be shown to certain human beings. In Hebrew, the term for worship is *shakhah*. It is appropriately used for humans in a large number of passages.

For example, in Genesis 37:7–9, Joseph relates two dreams that God gave him concerning how his family would honor him in coming years. Translated literally, the passage states: " 'Behold, we were binding sheaves in the field, and lo, my sheaf arose and stood upright; and behold, your sheaves gathered round it, and worshiped [*shakhah*] my sheaf.' . . . Then he dreamed another dream, and told it to his brothers, and said, 'Behold, I have dreamed another dream; and behold, the sun, the moon, and eleven stars were worshiping [*shakhah*] me.' "

In Genesis 49, Jacob pronounces a prophetic blessing on his sons, and concerning Judah he states: "Judah, your brothers shall praise you; your hand shall be on the neck of your enemies; your father's sons shall worship [*shakhah*] you" (Gen. 49:8). And in Exodus 18:7, Moses honored his father-in-law, Jethro: "Moses went out to meet his father-in-law, and worshiped [*shakhah*] him and kissed him; and they asked each other of their welfare, and went into the tent."

None of these passages were discussing the worship of adoration, the kind of worship given to God.

Honoring Saints

Consider how honor is given. We regularly give it to public officials. In the United States it is customary to address a judge as "Your Honor." In the marriage ceremony it used to be said that the wife would "love, honor, and obey" her husband. Letters to legislators are addressed to "the Honorable So-and-So." And just about anyone, living or dead, who bears an exalted rank is said to be worthy of honor, and this is particularly true of historical figures, as when children are (or at least used to be) instructed to honor the founding fathers of America.

These practices are entirely biblical. We are explicitly commanded at numerous points in the Bible to honor certain people. One of the most important commands on this subject is the command to honor one's parents: "Honor your father and your mother, that your days may be long in the land which the Lord your God gives you" (Ex. 20:12). God considered this command so important that he repeated it multiple times in the Bible (cf. Lev. 19:3; Deut. 5:16; Matt. 15:4; Luke 18:20; Eph. 6:2). It was also important to give honor to one's elders in general: "You shall rise up before the hoary head, and honor the face of an old man, and you shall fear your God: I am the Lord" (Lev. 19:32). It was also important to specially honor religious leaders: "And you shall make holy garments for Aaron your brother [the high priest], for glory and for beauty" (Ex. 28:2).

The New Testament also stresses the importance of honoring others. The apostle Paul commanded: "Pay all of them their dues, taxes to whom taxes are due, revenue to whom revenue is due, respect to whom respect is due, honor to whom honor is due" (Rom. 13:7). He also stated this as a principle regarding one's employers: "Slaves, be obedient to those who are your earthly masters, with fear and trembling, in singleness of heart, as to Christ" (Eph. 6:5). "Let all who are under the yoke of slavery regard their masters as worthy of all honor, so that the name of God and the teaching may not be defamed" (1 Tim. 6:1). Perhaps the broadest command to honor others is found in 1 Peter: "Honor all men. Love the brotherhood. Fear God. Honor the emperor" (1 Pet. 2:17).

The New Testament also stresses the importance of honoring religious figures. Paul spoke of the need to give them special honor: "Let the presbyters [priests] who rule well be considered worthy of double honor, especially those who labor in preaching and teaching" (1 Tim. 5:17). Christ himself promised special blessings to those who honor religious figures: "He who receives a prophet because he is a prophet shall receive a prophet's reward, and he who receives a righteous man [a saint] because he is a righteous man shall receive a righteous man's reward" (Matt. 10:41).

So, if there can be nothing wrong with honoring the living, who still have an opportunity to ruin their lives through sin, there certainly can be no argument against giving honor to saints whose lives are done and who ended them in sanctity. If people should be honored in general, God's special friends certainly should be honored.

Statue Worship?

People who do not know better sometimes say that Catholics worship statues. Not only do Catholics not worship statues, but they do not even honor statues. After all, a statue is nothing but a carved block of marble or a chunk of plaster, and no one gives honor to marble yet unquarried or to plaster still in the mixing bowl.

The fact that someone kneels before a statue to pray does not mean that he is praying *to* the statue, just as the fact that someone kneels with a Bible in his hands to pray does not mean that he is worshiping the Bible. Statues or paintings or other artistic devices are used to recall to the mind the person or thing depicted. Just as it is easier to remember one's mother by looking at her photograph, so it is easier to recall the lives of the saints by looking at representations of them.

The use of statues and icons for liturgical purposes (as opposed to idols) also had a place in the Old Testament. In Exodus 25:18–20, God commanded: "And you shall make two cherubim of gold; of hammered work shall you make them, on the two ends of the mercy seat. Make one cherub on the one end, and one cherub on the other end; of one piece with the mercy seat shall you make the cherubim on its two ends. The cherubim shall spread out their wings above, overshadowing the mercy seat with their wings, their faces one to another; toward the mercy seat shall the faces of the cherubim be."

In Numbers 21:8–9, he told Moses: " 'Make a fiery serpent, and set it on a pole; and every one who is bitten, when he sees it, shall live.' So Moses made a bronze serpent, and set it on a pole; and if a serpent bit any man, he would look at the bronze serpent and live." This shows the actual ceremonial use of a statue (looking to it) in order to receive a blessing from God (healing from a snakebite). In John 3:14, Jesus tells us that he himself is what the bronze serpent represented, so it was a symbolic representation of Jesus. There was no problem with this statue—God had commanded it to be made—so long as people did not worship it. When they did, the righteous king Hezekiah had it destroyed (cf. 2 Kgs. 18:4). This clearly shows the difference between the proper religious use of statues and idolatry.

When the time came to build the temple in Jerusalem, God inspired David's plans for it, which included "his plan for the golden chariot of the cherubim that spread their wings and covered the ark of the covenant of the Lord. All this he made clear by the writing from the hand of the Lord concerning it, all the work to be done according to the plan" (1 Chr. 28:18–19).

In obedience to this divinely inspired plan, Solomon built two gigantic golden statues of cherubim: "In the most holy place he made two cherubim of wood and overlaid them with gold. The wings of the cherubim together extended twenty cubits: one wing of the one, of five cubits, touched the wall of the house, and its other wing, of five cubits, touched the wing of the other cherub; and of this cherub, one wing, of five cubits, touched the wall of the house, and the other wing, also of five cubits, was joined to the wing of the first cherub. The wings of these cherubim extended twenty cubits; the cherubim stood on their feet, facing the nave. And he made the veil of blue and purple and crimson fabrics and fine linen, and worked cherubim on it" (2 Chr. 3:10–14).

Imitation Is the Biblical Form of Honor

The most important form of honoring the saints, to which all the other forms are related, is the imitation of them in their relationship with God. Paul wrote extensively about the importance of spiritual imitation. He stated: "I urge you, then, be imitators of me. Therefore I sent to you Timothy, my beloved and faithful child in the Lord, to remind you of my ways in Christ, as I teach them everywhere in every church" (1 Cor. 4:16–17). Later he told the same group: "Be imitators of me, as I am of Christ. I commend you because you remember me in everything and maintain the traditions even as I have delivered them to you" (1 Cor. 11:1–2). The author of the letter to the Hebrews also stresses the importance of imitating true spiritual leaders: "Remember your leaders, those who spoke to you the word of God; consider the outcome of their life, and imitate their faith" (Heb. 13:7).

One of the most important passages on imitation is found in Hebrews. Chapter 11 of that book, the Bible's well-known "hall of fame" chapter, presents numerous examples of the Old Testament saints for our imitation. Then comes the author's famous exhortation: "Therefore, since we are surrounded by so great a cloud of witnesses, let us also lay aside every weight, and sin which clings so closely, and let us run with perseverance the race that is set before us" (Heb. 12:1)—the race that the saints have run before us.

12

Do Catholics Worship Statues?

"Catholics worship statues!" People still make this ridiculous claim. Because Catholics have statues in their churches, goes the accusation, they are violating God's commandment "You shall not make for yourself a graven image, or any likeness of anything that is in heaven above, or that is in the earth beneath, or that is in the water under the earth: you shall not bow down to them or serve them" (Ex. 20:4–5); "Alas, this people have sinned a great sin; they have made for themselves gods of gold" (Ex. 32:31).

It is right to warn people against the sin of idolatry when they are committing it. But calling Catholics idolaters because they have images of Christ and the saints is based on misunderstanding or ignorance of what the Bible says about the purpose and uses (both good and bad) of statues.

Anti-Catholic writer Loraine Boettner, in his book *Roman Catholicism*, makes the blanket statement that "God has forbidden the use of images in worship" (281). Yet if people were to "search the scriptures" (John 5:39), they would find the opposite is true. God forbade the *worship* of statues, but he did not forbid the *religious use* of statutes. Instead, he actually *commanded* their use in religious contexts!

God Said to Make Them

People who oppose religious statuary forget about the many passages where the Lord *commands* the making of statues. For example: "And you shall make two cherubim of gold [i.e., two gold statues of angels]; of hammered work shall you make them, on the two ends of the mercy seat. Make one cherub on the one end, and one cherub on the other end; of one piece of the mercy seat shall you make the cherubim on its two ends. The cherubim shall spread out their wings above, overshadowing the mercy seat with their wings, their faces one to another; toward the mercy seat shall the faces of the cherubim be" (Ex. 25:18–20). David gave Solomon the plan "for the altar of incense made of refined gold, and its weight; also his plan for the golden chariot of the cherubim that spread their wings and covered the ark of the covenant of the Lord. All this he made clear by the writing of the hand of the Lord concerning it, all the work to be done according to the plan" (1 Chr. 28:18–19). David's plan for the temple, which the biblical author tells us was "by the writing of the hand of the Lord concerning it," included statues of angels.

Similarly Ezekiel 41:17–18 describes graven (carved) images in the idealized temple he was shown in a vision, for he writes, "On the walls round about in the inner room and [on] the nave were carved likenesses of cherubim."

The Religious Use of Images

During a plague of serpents sent to punish the Israelites during the Exodus, God told Moses to " 'make [a statue of] a fiery serpent, and set it on a pole; and every one who is bitten, when he sees it, shall live.' So Moses made a bronze serpent, and set it on a pole; and if a serpent bit any man, he would look at the bronze serpent and live" (Num. 21:8–9).

One had to *look* at the bronze statue of the serpent to be healed, which shows that statues could be used ritually, not merely as religious decorations.

Catholics use statues, paintings, and other artistic devices to recall the person or thing depicted. Just as it helps to remember one's mother by looking at her photograph, so it helps to recall the example of the saints by looking at pictures of them. Catholics also use statues as teaching tools. In the early Church they were especially useful for the instruction of the illiterate. Many Protestants have pictures of Jesus and other Bible pictures in Sunday school for teaching children. Catholics also use statues to commemorate certain people and events, much as Protestant churches have three-dimensional nativity scenes at Christmas.

If one measured Protestants by the same rule, then by using these "graven" images, they would be practicing the "idolatry" of which they accuse Catholics. But there's no idolatry going on in these situations. God forbids the *worship* of images as gods, but he doesn't ban the making of images. If he had, religious movies, videos, photographs, paintings, and all similar things would be banned. But, as the case of the bronze serpent shows, God does not even forbid the ritual use of religious images.

It is when people begin to adore a statue as a god that the Lord becomes angry. Thus when people *did* start to worship the bronze serpent as a snake-god (whom they named "Nehushtan"), the righteous King Hezekiah had it destroyed (cf. 2 Kgs. 18:4).

What about Bowing?

Sometimes anti-Catholics cite Deuteronomy 5:9, where God said concerning idols, "You shall not bow down to them." Since many Catholics sometimes bow or kneel in front of statues of Jesus and the saints, anti-Catholics confuse the legitimate veneration of a sacred image with the sin of idolatry.

Though bowing can be used as a posture in worship, not all bowing is worship. In Japan, people show respect by bowing in greeting (the equivalent of the Western handshake). Similarly, a person can kneel before a king without worshiping him as a god. In the same way, a Catholic who may kneel in front of a statue while praying isn't worshiping the statue or even praying to *it* any more than the Protestant who kneels with a Bible in his hands when praying is worshiping the Bible or praying to *it*.

Hiding the Second Commandment?

Another charge sometimes made by Protestants is that the Catholic Church "hides" the second commandment. This is because in Catholic catechisms, the first commandment is often listed as "You shall have no other gods before me" (Ex. 20:3), and the second is listed as "You shall not take the name of the Lord in vain" (Ex. 20:7). From this, it is argued that Catholics have deleted the prohibition of idolatry to justify their use of religious statues. But this is false. Catholics simply group the commandments differently from most Protestants.

In Exodus 20:2–17, which gives the Ten Commandments, there are actually fourteen imperative statements. To arrive at Ten Commandments, some statements have to be grouped together, and there is more than one way of doing this. Since, in the ancient world, polytheism and idolatry were always united—idolatry being the outward expression of polytheism—the historical Jewish numbering of the Ten Commandments has always grouped together the imperatives "You shall have no other gods before me" (v. 3) and "You shall not make for yourself a graven image" (v. 4). The historical Catholic numbering follows the Jewish numbering on this point, as does the historical Lutheran numbering. Martin Luther recognized that the imperatives against polytheism and idolatry are two parts of a single command.

Jews and Christians abbreviate the commandments so that they can be remembered using a summary, ten-point formula. For example, Jews, Catholics, and Protestants typically summarize the Sabbath commandment as "Remember the Sabbath to keep it holy," though the commandment's actual text takes four verses (Ex. 20:8–11).

When the prohibition of polytheism/idolatry is summarized, Jews, Catholics, and Lutherans abbreviate it as "You shall have no other gods before me." This is no attempt to "hide" the idolatry prohibition. (Jews and Lutherans don't even use statues of saints and angels.) It is to make learning the Ten Commandments easier.

The Catholic Church is not dogmatic about how the Ten Commandments are to be numbered, however. The *Catechism of the Catholic Church* says, "The division and numbering of the commandments have varied in the course of history. The present catechism follows the division of the commandments established by Augustine, which has become traditional in the Catholic Church. It is also that of the Lutheran confession. The Greek Fathers worked out a slightly different division, which is found in the Orthodox churches and Reformed communities" (CCC 2066).

The Form of God?

Some anti-Catholics appeal to Deuteronomy 4:15–18 in their attack on religious statues: "Since you saw no form on the day that the Lord spoke to you at Horeb out of the midst of the fire, beware lest you act corruptly by making a graven image for yourselves, in the form of any figure, the likeness of male or female, the likeness of any beast that is on the earth, the likeness of any winged bird that flies in the air, the likeness of anything that creeps on the ground, the likeness of any fish that is in the water under the earth."

We've already shown that God doesn't prohibit the making of statues or images of various creatures for religious purposes (cf. 1 Kgs. 6:29–32; 8:6–66; 2 Chr. 3:7–14). But what about statues or images that represent God? Many Protestants would say that's wrong because Deuteronomy 4 says the Israelites did not see God under any form when he made the covenant with them, so we should therefore not make symbolic representations of God either. But does Deuteronomy 4 forbid such representations?

The Answer Is No

Early in its history, Israel was forbidden to make any depictions of God because he had not revealed himself in a visible form. Given the pagan culture surrounding them, the Israelites might have been tempted to worship God in the form of an animal or some natural object (e.g., a bull or the sun).

But God later *did* reveal himself under visible forms, such as in Daniel 7:9: "As I looked, thrones were placed and one that was ancient of days took his seat; his raiment was white as snow, and the hair of his head like pure wool; his throne was fiery flames, its wheels were burning fire." Protestants make depictions of the Father under this form when they do illustrations of Old Testament prophecies.

The Holy Spirit revealed himself under at least two visible forms —that of a dove, at the baptism of Jesus (Matt. 3:16; Mark 1:10; Luke 3:22; John 1:32), and as tongues of fire, on the day of Pentecost (Acts 2:1–4). Protestants use these images when drawing or painting these biblical episodes and when they wear Holy Spirit lapel pins or place dove emblems on their cars.

But, more important, in the Incarnation of Christ his Son, God showed mankind an icon of himself. Paul said, "He is the *image* (Greek: *ikōn*) of the invisible God, the firstborn of all creation." Christ is the tangible, divine "icon" of the unseen, infinite God.

We read that when the magi were "going into the house they *saw the child* with Mary his mother, and they fell down and worshiped him. Then, opening their treasures, they offered him gifts, gold, frankincense, and myrrh" (Matt. 2:11). Though God did not reveal a form for himself on Mount Horeb, he did reveal one in the house in Bethlehem.

The bottom line is that when God made the New Covenant with us, he *did* reveal himself under a visible form in Jesus Christ. For that reason, we *can* make representations of God in Christ. Even Protestants use all sorts of religious images: Pictures of Jesus and other biblical persons appear on a myriad of Bibles, picture books, T-shirts, jewelry, bumper stickers, greeting cards, compact discs, and manger scenes. Christ is even symbolically represented through the *Ichthus* or "fish emblem."

Common sense tells us that, since God has revealed himself in various images, most especially in the incarnate Jesus Christ, it's not wrong for us to use images of these forms to deepen our knowledge and love of God. That's *why* God revealed himself in these visible forms, and that's why statues and pictures are made of them.

Idolatry Condemned by the Church

Since the days of the apostles, the Catholic Church has consistently condemned the sin of idolatry. The early Church Fathers warn against this sin, and Church councils also dealt with the issue.

The Second Council of Nicaea (787), which dealt largely with the question of the religious use of images and icons, said, "The one who redeemed us from the darkness of idolatrous insanity, Christ our God, when he took for his bride his holy Catholic Church . . . promised he would guard her and assured his holy disciples saying, 'I am with you every day until the consummation of this age.' . . . To this gracious offer some people paid no attention; being hoodwinked by the treacherous foe they abandoned the true line of reasoning . . . and they failed to distinguish the holy from the profane, asserting that the icons of our Lord and of his saints were no different from the wooden images of satanic idols."

The *Catechism of the Council of Trent* (1566) taught that idolatry is committed "by worshiping idols and images as God, or believing that they possess any divinity or virtue entitling them to our worship, by praying to, or reposing confidence in them" (374).

"Idolatry is a perversion of man's innate religious sense. An idolater is someone who 'transfers his indestructible notion of God to anything other than God'" (CCC 2114).

The Church absolutely recognizes and condemns the sin of idolatry. What anti-Catholics fail to recognize is the distinction between thinking a piece of stone or plaster is a god and desiring to visually remember Christ and the saints in heaven by making statues in their honor. The making and use of religious statues is a *thoroughly* biblical practice. Anyone who says otherwise doesn't know his Bible.

13

Relics

Many non-Catholics particularly shy away from the sacramental aspects of Catholicism—and not from the seven sacraments only. What they dislike is the mixing of spirit and matter, the gift of something spiritual—grace—by means of physical things. That, after all, is what the sacraments are. This tendency to drive a wedge between spirit and matter stems from age-old heresies known as Dualism, Marcionism, and Manichaeism. Marcion in particular taught that the God of the Old Testament was evil in creating matter, but the God of the New Testament is a different and good God, who raises us to the level of spirit. The less one is entrapped by matter, the closer one is to God. Needless to say, this does not fit well with the sacraments—or with the Incarnation!

In the sacraments, common material things, such as water, wine, bread, oil, and the imposition of hands, result in the giving of grace. Related to the sacraments are the sacramentals, objects such as medals, blessed palms, holy water, and ashes. Their use can lead people to receive or respond to grace. Many non-Catholics wrongly believe that the Church teaches that these sacramentals actually provide grace. But one of the biggest problems for non-Catholics are the relics of saints—the bones, ashes, clothing, or personal possessions of the apostles and other holy people that are held in reverence by the Church and sometimes associated with miraculous healings and other acts of God.

This is how Bart Brewer, an ex-priest and the head of Mission to Catholics International, phrases the complaint in his autobiography, *Pilgrimage from Rome*:

"Another dogma that has bothered Catholics for centuries is the veneration of relics and the claims that they have magical powers. Even Martin Luther wondered how there could be twenty-

six apostles buried in Germany, when there were only twelve in
the entire Bible! It is said that if all the pieces of the cross displayed in Catholic churches were assembled together, it would
take a ten-ton truck to carry them. It is clear that most 'relics' are
frauds. Furthermore, there is nothing in the Bible that supports
the veneration of relics, even if they are genuine" (132).

This is a unique paragraph in that each sentence in it contains
one or two blunders. Let's go through them.

The first is the claim that the veneration of relics has "bothered
Catholics for centuries." Considering the high regard Catholics
have had for relics throughout the years, this is absurd. It hasn't
been Catholics who have been bothered—it has been non-Catholics (and ex-Catholics).

What's more, the Church does not claim that relics have "magical powers." Note that Brewer cites no Catholic work that makes
such a claim—because there isn't any. The sacramental system is
the opposite of magic. In magic, something material is regarded
as the cause of something spiritual; in other words, a lower cause
is expected to produce a higher effect.

No Magic in Sacraments

The sacraments (and, derivatively, sacramentals and relics) don't
compel God to work in a certain way. Their use depends on God,
who established their efficacy, so their effects are divine, not natural, in their origin. It is God who sanctions the use of relics; it
is not a matter of men "overpowering" God through their own
powers or the powers of nature, which is what magic amounts to.

When Jesus healed the blind man in John 9:1–7, did the Lord
use magic mud and spittle? Was it actually a magic potion he
mixed in the clay, or was it simply that Jesus saw fit to use matter in association with the conferral of his grace? The Lord is no
dualist. He made matter, he loves matter, and he had no qualms
about becoming matter himself to accomplish our redemption.

In the next sentence Brewer casts ridicule on relics by referring to Luther's comment, but the rejoinder should have been obvious to him. Apart from the fact that there are more than twelve apostles mentioned in the Bible (there are at least sixteen, counting Paul, Barnabas, James the Just, and Matthias), there is no reason to think that the whole of a saint's skeleton must be kept in one reliquary. In fact, from what we know about the way early Christians preserved the bones of those killed during the persecutions, that would be unusual. More commonly, the saint's bones were divided up, so various communities could have a portion of his relics: the skull here, a hand there, other bones elsewhere. So it would be proper for several cities to claim to have the relics of a single saint.

Ten-Ton Truck or Warship?

Now for the classic argument. As Brewer phrases it, if all the alleged pieces of the true cross were gathered together, "it would take a ten-ton truck to carry them." That's a modern way to put the charge. It used to be said the pieces would be enough to build a warship, but warships aren't made out of wood any longer.

Either way, the charge is nonsense. In 1870 a Frenchman, Rohault de Fleury, catalogued all the relics of the true cross, including relics that were said to have existed but were lost. He measured the existing relics and estimated the volume of the missing ones. Then he added up the figures and discovered that the fragments, if glued together, would not have made up more than one-third of a cross. The scandal wasn't that there was too much wood. The scandal was that most of the true cross, after being unearthed in Jerusalem in the fourth century, was lost again!

Brewer's next charge is this: "It is clear that most 'relics' are frauds." It isn't clear at all. Certainly nothing he said indicates that. Have there been any frauds? Sure. But in most cases, relics are either known to be genuine or there is some reason to think they may be genuine, even if complete proof is impossible.

Take the famous Shroud of Turin, which scientists have been

examining for some years. The scientists admit their experiments cannot establish that the shroud is the actual burial cloth of Christ —they admit that is impossible—but they also say they might be able to eliminate the possibility of forgery. That is, they apparently are demonstrating that the shroud was a burial cloth that was wrapped around someone who was crucified in the same manner as Christ, perhaps at about the same time he was crucified (there is considerable dispute about the age of the shroud, and the carbon-14 tests that have been performed on the shroud have been defective), and in the same area he was crucified.

Most relics cannot be fakes because most relics are the bones of ordinary saints of history who were well known and whose remains were never lost in the first place.

The Church has never pronounced that any particular relic— even that of the cross—is genuine. But, the Church does approve of honor being given to the relics that can with reasonable probability be considered authentic.

Is There Room for Doubt?

Will there always be room for doubt for those who seek it? Sure. And if that is the case with the Shroud of Turin, it is more the case with most other relics.

The skeptic will always be able to say, "This might not have been so-and-so's," or "You might be mistaken," and we'd have to admit that's true. There might have been a mistake, or fakes might have been substituted for the real relics.

We evaluate relics the same way we evaluate the bona fides of anything else. Did George Washington really sleep in a particular bed? We have to do some detective work to find out. We may never know for sure. We may have to rely on probabilities. On the other hand, we might have incontrovertible proof that could be disbelieved only by the skeptic who insists George Washington never existed at all.

It's the same with relics. Some are beyond doubt. Others are so highly probable that it would be rash to doubt. Others are merely probable. And some, yes, are improbable (though we wouldn't want to toss out even most of those, in case we err and toss out something that really is a relic).

No Veneration?

Finally, Brewer claims that "there is nothing in the Bible that supports the veneration of relics, even if they are genuine." Again, not so.

One of the most moving accounts of the veneration of relics is that of the very body of Christ itself. Rather than leaving his body on the cross, to be taken down and disposed of by the Romans (as was the customary practice), Joseph of Arimathea courageously interceded with Pilate for Christ's body (cf. Mark 15:43; John 19:38). He donated his own, newly hewn tomb as Christ's resting place (cf. Matt. 27:60). Nicodemus came and donated over a hundred pounds of spices to wrap inside Jesus' grave clothes (cf. John 19:39), that amount of spices being used only for the most honored dead. And after he was buried, the women went to reverently visit the tomb (cf. Matt. 28:1) and to further anoint Christ's body with spices even though it had already been sealed inside the tomb (cf. Mark 16:1; Luke 24:1). These acts of reverence were more than just the usual courtesy shown to the remains of the dead; they were special respect shown to the body of a most holy man—in this case, the holiest man who has ever lived, for he was God Incarnate.

Relics in Early Christianity

The veneration of relics is seen explicitly as early as the account of Polycarp's martyrdom written by the Smyrnaeans in A.D. 156. In it, the Christians describe the events following his burning at the stake: "We took up his bones, which are more valuable than

precious stones and finer than refined gold, and laid them in a
suitable place, where the Lord will permit us to gather ourselves
together, as we are able, in gladness and joy and to celebrate the
birthday of his martyrdom."

In speaking of the veneration of relics in the early Church, the
anti-Catholic historian Adolph Harnack writes that "no Church
doctor of repute restricted it. All of them rather, even the Cap-
padocians, countenanced it. The numerous miracles which were
wrought by bones and relics seemed to confirm their worship.
The Church therefore would not give up the practice, although
a violent attack was made upon it by a few cultured heathens and
besides by the Manichaeans" (Harnack, *History of Dogma*, tr., IV,
313).

In the fourth century the great biblical scholar Jerome declared,
"We do not worship, we do not adore, for fear that we should
bow down to the creature rather than to the Creator, but we venerate the relics of the martyrs in order the better to adore him
whose martyrs they are" (*Ad Riparium*, I, PL XXII, 907).

Relics in Scripture

Keep in mind what the Church says about relics. It doesn't say
there is some magical power in them. There is nothing in the relic
itself, whether a bone of the apostle Peter or water from Lourdes,
that has any curative ability. The Church just says that relics may
be the occasion of God's miracles, and in this the Church follows
Scripture.

The use of the bones of Elisha brought a dead man to life: "So
Elisha died, and they buried him. Now bands of Moabites used to
invade the land in the spring of the year. And as a man was being
buried, lo, a marauding band was seen and the man was cast into
the grave of Elisha; and as soon as the man touched the bones of
Elisha, he revived, and stood on his feet" (2 Kgs. 13:20–21). This
is an unequivocal biblical example of a miracle being performed
by God through contact with the relics of a saint!

Similar are the cases of the woman cured of a hemorrhage by touching the hem of Christ's cloak (cf. Matt. 9:20–22) and the sick who were healed when Peter's shadow passed over them (cf. Acts 5:14–16). "And God did extraordinary miracles by the hands of Paul, so that handkerchiefs or aprons were carried away from his body to the sick, and diseases left them and the evil spirits came out of them" (Acts 19:11–12).

If these aren't examples of the use of relics, what are? In the case of Elisha, a Lazarus-like return from the dead was brought about through the prophet's bones. In the New Testament cases, physical things (the cloak, the shadow, handkerchiefs and aprons) were used to effect cures. There is a perfect congruity between present-day Catholic practice and ancient practice. If you reject all Catholic relics today as frauds, you should also reject these biblical accounts as frauds.

14

"Brethren of the Lord"

When Catholics call Mary the "Blessed Virgin," they mean she remained a virgin throughout her life. When Protestants refer to Mary as "virgin," they mean she was a virgin only until Jesus' birth. They believe that she and Joseph later had children whom Scripture refers to as "the brethren of the Lord." The disagreement arises over biblical verses that use the terms *brethren*, *brother*, and *sister*.

There are about ten instances in the New Testament where "brothers" and "sisters" of the Lord are mentioned: Matthew 12:46, Matthew 13:55, Mark 3:31–34, Mark 6:3, Luke 8:19–20, John 2:12, John 7:3–10, Acts 1:14, and 1 Corinthians 9:5.

When trying to understand these verses, note that the term *brother* (Greek: *adelphos*) has a wide meaning in the Bible. It is not restricted to the literal meaning of a full brother or half-brother. The same goes for *sister* (*adelphe*) and the plural form *brothers* (*adelphoi*). The Old Testament shows that the word for "brother" had a wide semantic range of meaning and could refer to any male relative from whom you are not descended (male relatives from whom you are descended are known as "fathers") and who are not descended from you (your male descendants, regardless of the number of generations removed, are your "sons"), as well as kinsmen such as cousins, those who are members of the family by marriage or by law rather than by blood, and even friends or mere political allies (cf. 2 Sam. 1:26; Amos 1:9).

Lot, for example, is called Abraham's brother (cf. Gen. 14:14), even though, being the son of Haran, Abraham's brother (cf. Gen. 11:26–28), he was actually Abraham's nephew. Similarly, Jacob is called the brother of his uncle Laban (cf. Gen. 29:15). Kish and Eleazar were the sons of Mahli. Kish had sons of his own, but Eleazar had no sons, only daughters, who married their "brethren," the sons of Kish. These "brethren" were really their cousins (1 Chr. 23:21–22).

The terms for "brothers," "brother," and "sister" did not refer only to close relatives. Sometimes they meant kinsmen (cf. Deut. 23:7; Neh. 5:7; Jer. 34:9), as in the reference to the forty-two "brethren" of King Azariah (cf. 2 Kgs. 10:13–14).

No Word for "Cousin"

Because neither Hebrew nor Aramaic (the language spoken by Christ and his disciples) had a special word meaning "cousin," speakers of those languages could use either the word for "brother" or a circumlocution, such as "the son of my uncle." But circumlocutions are clumsy, so the Jews often used the word for "brother."

The writers of the New Testament were brought up using the Aramaic equivalent of "brothers" to mean both cousins and sons of the same father—plus other relatives and even non-relatives. When they wrote in Greek, they did the same thing the translators of the Septuagint did. (The Septuagint was the Greek version of the Hebrew Bible; it was translated by Hellenistic Jews a century or two before Christ's birth and was the version of the Bible from which most of the Old Testament quotations found in the New Testament are taken.)

In the Septuagint the Hebrew word that includes both brothers and cousins was translated as *adelphos*, which in Greek usually has the narrow meaning that the English *brother* has. Unlike Hebrew or Aramaic, Greek has a separate word for cousin, *anepsios*, but the translators of the Septuagint used *adelphos*, even for true cousins.

You might say they transliterated instead of translated, importing the Jewish idiom into the Greek Bible. They took an exact equivalent of the Hebrew word for "brother" and did not use *adelphos* in one place (for sons of the same parents), and *anepsios* in another (for cousins). This same usage was employed by the writers of the New Testament and passed into English translations of the Bible. To determine what *brethren* or *brother* or *sister* means in any one verse, we have to look at the context. When we do that, we see that insuperable problems arise if we assume that Mary had children other than Jesus.

When the angel Gabriel appeared to Mary and told her that she would conceive a son, she asked, "How can this be, since I have no husband?" (Luke 1:34). From the Church's earliest days, as the Fathers interpreted this Bible passage, Mary's question was taken to mean that she had made a vow of lifelong virginity, even in marriage. (This was not common, but neither was it unheard of.) If she had not taken such a vow, the question would make no sense.

Mary knew how babies are made (otherwise she wouldn't have asked the question she did). If she had anticipated having children in the normal way and did not intend to maintain a vow of virginity, she would hardly have to ask *how* she was to have a child, since conceiving a child in the natural way would be expected by a newlywed wife. Her question makes sense only if there was an apparent (but not a real) conflict between keeping a vow of virginity and acceding to the angel's request. A careful look at the New Testament shows that Mary kept her vow of virginity and never had any children other than Jesus.

When Jesus was found in the temple at age twelve, the context suggests that he was the only son of Mary and Joseph. There is no hint in this episode of any other children in the family (cf. Luke 2:41–51). Jesus grew up in Nazareth, and the people of Nazareth referred to him as "the son of Mary" (Mark 6:3), not as "*a* son of Mary." In fact, others in the Gospels are never referred to as Mary's sons, not even when they are called Jesus' "brethren." If they were in fact her sons, this would be strange usage.

Also, the attitude taken by the "brethren of the Lord" implies that they are his elders. In ancient and, particularly, in Eastern societies (remember, Palestine is in Asia), older sons gave advice to younger, but younger seldom gave advice to older—it was considered disrespectful to do so. But we find Jesus' "brethren" saying to him that Galilee was no place for him and that he should go to Judea so he could make a name for himself (John 7:3–4).

Another time, they sought to restrain him for his own benefit: "And when his family heard it, they went out to seize him, for people were saying, 'He is beside himself' " (Mark 3:21). This kind of behavior could make sense for ancient Jews only if the "brethren" were older than Jesus, but that alone eliminates them as his biological brothers, since Jesus was Mary's "first-born son" (Luke 2:7).

Consider what happened at the foot of the cross. When he was dying, Jesus entrusted his Mother to the apostle John (John 19:26–27). The Gospels mention four of his "brethren": James, Joseph, Simon, and Jude. It is hard to imagine why Jesus would have disregarded family ties and made this provision for his Mother if these four were also her sons.

Fundamentalist Arguments

Fundamentalists insist that "brethren of the Lord" must be interpreted in the strict sense. They most commonly make two arguments based on Matthew 1:25: "And he did not know her until (Greek: *heos*, also translated into English as *till*) she brought forth her firstborn son." They first argue that the natural inference from *till* is that Joseph and Mary afterward lived together as husband and wife, in the usual sense, and had several children. Otherwise, why would Jesus be called "firstborn"? Doesn't that mean there must have been at least a second-born, perhaps a third-born, and so on? But they are using a narrow, modern meaning of *until*, instead of the meaning it had when the Bible was written. In the Bible, it means only that some action did not happen up to a certain point; it does not imply that the action did happen later, which is the modern sense of the term. In fact, if the modern sense is forced on the Bible, some ridiculous meanings result.

Consider this line: "Michal the daughter of Saul had no children till the day of her death" (2 Sam. 6:23). Are we to assume she had children *after* her death?

There is also the burial of Moses. The book of Deuteronomy says that no one knew the location of his grave "until this present day" (Deut. 34:6, Knox). But we know that no one has known since that day either.

The examples could be multiplied, but you get the idea— nothing can be proved from the use of the word *till* in Matthew 1:25. Recent translations give a better sense of the verse: "He had no relations with her at any time before she bore a son" (*New American Bible*); "He had not known her when she bore a son" (Knox).

Fundamentalists claim Jesus could not be Mary's "firstborn" unless there were other children that followed him. But this shows ignorance of the way the ancient Jews used the term. For them it meant the child that opened the womb (cf. Ex. 13:2; Num. 3:12). Under the Mosaic law, it was the firstborn son that was to be sanctified (cf. Ex. 34:20). Did this mean that the parents had to wait until a second son was born before they could call their first the "firstborn"? Hardly. The first male child of a marriage was termed the "firstborn" even if he turned out to be the only child of the marriage.

The Holy Family

Fundamentalists say it would have been repugnant for Mary and Joseph to enter a marriage and remain celibate. They call such marriages "unnatural" arrangements. Certainly they were unusual, but not as unusual as having the Son of God in one's family, and not nearly as unusual as having a virgin give birth to a child! The Holy Family was not an average family, nor should we expect its members to act as members of an average family would.

The circumstances demanded sacrifice by Mary and Joseph. This was a special family, set aside for the nurturing of the Son of God. No greater dignity could be given to marriage than that.

Backing up the testimony of Scripture regarding Mary's perpetual virginity is the testimony of the early Christian Church.

Consider the controversy between Jerome and Helvidius, writing around 380. Helvidius first brought up the notion that the "brothers of the Lord" were children born to Mary and Joseph after Jesus' birth. The great Scripture scholar Jerome at first declined to comment on Helvidius's remarks because they were a "novel, wicked, and a daring affront to the faith of the whole world." At length, though, Jerome's friends convinced him to write a reply, which turned out to be his treatise called *On the Perpetual Virginity of the Blessed Mary.* He used not only the scriptural arguments given above, but earlier Christian writers, such as Ignatius, Polycarp, Irenaeus, and Justin Martyr. Helvidius was unable to come up with a reply, and his theory remained in disrepute and was unheard of until recent times.

So, if it is established that the "brethren of the Lord" were not Jesus' brothers or half-brothers through Mary, who were they?

Prior to the time of Jerome, the standard theory was that they were Jesus' "brothers" who were sons of Joseph though not of Mary. According to this view, Joseph was a widower at the time he married Mary. He had children from his first marriage (who would be older than Jesus, explaining their attitude toward him). This is mentioned in a number of early Christian writings. One work, known as the *Protoevangelium of James* (A.D. 125) records that Joseph was selected from a group of widowers to serve as the husband and protector of Mary, who was a virgin consecrated to God. When he was chosen, Joseph objected: "I have children, and I am an old man, and she is a young girl" (4:8).

Today, the most commonly accepted view is that they were Jesus' cousins. Of the four "brethren" who are named in the Gospels, consider, for the sake of argument, only James. Similar reasoning can be used for the other three. We know that James the younger's mother was named Mary. Look at the descriptions of the women standing beneath the cross: "There were also many women there . . . among whom were Mary Magdalene, and Mary the mother of James and Joseph, and the mother of the sons of Zebedee" (Matt. 27:56); "there were also women looking on from afar, among whom were Mary Magdalene, and Mary the mother of James the younger and of Joses, and Salome" (Mark 15:40). Then look at what John says: "But standing by the cross of Jesus were his mother, and his mother's sister, Mary the wife of Clopas, and Mary Magdalene" (John 19:25). If we compare these parallel accounts of the scene of the crucifixion, we see that the mother of James and Joseph must be the wife of Clopas. So far, so good.

An argument against this, though, is that James is elsewhere described as the son of Alphaeus (cf. Matt. 10:3), which would mean this Mary, whoever she was, was the wife of both Clopas and Alphaeus. But Alphaeus and Clopas are the same person, since the Aramaic name for Alphaeus could be rendered in Greek either as Alphaeus or as Clopas. Another possibility is that Alphaeus took a Greek name similar to his Jewish name, the way that Saul took the name Paul.

So it's probable that James the younger is the son of Mary and Clopas. The second-century historian Hegesippus explains that Clopas was the brother of Joseph, the foster-father of Jesus. James would thus be Joseph's nephew and a cousin of Jesus, who was Joseph's putative son.

This identification of the "brethren of the Lord" as Jesus' first cousins is open to legitimate question—they might even be relatives more distantly removed—but our inability to determine for certain their exact status strictly on the basis of the biblical evidence (or lack of it, in this case) says nothing at all about the main point, which is that the Bible demonstrates that they were not the Blessed Virgin Mary's children.

15

Immaculate Conception
and Assumption

The Marian doctrines are, for Fundamentalists, among the most bothersome of the Catholic Church's teachings. In this chapter we'll briefly examine two Marian doctrines that Fundamentalist writers frequently object to: the Immaculate Conception and the Assumption.

The Immaculate Conception

It's important to understand what the doctrine of the Immaculate Conception is and what it is not. Some people think the term refers to Christ's conception in Mary's womb without the intervention of a human father, but that is the Virgin Birth. Others think the Immaculate Conception means that Mary was conceived "by the power of the Holy Spirit," in the way Jesus was, but that, too, is incorrect. The Immaculate Conception means that Mary, whose conception was brought about the normal way, was conceived without original sin or its stain—that's what "immaculate" means: without stain. The essence of original sin consists in the deprivation of sanctifying grace, and its stain is a corrupt nature. Mary was preserved from these defects by God's grace; from the first instant of her existence she was in the state of sanctifying grace and was free from the corrupt nature that original sin brings.

When discussing the Immaculate Conception, an implicit reference may be found in the angel's greeting to Mary. The angel Gabriel said, "Hail, full of grace, the Lord is with you!" (Luke 1:28). The phrase "full of grace" is a translation of the Greek word *kecharitōmenē*. It therefore expresses a characteristic quality of Mary.

The traditional translation, "full of grace," is better than the one found in many recent versions of the New Testament, which give something along the lines of "highly favored daughter." Mary was indeed a highly favored daughter of God, but the Greek implies more than that (and it never mentions the word for "daughter"). The grace given to Mary is permanent and of a unique kind. *Kecharitomene* is a perfect passive participle of *charitoo*, meaning "to fill or endow with grace." Since this term is in the perfect tense, it indicates that Mary was graced in the past but with continuing effects in the present. So, the grace Mary enjoyed was not a result of the angel's visit. In fact, Catholics hold, it extended over the whole of her life, from conception onward. She was in a state of sanctifying grace from the first moment of her existence.

Fundamentalists' Objections

Fundamentalists' chief reason for objecting to the Immaculate Conception and Mary's consequent sinlessness is that we are told that "all have sinned" (Rom. 3:23). Besides, they say, Mary said her "spirit rejoices in God my Savior" (Luke 1:47), and only a sinner needs a Savior.

Let's take the second citation first. Mary, too, required a Savior. Like all other descendants of Adam, she was subject to the necessity of contracting original sin. But by a special intervention of God, undertaken at the instant she was conceived, she was preserved from the stain of original sin and its consequences. She was therefore redeemed by the grace of Christ, but in a special way—by anticipation.

Consider an analogy: Suppose a man falls into a deep pit, and someone reaches down to pull him out. The man has been "saved" from the pit. Now imagine a woman walking along, and she too is about to topple into the pit, but at the very moment that she is to fall in, someone holds her back and prevents her. She too has been saved from the pit, but in an even better way: She was not simply taken out of the pit; she was prevented from getting stained by the mud in the first place. This is the illustration Christians have used for two thousand years to explain how Mary was saved by Christ. By receiving Christ's grace at her conception, she had his grace applied to her before she was able to become mired in original sin and its stain.

The Second Vatican Council states that she was "redeemed, in a more exalted fashion, by reason of the merits of her Son" (*Lumen Gentium* 56). She has more reason to call God her Savior than we do, because he saved her in an even more glorious manner!

But what about Romans 3:23, "all have sinned"? Have all people committed actual sins? Consider a child below the age of reason. By definition he can't sin, since sinning requires the ability to reason and the ability to intend to sin. This is indicated by Paul later in the letter to the Romans when he speaks of the time when Jacob and Esau were unborn babies as a time when they "had done nothing either good or bad" (Rom. 9:11).

We also know of another very prominent exception to the rule: Jesus (cf. Heb. 4:15). So if Paul's statement in Romans 3 includes an exception for the New Adam (Jesus), one may argue that an exception for the New Eve (Mary) can also be made.

Paul's comment seems to have one of two meanings. It might be that it refers not to absolutely everyone, but just to the mass of mankind (which means young children and other special cases, like Jesus and Mary, would be excluded without having to be singled out). If not that, then it would mean that everyone, without exception, is subject to *original* sin, which is true for a young child, for the unborn, even for Mary—but she, though due to be subject to it, was preserved by God from it and its stain.

The objection is also raised that if Mary were without sin, she would be equal to God. In the beginning, God created Adam, Eve, and the angels without sin, but none were equal to God. Most of the angels never sinned, and all souls in heaven are without sin. This does not detract from the glory of God, but manifests it by the work he has done in sanctifying his creation. Sinning does not make one human. On the contrary, it is when man is without sin that he is most fully what God intends him to be.

The doctrine of the Immaculate Conception was officially defined by Pope Pius IX in 1854. When Fundamentalists claim that the doctrine was "invented" at this time, they misunderstand both the history of dogmas and what prompts the Church to issue, from time to time, definitive pronouncements regarding faith or morals. They are under the impression that no doctrine is believed until the pope or an ecumenical council issues a formal statement about it.

Actually, doctrines are defined formally only when there is a controversy that needs to be cleared up or when the magisterium (the Church in its office as teacher; cf. Matt. 28:18–20; 1 Tim. 3:15; 4:11) thinks that the faithful can be helped by particular emphasis being drawn to some already-existing belief. The definition of the Immaculate Conception was prompted by the latter motive; it did not come about because there were widespread doubts about the doctrine. In fact, the Vatican was deluged with requests from people desiring the doctrine to be officially proclaimed. Pope Pius IX, who was highly devoted to the Blessed Virgin, hoped the definition would inspire others in their devotion to her.

The Assumption

The doctrine of the Assumption says that at the end of her life on earth Mary was assumed, body and soul, into heaven, just as Enoch, Elijah, and perhaps others had been before her. It is also necessary to keep in mind what the Assumption is not. Some people think that Catholics believe Mary "ascended" into heaven. That is not correct. Christ, by his own power, ascended into heaven. Mary was assumed or taken up into heaven by God. She did not do it under her own power.

The Church has never formally defined whether she died or not, and the integrity of the doctrine of the Assumption would

130 THE ESSENTIAL CATHOLIC SURVIVAL GUIDE

not be impaired if she did not in fact die, but the almost universal consensus is that she did die. Pope Pius XII, in *Munificentissimus Deus* (1950), defined that Mary, "after the completion of her earthly life [note the silence regarding her death], was assumed body and soul into the glory of heaven."

The possibility of a bodily assumption before the Second Coming is suggested by Matthew 27:52–53: "The tombs also were opened, and many bodies of the saints who had fallen asleep were raised, and coming out of the tombs after his resurrection they went into the holy city and appeared to many." Did all these Old Testament saints die and have to be buried all over again? There is no record of that, but it is recorded by early Church writers that they were assumed into heaven, or at least into that temporary state of rest and happiness often called "paradise," where the righteous people from the Old Testament era waited until Christ's Resurrection (cf. Luke 16:22; 23:43; Heb. 11:1–40; 1 Pet. 4:6), after which they were brought into the eternal bliss of heaven.

No Remains

There is also what might be called the negative historical proof for Mary's Assumption. It is easy to document that, from the first, Christians gave homage to saints, including many about whom we now know little or nothing. Cities vied for the title of the last resting place of the most famous saints. Rome, for example, houses the tombs of Peter and Paul, Peter's tomb being under the high altar of St. Peter's Basilica in Rome. In the early Christian centuries, relics of saints were zealously guarded and highly prized. The bones of those martyred in the Coliseum, for instance, were quickly gathered up and preserved. There are many accounts of this in the biographies of those who gave their lives for the faith.

It is agreed that Mary ended her life in Jerusalem, or perhaps in Ephesus. However, neither those cities nor any other claimed her remains, though there are claims about possessing her (temporary) tomb. And why did no city claim the bones of Mary?

Apparently because there weren't any bones to claim, and people knew it. Here was Mary, certainly the most privileged of all the saints (and certainly the most saintly), but we have no record of her bodily remains being venerated anywhere.

Complement to the Immaculate Conception

Over the centuries, the Fathers and the Doctors of the Church spoke often about the fittingness of the privilege of Mary's Assumption. The speculative grounds considered include Mary's freedom from sin, her motherhood of God, her perpetual virginity, and—the key—her union with the salvific work of Christ.

The dogma is especially fitting when one examines the honor that was given to the Ark of the Covenant. It contained manna (bread from heaven), stone tablets of the Ten Commandments (the word of God), and the staff of Aaron (a symbol of Israel's high priesthood). Because of its contents, it was made of incorruptible wood, and Psalm 132:8 said, "Arise, O Lord, and go to thy resting place, thou and the ark of thy might." If this vessel was given such honor, how much more should Mary be kept from corruption, since she is the new ark—who carried the real bread from heaven, the Word of God, and the high priest of the New Covenant, Jesus Christ.

Some argue that the new ark is not Mary, but the body of Jesus. Even if this were the case, it is worth noting that 1 Chronicles 15:14 records that the persons who bore the ark were to be sanctified. There would be no sense in sanctifying men who carried a box and not sanctifying the womb that carried God himself! After all, wisdom will not dwell "in a body enslaved to sin" (Wis. 1:4).

But there is more than just fittingness. After all, if Mary is immaculately conceived, then it would follow that she would not suffer the corruption in the grave, which is a consequence of sin (cf. Gen. 3:19).

Mary's Cooperation

Mary freely and actively cooperated in a unique way with God's plan of salvation (cf. Luke 1:38; Gal. 4:4). Like any mother, she was never separated from the suffering of her Son (cf. Luke 2:35), and Scripture promises that those who share in the sufferings of Christ will share in his glory (cf. Rom. 8:17). Since she suffered a unique interior martyrdom, it is appropriate that Jesus would honor her with a unique glory.

All Christians believe that one day we will all be raised in a glorious form and then caught up and rendered immaculate to be with Jesus forever (cf. 1 Thess. 4:17; Rev. 21:27). As the first person to say "yes" to the good news of Jesus (cf. Luke 1:38), Mary is in a sense the prototypical Christian, and received early the blessings we will all one day be given.

The Bible Only?

Since the Immaculate Conception and Assumption are not explicit in Scripture, Fundamentalists conclude that the doctrines are false. Here, of course, we get into an entirely separate matter, the question of *sola scriptura*, or the Protestant "Bible only" theory. There is no room here to consider that idea. Let it just be said that if the position of the Catholic Church is true, then the notion of *sola scriptura* is false. There is then no problem with the Church officially defining a doctrine that is not explicitly in Scripture, so long as it is not in contradiction to Scripture.

The Catholic Church was commissioned by Christ to teach all nations and teach them infallibly—guided, as he promised, by the Holy Spirit until the end of the world (cf. John 14:26; 16:13). The mere fact that the Church teaches that something is definitely true is a guarantee that it is true (cf. Matt. 28:18–20; Luke 10:16; 1 Tim. 3:15).

16

The Rosary

The word *rosary* comes from Latin and means "a garland of roses," the rose being one of the flowers used to symbolize the Virgin Mary. If you were to ask what object is most emblematic of Catholics, people would probably say, "The rosary, of course." We're familiar with the images: the silently moving lips of the old woman fingering her beads, the oversized rosary hanging from the waist of the wimpled nun, and more recently, the merely decorative rosary hanging from the rearview mirror.

After Vatican II the rosary fell into relative disuse. The same is true for Marian devotions as a whole. But in recent years the rosary has made a comeback, and not just among Catholics. Many Protestants now say the rosary, recognizing it as a truly biblical form of prayer—after all, the prayers that comprise it come mainly from the Bible.

The rosary is a devotion in honor of the Virgin Mary. It consists of a set number of specific prayers. First are the introductory prayers: one Apostles' Creed (*Credo*), one Our Father (the *Pater Noster* or the Lord's Prayer), three Hail Marys (*Ave Maria*), one Glory Be (*Gloria Patri*).

The Apostles' Creed

The Apostles' Creed is so called not because it was composed by the apostles themselves, but because it expresses their teachings. The original form of the creed came into use around A.D. 125, and the present form dates from the fifth century. It reads this way:

"I believe in God, the Father Almighty, Creator of heaven and earth, and in Jesus Christ, his only Son, our Lord, who was conceived by the Holy Spirit, born of the Virgin Mary, suffered under Pontius Pilate, was crucified, died, and was buried. He descended into hell. The third day he arose again from the dead. He ascended into heaven and is seated at the right hand of the Father. From thence he shall come to judge the living and the dead. I believe in the Holy Spirit, the holy Catholic Church, the communion of saints, the forgiveness of sins, the resurrection of the body, and the life everlasting. Amen."

Traditional Protestants are able to recite the Apostles' Creed without qualms, meaning every line of it, though to some lines they must give meanings different from those given by Catholics, who composed the creed. For instance, we refer to "the holy Catholic Church," meaning a particular, identifiable Church on earth. Protestants typically reinterpret this to refer to an "invisible church" consisting of all "true believers" in Jesus.

Protestants, when they say the prayer, refer to the (lowercased) "holy catholic church," using *catholic* merely in the sense of "universal," not implying any connection with the (uppercase) Catholic Church, which is based in Rome. (This is despite the fact that the term *Catholic* was already used to refer to a particular, visible Church by the second century and had already lost its broader meaning of "universal").

Despite these differences, Protestants embrace the Apostles' Creed without reluctance, seeing it as embodying basic Christian truths as they understand them.

The Lord's Prayer

The next prayer in the rosary—the Our Father or *Pater Noster* (from its opening words in Latin), also known as the Lord's Prayer —is even more acceptable to Protestants because Jesus himself taught it to his disciples.

It is given in the Bible in two slightly different versions (cf. Matt. 6:9–13; Luke 11:2–4). The one given in Matthew is the one we say. (We won't reproduce it here. All Christians should have it memorized.)

The Hail Mary

The next prayer in the rosary, and the prayer that is really at the center of the devotion, is the Hail Mary. Since the Hail Mary is a prayer to Mary, many Protestants assume that it's unbiblical. Quite the contrary, actually. Let's look at it.

The prayer begins, "Hail Mary, full of grace, the Lord is with thee." This is nothing other than the greeting the angel Gabriel gave Mary in Luke 1:28 (*Confraternity Version*). The next part reads this way:

"Blessed art thou among women, and blessed is the fruit of thy womb, Jesus." This was exactly what Mary's relative Elizabeth said to her in Luke 1:42. The only thing that has been added to these two verses are the names Jesus and Mary, to make clear who is being referred to. So the first part of the Hail Mary is entirely biblical.

The second part of the Hail Mary is not taken straight from Scripture, but it is entirely biblical in the thoughts it expresses. It reads:

"Holy Mary, Mother of God, pray for us sinners, now and at the hour of our death. Amen."

Let's look at the first words. Some Protestants object to saying "Holy Mary" because they claim that Mary was a sinner like the rest of us. But Mary was a Christian (the first Christian, actually —the first to accept Jesus: cf. Luke 1:45), and the Bible describes Christians in general as holy. In fact, they are called saints, which means "holy ones" (cf. Eph. 1:1; Phil. 1:1, Col. 1:2). Furthermore, as the Mother of Jesus Christ, the incarnate second Person of the Blessed Trinity, Mary was certainly a very holy woman.

Some Protestants object to the title "Mother of God," but suffice it to say that the title does not mean that Mary is older than God; it means the person who was born of her was a divine person, not a human person. (Jesus is one person, the divine, but has two natures, the divine and the human. It is incorrect to say that he is a human person.) The denial that Mary had God in her womb is a heresy known as Nestorianism (which claims that Jesus was two persons, one divine and one human), which has been condemned since the early fifth century and which the Reformers and Protestant Bible scholars have always rejected.

Another Mediator?

The most problematic line for non-Catholics is usually the last: "Pray for us sinners, now and at the hour of our death." Many non-Catholics think such a request denies the teaching of 1 Timothy 2:5: "For there is one God, and there is one mediator between God and men, the man Christ Jesus." But in the preceding four verses, Paul instructs Christians to pray for each other, meaning that it cannot interfere with Christ's mediatorship: "I urge that supplications, prayers, intercessions, and thanksgivings be made for all men. . . . This is good, and it is acceptable in the sight of God our Savior" (1 Tim. 2:1–3).

We know this exhortation to pray for others applies to the saints in heaven who, as Revelation 5:8 reveals, intercede for us by offering our prayers to God: "The twenty-four elders fell down before the Lamb, each holding a harp, and with golden bowls full of incense, which are the prayers of the saints."

The Glory Be

The fourth prayer found in the rosary is the Glory Be, sometimes called the *Gloria* or *Gloria Patri*. The last two names are taken from the opening words of the Latin version of the prayer, which in English reads:

"Glory be to the Father, and to the Son, and to the Holy Spirit. As it was in the beginning, is now, and ever shall be, world without end. Amen." The *Gloria* is a brief hymn of praise in which all Christians can join. It has been used since the fourth century (though its present form is from the seventh) and traditionally has been recited at the end of each psalm in the Divine Office.

The Closing Prayer

We've covered the opening prayers of the rosary. In fact, we've covered all the prayers of the rosary except the very last one, which is usually the Hail Queen (*Salve Regina*), sometimes called the Hail Holy Queen. It's the most commonly recited prayer in praise of Mary, after the Hail Mary itself, and was composed at the end of the eleventh century. It generally reads like this (there are several variants):

"Hail holy Queen, Mother of mercy, our life, our sweetness, and our hope! To thee do we cry, poor banished children of Eve. To thee do we send up our sighs, mourning and weeping in this valley of tears. Turn, then, most gracious advocate, thine eyes of mercy toward us, and after this, our exile, show unto us the blessed fruit of thy womb, Jesus. O clement, O loving, O sweet Virgin Mary."

So those are the prayers of the rosary. Between the introductory prayers and the concluding prayer is the meat of the rosary: the decades. Each decade—there are fifteen in a full rosary (which takes about forty-five minutes to say)—is composed of ten Hail Marys. Each decade is bracketed between an Our Father and a Glory Be, so each decade actually has twelve prayers.

Each decade is devoted to a mystery regarding the life of Jesus or his Mother. Here the word *mystery* refers to a truth of the faith, not to something incomprehensible (as in "It's a mystery to me!"). The fifteen mysteries are divided into three groups of five: the joyful, the sorrowful, the glorious. When people speak of "saying the rosary" they usually mean saying any set of five (which takes about fifteen minutes) rather than the recitation of all fifteen mysteries. Let's look at the mysteries.

Meditation the Key

First we must understand that they are meditations. When Catholics recite the twelve prayers that form a decade of the rosary, they meditate on the mystery associated with that decade. If they merely recite the prayers, whether vocally or silently, then they are missing the essence of the rosary. It isn't just a recitation of prayers, but a meditation on the grace of God. Critics, not knowing about the meditation part, imagine that the rosary must be boring, uselessly repetitious, and meaningless. Their criticism carries weight if you reduce the rosary to a formula. Christ forbade meaningless repetition (cf. Matt. 6:7), but the Bible itself prescribes some prayers that involve repetition. Look at Psalm 136, which is a litany (a prayer with a recurring refrain) meant to be sung in the Jewish temple. In the psalm the refrain is "His mercy endures forever." Sometimes in Psalm 136 the refrain starts before a sentence is finished, meaning it is more repetitious than the rosary, though this prayer was written directly under the inspiration of God.

It is the meditation on the mysteries that gives the rosary its staying power.

The joyful mysteries are these: the Annunciation (Luke 1:26–38), the Visitation (Luke 1:40–56), the Nativity (Luke 2:6–20), the presentation of Jesus in the temple (Luke 2:21–39), and the finding of the child Jesus in the temple (Luke 2:41–51).

Then come the sorrowful mysteries: the agony in the garden (Matt. 26:36–46), the scourging (Matt. 27:26), the crowning with thorns (Matt. 27:29), the carrying of the cross (John 19:17), and the Crucifixion (Luke 23:33–46).

The final mysteries are the Glorious: the Resurrection (Luke 24:1–12), the Ascension (Luke 24:50–51), the descent of the Holy Spirit (Acts 2:1–4), the Assumption of Mary into heaven (Rev. 12), and her coronation (cf. Rev. 12:1).

In 2002, Pope John Paul II introduced the *luminous mysteries*, which have to do with the earthly ministry of Jesus: the baptism of Jesus (Matt. 3:13–17; Mark 1.9–11, Luke 3.21–22), the wedding in Cana (John 2:1–11), the proclaiming of the kingdom (Matt. 10:7–8), the Transfiguration (Matt. 17:1–9; Mark 9:2–10; Luke 9:28–36), and the institution of the Eucharist (Matt. 26:26–29; Mark 14:22–25; Luke 22:19–20).

With the exception of the last two glorious mysteries, each mystery is explicitly scriptural. True, the Assumption and coronation of Mary are not explicitly stated in the Bible, but they are not contrary to it, so there is no reason to reject them out of hand. Given the scriptural basis of most of the mysteries, it is little wonder that many Protestants, once they understand the meditations that are the essence of the rosary, happily take it up as a devotion. We've looked at the prayers found in the rosary and the mysteries around which it is formed. Now let's see how it was formed historically

The Secret of Paternoster Row

It's commonly said that St. Dominic, the founder of the Order of Preachers (the Dominicans), instituted the rosary. Not so. Certain parts of the rosary predated Dominic; others arose only after his death.

Centuries before Dominic, monks had begun to recite all 150 psalms on a regular basis. As time went on, it was felt that the lay brothers, known as the *conversi*, should have some form of prayer of their own. Since the *conversi* couldn't read the psalms, they couldn't recite them with the monks. They needed an easily remembered prayer.

The prayer first chosen was the Our Father, and, depending on the circumstances, it was said either fifty or a hundred times. These *conversi* used rosaries to keep count, and the rosaries were known then as *Paternosters* ("Our Fathers").

In England there arose a craftsmen's guild of some importance, the members of which made these rosaries. In London, you can find a street named Paternoster Row, which preserves the memory of the area where these craftsmen worked.

The rosaries that were originally used to count Our Fathers came to be used, during the twelfth century, to count Hail Marys —or, more properly, the first half of what we now call the Hail Mary. (The second half was added some time later.)

Both Catholics and non-Catholics, as they learn more about the rosary and make more frequent use of it, come to see how its meditations bring to mind the sweet fragrance not only of the Mother of God, but of Christ himself.

17

Infant Baptism

Fundamentalists often criticize the Catholic Church's practice of baptizing infants. According to them, baptism is for adults and older children, because it is to be administered only after one has undergone a "born again" experience—that is, after one has "accepted Jesus Christ as his personal Lord and Savior." At the instant of acceptance, when he is "born again," the adult becomes a Christian and his salvation is assured forever. Baptism follows, though it has no actual salvific value. In fact, one who dies before being baptized but after "being saved" goes to heaven anyway.

As Fundamentalists see it, baptism is not a sacrament (in the true sense of the word), but an ordinance. It does not in any way convey the grace it symbolizes; rather, it is merely a public manifestation of the person's conversion. Since only an adult or older child can be converted, baptism is inappropriate for infants or for children who have not yet reached the age of reason (generally considered to be about age seven). Most Fundamentalists say that during the years before they reach the age of reason infants and young children are automatically saved. Only after a person reaches the age of reason does he need to "accept Jesus" in order to reach heaven.

Since the New Testament era, the Catholic Church has always understood baptism differently, teaching that it is a sacrament that accomplishes several things, the first of which is the remission of sin—both original sin and actual sin (only original sin in the case of infants and young children, since they are incapable of actual sin, and both original and actual sin in the case of older persons).

Peter explained what happens at baptism when he said, "Repent, and be baptized every one of you in the name of Jesus Christ for the forgiveness of your sins; and you shall receive the gift of the Holy Spirit" (Acts 2:38). But he did not restrict this teaching to adults. He added, "For the promise is to you *and to your children* and to all that are far off, every one whom the Lord our God calls to him" (2:39). We also read: "Rise and be baptized, and wash away your sins, calling on his name" (Acts 22:16). These commands are universal, not restricted to adults. Further, these commands make clear the necessary connection between baptism and salvation, a connection explicitly stated in 1 Peter 3:21: "Baptism . . . now saves you, not as a removal of dirt from the body but as an appeal to God for a clear conscience, through the resurrection of Jesus Christ."

Christ Calls All to Baptism

Although Fundamentalists are the most recent critics of infant baptism, opposition to infant baptism is not a new phenomenon. In the Middle Ages, some groups developed that rejected infant baptism, such as the Waldenses and Catharists. Later, the Anabaptists ("re-baptizers") echoed them, claiming that infants are incapable of being baptized validly. But the Christian Church has always held that Christ's law applies to infants as well as adults, for Jesus said that no one can enter heaven unless he has been born again of water and the Holy Spirit (cf. John 3:5). His words can be taken to apply to anyone capable of belonging to his kingdom. He asserted such even for children: "Let the children come to me, and do not hinder them; for to such belongs the kingdom of heaven" (Matt. 19:14).

More detail is given in Luke's account of this event, which reads: "Now they were bringing even infants to him that he might touch them; and when the disciples saw it, they rebuked them. But Jesus called them to him, saying, 'Let the children come to me, and do not hinder them; for to such belongs the kingdom of God' " (Luke 18:15–16).

Now Fundamentalists say that this event does not apply to young children or infants since it implies that the children to which Christ was referring were able to approach him on their own. (Older translations have, "Suffer the little children to come unto me," which seems to suggest they could do so under their own power.) Fundamentalists conclude that the passage refers only to children old enough to walk, and, presumably, capable of sinning. But the text in Luke 18:15 says, "Now they were bringing even *infants* to him" (Greek: *Prosepheron de autō kai ta brephā*). The Greek word *brephe* means "infants"—children who are quite unable to approach Christ on their own and who could not possibly make a conscious decision to "accept Jesus as their personal Lord and Savior." And that is precisely the problem. Fundamentalists refuse to permit the baptism of infants and young children, because they are not yet capable of making such a conscious act. But notice what Jesus said: "To such [referring to the infants and children who had been brought to him] belongs the kingdom of heaven." The Lord did not require them to make a conscious decision. He says that they are precisely the kind of people who *can* come to him and receive the kingdom. So on what basis, Fundamentalists should be asked, can infants and young children be excluded from the sacrament of baptism? If Jesus said "let them come unto me," who are we to say "no," and withhold baptism from them?

In Place of Circumcision

Furthermore, Paul notes that baptism has replaced circumcision (cf. Col. 2:11-12). In that passage, he refers to baptism as "the circumcision of Christ" and "the circumcision made without hands." Of course, usually only infants were circumcised under the Old Law; circumcision of adults was rare, since there were few converts to Judaism. If Paul meant to exclude infants, he would not have chosen circumcision as a parallel for baptism.

This comparison between who could receive baptism and circumcision is an appropriate one. In the Old Testament, if a man wanted to become a Jew, he had to believe in the God of Israel and be circumcised. In the New Testament, if one wants to become a Christian, one must believe in God and Jesus and be baptized. In the Old Testament, those born into Jewish households could be circumcised in anticipation of the Jewish faith in which they would be raised. Thus in the New Testament, those born in Christian households can be baptized in anticipation of the Christian faith in which they will be raised. The pattern is the same: If one is an adult, one must have faith before receiving the rite of membership; if one is a child too young to have faith, one may be given the rite of membership in the knowledge that one will be raised in the faith. This is the basis of Paul's reference to baptism as "the circumcision of Christ"—that is, the Christian equivalent of circumcision.

Were Only Adults Baptized?

Fundamentalists are reluctant to admit that the Bible nowhere says that baptism is to be restricted to adults, but when pressed, they will. They just conclude that that is what should be taken as meaning, even if the text does not explicitly support such a view. Naturally enough, the people whose baptisms we read about in Scripture (and few are individually identified) are adults, because they were converted as adults. This makes sense, because Christianity was just beginning—there were no "cradle Christians," people brought up from childhood in Christian homes.

Even in the books of the New Testament that were written later in the first century, during the time when children were raised in the first Christian homes, we never—not even once—find an example of a child raised in a Christian home who is baptized only upon making a "decision for Christ." Rather, it is always assumed that the children of Christian homes are already Christians, that they have already been "baptized into Christ" (Rom. 6:3). If infant baptism were not the rule, then we should have references to the children of Christian parents joining the Church only after they had come to the age of reason, and there are no such records in the Bible.

Specific Biblical References?

But, one might ask, does the Bible ever say that infants or young children can be baptized? The indications are clear. In the New Testament we read that Lydia was converted by Paul's preaching and that "she was baptized, with her household" (Acts 16:15). The Philippian jailer whom Paul and Silas had converted to the faith was baptized that night along with his household. We are told that "the same hour of the night . . . he was baptized, with all his family" (Acts 16:33). And in his greetings to the Corinthians, Paul recalled that "I did baptize also the household of Stephanas" (1 Cor. 1:16).

In all these cases, whole households or families were baptized. This means more than just the spouse; the children too were included. If the text of Acts referred simply to the Philippian jailer and his wife, then we would read that "he and his wife were baptized," but we do not. Thus his children must have been baptized as well. The same applies to the other cases of household baptism in Scripture.

Granted, we do not know the exact age of the children; they may have been past the age of reason, rather than infants. Then again, they could have been babes in arms. More probably, there were both younger and older children. Certainly there were children younger than the age of reason in some of the households that were baptized, especially if one considers that society at this time had no reliable form of birth control. Furthermore, given the New Testament pattern of household baptism, if there were to be exceptions to this rule (such as infants), they would be explicit.

Catholics from the First

The present Catholic attitude accords perfectly with early Christian practices. Origen, for instance, wrote in the third century that "according to the usage of the Church, baptism is given even to infants" (*Homilies on Leviticus*, 8:3:11 [A.D. 244]). The Council of Carthage, in 253, condemned the opinion that baptism should be withheld from infants until the eighth day after birth. Later, Augustine taught, "The custom of Mother Church in baptizing infants is certainly not to be scorned . . . nor is it to be believed that its tradition is anything except apostolic" (*Literal Interpretation of Genesis* 10:23:39 [A.D. 408]).

No Cry of "Invention!"

None of the Fathers or councils of the Church were claiming that the practice was contrary to Scripture or Tradition. They agreed that the practice of baptizing infants was the customary and appropriate practice since the days of the early Church. The only uncertainty seemed to be when—exactly—an infant should be baptized. Further evidence that infant baptism was the accepted practice in the early Church is the fact that if infant baptism had been opposed to the religious practices of the first believers, why do we have no record of early Christian writers condemning it?

But Fundamentalists try to ignore the historical writings from the early Church, which clearly indicate the legitimacy of infant baptism. They attempt to sidestep appeals to history by saying that baptism requires faith and, since children are incapable of having faith, they cannot be baptized. It is true that Christ prescribed instruction and actual faith for adult converts (cf. Matt. 28:19–20), but his general law on the necessity of baptism (cf. John 3:5) puts no restriction on the subjects of baptism. Although infants are included in the law he establishes, requirements of that law that are impossible to meet because of their age are not applicable to them. They cannot be expected to be instructed and have faith when they are incapable of receiving instruction or manifesting faith. The same was true of circumcision: Faith in the Lord was necessary for an adult convert to receive it, but it was not necessary for the children of believers.

Furthermore, the Bible never says, "Faith in Christ is necessary for salvation except for infants"; it simply says, "Faith in Christ is necessary for salvation." Yet Fundamentalists must admit there is an exception for infants unless they wish to condemn instantaneously all infants to hell. Therefore, the Fundamentalist himself makes an exception for infants regarding the necessity of faith for salvation. He can thus scarcely criticize the Catholic for making the exact same exception for baptism, especially if, as Catholics believe, baptism is an instrument of salvation.

It becomes apparent, then, that the Fundamentalist position on infant baptism is not really a consequence of the Bible's strictures but of the demands of Fundamentalism's idea of salvation. In reality, the Bible indicates that infants are to be baptized, that they too are meant to inherit the kingdom of heaven. Further, the witness of the earliest Christian practices and writings must once and for all silence those who criticize the Catholic Church's teaching on infant baptism. The Catholic Church is merely continuing the tradition established by the first Christians, who heeded the words of Christ: "Let the children come to me, and do not hinder them; for to such belongs the kingdom of God" (Luke 18:16).

18

Baptism: Immersion Only?

Although Latin-rite Catholics are usually baptized by infusion (pouring), they know that immersion (dunking) and sprinkling are also valid ways to baptize. Fundamentalists, however, regard only baptism by immersion as true baptism, concluding that most Catholics are not validly baptized at all.

Although the New Testament contains no explicit instructions on how to physically administer the water of baptism, Fundamentalists argue that the Greek word *baptizo* found in the New Testament means "to immerse." They also maintain that only immersion reflects the symbolic significance of being "buried" and "raised" with Christ (see Romans 6:3–4).

It is true that *baptizo* often means "immersion." For example, the Greek version of the Old Testament tells us that Naaman, at Elisha's direction, "went down and *dipped himself* [the Greek word here is *baptizo*] seven times in the Jordan" (2 Kgs. 5:14, *Septuagint*, emphasis added).

But immersion is not the only meaning of *baptizo*. Sometimes it just means washing up. Thus Luke 11:38 reports that, when Jesus ate at a Pharisee's house, "the Pharisee was astonished to see that he did not first wash [*baptizo*] before dinner." They did not practice immersion before dinner, but, according to Mark, the Pharisees "do not eat unless they wash [*nipto*] their hands, observing the tradition of the elders; and when they come from the market place, they do not eat unless they *wash themselves* [*baptizo*]" (Mark 7:3–4a, emphasis added). So *baptizo* can mean cleansing or ritual washing as well as immersion.

A similar range of meanings can be seen when *baptizo* is used metaphorically. Sometimes a figurative "baptism" is a sort of "immersion"; but not always. For example, speaking of his future suffering and death, Jesus said, "I have a baptism [*baptisma*] to be baptized [*baptizo*] with; and how I am constrained until it is accomplished!" (Luke 12:50). This might suggest that Christ would be "immersed" in suffering. On the other hand, consider the case of being baptized with the Holy Spirit."

In Acts 1:4–5 Jesus charged his disciples "not to depart from Jerusalem, but to wait for the promise of the Father, which, he said, 'you heard from me, for John baptized with water, but before many days you shall be baptized with the Holy Spirit.' " Did this mean they would be "immersed" in the Spirit? No: Three times Acts 2 states that the Holy Spirit was *poured* out on them when Pentecost came (2:17, 18, 33). Later Peter referred to the Spirit *falling* upon them and also on others after Pentecost, explicitly identifying these events with the promise of being "baptized with the Holy Spirit" (Acts 11:15–17). These passages demonstrate that the meaning of *baptizo* is broad enough to include "pouring."

Christian Baptism

The Fundamentalist contention that *baptizo* always means immersion is an oversimplification. This is especially true because in Christian usage the word had a highly particular meaning distinct from the term's ordinary, everyday usage.

The same principle can be seen with other special Christian terms, such as *Trinity* and *agape* (divine love), that were originally ordinary Greek words with no special religious significance. The earliest evidence of anyone referring to God as a "Trinity" is a letter by Theophilus of Antioch (*Ad Autolycum* [A.D. 181]). Before the Christian usage, a "trinity" (*triad* in Greek) was simply any group of three things.

However, as Christians made theological use of the term, it quickly gained a new, technical sense, referring specifically to the three Persons of the Godhead. When Christians professed that God is a "Triad," they did not mean a group of three gods but one God in three Persons. Here, an everyday word was being used in a special, theological sense.

The same is true of *agape*, originally a general term for any sort of "love" very much like the English word. But it quickly became used in Christian circles as the name of a common fellowship (love) meal among Christians (cf. Jude 12).

In the same way, *baptizo* acquired a specialized Christian usage distinct from its original meaning. In fact, it already had a complex history of specifically religious usages even before Christians adopted it. Long before Jesus' day, Gentile converts to Judaism were "baptized" as well as circumcised. Then John the Baptist performed a "baptism of repentance" for Jews as a dramatic prophetic gesture indicating that they were as much in need of conversion as pagans were. Through these usages *baptizo* acquired associations of initiation, conversion, and repentance.

Given this history, it was natural for Jesus and his followers to use the same word for Christian baptism, though it was not identical to either the Jewish baptism or that of John. But it is completely misguided to try to determine the meaning of the word in its Christian sense merely on the basis of ordinary secular usage. It would be like thinking that the doctrine of the Trinity is polytheism or that the New Testament exhortation to "love one another" means only to be fond of each other. To understand what Christian baptism entailed, we must examine not what the word meant in other contexts but what it meant and how it was practiced *in a Christian context*.

Inner and Outer Baptism

One important aspect of Christian baptism in the New Testament is the clear relationship between being baptized with water and being "baptized with the Holy Spirit," or "born again." This chapter is primarily concerned with the *mode* of baptism, not its *effects*. (For more on the relationship between baptism and rebirth, see John 3:5; Acts 2:38, 19:2–3, 22:16; Romans 6:3–4;

Colossians 2:11–12; Titus 3:5; and 1 Peter 3:21.) But even non-Catholic Christians must admit that the New Testament clearly associates water baptism with Spirit baptism and rebirth (even if they do not interpret this relationship as cause and effect).

Right from the beginning, as soon as the Holy Spirit was given on Pentecost, water and Spirit went hand in hand: "Repent, and be baptized every one of you in the name of Jesus Christ for the forgiveness of your sins; and you shall receive the gift of the Holy Spirit" (Acts 2:38).

In Acts 10:44, the first Gentiles to whom Peter preached received the Holy Spirit even before their water baptism. This is always possible, for God is free to operate outside the sacraments as well as within them. In this case it was fitting for the Spirit to be given before baptism, in order to show God's acceptance of believing Gentiles. Even under these circumstances, however, the connection to water baptism is still evident from Peter's response: "Can anyone withhold the water for baptizing these people who have received the Holy Spirit just as we have?" (Acts 10:47).

Still later in Acts, when Paul found people who did not have the Spirit, he immediately questioned whether they had received Christian water baptism. Upon learning that they had not, he baptized them and laid hands on them, and they received the Spirit (Acts 19:1–6).

These passages illustrate the connection between water and Spirit first made by Jesus himself: "Unless a man is born of water and the Spirit, he cannot enter the kingdom of God" (John 3:5).

Earlier we saw that the "baptism of the Holy Spirit" was depicted as "pouring." But these passages show that the "baptism" or "pouring" of the Spirit is itself closely related to water baptism.

This provides some balance to the Fundamentalist argument that only baptism by immersion adequately symbolizes death and resurrection with Jesus. It is true that immersion *best* represents death and resurrection, bringing out more fully the meaning of the sacrament than pouring or sprinkling (cf. *Catechism of the Catholic Church* 1239). (Immersion is actually the usual mode of baptizing in the Catholic Church's Eastern rites.) On the other hand, *pour-*

ing best represents the *infusion* of the Holy Spirit also associated with water baptism. And all three modes adequately suggest the sense of cleansing signified by baptism. No one mode has exclusive symbolical validity over the others.

Physical Difficulties

After Peter's first sermon, three thousand people were baptized in Jerusalem (Acts 2:41). Archaeologists have demonstrated that there was no sufficient water supply for so many to have been immersed. Even if there had been, the natives of Jerusalem would scarcely have let their city's water supply be polluted by three thousand unwashed bodies plunging into it. These people must have been baptized by pouring or sprinkling.

Even today practical difficulties can render immersion nearly or entirely impossible for some individuals: for example, people with certain medical conditions—the bedridden, quadriplegics, individuals with tracheotomies or in negative pressure ventilators (iron lungs). Again, those who have recently undergone certain procedures (such as open-heart surgery) cannot be immersed and may not wish to defer baptism until their recovery.

Other difficulties arise in certain environments. For example, immersion may be nearly or entirely impossible for desert nomads or Eskimos. Or consider those in prison—not in America, where religious freedom gives prisoners the right to be immersed if they desire—but in a more hostile setting, such as a Muslim regime, where baptisms must be done in secret, without adequate water for immersion.

What are we to do in these and similar cases? Shall we deny people the sacrament because immersion is impractical or impossible for them? Ironically, the Fundamentalist, who acknowledges that baptism is commanded but thinks it isn't essential for salvation, may make it impossible for many people to be baptized at all in obedience to God's command. The Catholic, who believes baptism confers grace and is normatively necessary for salvation, maintains that God wouldn't require a form of baptism that, for some people, is impossible.

Baptism in the Early Church

That the early Church permitted pouring instead of immersion is demonstrated by the *Didache*, a Syrian liturgical manual that was widely circulated among the churches in the first few centuries of Christianity, perhaps the earliest Christian writing outside the New Testament.

The *Didache* was written around A.D. 70 and, though not inspired, is a strong witness to the sacramental practice of Christians in the apostolic age. In its seventh chapter, the *Didache* reads, "Concerning baptism, baptize in this manner: Having said all these things beforehand, baptize in the name of the Father and of the Son and of the Holy Spirit in living water [that is, in running water, as in a river]. If there is no living water, baptize in other water; and, if you are not able to use cold water, use warm. If you have neither, pour water three times upon the head in the name of the Father, Son, and Holy Spirit." These instructions were composed either while some of the apostles and disciples were still alive or during the next generation of Christians, and they represent an already established custom.

The testimony of the *Didache* is seconded by other early Christian writings. Hippolytus of Rome said, "If water is scarce, whether as a constant condition or on occasion, then use whatever water is available" (*The Apostolic Tradition*, 21 [A.D. 215]). Pope Cornelius I wrote that, as Novatian was about to die, "he received baptism in the bed where he lay, by pouring" (*Letter to Fabius of Antioch* [A.D. 251]; cited in Eusebius, *Ecclesiastical History*, 6:4311).

Cyprian advised that no one should be "disturbed because the sick are poured upon or sprinkled when they receive the Lord's grace" (*Letter to a Certain Magnus* 69:12 [A.D. 255]). Tertullian described baptism by saying that it is done "with so great simplicity, without pomp, without any considerable novelty of preparation, and finally, without cost, a man is baptized in water, and amid the utterance of some few words, is sprinkled, and then rises again, not much (or not at all) the cleaner" (*On Baptism*, 2 [A.D. 203]). Obviously, Tertullian did not consider baptism by immersion the only valid form, since he says one is only sprinkled and thus comes up from the water "not much (or not at all) the cleaner."

Ancient Christian Mosaics Show Pouring

Then there is the artistic evidence. Much of the earliest Christian artwork depicts baptism—but not baptism by immersion! If the recipient of the sacrament is in a river, he is shown standing in the river while water is poured over his head from a cup or shell. Tile mosaics in ancient churches and paintings in the catacombs depict baptism by pouring. Baptisteries in early cemeteries are clear witnesses to baptisms by infusion. The entire record of the early Church—as shown in the New Testament, in other writings, and in monumental evidence—indicates that the mode of baptism was not restricted to immersion.

Other archaeological evidence confirms the same thing. An early Christian baptistery was found in a church in Jesus' hometown of Nazareth, yet this baptistery, which dates from the second century, was too small and narrow in which to immerse a person.

19

Christ in the Eucharist

Protestant attacks on the Catholic Church often focus on the Eucharist. This demonstrates that opponents of the Church—mainly Evangelicals and Fundamentalists—recognize one of Catholicism's core doctrines. What's more, the attacks show that Fundamentalists are not always literalists. This is seen in their interpretation of the key biblical passage in which Christ speaks about the sacrament that will be instituted at the Last Supper: John 6. Let's examine the last half of that chapter.

John 6:30 begins a colloquy that took place in the synagogue at Capernaum. The Jews asked Jesus what sign he could perform so that they might believe in him. As a challenge, they noted that "our fathers ate the manna in the wilderness." Could Jesus top that? He told them the real bread from heaven comes from the Father. "Give us this bread always," they said. Jesus replied, "I am the bread of life; he who comes to me shall not hunger, and he who believes in me shall never thirst." At this point the Jews understood him to be speaking metaphorically.

Again and Again

Jesus first repeated what he said, then summarized: " 'I am the living bread which came down from heaven; if any one eats of this bread, he will live for ever; and the bread which I shall give for the life of the world is my flesh.' The Jews then disputed among themselves, saying, 'How can this man give us his flesh to eat?' " (John 6:51–52).

His listeners were stupefied because now they understood Jesus *literally*—and correctly. He again repeated his words, but with even greater emphasis, and introduced the statement about drinking his blood: "Truly, truly, I say to you, unless you eat the flesh of the Son of man and drink his blood, you have no life in you; he who eats my flesh and drinks my blood has eternal life, and I will raise him up at the last day. For my flesh is food indeed, and my blood is drink indeed. He who eats my flesh and drinks my blood abides in me, and I in him" (John 6:53–56).

No Corrections

Notice that Jesus made no attempt to soften what he said, no attempt to correct "misunderstandings," for there were none. Our Lord's listeners understood him perfectly well. They no longer thought he was speaking metaphorically. If they *had*, if they mistook what he said, why no correction?

On other occasions when there was confusion, Christ explained just what he meant (cf. Matt. 16:5–12). Here, where any misunderstanding would be fatal, there was no effort by Jesus to correct. Instead, he repeated himself for greater emphasis.

In John 6:60 we read: "Many of his disciples, when they heard it, said, 'This is a hard saying; who can listen to it?' " These were his disciples, people used to his remarkable ways. He warned them not to think carnally, but spiritually: "It is the spirit that gives life, the flesh is of no avail; the words that I have spoken to you are spirit and life" (John 6:63; cf. 1 Cor. 2:12–14).

But he knew some did not believe. (It is here, in the rejection of the Eucharist, that Judas fell away; look at John 6:64.) "After this, many of his disciples drew back and no longer went about with him" (John 6:66).

This is the only record we have of any of Christ's followers forsaking him for purely doctrinal reasons. If it had all been a misunderstanding, if they erred in taking a metaphor in a literal sense, why didn't he call them back and straighten things out? Both the Jews, who were suspicious of him, and his disciples, who had accepted everything up to this point, would have remained with him had he said he was speaking only symbolically.

But he did not correct these protesters. Twelve times he said he was the bread that came down from heaven; four times he said they would have to eat my flesh and drink my blood." John 6 was an extended promise of what would be instituted at the Last Supper—and it was a promise that could not be more explicit. Or so it would seem to a Catholic. But what do Fundamentalists say?

Merely Figurative?

They say that in John 6 Jesus was not talking about physical food and drink, but about spiritual food and drink. They quote John 6:35: "Jesus said to them, 'I am the bread of life; he who comes to me shall not hunger, and he who believes in me shall never thirst.'" They claim that coming to him is bread, having faith in him is drink. Thus, eating his flesh and blood merely means believing in Christ.

But there is a problem with that interpretation. As Fr. John A. O'Brien explains, "The phrase 'to eat the flesh and drink the blood,' when used figuratively among the Jews, as among the Arabs of today, meant to inflict upon a person some serious injury, especially by calumny or by false accusation. To interpret the phrase figuratively then would be to make our Lord promise life everlasting to the culprit for slandering and hating him, which would reduce the whole passage to utter nonsense" (O'Brien, *The Faith of Millions*, 215). For an example of this use, see Micah 3:3.

Fundamentalist writers who comment on John 6 also assert that one can show that Christ was speaking only metaphorically by comparing verses like John 10:9 ("I am the door") and John 15:1 ("I am the true vine"). The problem is that there is not a connection to John 6:35, "I am the bread of life." "I am the door" and "I am the vine" make sense as metaphors because Christ is like a door—we go to heaven through him—and he is also like a vine—we get our spiritual sap through him. But Christ takes John 6:35 far beyond symbolism by saying, "For my flesh is food indeed, and my blood is drink indeed" (John 6:55).

He continues: "As the living Father sent me, and I live because of the Father, so he who eats me will live because of me" (John 6:57). The Greek word used for "eats" (*trogon*) is very blunt and has the sense of "chewing" or "gnawing." This is not the language of metaphor.

Their Main Argument

For Fundamentalist writers, the scriptural argument is capped by an appeal to John 6:63: "It is the spirit that gives life, the flesh is of no avail; the words that I have spoken to you are spirit and life." They say this means that eating real flesh is a waste. But does this make sense?

Are we to understand that Christ had just commanded his disciples to eat his flesh, then said their doing so would be pointless? Is that what "the flesh is of no avail" means? "Eat my flesh, but you'll find it's a waste of time"—is that what he was saying? Hardly.

The fact is that Christ's flesh avails much! If it were of no avail, then the Son of God incarnated for no reason, he died for no reason, and he rose from the dead for no reason. Christ's flesh profits us more than anyone else's in the world. If it profits us nothing, so that the incarnation, death, and resurrection of Christ are of no avail, then "your faith is futile and you are still in your sins. Then those also who have fallen asleep in Christ have perished" (1 Cor. 15:17b–18).

In John 6:63 "flesh is of no avail" refers to mankind's inclination to think using only what their natural human reason would tell them rather than what God would tell them. Thus in John 8:15–16 Jesus tells his opponents: "You judge according to the flesh, I judge no one. Yet even if I do judge, my judgment is true, for it is not I alone that judge, but I and he who sent me." So natural human judgment, unaided by God's grace, is unreliable; but God's judgment is always true.

And were the disciples to understand the line "The words that I have spoken to you are spirit and life" as nothing but a circumlocution (and a very clumsy one at that) for symbolic"? No one can come up with such interpretations unless he first holds to the Fundamentalist position and thinks it necessary to find a rationale, no matter how forced, for evading the Catholic interpretation. In John 6:63, *flesh* does not refer to Christ's own flesh—the context makes this clear—but to mankind's inclination to think on a natural, human level. "The words that I have spoken to you are spirit" does not mean, "What I have just said is symbolic." The word *spirit* is never used that way in the Bible. The line means that what Christ has said will be understood only through faith —only by the power of the Spirit and the drawing of the Father (cf. John 6:37, 44–45, 65).

Paul Confirms This

Paul wrote to the Corinthians: "The cup of blessing which we bless, is it not a participation in the blood of Christ? The bread which we break, is it not a participation in the body of Christ?" (1 Cor. 10:16). So when we receive Communion, we actually participate in the body and blood of Christ; we do not just eat symbols of them. Paul also said, "Whoever, therefore, eats the bread and drinks the cup of the Lord in an unworthy manner will be guilty of profaning the body and blood of the Lord. . . . For any one who eats and drinks without discerning the body eats and drinks judgment on himself" (1 Cor. 11:27, 29). To "be guilty of profaning the body and blood" of someone meant to be guilty of a crime as serious as homicide. How could eating mere bread and wine unworthily be so serious? Paul's comment makes sense only if the bread and wine became the real body and blood of Christ.

What Did the First Christians Say?

Anti-Catholics also claim that the early Church took this chapter symbolically. Is that so? Let's see what some early Christians thought, keeping in mind that we can learn much about how Scripture should be interpreted by examining the writings of early Christians.

Ignatius of Antioch, who had been a disciple of the apostle John and who wrote a letter to the Smyrnaeans about A.D. 110, said, referring to "those who hold heterodox opinions," that "they abstain from the Eucharist and from prayer, because they do not confess that the Eucharist is the flesh of our Savior Jesus Christ, flesh that suffered for our sins and that the Father, in his goodness, raised up again" (*Letter to the Smyrnaeans* 6:2, 7:1).

Forty years later, Justin Martyr wrote, "Not as common bread or common drink do we receive these; but since Jesus Christ our Savior was made incarnate by the word of God and had both flesh and blood for our salvation, so too, as we have been taught, the food which has been made into the Eucharist by the eucharistic prayer set down by him, and by the change of which our blood and flesh is nourished, . . . is both the flesh and the blood of that incarnated Jesus" (*First Apology* 66:1–20).

Origen, in a homily written about A.D. 244, attested to belief in the Real Presence. "I wish to admonish you with examples from your religion. You are accustomed to take part in the divine mysteries, so you know how, when you have received the body of the Lord, you reverently exercise every care lest a particle of it fall and lest anything of the consecrated gift perish. You account yourselves guilty, and rightly do you so believe, if any of it be lost through negligence" (*Homilies on Exodus* 13:3).

Cyril of Jerusalem, in a catechetical lecture presented in the mid-300s, said, "Do not, therefore, regard the bread and wine as simply that, for they are, according to the Master's declaration, the body and blood of Christ. Even though the senses suggest to you the other, let faith make you firm. Do not judge in this matter by taste, but be fully assured by faith, not doubting that you have been deemed worthy of the body and blood of Christ" (*Catechetical Discourses: Mystagogic* 4:22:9).

In a fifth-century homily, Theodore of Mopsuestia seemed to be speaking to today's Evangelicals and Fundamentalists: "When [Christ] gave the bread he did not say, 'This is the *symbol* of my body,' but, 'This *is* my body.' In the same way, when he gave the cup of his blood he did not say, 'This is the *symbol* of my blood,' but, 'This *is* my blood,' for he wanted us to look upon the [eucharistic elements], after their reception of grace and the coming of the Holy Spirit, not according to their nature, but to receive them as they are, the body and blood of our Lord" (*Catechetical Homilies* 5:1).

Unanimous Testimony

Whatever else might be said, the early Church took John 6 literally. In fact, there is no record from the early centuries that implies that Christians doubted the constant Catholic interpretation. There exists no document in which the literal interpretation is opposed and only the metaphorical accepted.

Why do Fundamentalists and Evangelicals reject the plain, literal interpretation of John 6? For them, Catholic sacraments are out because they imply a spiritual reality—grace—being conveyed by means of matter. This seems to them to be a violation of the divine plan. For many Protestants, matter is not to be used but to be overcome or avoided.

One suspects that, had they been asked by the Creator their opinion of how to bring about mankind's salvation, Fundamentalists would have advised him to adopt a different approach. How much cleaner things would be if spirit never dirtied itself with matter! But God approves of matter—he approves of it because he created it—and he approves of it so much that he comes to us under the appearances of bread and wine, just as he does in the physical form of the incarnate Christ.

20

The Institution of the Mass

Many non-Catholics do not understand the Mass. Television evangelist Jimmy Swaggart wrote, "The Roman Catholic Church teaches that the Holy Mass is an expiatory sacrifice, in which the Son of God is actually sacrificed anew on the cross" (Swaggart, *Catholicism and Christianity*). The late Loraine Boettner, the dean of anti-Catholic Fundamentalists, said the Mass is a "jumble of medieval superstition."

Vatican II puts the Catholic position succinctly:

"At the Last Supper, on the night he was betrayed, our Savior instituted the eucharistic sacrifice of his body and blood. He did this in order to perpetuate the sacrifice of the cross throughout the centuries until he should come again, and so to entrust to his beloved spouse, the Church, a memorial of his death and resurrection: a sacrament of love, a sign of unity, a bond of charity, a paschal banquet in which Christ is consumed, the mind is filled with grace, and a pledge of future glory is given to us" (*Sacrosanctum Concilium* 47).

Even a modestly informed Catholic can set an inquirer right and direct him to biblical accounts of Jesus' final night with his disciples. Turning to the text, we read, "And he took bread, and when he had given thanks he broke it and gave it to them, saying, 'This is my body which is given for you. Do this in remembrance of me'" (Luke 22:19).

The Greek here and in the parallel Gospel passages (cf. Matt. 26:26; Mark 14:22) reads: *Touto estin to soma mou*. Paul's version differs slightly: *Touto mou estin to soma* (1 Cor. 11:24). They all translate as "This is my body." The verb *estin* is the equivalent of the English *is* and can mean "is really" or "is figuratively." The usual meaning of *estin* is the former (check any Greek grammar book), just as, in English, the verb *is* usually is taken literally.

Fundamentalists insist that when Christ says, "This is my body," he is speaking figuratively. But this interpretation is precluded by Paul's discussion of the Eucharist in 1 Corinthians 11:23–29 and by the whole tenor of John 6, the chapter where the Eucharist is promised. The Greek word for "body" in John 6:54 is *sarx*, which means physical flesh, and the word for "eats" (*trōgōn*) translates as "gnawing" or "chewing." This is certainly not the language of metaphor.

No "Figurative Presence"

The literal meaning cannot be avoided except through violence to the text—and through the rejection of the universal understanding of the early Christian centuries. The writings of Paul and John reflect belief in the Real Presence. There is no basis for forcing anything else out of the lines, and no writer tried to do so until the early Middle Ages. Christ did not institute a Figurative Presence. Some Fundamentalists say the word *is* is used because Aramaic, the language Christ spoke, had no word for "represents." Those who make this feeble claim are behind the times, since, as Nicholas Cardinal Wiseman showed a century ago, Aramaic has about three dozen words that can mean "represents."

The Catholic Position

The Church teaches that the Mass is the re-presentation of the sacrifice of Calvary, which also is invariably misunderstood by anti-Catholics. The Catholic Church does *not* teach that the Mass is a re-crucifixion of Christ, who does *not* suffer and die again in the Mass.

Yet, it is more than just a memorial service. John A. O'Brien, writing in *The Faith of Millions*, says, "The manner in which the sacrifices are offered is alone different: On the cross Christ really shed his blood and was really slain; in the Mass, however, there is no real shedding of blood, no real death; but the separate consecration of the bread and of the wine symbolizes the separation of the body and blood of Christ and thus symbolizes his death upon the cross. The Mass is the renewal and perpetuation of the sacrifice of the cross in the sense that it offers [Jesus] anew to God . . . and thus commemorates the sacrifice of the cross, reenacts it symbolically and mystically, and applies the fruits of Christ's death upon the cross to individual human souls. All the efficacy of the Mass is derived, therefore, from the sacrifice of Calvary" (306).

"Once for All"

The Catholic Church specifically says that Christ does not die again—his death is once for all. It would be something else if the Church were to claim that he does die again, but it does not make that claim. Through his intercessory ministry in heaven and through the Mass, Jesus continues to offer himself to his Father as a living sacrifice, and he does so in what the Church specifically states is "an unbloody manner"—one that does not involve a new crucifixion.

The Language of Appearances

Loraine Boettner mounts another charge. In chapter 8 of *Roman Catholicism*, when arguing that the meal instituted by Christ was strictly symbolic, he gives a cleverly incomplete quotation. He writes, "Paul too says that the bread remains bread: 'Wherefore whosoever shall eat the bread and drink the cup of the Lord in an unworthy manner. . . . But let each man prove himself, and so let him eat of the bread, and drink of the cup' (1 Cor. 11:27–28)."

The part of verse 27 represented by the ellipsis is crucial. It reads, "shall be guilty of the body and blood of the Lord." Why does Boettner omit this? Because to be guilty of someone's body and blood is to commit a crime against his body and blood, not just against symbols of them. The omitted words clearly imply that the bread and wine become Christ himself.

Profaning the Eucharist was so serious that the stakes could be life and death. In the next two verses (29–30), Paul states, "For any one who eats and drinks without discerning the body eats and drinks judgment upon himself. That is why many of you are weak and ill, and some have died."

Boettner's omitted statements reveal that when Paul uses the term *bread*, he's using the language of appearances, what scholars call "phenomenological language." In this form of speech, something is described according to how it appears rather than according to its fundamental nature. "The sun rose" is an example of phenomenological language. From our perspective, it *appears* that the sun rises, though we know that what we see is actually caused by the earth's rotation.

Scripture uses phenomenological language regularly—as, for example, when it describes angels appearing in human guise as "men" (cf. Gen. 19:1–11; Luke 24:4–7, 23; Acts 1:10–11). Since the Eucharist still *appears* as bread and wine, Catholics from Paul's time on have referred to the consecrated elements using phenomenological language while recognizing that this is only description according to appearances and that it is actually Jesus who is present.

We are not merely symbolically commemorating Jesus in the Eucharist but actually participating in his body and blood, as Paul states, "The cup of blessing which we bless, is it not a participation in the blood of Christ? The bread which we break, is it not a participation in the body of Christ?" (1 Cor. 10:16).

The Manner of Melchizedek

The Old Testament predicted that Christ would offer a true sacrifice to God using the elements of bread and wine. In Genesis 14:18, Melchizedek, the king of Salem (that is, Jerusalem) and a priest, offered sacrifice under the form of bread and wine. Psalm 110 predicted that Christ would be a priest "after the order of Melchizedek," that is, offering a sacrifice in bread and wine. We must look for some sacrifice other than Calvary, since it was not under the form of bread and wine. The Mass meets that need.

Furthermore, "according to the order of Melchizedek" means "in the manner of Melchizedek." (*Order* does not refer to a religious order, as there was no such thing in Old Testament days.) The only "manner" shown by Melchizedek was the use of bread and wine. A priest sacrifices the items offered—that is the main task of all priests, in all cultures, at all times—so the bread and wine must have been what Melchizedek sacrificed.

Fundamentalists sometimes say that Christ followed the example of Melchizedek at the Last Supper but that it was a rite that was not to be continued. They undermine their case against the Mass in saying this, since such an admission shows, at least, that the Last Supper was truly sacrificial. The key, though, is that they overlook that Christ said, "Do this in remembrance of me" (Luke 22:19). Clearly, he wasn't talking about a one-time thing.

"Do this in remembrance of me" can also be translated as "Offer this as my memorial sacrifice." The Greek term for "remembrance" is *anamnesis*, and every time it occurs in the Protestant Bible (whether in the New Testament or the Greek Old Testament), it occurs in a sacrificial context. For example, it appears in the Greek translation of Numbers 10:10: "On the day of your gladness also, and at your appointed feasts, and at the beginnings of your months, you shall blow the trumpets over your burnt offerings and over the sacrifices of your peace offerings; they shall serve you for remembrance [*anamnesis*] before your God: I am the Lord your God." Thus the Eucharist is a remembrance, a memorial offering we present to God to plead the merits of Christ on the cross.

Fundamentalists disbelieve claims about the antiquity of the Mass's sacrificial aspects, even if they think the Mass, in the form of a mere commemorative meal, goes all the way back to the Last Supper. Many say the Mass as a sacrifice was not taught until the Middle Ages, alleging that Innocent III was the first pope to teach the doctrine.

But he merely insisted on a doctrine that had been held from the first but was being publicly doubted in his time. He formalized, but did not invent, the notion that the Mass is a sacrifice. Jimmy Swaggart, for one, goes further back than do many Fundamentalists, claiming, "By the third century the idea of sacrifice had begun to intrude." Still other Fundamentalists say Cyprian of Carthage, who died in 258, was the first to make noises about a sacrifice.

But Irenaeus, writing *Against Heresies* in the second century, beat out Cyprian when he wrote of the sacrificial nature of the Mass, and Irenaeus was beaten out by Clement of Rome, who wrote, in the first century, about those "from the episcopate who blamelessly and holily have offered its sacrifices" (*Letter to the Corinthians* 44:1).

Furthermore, Clement was beaten out by the *Didache* (a Syrian liturgical manual written around A.D. 70), which stated, "On the Lord's Day . . . gather together, break bread and offer the Eucharist, after confessing your transgressions so that your sacrifice may be pure. Let no one who has a quarrel with his neighbor join you until he is reconciled, lest our sacrifice be defiled. For this is that which was proclaimed by the Lord: 'In every place and time let there be offered to me a clean sacrifice. For I am a great king,' says the Lord, 'and my name is wonderful among the gentiles' [cf. Mal. 1:11]" (14:1–3).

It isn't possible to get closer to New Testament times than this, because Clement and the author of the *Didache* were writing during New Testament times. After all, at least one apostle (John) was still alive.

A Misreading

Fundamentalists are particularly upset about the Catholic notion that the sacrifice on Calvary is somehow continued through the centuries by the Mass. They think Catholics are trying to have it both ways. The Church on the one hand says that Calvary is "perpetuated," which seems to mean that the same act of killing, the same letting of blood, is repeated again and again. This violates the "once for all" idea. On the other hand, what Catholics call a sacrifice seems to have no relation to biblical sacrifices, since it does not look the same; after all, no splotches of blood are to be found on Catholic altars.

"We must, of course, take strong exception to such pretended sacrifice," Boettner instructs. "We cannot regard it as anything other than a deception, a mockery, and an abomination before God. The so-called sacrifice of the Mass certainly is not identical with that on Calvary, regardless of what the priests may say. There is in the Mass no real Christ, no suffering, and no bleeding. And a bloodless sacrifice is ineffectual. The writer of the book of Hebrews says that 'apart from shedding of blood there is no remission' of sin (9:22); and John says, 'The blood of Jesus his Son cleanseth us from all sin' (1 John 1:7). Since admittedly there is no blood in the Mass, it simply cannot be a sacrifice for sin" (174).

Boettner misreads chapter 9 of Hebrews, which begins with an examination of the Old Covenant. Moses is described as taking the blood of calves and goats and using it in the purification of the tabernacle (cf. Heb. 9:19–21; see Ex. 24:6–8 for the origins of this). Under the Old Law, a repeated blood sacrifice was necessary for the remission of sins. Under the Christian dispensation, blood (Christ's) is shed only once, but it is continually offered to the Father.

"But how can that be?" ask Fundamentalists. They have to keep in mind that "Jesus Christ is the same yesterday and today and for ever" (Heb. 13:8). What Jesus did in the past is present to God now, and God can make the sacrifice of Calvary present to us at

Mass. "For as often as you eat this bread and drink the cup, you proclaim the Lord's death until he comes" (1 Cor. 11:26).

Jesus does not offer himself to God as a bloody, dying sacrifice in the Mass, but as we offer ourselves, a "living sacrifice" (Rom. 12:1). As this passage indicates, the offering of sacrifice does not require death or the shedding of blood. If it did, we could not offer ourselves as living sacrifices to God. Jesus, having shed his blood once for all on the cross, now offers himself to God in a continual, unbloody manner as a holy, living sacrifice on our behalf.

21

Who Can Receive Communion?

The Holy Eucharist is the most important of the seven sacraments because, in this and in no other sacrament, we receive the very body and blood, soul and divinity of Jesus Christ. Innumerable, precious graces come to us through the reception of Holy Communion.

Communion is an intimate encounter with Christ in which we sacramentally receive Christ into our bodies, that we may be more completely assimilated into his. "The Eucharist builds the Church" (*Redemptor Hominis* 20), as Pope John Paul II said. It deepens unity with the Church, more fully assimilating us into Christ (cf. 1 Cor. 12:13; CCC 1396).

The Eucharist also strengthens the individual because in it Jesus himself, the Word made flesh, forgives our venial sins and gives us the strength to resist mortal sin. It is also the very channel of eternal life: Jesus himself.

In John's Gospel, Jesus summarized the reasons for receiving Communion when he said:

"Truly, truly, I say to you, unless you eat the flesh of the Son of man and drink his blood, you have no life in you; he who eats my flesh and drinks my blood has eternal life, and I will raise him up at the last day. For my flesh is food indeed, and my blood is drink indeed. He who eats my flesh and drinks my blood abides in me, and I in him. As the living Father sent me, and I live because of the Father, so he who eats me will live because of me. This is the bread which came down from heaven, not such as the fathers ate and died; he who eats this bread will live for ever" (John 6:53–58).

Because of the gravity of Jesus' teaching on receiving the Eucharist, the Church encourages Catholics to receive frequent

Communion, even daily Communion if possible, and mandates reception of the Eucharist at least once a year during the Easter season. Before going to Communion, however, there are several things one needs to know.

Catholics and Communion

The Church sets out specific guidelines regarding how we should prepare ourselves to receive the Lord's body and blood in Communion. To receive Communion worthily, you must be in a state of grace, have made a good confession since your last mortal sin, believe in transubstantiation, observe the eucharistic fast, and, finally, not be under an ecclesiastical censure such as excommunication.

First, you must be in a state of grace. "Whoever, therefore, eats the bread or drinks the cup of the Lord in an unworthy manner will be guilty of profaning the body and blood of the Lord. Let a man examine himself, and so eat of the bread and drink of the cup" (1 Cor. 11:27–28). This is an absolute requirement that can never be dispensed. To receive the Eucharist without sanctifying grace in your soul profanes the Eucharist in the most grievous manner.

A mortal sin is *any* sin whose matter is grave and that has been committed willfully and with knowledge of its seriousness. Grave matter includes, but is not limited to, murder, receiving or participating in an abortion, homosexual acts, having sexual intercourse outside of marriage or in an invalid marriage, and deliberately engaging in impure thoughts (cf. Matt. 5:28–29). Scripture contains lists of mortal sins (for example, 1 Cor. 6:9–10 and Gal. 5:19–21). For further information on what constitutes a mortal sin, see the *Catechism of the Catholic Church*.

Out of habit and out of fear of what those around them will think if they do not receive Communion, some Catholics, in a state of mortal sin, choose to go forward and offend God rather than stay in the pew while others receive the Eucharist. The Church's ancient teaching on this particular matter is expressed in the *Didache*, an early Christian document written around A.D. 70, which states: "Whosoever is holy [i.e., in a state of sanctifying grace], let him approach. Whosoever is not, let him repent" (*Didache* 10).

Second, you must have been to confession since your last mortal sin. The *Didache* witnesses to this practice of the early Church. "But first make confession of your faults, so that your sacrifice may be a pure one" (*Didache* 14).

The 1983 *Code of Canon Law* indicates that the same requirement applies today. "A person who is conscious of a grave sin is not to . . . receive the body of the Lord without prior sacramental confession unless a grave reason is present and there is no opportunity of confessing; in this case the person is to be mindful of the obligation to make an act of perfect contrition, including the intention of confessing as soon as possible" (CIC 916).

The requirement for sacramental confession can be dispensed if four conditions are fulfilled: (1) there must be a grave reason to receive Communion (for example, danger of death), (2) it must be physically or morally impossible to go to confession first, (3) the person must already be in a state of grace through perfect contrition, and (4) he must resolve to go to confession as soon as possible.

Third, you must believe in the doctrine of transubstantiation. "For any one who eats and drinks without discerning the body eats and drinks judgment upon himself" (1 Cor. 11:29). Transubstantiation means more than the Real Presence. According to transubstantiation, the bread and wine are actually transformed into the actual body, blood, soul, and divinity of Christ, with only the appearances of bread and wine remaining. This is why, at the Last Supper, Jesus held what *appeared* to be bread and wine, yet said: "This *is* my body. . . . This *is* my blood" (Mark 14:22–24, cf. Luke 22:14–20). If Christ were merely present alongside bread and wine, he would have said "This *contains* my body. . . . This *contains* my blood," which he did not say.

Fourth, you must observe the eucharistic fast. Canon law states,

"One who is to receive the most Holy Eucharist is to abstain from any food or drink, with the exception only of water and medicine, for at least the period of one hour before Holy Communion" (CIC 919 §1). Elderly people, those who are ill, and their caretakers are aroused from the eucharistic fast (cf. CIC 191 §3). Priests and deacons may not dispense one obligated by the eucharistic fast unless the bishop has expressly granted such power to them (cf. CIC 89).

Finally, one must not be under an ecclesiastical censure. Canon law mandates, "Those who are excommunicated or interdicted after the imposition or declaration of the penalty and others who obstinately persist in manifest grave sin are not to be admitted to Holy Communion" (CIC 915).

Provided they are in a state of grace and have met the above requirements, Catholics should receive the Eucharist frequently (cf. CIC 898).

Other Christians and Communion

The guidelines for receiving Communion, which are issued by the U.S. bishops and published in many missalettes, explain, "We welcome our fellow Christians to this celebration of the Eucharist as our brothers and sisters. We pray that our common baptism and the action of the Holy Spirit in this Eucharist will draw us closer to one another and begin to dispel the sad divisions that separate us. We pray that these will lessen and finally disappear, in keeping with Christ's prayer for us 'that they may all be one' (John 17:21).

"Because Catholics believe that the celebration of the Eucharist is a sign of the reality of the oneness of faith, life, and worship, members of those churches with whom we are not yet fully united are ordinarily not admitted to Communion. Eucharistic sharing in exceptional circumstances by other Christians requires permission according to the directives of the diocesan bishop and the provisions of canon law."

Scripture is clear that partaking of the Eucharist is among the highest signs of Christian unity: "Because there is one bread, we who are many are one body, for we all partake of the one bread" (1 Cor. 10:17). For this reason, it is normally impossible for non-Catholic Christians to receive Holy Communion, for to do so would be to proclaim a unity to exist that, regrettably, does not.

Another reason that many non-Catholics may not ordinarily receive Communion is for their own protection, since many reject the doctrine of the Real Presence of Christ in the Eucharist. Scripture warns that it is very dangerous for one not believing in the Real Presence to receive Communion: "For any one who eats and drinks without discerning the body eats and drinks judgment upon himself. That is why many of you are weak and ill, and some have died" (1 Cor. 11:29–30).

Possible Exceptions

However, there are circumstances when non-Catholics may receive Communion from a Catholic priest. This is especially the case when it comes to Eastern Orthodox Christians, who share the same faith concerning the nature of the sacraments:

"Catholic ministers may licitly administer the sacraments of penance, Eucharist and anointing of the sick to members of the oriental churches, which do not have full Communion with the Catholic Church, if they ask on their own for the sacraments and are properly disposed. This holds also for members of other churches, which in the judgment of the Apostolic See are in the same condition as the oriental churches as far as these sacraments are concerned" (CIC 844 §3).

Christians in these churches should, of course, respect their own church's guidelines regarding when it would be permissible for them to receive Communion in a Catholic church.

The circumstances in which Protestants are permitted to receive Communion are more limited, though it is still possible for them to do so under certain specifically defined circumstances.

Canon law explains the parameters: "If the danger of death is present or other grave necessity, in the judgment of the diocesan bishop or the conference of bishops, Catholic ministers may licitly administer these sacraments to other Christians who do not have full Communion with the Catholic Church, who cannot approach a minister of their own community and on their own ask for it, provided they manifest Catholic faith in these sacraments and are properly disposed" (CIC 844 §4).

It is important to remember that, under the rubrics specified above, even in those rare circumstances when non-Catholics are able to receive Communion, the same requirements apply to them as to Catholics.

Non-Christians and Communion

The U.S. bishops' guidelines for receiving Communion state: "We also welcome to this celebration those who do not share our faith in Jesus Christ. While we cannot admit them to Communion, we ask them to offer their prayers for the peace and the unity of the human family."

Because they have not received baptism, the gateway to the other sacraments, non-Christians cannot receive Communion. However, in emergency situations, they can be received into the Church via baptism, even if no priest is present, and an extraordinary minister of Holy Communion may bring them Communion as Viaticum.

How to Receive Communion

Communion may be received either in the hand or on the tongue. Around the year A.D. 390, Cyril of Jerusalem indicated that the early Church practiced Communion in the hand when he instructed his audience: "Approaching, therefore, come not with thy wrists extended, or thy fingers open; but make thy left hand as if a throne for thy right, which is on the eve of receiving the

King. And having hallowed thy palm, receive the body of Christ, saying after it, 'Amen.' Then after thou hast with carefulness hallowed thine eyes by the touch of the holy body, partake thereof; giving heed lest thou lose any of it; for what thou losest is a loss to thee as it were from one of thine own members. For tell me, if anyone gave thee gold dust, wouldst thou not with all precaution keep it fast, being on thy guard against losing any of it, and suffering loss?" (*Catechetical Lectures* 23:22).

The Congregation of the Sacraments and Divine Worship permitted the U.S. Bishops' Conference to authorize reception of Communion in the hand on July 25, 1977, provided the local bishop implements the practice in his diocese. Once implemented, the option to receive Communion either in the hand or on the tongue always remains with the communicant. No priest, deacon, acolyte, or extraordinary minister of Holy Communion may refuse a communicant Communion on the tongue. Likewise, once the local bishop has introduced Communion in the hand, none may refuse a communicant Communion in the hand (except when Communion is being given by intinction, in which case it must be given on the tongue).

Finally, after you have received Communion, it is appropriate to stay after Mass and thank Jesus for coming to you in the Holy Eucharist. The Church mandates that "the faithful are to be recommended not to omit to make a proper thanksgiving after Communion. They may do this during the celebration with a period of silence, with a hymn, psalm or other song of praise, or also after the celebration, if possible by staying behind to pray for a suitable time" (*Inaestimabile Donum* 17).

After receiving Jesus into one's own body and being drawn more closely into his, how could one do any less?

22

Anointing of the Sick

The anointing of the sick is administered to bring spiritual and even physical strength during an illness, especially near the time of death. It is most likely one of the last sacraments one will receive. A sacrament is an outward sign established by Jesus Christ to confer inward grace. In more basic terms, it is a rite that is performed to convey God's grace to the recipient through the power of the Holy Spirit.

The sacrament's name has changed over time. It was once called extreme unction, which means "the last anointing," and has been referred to as part of the "last rites." The *Catechism of the Catholic Church* calls it "the anointing of the sick" (CCC 1511).

The Sacrament's Institution

Like all the sacraments, holy anointing was instituted by Jesus Christ during his earthly ministry. The *Catechism* explains, "This sacred anointing of the sick was instituted by Christ our Lord as a true and proper sacrament of the New Testament. It is alluded to indeed by Mark but is recommended to the faithful and promulgated by James the apostle and brother of the Lord" (CCC 1511; cf. Mark 6:13; Jas. 5:14–15).

The anointing of the sick conveys several graces and imparts gifts of strengthening in the Holy Spirit against anxiety, discouragement, and temptation. It conveys peace and fortitude (CCC 1520). These graces flow from the atoning death of Jesus Christ, for "this was to fulfill what was spoken by the prophet Isaiah, 'He took our infirmities and bore our diseases'" (Matt. 8:17).

Mark refers to the sacrament when he recounts how Jesus

sent out the twelve disciples to preach, and "they cast out many demons, and anointed with oil many that were sick and healed them" (Mark 6:13). In his epistle, James says, "Is any among you sick? Let him call for the elders of the church, and let them pray over him, anointing him with oil in the name of the Lord; and the prayer of faith will save the sick man, and the Lord will raise him up; and if he has committed sins, he will be forgiven" (Jas. 5:14-15).

The early Church Fathers recognized this sacrament's role in the life of the Church. Around A.D. 250, Origen wrote that the penitent Christian "does not shrink from declaring his sin to a priest of the Lord and from seeking medicine . . . [of] which the apostle James says: 'If then there is anyone sick, let him call the presbyters of the Church, and let them impose hands upon him, anointing him with oil in the name of the Lord; and the prayer of faith will save the sick man, and if he be in sins, they shall be forgiven him'" (*Homilies on Leviticus* 2:4).

In the year 350, Bishop Serapion wrote, "We beseech you, Savior of all men, you that have all virtue and power, Father of our Lord and Savior Jesus Christ, and we pray that you send down from heaven the healing power of the only begotten [Son] upon this oil, so that for those who are anointed . . . it may be effected for the casting out of every disease and every bodily infirmity . . . for good grace and remission of sins" (*The Sacramentary of Serapion* 29:1).

The Sacrament's Effects

"The special grace of the sacrament of the anointing of the sick has as its effects: the uniting of the sick person to the Passion of Christ, for his own good and that of the whole Church; the strengthening, peace, and courage to endure in a Christian manner the sufferings of illness or old age; the forgiveness of sins, if the sick person was not able to obtain it through the sacrament of penance; the restoration of health, if it is conducive to the salvation of his soul; the preparation for passing over to eternal life" (CCC 1532).

Does a person have to be dying to receive this sacrament? No. The Catechism says, "The anointing of the sick is not a sacrament for those only who are at the point of death. Hence, as soon as anyone of the faithful begins to be in danger of death from sickness or old age, the fitting time for him to receive this sacrament has certainly already arrived" (CCC 1514).

Does God Always Heal?

Today some Christians go to extremes in their expectation of divine healing. On one hand, some say that if a Christian is not healed of all his diseases, this reflects his lack of faith. Others claim that divine healings were only for the apostolic age, when all diseases were healed instantly and automatically. Both extremes are wrong.

God does not always heal the physical infirmities that afflict us. Paul preached to the Galatians while he was afflicted by a "bodily ailment" (Gal. 4:13). He also mentions that he had to leave his companion Trophimus in the town of Miletus because he was too sick to travel (cf. 2 Tim. 4:20). In his first letter to Timothy, Paul urges his young protégé to "no longer drink only water, but to use a little wine for the sake of your stomach and your frequent ailments" (1 Tim. 5:23).

The last passage is especially informative. Not only does it reveal that illnesses were not always healed in the apostolic age, but it also shows an apostle's practical advice to a fellow Christian on how to deal with an illness. Notice that Paul does not tell Timothy to pray harder and have more faith that God will heal him from his ailments. Rather, he tells him how to manage the illness through medicinal means.

Some argue that healings were always instantaneous and were

only for those living during the apostolic age, but that afterward the gift of healing disappeared. The problem with that theory is that the Bible tells us otherwise. For example, when Jesus healed the blind man at Bethsaida, he laid his hands upon him twice before the man was fully healed (Mark 8:22–26).

Finally, we have a standing command of the New Testament in James 5:14–15, cited earlier. This command is never revoked anywhere in the Bible, and there are no statements anywhere that God will cease to heal. Thus the command is in effect to this very day.

Of course, our healing, like all things, is subject to God's will. As James pointed out just a chapter earlier, "You do not know about tomorrow. What is your life? For you are a mist that appears for a little time and then vanishes. Instead you ought to say, '*If the Lord wills, we shall live* and we shall do this or that'" (Jas. 4:14–15, emphasis added). We have a promise of healing, but not an unqualified one. It is conditional on the will of God.

Why Doesn't God Always Heal?

If God can heal us, why doesn't he? Why isn't it always his will to do so? One answer to this question is found in the spiritual discipline and training that can result from facing illness and adversity. Scripture asks, "Have you forgotten the exhortation which addresses you as sons?—'My son, do not regard lightly the discipline of the Lord, nor lose courage when you are punished by him. For the Lord disciplines him whom he loves, and chastises every son whom he receives' [Prov. 3:11–12]. It is for discipline that you have to endure. God is treating you as sons; for what son is there whom his father does not discipline? If you are left without discipline, in which all have participated, then you are illegitimate children and not sons. Besides this, we have had earthly fathers to discipline us and we respected them. Shall we not much more be subject to the Father of spirits and live? For they disciplined us for a short time at their pleasure, but he disciplines us for our good, that we may share his holiness. For the moment all discipline seems painful rather than pleasant; later it yields the peaceful fruit of righteousness to those who have been trained by it" (Heb. 12:5-11).

The Value of Suffering

Sometimes God allows us to undergo sickness as a form of discipline and training in righteousness. God often permits these trials for our sanctification, as Paul himself learned when he prayed that God would remove from him an angel of Satan who was afflicting him: "And to keep me from being too elated by the abundance of revelations, a thorn was given me in the flesh, a messenger [Greek: *angelos*] of Satan, to harass me, to keep me from being too elated. Three times I besought the Lord about this, that it should leave me; but he said to me, 'My grace is sufficient for you, for my power is made perfect in weakness.' I will all the more gladly boast of my weaknesses, that the power of Christ may rest upon me" (2 Cor. 12:7-9).

Even though we must face a certain amount of suffering and affliction in this life, we know God's grace is sufficient to sustain us. All of God's graces, including physical health, are bestowed to lead to the salvation of our souls. The Catholic Church teaches that the sacrament brings "the restoration of health, if it is conducive to the salvation of his soul" (CCC 1532).

God also uses our suffering to help others. If Paul had not become ill while on his first missionary journey and been forced to stop traveling, he would not have preached to the Galatians, for he tells them, "You know it was because of a bodily ailment that I preached the gospel to you at first" (Gal. 4:13). If he had not preached to the Galatians, he would not have later written them the epistle that appears in our New Testament. God used Paul's illness to bring salvation to the Galatians and bring us a work of Scripture, through which we are still receiving benefits from God.

This is just one example of how God used suffering to bring about good. Therefore, if we suffer, we should look upon it as an opportunity for good, such as by offering up our sufferings for our own sanctification and for our departed brothers and sisters in Christ.

This applies also to the physical suffering of death, which will come for each of us one day. The Bible reminds us, "As for man, his days are like grass; he flourishes like a flower of the field; for the wind passes over it, and it is gone, and its place knows it no more" (Ps. 103:15–16).

The "Last Rites"

Though the psalmist teaches us to ponder our mortality, he immediately comforts us by saying, "But the steadfast love of the Lord is from everlasting to everlasting upon those who fear him, and his righteousness to children's children, to those who keep his covenant and remember to do his commandments" (Ps. 103:17–18).

In his steadfast love for us, the Lord gives us the sacraments involved in the last rites to comfort us in our final days and prepare us for the journey ahead. "These include penance (or confession), confirmation (when lacking), anointing of the sick . . . and Viaticum (which is meant to be the last reception of Communion for the journey from this life to eternity). . . . The present ritual orders these sacraments in two ways. The 'continuous rites of penance and anointing' include: Introductory Rites, Liturgy of Penance, Liturgy of Confirmation, Liturgy of Anointing, Liturgy of Viaticum, and Concluding Rites. The 'rite for emergencies' includes the sacrament of penance, Apostolic Pardon, Lord's Prayer, Communion as Viaticum, prayer before anointing, anointing, concluding prayer, blessing, sign of peace" (Fr. Peter Stravinskas, *Catholic Encyclopedia*, 572).

The most important part of the last rites is the reception of the Lord in one's final Communion, also called "Viaticum" (Latin = that which you take on the road, i.e., provisions for a journey). This special Communion prepares us to travel with the Lord on the final part of our journey. The comfort of viaticum has been valued by Christians since the beginning of Church history. The first ecumenical council, held at Nicaea in 325, decreed: "Concerning the departing, the ancient canonical law is still to be maintained, to wit, that, if any man be at the point of death, he must not be deprived of the last and most indispensable viaticum" (canon 13). Having repented of our sins and received reconciliation, we travel with the Lord Jesus out of this earthly life and to eternal happiness with him in heaven.

From the earliest times, the sacrament of the anointing of the sick was cherished among Christians not only in immediate danger of death but even at the beginning sign of danger from illness or old age. A sermon of Caesar of Arles (c. A.D. 470–542) contains the following: "As often as some infirmity overtakes a man, let him who is ill receive the body and blood of Christ; let him humbly and in faith ask the presbyters for blessed oil, to anoint his body, so that what was written may be fulfilled in him: 'Is anyone among you sick? Let him bring in the presbyters, and let them pray over him, anointing him with oil; and the prayer of faith will save the sick man, and the Lord will raise him up; and if he be in sins, they will be forgiven him. . . . See to it, brethren, that whoever is ill hasten to the church, both that he may receive health of body and will merit to obtain the forgiveness of his sins" (*Sermons* 13[325]:3).

John Chrysostom

"The priests of Judaism had power to cleanse the body from leprosy—or rather, not to cleanse it at all, but to declare a person as having been cleansed. . . . Our priests have received the power

THE ESSENTIAL CATHOLIC SURVIVAL GUIDE

not of treating with the leprosy of the body, but with spiritual uncleanness; not of declaring cleansed, but of actually cleansing. . . . Priests accomplish this not only by teaching and admonishing, but also by the help of prayer. Not only at the time of our regeneration [in baptism], but even afterward, they have the authority to forgive sins: 'Is there anyone among you sick? Let him call in the priests of the church, and let them pray over him, anointing him with oil in the name of the Lord. And the prayer of faith shall save the sick man, and the Lord shall raise him up, and if he has committed sins, he shall be forgiven' " (*On the Priesthood* 3:6:190ff [A.D. 387]).

23

Call No Man Father?

Many Protestants claim that when Catholics address priests as "father," they are engaging in an unbiblical practice that Jesus forbade: "Call no man your father on earth, for you have one Father, who is in heaven" (Matt. 23:9).

In his tract *10 Reasons Why I Am Not a Roman Catholic*, Fundamentalist anti-Catholic writer Donald Maconaghie quotes this passage as support for his charge that "the papacy is a hoax."

Bill Jackson, another Fundamentalist who runs a full-time anti-Catholic organization, says in his *Christian's Guide to Roman Catholicism* that a "study of Matthew 23:9 reveals that Jesus was talking about being called father as a title of religious superiority . . . [which is] the basis for the [Catholic] hierarchy" (53).

How should Catholics respond to such objections?

The Answer

To understand why the charge does not work, one must first understand the use of the word *father* in reference to our earthly fathers. No one would deny a little girl the opportunity to tell someone that she loves her father. Common sense tells us that Jesus wasn't forbidding this type of use of the word *father*.

In fact, to forbid it would rob the address "Father" of its meaning when applied to God, for there would no longer be any earthly counterpart for the analogy of divine Fatherhood. The concept of God's role as Father would be meaningless if we obliterated the concept of earthly fatherhood.

But in the Bible the concept of fatherhood is not restricted to just our earthly fathers and God. It is used to refer to people other than biological or legal fathers and is used as a sign of respect to those with whom we have a special relationship.

For example, Joseph tells his brothers of a special fatherly relationship God had given him with the king of Egypt: "So it was not you who sent me here, but God; and he has made me a father to Pharaoh, and lord of all his house and ruler over all the land of Egypt" (Gen. 45:8).

Job indicates he played a fatherly role with the less fortunate: "I was a father to the poor, and I searched out the cause of him whom I did not know" (Job 29:16). And God himself declares that he will give a fatherly role to Eliakim, the steward of the house of David: "In that day I will call my servant Eliakim, the son of Hilkiah, and I will clothe him with [a] robe, and will bind [a] girdle on him, and will commit . . . authority to his hand; and he shall be a father to the inhabitants of Jerusalem and to the house of Judah" (Is. 22:20–21).

This type of fatherhood not only applies to those who are wise counselors (like Joseph) or benefactors (like Job) or both (like Eliakim); it also applies to those who have a fatherly spiritual relationship with one. For example, Elisha cries, "My father, my father!" to Elijah as the latter is carried up to heaven in a whirlwind (2 Kgs. 2:12). Later, Elisha himself is called a father by the king of Israel (2 Kgs. 6:21).

A Change with the New Testament?

Some Fundamentalists argue that this usage changed with the New Testament—that while it may have been permissible to call certain men "father" in the Old Testament, since the time of Christ, it's no longer allowed. This argument fails for several reasons.

First, as we've seen, the imperative "call no man father" does not apply to one's biological father. It also doesn't exclude calling one's ancestors "father," as is shown in Acts 7:2, where Stephen refers to "our father Abraham," or in Romans 9:10, where Paul speaks of "our father Isaac."

Second, there are numerous examples in the New Testament of the term *father* being used as a form of address and reference, even for men who are not biologically related to the speaker. There are, in fact, so many uses of *father* in the New Testament that the Fundamentalist interpretation of Matthew 23 (and the objection to Catholics calling priests "father") must be wrong, as we shall see.

Third, a careful examination of the context of Matthew 23 shows that Jesus didn't intend for his words here to be understood literally. The whole passage reads, "But you are not to be called 'rabbi,' for you have one teacher, and you are all brethren. And call no man your father on earth, for you have one Father, who is in heaven. Neither be called 'masters,' for you have one master, the Christ" (Matt. 23:8–10).

The first problem is that although Jesus seems to prohibit the use of the term *teacher*, Christ himself appointed certain men to be teachers in his Church: "Go therefore and make disciples of all nations . . . *teaching* them to observe all that I have commanded you" (Matt. 28:19–20). Paul speaks of his commission as a teacher: "For this I was appointed a preacher and apostle . . . a teacher of the Gentiles in faith and truth" (1 Tim. 2:7); "for this gospel I was appointed a preacher and apostle and teacher" (2 Tim. 1:11). He also reminds us that the Church has an office of teacher: "God has appointed in the church first apostles, second prophets, third teachers" (1 Cor. 12:28), and "his gifts were that some should be apostles, some prophets, some evangelists, some pastors and teachers" (Eph. 4:11). There is no doubt that Paul was not violating Christ's teaching in Matthew 23 by referring so often to others as "teachers."

Fundamentalists themselves slip up on this point by calling all sorts of people "doctor," for example, medical doctors as well as professors and scientists who have Ph.D. degrees (i.e., doctorates). What they fail to realize is that *doctor* is simply the Latin word for "teacher." Even "Mister" and "Mistress" ("Mrs.") are forms of the word *master*, also mentioned by Jesus. So if his words in Matthew 23 were meant to be taken literally, Fundamentalists would be just as guilty for using the words *teacher* and *doctor* and *mister* as Catholics for saying "father." But that would clearly be a misunderstanding of Christ's words.

So What Did Jesus Mean?

Jesus criticized Jewish leaders who love "the place of honor at feasts and the best seats in the synagogues, and salutations in the market places, and being called rabbi by men" (Matt. 23:6–7). His admonition here is a response to the Pharisees' proud hearts and their grasping after marks of status and prestige.

He was using hyperbole (exaggeration to make a point) to show the scribes and Pharisees how sinful and proud they were for not looking humbly to God as the source of all authority and fatherhood and teaching, and instead setting themselves up as the ultimate authorities, father figures, and teachers.

Christ used hyperbole often, for example when he declared, "If your right eye causes you to sin, pluck it out and throw it away; it is better that you lose one of your members than that your whole body be thrown into hell" (Matt. 5:29; cf. 18:9; Mark 9:47). Christ certainly did not intend this to be applied literally, for otherwise all Christians would be blind amputees (cf. 1 John 1:8; 1 Tim. 1:15). We are all subject to "the lust of the flesh and the lust of the eyes and the pride of life" (1 John 2:16).

Since Jesus is demonstrably using hyperbole when he says not to call anyone our father—else we would not be able to refer to our earthly fathers as such—we must read his words carefully and with sensitivity to the presence of hyperbole if we wish to understand what he is saying.

Jesus is not forbidding us to call men "fathers" who actually are such—either literally or spiritually. (See below on the apostolic example of spiritual fatherhood.) To refer to such people as fathers is only to acknowledge the truth, and Jesus is not against that. He is warning people against *inaccurately* attributing fatherhood—or a particular *kind or degree* of fatherhood—to those who do not have it.

As the apostolic example shows, some individuals genuinely do have a spiritual fatherhood, meaning that they can be referred to as spiritual fathers. What must not be done is to confuse their form of spiritual paternity with that of God. Ultimately, God is our supreme protector, provider, and instructor. Correspondingly, it is wrong to view any individual other than God as having these roles.

Throughout the world, some people have been tempted to look upon religious leaders who are mere mortals as if they were an individual's supreme source of spiritual instruction, nourishment, and protection. The tendency to turn mere men into "gurus" is worldwide.

This was also a temptation in the Jewish world of Jesus' day, when famous rabbinical leaders, especially those who founded important schools, such as Hillel and Shammai, were highly exalted by their disciples. It is this elevation of an individual man—the formation of a "cult of personality" around him—of which Jesus is speaking when he warns against attributing to someone an undue role as master, father, or teacher.

He is not forbidding the perfunctory use of honorifics or forbidding us to recognize that the person *does* have a role as a spiritual father and teacher. The example of his own apostles shows us that.

The Apostles Show the Way

The New Testament is filled with examples of and references to spiritual father-son and father-child relationships. Many people are not aware just how common these are, so it is worth quoting some of them here.

Paul regularly referred to Timothy as his child: "Therefore I sent to you Timothy, my beloved and faithful child in the Lord, to remind you of my ways in Christ" (1 Cor. 4:17); "to Timothy, my true child in the faith: Grace, mercy, and peace from God the Father and Christ Jesus our Lord" (1 Tim. 1:2); "to Timothy, my beloved child: Grace, mercy, and peace from God the Father and Christ Jesus our Lord" (2 Tim. 1:2).

He also referred to Timothy as his son: "This charge I commit to you, Timothy, my son, in accordance with the prophetic utterances which pointed to you, that inspired by them you may wage the good warfare" (1 Tim 1:18); "you then, my son, be strong in the grace that is in Christ Jesus" (2 Tim. 2:1); "but Timothy's worth you know, how as a son with a father he has served with me in the gospel" (Phil. 2:22).

Paul also referred to others of his converts in this way: "To Titus, my true child in a common faith: Grace and peace from God the Father and Christ Jesus our Savior" (Titus 1:4); "I appeal to you for my child, Onesimus, whose father I have become in my imprisonment" (Philem. 10). None of these men were Paul's literal, biological sons. Rather, Paul is emphasizing his spiritual fatherhood with them.

Spiritual Fatherhood

Perhaps the most pointed New Testament reference to the theology of the spiritual fatherhood of priests is Paul's statement that "I do not write this to make you ashamed, but to admonish you as my beloved children. For though you have countless guides in Christ, you do not have many fathers. *For I became your father in Christ Jesus through the gospel*" (1 Cor. 4:14–15, emphasis added).

Peter followed the same custom, referring to Mark as his son: "She who is at Babylon, who is likewise chosen, sends you greetings; and so does my son Mark" (1 Pet. 5:13). The apostles sometimes referred to entire churches under their care as their children. Paul writes, "Here for the third time I am ready to come to you. And I will not be a burden, for I seek not what is yours but you; for children ought not to lay up for their parents, but parents for their children" (2 Cor. 12:14). "My little children, with whom I am again in travail until Christ be formed in you!" (Gal. 4:19).

John said, "My little children, I am writing this to you so that you may not sin; but if any one does sin, we have an advocate with the Father, Jesus Christ the righteous" (1 John 2:1). "No greater joy can I have than this, to hear that my children follow the truth" (3 John 4). In fact, John also addresses men in his congregations as "fathers" (1 John 2:13–14).

By referring to these people as their spiritual sons and spiritual children, Peter, Paul, and John imply their own roles as spiritual fathers. Since the Bible frequently speaks of this spiritual fatherhood, we Catholics acknowledge it and follow the custom of the apostles by calling priests "father." Failure to acknowledge this is a failure to recognize and honor a great gift God has bestowed on the Church: the spiritual fatherhood of the priesthood.

Catholics know that as members of a parish, they have been committed to a priest's spiritual care. Thus they have great filial affection for priests and call them "father." Priests, in turn, follow the apostles' biblical example by referring to members of their flock as "my son" or "my child" (cf. Gal. 4:19; 1 Tim. 1:18; 2 Tim. 2:1; Philem. 10; 1 Pet. 5:13; 1 John 2:1; 3 John 4).

All of these passages were written under the inspiration of the Holy Spirit, and they express the infallibly recorded truth that Christ's ministers do have a role as spiritual fathers. Jesus is not against acknowledging that. It is he who gave these men their role as spiritual fathers, and it is his Holy Spirit who recorded this role for us in the pages of Scripture. To acknowledge spiritual fatherhood is to acknowledge the truth, and no amount of anti-Catholic grumbling will change that fact.

24

Celibacy and the Priesthood

Fundamentalist attacks on priestly celibacy come in a number of different forms, not all compatible with one another. There is almost no other subject about which so many *different* confusions exist.

The first and most basic confusion is thinking of priestly celibacy as a dogma or doctrine—a central and irreformable part of the faith, believed by Catholics to come from Jesus and the apostles. Thus some Fundamentalists make a great deal of a biblical reference to Peter's mother-in-law (Mark 1:30), apparently supposing that, if Catholics only knew that Peter had been married, they would be unable to regard him as the first pope. Again, Fundamentalist timelines of "Catholic inventions" (a popular literary form) assign "mandatory priestly celibacy" to this or that year in Church history, as if prior to this requirement the Church could not have been Catholic.

These Fundamentalists are often surprised to learn that even today celibacy is not the rule for all Catholic priests. In fact, for Eastern rite Catholics, married priests are the *norm*, just as they are for Orthodox and Oriental Christians.

Even in the Eastern churches, though, there have always been some restrictions on marriage and ordination. Although married men may become priests, unmarried priests may not marry, and married priests, if widowed, may not remarry. Moreover, there is an ancient Eastern discipline of choosing bishops from the ranks of the celibate monks, so their bishops are all unmarried.

The tradition in the Western or Latin-rite Church has been for priests as well as bishops to take vows of celibacy, a rule that has been firmly in place since the early Middle Ages. Even today, though, exceptions are made. For example, there are married

Latin-rite priests who are converts from Lutheranism and Epis-
copalianism.

As these variations and exceptions indicate, priestly celibacy is
not an unchangeable dogma but a disciplinary rule. The fact that
Peter was married is no more contrary to the Catholic faith than
the fact that the pastor of the nearest Maronite Catholic church
is married.

Is Marriage Mandatory?

Another, quite different Fundamentalist confusion is the notion
that celibacy is unbiblical or even "unnatural." Every man, it is
claimed, must obey the biblical injunction to "be fruitful and multiply" (Gen. 1:28), and Paul commands that "each man should have
his own wife and each woman her own husband" (1 Cor. 7:2).
It is even argued that celibacy somehow "causes" illicit sexual behavior or perversion or at least correlates with higher incidence
of it.

All of this is false. Although most people are at some point
in their lives called to the married state, the vocation of celibacy
is explicitly advocated—as well as practiced—by both Jesus and
Paul.

Far from "commanding" marriage in 1 Corinthians 7, in that
very chapter Paul actually endorses celibacy for those capable of
it: "To the unmarried and the widows I say that it is well for them
to remain single as I do. But if they cannot exercise self-control,
they should marry. For it is better to marry than to be aflame with
passion" (7:8–9).

It is only because of this "temptation to immorality" (7:2) that
Paul gives the teaching about each man and woman having a spouse
and giving each other their "conjugal rights" (7:3). He specifically
clarifies, "I say this *by way of concession, not of command.* I wish that
all were as I myself am. But each has his own special gift from God,
one of one kind and one of another" (7:6–7, emphasis added).

Paul even goes on to make a case for *preferring* celibacy to marriage: "Are you free from a wife? Do not seek marriage. . . . Those who marry will have worldly troubles, and I would spare you that. . . . The unmarried man is anxious about the affairs of the Lord, how to please the Lord; but the married man is anxious about worldly affairs, how to please his wife, and his interests are divided. And the unmarried woman or girl is anxious about the affairs of the Lord, how to be holy in body and spirit; but the married woman is anxious about worldly affairs, how to please her husband" (7:27–34).

Paul's conclusion: He who marries "does well; and he who refrains from marriage will do better" (7:38).

Paul was not the first apostle to conclude that celibacy is, in some sense, "better" than marriage. After Jesus' teaching in Matthew 19 on divorce and remarriage, the disciples exclaimed, "If such is the case of a man with his wife, it is not expedient to marry" (Matt 19:10). This remark prompted Jesus' teaching on the value of celibacy "for the sake of the kingdom":

"Not all men can receive this saying, but only those to whom it is given. For there are eunuchs who have been so from birth, and there are eunuchs who have been made eunuchs by men, and there are eunuchs who have made themselves eunuchs for the sake of the kingdom of heaven. He who is able to receive this, let him receive it" (Matt. 19:11–12).

Notice that this sort of celibacy "for the sake of the kingdom" is a gift, a call that is not granted to all—or even most people— but is granted to some. Other people are called to marriage. It is true that too often individuals in both vocations fall short of the requirements of their state, but this does not diminish either vocation, nor does it mean that the individuals in question were "not really called" to that vocation. The sin of a priest doesn't necessarily prove that he never should have taken a vow of celibacy any more than the sin of a married man or woman proves that he or she never should have gotten married. It is possible for us to fall short of our own true calling.

Celibacy is neither unnatural nor unbiblical. "Be fruitful and multiply" is not binding upon every individual; rather, it is a general precept for the human race. Otherwise, every unmarried man and woman of marrying age would be in a state of sin by remaining single, and Jesus and Paul would be guilty of advocating sin as well as committing it.

"The Husband of One Wife"

Another Fundamentalist argument is that marriage is mandatory *for Church leaders*. Paul says that a bishop must be "the husband of one wife" and "must manage his own household well, keeping his children submissive and respectful in every way; for if a man does not know how to manage his own household, how can he care for God's church?" (1 Tim. 3:2, 4–5). This means, they argue, that only a man who has demonstrably looked after a family is fit to care for God's Church. An unmarried man, it is implied, is somehow untried or unproven.

This interpretation leads to obvious absurdities. For one, if "the husband of one wife" really meant that a bishop *had* to be married, then by the same logic "keeping his children submissive and respectful in every way" would mean that he *had* to have children. Childless husbands (or even fathers of only *one* child, since Paul uses the plural) would not qualify.

In fact, following this style of interpretation to its final absurdity, since Paul speaks of bishops meeting these requirements (not of their *having met* them, or of *candidates* for bishop meeting them), it would even follow that an ordained bishop whose wife or children died would become unqualified for ministry! Clearly such excessive literalism must be rejected.

The theory that Church leaders must be married also contradicts the obvious fact that Paul himself, an eminent Church leader, was single and happy to be so. Unless Paul was a hypocrite, he could hardly have imposed a requirement on bishops that he did not himself meet. Consider, too, the implications regarding Paul's positive attitude toward celibacy in 1 Corinthians 7: The married have worldly anxieties and divided interests, yet *only* they are qualified to be bishops, whereas the unmarried have single-minded devotion to the Lord, yet they are barred from ministry!

The suggestion that the unmarried man is somehow untried or unproven is equally absurd. Each vocation has its own proper challenges: The celibate man must exercise self-control (cf. 1 Cor. 7:9), the husband must love and care for his wife selflessly (cf. Eph. 5:25), and the father must raise his children well (cf. 1 Tim. 3:4). *Every* man must meet Paul's standard of "managing his household well," even if his "household" is only himself. If anything, the chaste celibate man meets a *higher* standard than the respectable family man.

Clearly, the point of Paul's requirement that a bishop be "the husband of one wife" is not that he *must* have one wife, but that he must have *only* one wife. Expressed conversely, Paul is saying that a bishop must *not* have unruly or undisciplined children (not that he *must* have children who are well behaved), and must not be married *more than once* (not that he must be married).

It is precisely those who are uniquely "anxious about the affairs of the Lord" (1 Cor. 7:32), those to whom it has been given to renounce marriage "for the sake of the kingdom of heaven" (Matt. 19:12), who are ideally suited to follow in the footsteps of those who have left everything to follow Christ (cf. Matt. 19:27): the calling of the clergy and consecrated religious (i.e., monks and nuns).

Thus Paul warned Timothy, a young bishop, that those called to be soldiers of Christ must avoid "civilian pursuits": "Share in suffering as a good soldier of Christ Jesus. No soldier on service gets entangled in civilian pursuits, since his aim is to satisfy the one who enlisted him" (2 Tim. 2:3–4). In light of Paul's remarks in 1 Corinthians 7 about the advantages of celibacy, marriage and family clearly stand out in connection with these "civilian pursuits."

An example of ministerial celibacy can also be seen in the Old Testament. The prophet Jeremiah, as part of his prophetic ministry, was forbidden to take a wife: "The word of the Lord came to me: 'You shall not take a wife, nor shall you have sons or daughters in this place'" (Jer. 16:1–2). Of course, this is different from Catholic priestly celibacy, which is not divinely ordained, yet the divine precedent still supports the legitimacy of the human institution.

Forbidden to Marry?

Yet none of these passages give us an example of humanly mandated celibacy. Jeremiah's celibacy was mandatory, but it was from the Lord. Paul's remark to Timothy about "civilian pursuits" is only a general admonition, not a specific command. And even in 1 Corinthians 7, Paul qualifies his strong endorsement of celibacy by adding: "I say this for your own benefit, not to lay any restraint upon you, but to promote good order and to secure your undivided devotion to the Lord" (7:35).

This brings us to Fundamentalism's last line of attack: that, by *requiring* at least some of its clerics and its religious not to marry, the Catholic Church falls under Paul's condemnation in 1 Timothy 4:3 against apostates who "forbid marriage."

In fact, the Catholic Church forbids no one to marry. No one is required to take a vow of celibacy. Those who do take the vow do so voluntarily. They renounce marriage (cf. Matt. 19:12); no one forbids it to them. Any Catholic who doesn't wish to take such a vow doesn't have to, and he is almost always free to marry with the Church's blessing. The Church simply elects candidates for the priesthood (or, in the Eastern rites, for the episcopacy) from among those who voluntarily renounce marriage.

But is there scriptural precedent for this practice of restricting membership in a group to those who take a voluntary vow of celibacy? Yes. Paul, in 1 Timothy 5:9–16, mentions an order of widows pledged not to remarry, in particular advising: "But refuse to enroll younger widows; for when they grow wanton against Christ they desire to marry, and so they incur condemnation for having violated their first pledge" (5:11–12).

This "first pledge" broken by remarriage cannot refer to previous wedding vows, for Paul does not condemn widows for remarrying (Rom. 7:2–3). It can refer only to a *vow not to remarry* taken by widows enrolled in this group. In effect, they were an early form of women religious—New Testament nuns. The New Testament Church *did* contain orders with mandatory celibacy, just as the Catholic Church does today.

Such orders are not, then, what Paul meant when he warned against forbidding marriage. The real culprits here are the many Gnostic sects through the ages that denounced marriage, sex, and the body as intrinsically evil. Some early heretics fit this description, as did the medieval Albigensians and Catharists (whom, ironically, some anti-Catholic writers admire in ignorance, purely because they insisted on using their own vernacular translation of the Bible).

The Dignity of Celibacy and Marriage

Most Catholics marry, and all Catholics are taught to venerate marriage as a holy institution—a sacrament, an action of God upon our souls, one of the holiest things we encounter in this life.

In fact, it is precisely the holiness of marriage that makes celibacy precious, for only what is good and holy in itself can be given up for God as a sacrifice. Just as fasting presupposes the goodness of food, celibacy presupposes the goodness of marriage. To despise celibacy, therefore, is to undermine marriage itself, as the early Fathers pointed out.

Celibacy is also a life-affirming institution. In the Old Testament, where celibacy was almost unknown, the childless were often despised by others and themselves. Only through children, it was felt, did one acquire value. By renouncing marriage, the celibate affirms the intrinsic value of each human life in itself, regardless of offspring.

Finally, celibacy is an eschatological sign to the Church, a living-out in the present of the universal celibacy of heaven: "For in the resurrection they neither marry nor are given in marriage, but are like angels in heaven" (Matt. 22:30).

25

The Forgiveness of Sins

All pardon for sins ultimately comes from Christ's finished work on Calvary, but how is this pardon received by individuals? Did Christ leave us any means within the Church to take away sin? The Bible says he gave us two means.

Baptism was given to take away the sin inherited from Adam (original sin) and any sins we personally committed before baptism—sins we personally commit are called actual sins, because they come from our own acts. Thus on the day of Pentecost, Peter told the crowds, "Repent, and be baptized every one of you in the name of Jesus Christ for the forgiveness of your sins; and you shall receive the gift of the Holy Spirit" (Acts 2:38), and when Paul was baptized he was told, "And now why do you wait? Rise and be baptized, and wash away your sins, calling on his name" (Acts 22:16). And so Peter later wrote, "Baptism . . . now saves you, not as a removal of dirt from the body but as an appeal to God for a clear conscience, through the resurrection of Jesus Christ" (1 Pet. 3:21).

For sins committed after baptism, a different sacrament is needed. It has been called penance, confession, and reconciliation, each word emphasizing one of its aspects. During his life, Christ forgave sins, as in the case of the woman caught in adultery (John 8:1–11) and the woman who anointed his feet (Luke 7:48). He exercised this power in his human capacity as the Messiah or Son of man, telling us, "the Son of man has authority on earth to forgive sins" (Matt. 9:6), which is why the Gospel writer himself explains that God "had given such authority to men" (Matt. 9:8).

Since he would not always be with the Church visibly, Christ gave this power to other men so the Church, which is the continuation of his presence throughout time (cf. Matt. 28:20), would be able to offer forgiveness to future generations. He gave his power to the apostles, and it was a power that could be passed on to their successors and agents, since the apostles wouldn't always be on earth either, but people would still be sinning.

God had sent Jesus to forgive sins, but after his Resurrection, Jesus told the apostles, " 'As the Father has sent me, even so I send you.' And when he had said this, he breathed on them, and said to them, 'Receive the Holy Spirit. If you forgive the sins of any, they are forgiven; if you retain the sins of any, they are retained' " (John 20:21–23). (This is one of only two times we are told that God breathed on man, the other being in Genesis 2:7, when he made man a living soul. It emphasizes how important the establishment of the sacrament of penance is.)

The Commission

Christ told the apostles to follow his example: "As the Father has sent me, even so I send you" (John 20:21). Just as the apostles were to carry Christ's message to the whole world, so they were to carry his forgiveness: "Truly, I say to you, whatever you bind on earth shall be bound in heaven, and whatever you loose on earth shall be loosed in heaven" (Matt. 18:18).

This power was understood as coming from God: "All this is from God, who through Christ reconciled us to himself and gave us the ministry of reconciliation" (2 Cor. 5:18). Indeed, confirms Paul, "we are ambassadors for Christ" (2 Cor. 5:20).

Some say that any power given to the apostles died with them. Not so. Some powers must have, such as the ability to write Scripture. But the powers necessary to maintain the Church as a living, spiritual society had to be passed down from generation to generation. If they ceased, the Church would cease, except as a quaint abstraction. Christ ordered the apostles to, "Go therefore and make disciples of all nations." It would take much time. And he promised them assistance: "Lo, I am with you always, to the close of the age" (Matt. 28:19–20).

If the disciples believed that Christ instituted the power to sacramentally forgive sins in his stead, we would expect the apostles'
successors—the bishops—and Christians of later years to act as
though such power was legitimately and habitually exercised. If,
on the other hand, the sacramental forgiveness of sins was what
Fundamentalists term it—an "invention"—and if it was something foisted upon the young Church by ecclesiastical or political
leaders, we'd expect to find records of protest. In fact, in early
Christian writings we find no sign of protests concerning sacramental forgiveness of sins. Quite the contrary. We find that confessing to a priest was accepted as part of the original deposit of
faith handed down from the apostles.

Lots of Gumption

Loraine Boettner, in his book *Roman Catholicism*, claims "auricular
confession to a priest instead of to God" was instituted in 1215
at the Fourth Lateran Council. This is an extreme example, even
for a committed anti-Catholic. Few people have the gumption
to place the "invention" of confession so late, since there is so
much early Christian writing—a good portion of it one thousand
or more years before that council—that refers to the practice of
confession as something already long-established.

Actually, the Fourth Lateran Council did discuss confession.
To combat the lax morals of the time, the Council regulated the
already-existing duty to confess one's sins by saying that Catholics
should confess any mortal sins at least once a year. To issue an official decree about how frequently a sacrament must be celebrated
is hardly the same as "inventing" that sacrament.

The earliest Christian writings, such as the first-century *Didache*, are indefinite on the procedure for confession to be used
in the forgiveness of sins, but a verbal confession is listed as part
of the Church's requirement by the time of Irenaeus (A.D. 180).
He wrote that the disciples of the Gnostic heretic Marcus "have
deluded many women. . . . Their consciences have been branded

as with a hot iron. Some of these women make a public confession, but others are ashamed to do this, and in silence, as if withdrawing themselves from the hope of the life of God, they either apostatize entirely or hesitate between the two courses" (*Against Heresies* 1:22).

The sacrament of penance is clearly in use, for Irenaeus speaks of making an outward confession (versus remaining silent) upon which the hope of eternal life hangs, but it is not yet clear from Irenaeus just how, or to whom, confession is to be made. Is it privately to the priest, or before the whole congregation, with the priest presiding? The one thing we can say for sure is that the sacrament is understood by Irenaeus as having originated in the infant Church.

Later writers, such as Origen (241), Cyprian (251), and Aphraates (337), are clear in saying confession is to be made to a priest. (In their writings the whole process of penance is termed *exomologesis*, which means confession—the confession was seen as the main part of the sacrament.) Cyprian writes that the forgiveness of sins can take place only "through the priests." Ambrose says "this right is given to priests only." Pope Leo I says absolution can be obtained only through the prayers of the priests. These utterances are not taken as novel, but as reminders of accepted belief. We have no record of anyone objecting, of anyone claiming these men were pushing an "invention."

Confession Implied

Note that the power Christ gave the apostles was twofold: to forgive sins or to hold them bound, which means to retain them unforgiven. Several things follow from this. First, the apostles could not know what sins to forgive and what not to forgive unless they were first told the sins by the sinner. This implies confession. Second, their authority was not merely to proclaim that God had already forgiven sins or that he would forgive sins if there were proper repentance.

Such interpretations don't account for the distinction between forgiving and retaining—nor do they account for the importance given to the utterance in John 20:23. If God has already forgiven all of a man's sins, or will forgive them all (past and future) upon a single act of repentance, then it makes little sense to tell the apostles they have been given the power to "retain" sins, since forgiveness would be all-or-nothing and nothing could be "retained."

Furthermore, if at conversion we were forgiven all sins—past, present, and future—it would make no sense for Christ to require us to pray, "And forgive us our debts, as we also have forgiven our debtors," which he explained is required because "if you forgive men their trespasses, your heavenly Father also will forgive you; but if you do not forgive men their trespasses, neither will your Father forgive your trespasses" (Matt. 6:12–15).

If forgiveness really can be partial—not a once-for-all thing—how is one to tell which sins have been forgiven, which not, in the absence of a priestly decision? You can't very well rely on your own gut feelings. No, the biblical passages make sense only if the apostles and their successors were given a real authority.

Still, some people are not convinced. One is Paul Juris, a former priest, now a Fundamentalist, who has written a pamphlet on this subject. The pamphlet is widely distributed by organizations opposed to Catholicism. The cover describes the work as "a study of John 20:23, a much misunderstood and misused portion of Scripture pertaining to the forgiveness of sins." Juris mentions "two main schools of thought": the Catholic and the Fundamentalist positions.

He correctly notes that "among Christians, it is generally agreed that regular confession of one's sins is obviously necessary to remain in good relationship with God. So the issue is not whether we should or should not confess our sins. Rather, the real issue is, How does God say that our sins are forgiven or retained?"

Verse Slinging

This apparently reasonable approach sounds fine on the surface, but it masks what really happens next. Juris engages in verse slinging, listing as many verses as he can find that refer to God forgiving sins, in hopes that the sheer mass of verses will settle the question. But none of the verses he lists specifically interpret John 20:23, and none contradict the Catholic interpretation.

For instance, he cites verses like these: "Let it be known to you therefore, brethren, that through this man forgiveness of sins is proclaimed to you, and by him every one that believes is freed from everything from which you could not be freed by the law of Moses" (Acts 13:38–39); "and he said to them, 'Go into all the world and preach the gospel to the whole creation. He who believes and is baptized will be saved; but he who does not believe will be condemned'" (Mark 16:15–16).

Juris says that verses like these demonstrate that "all that was left for the disciples to do was to 'go' and 'proclaim' this wonderful good news (the gospel) to all men. As they proclaimed this good news of the gospel, those who believed the gospel, their sins would be forgiven. Those who rejected (did not believe) the gospel, their sins would be retained." Juris does nothing more than show that the Bible says God will forgive sins and that it is through Jesus that our sins are forgiven—things no one doubts. He does not remotely prove that John 20:23 is equivalent to a command to "go" and to "preach," that merely going and preaching are part of God's plan for saving people. He also sidesteps the evident problems in the Fundamentalist interpretation.

The passage says nothing about preaching the good news. Instead, Jesus is telling the apostles that they have been empowered to do something. He does not say, "When God forgives men's sins, they are forgiven." He uses the second person plural: *you.* And he talks about the apostles forgiving, not preaching. When he refers to retaining sins, he uses the same form: "When you hold them bound, they are held bound."

The best Juris can do is assert that John 20:23 means the apostles were given authority only to proclaim the forgiveness of sins —but asserting this is not proving it. His is a technique that often works because many readers believe that the Fundamentalist interpretation has been proven true. After all, if you propose to interpret one verse and accomplish that by listing irrelevant verses that refer to something other than the specific point in controversy, lazy readers will conclude that you have marshaled an impressive array of evidence. All they have to do is count the citations. Here's one for the Catholics, they say, looking at John 20:21–23, but ten or twenty for the Fundamentalists. The Fundamentalists must be right!

The Advantages

Is the Catholic who confesses his sins to a priest any better off than the non-Catholic who confesses directly to God? Yes. First, he seeks forgiveness the way Christ intended. Second, by confessing to a priest, the Catholic learns a lesson in humility, which is avoided when one confesses only through private prayer. Third, the Catholic receives sacramental graces the non-Catholic doesn't get; through the sacrament of penance sins are forgiven and graces are obtained. Fourth, the Catholic is assured that his sins are forgiven; he does not have to rely on a subjective "feeling." Lastly, the Catholic can also obtain sound advice on avoiding sin in the future.

During his lifetime Christ sent out his followers to do his work. Just before he left this world, he gave the apostles special authority, commissioning them to make God's forgiveness present to all people, and the whole Christian world accepted this, until just a few centuries ago. If there is an "invention" here, it is not the sacrament of penance but the notion that the sacramental forgiveness of sins is not to be found in the Bible or in early Christian history.

26

Primer on Indulgences

Those who claim that indulgences are no longer part of Church teaching have the admirable desire to distance themselves from abuses that occurred around the time of the Protestant Reformation. They also want to remove stumbling blocks that prevent non-Catholics from taking a positive view of the Church. As admirable as these motives are, the claim that indulgences are not part of Church teaching today is false.

This is proved by the *Catechism of the Catholic Church*, which states, "An indulgence is obtained through the Church who, by virtue of the power of binding and loosing granted her by Christ Jesus, intervenes in favor of individual Christians and opens for them the treasury of the merits of Christ and the saints to obtain from the Father of mercies the remission of the temporal punishment due for their sins." The Church does this not just to aid Christians "but also to spur them to works of devotion, penance, and charity" (CCC 1478).

Indulgences are part of the Church's infallible teaching. This means that no Catholic is at liberty to disbelieve in them. The Council of Trent "condemns with anathema those who say that indulgences are useless or that the Church does not have the power to grant them" (*Decree on Indulgences*). Trent's anathema places indulgences in the realm of infallibly defined teaching.

The pious use of indulgences dates back to the early days of the Church, and the principles underlying indulgences are found in the Bible itself. Catholics who are uncomfortable with indulgences do not realize how biblical they are. The principles behind indulgences are as clear in Scripture as those behind more familiar doctrines, such as the Trinity.

Before looking at those principles more closely, we should define indulgences. In his apostolic constitution on indulgences, Pope Paul VI said: "An indulgence is a remission before God of the temporal punishment due to sins whose guilt has already been forgiven, which the faithful Christian who is duly disposed gains under certain defined conditions through the Church's help when, as a minister of redemption, she dispenses and applies with authority the treasury of the satisfactions won by Christ and the saints" (*Indulgentiarum Doctrina* 1).

This technical definition can be phrased more simply as follows: "An indulgence is what we receive when the Church lessens the temporal (lasting only for a short time) penalties to which we may be subject even though our sins have been forgiven." To understand this definition, we need to look at the biblical principles behind indulgences.

Principle 1: Sin Results in Guilt and Punishment

When a person sins, he acquires certain liabilities: the liability of guilt and the liability of punishment. Scripture speaks of the former when it pictures guilt as clinging to our souls, making them discolored and unclean before God: "Though your sins are like scarlet, they shall be white as snow; though they are red like crimson, they shall become like wool" (Is. 1:18). This idea of guilt clinging to our souls appears in texts that picture forgiveness as a cleansing or washing and the state of our forgiven souls as clean and white (cf. Ps. 51:4, 9).

We incur not just guilt but liability for punishment when we sin: "I will punish the world for its evil, and the wicked for their iniquity; I will put an end to the pride of the arrogant, and lay low the haughtiness of the ruthless" (Is. 13:11). Judgment pertains even to the smallest sins: "For God will bring every deed into judgment, with every secret thing, whether good or evil" (Eccl. 12:14).

Principle 2: Punishments Are
Both Temporal and Eternal

The Bible indicates some punishments are eternal, lasting forever, but others are temporal. Eternal punishment is mentioned in Daniel 12:2: "And many of those who sleep in the dust of the earth shall awake, some to everlasting life, and some to shame and everlasting contempt."

We normally focus on the eternal penalties of sin, because they are the most important, but Scripture indicates temporal penalties are real and go back to the first sin humans committed: "To the woman he said, 'I will greatly multiply your pain in childbearing; in pain you shall bring forth children'" (Gen. 3:16).

Principle 3: Temporal Penalties May
Remain When a Sin Is Forgiven

When someone repents, God removes his guilt (cf. Is. 1:18) and any eternal punishment (cf. Rom. 5:9), but temporal penalties may remain. One passage demonstrating this is 2 Samuel 12, in which Nathan the prophet confronts David over his adultery:

"David said to Nathan, 'I have sinned against the Lord.' And Nathan said to David: 'The Lord also has put away your sin; you shall not die. Nevertheless, because by this deed you have utterly scorned the Lord, the child that is born to you shall die'" (2 Sam. 12:13–14). God forgave David, but David still had to suffer the loss of his son as well as other temporal punishments (cf. 2 Sam. 12:7–12). (For other examples, see: Numbers 14:13–23; 20:12; 27:12–14.)

Protestants realize that, while Jesus paid the price for our sins before God, he did not relieve our obligation to repair what we have done. They fully acknowledge that if you steal someone's car, you have to give it back; it isn't enough just to repent. God's forgiveness (and man's!) does not include letting you keep the stolen car.

Protestants also admit the principle of temporal penalties for sin, in practice, when discussing death. Scripture says death entered the world through original sin (cf. Gen. 3:22–24; Rom. 5:12). When we first come to God we are forgiven, and when we sin later we are able to be forgiven, yet that does not free us from the penalty of physical death. Even the forgiven die; a penalty remains after our sins are forgiven. This is a temporal penalty since physical death is temporary and we will be resurrected (cf. Dan. 12:2).

Principle 4: God Blesses Some People As a Reward to Others

In Matthew 9:1–8, Jesus heals a paralytic and forgives his sins after seeing the faith of his friends. Paul also tells us that "as regards election [the Jews] are beloved for the sake of their forefathers" (Rom. 11:28).

When God blesses one person as a reward to someone else, sometimes the specific blessing he gives is a reduction of the temporal penalties to which the first person is subject. For example, God promised Abraham that, if he could find a certain number of righteous men in Sodom, he was willing to defer the city's temporal destruction for the sake of the righteous (Gen. 18:16–33; cf. 1 Kgs. 11:11–13; Rom. 11:28–29).

Principle 5: God Remits Temporal Punishments through the Church

God uses the Church when he removes temporal penalties. This is the essence of the doctrine of indulgences. Earlier we defined indulgences as "what we receive when the Church lessens the temporal penalties to which we may be subject even though our sins have been forgiven." The members of the Church became aware of this principle through the sacrament of penance. From the beginning, acts of penance were assigned as part of the sacrament because the Church recognized that Christians must deal with temporal penalties, such as God's discipline and the need to compensate those our sins have injured.

In the early Church, penances were sometimes severe. For serious sins, such as apostasy, murder, and abortion, the penances could stretch over years, but the Church recognized that repentant sinners could shorten their penances by pleasing God through pious or charitable acts that expressed sorrow and a desire to make up for one's sin.

The Church also recognized that the duration of temporal punishments could be lessened through the involvement of other persons who had pleased God. Scripture tells us God gave the authority to forgive sins "to men" (Matt. 9:8) and to Christ's ministers in particular. Jesus told them, "As the Father has sent me, even so I send you. . . . Receive the Holy Spirit. If you forgive the sins of any, they are forgiven; if you retain the sins of any, they are retained" (John 20:21–23).

If Christ gave his ministers the ability to forgive the eternal penalty of sin, how much more would they be able to remit the temporal penalties of sin! Christ also promised his Church the power to bind and loose on earth, saying, "Truly, I say to you, whatever you bind on earth shall be bound in heaven, and whatever you loose on earth shall be loosed in heaven" (Matt. 18:18). As the context makes clear, binding and loosing cover Church discipline, and Church discipline involves administering and removing temporal penalties (such as barring from and readmitting to the sacraments). Therefore, the power of binding and loosing includes the administration of temporal penalties.

Principle 6: God Blesses Dead Christians
As a Reward to Living Christians

From the beginning the Church recognized the validity of praying
for the dead so that their transition into heaven (via purgatory)
might be swift and smooth. This meant praying for the lessening
or removal of temporal penalties holding them back from the full
glory of heaven. For this reason the Church teaches that "indulgences can always be applied to the dead by way of prayer" (II
3). The custom of praying for the dead is not restricted to the
Catholic faith. When a Jewish person's loved one dies, he prays a
prayer known as the Mourner's *Kaddish* for eleven months after
the death for the loved one's purification.

In the Old Testament, Judah Maccabee finds the bodies of soldiers who died wearing superstitious amulets during one of the
Lord's battles. Judah and his men "turned to prayer, beseeching
that the sin which had been committed might be wholly blotted
out" (2 Macc. 12:42).

The reference to the sin being "wholly blotted out" refers to
its temporal penalties. The author of 2 Maccabees tells us that for
these men Judah "was looking to the splendid reward that is laid
up for those who fall asleep in godliness" (12:45); he believed that
these men fell asleep in godliness, which would not have been the
case if they were in mortal sin. If they were not in mortal sin,
then they would not have eternal penalties to suffer, and thus the
complete blotting out of their sin must refer to temporal penalties
for their superstitious actions. Judah "took up a collection, man
by man, to the amount of two thousand drachmas of silver, and
sent it to Jerusalem to provide for a sin offering. In doing this
. . . he made atonement for the dead, that they might be delivered
from their sin" (12:43, 45).

Judah not only prayed for the dead, but he provided for them
the then-appropriate ecclesial action for lessening temporal penalties: a sin offering. Accordingly, we may take the now-appropriate

ecclesial action for lessening temporal penalties—indulgences—and apply them to the dead by way of prayer.

These six principles, which we have seen to be thoroughly biblical, are the underpinnings of indulgences. But the question of expiation often remains. Can we expiate our sins—and what does *expiate* mean, anyway?

Some criticize indulgences, saying they involve our making "expiation" for our sins, something only Christ can do. While this sounds like a noble defense of Christ's sufficiency, this criticism is unfounded, and most who make it do not know what the word *expiation* means or how indulgences work.

Protestant Scripture scholar Leon Morris comments on the confusion around the word *expiate*: "Most of us . . . don't understand 'expiation' very well. . . . Expiation is . . . making amends for a wrong. . . . Expiation is an impersonal word; one expiates a sin or a crime" (*The Atonement*, InterVarsity, 151). The *Wycliff Bible Encyclopedia* gives a similar definition: "The basic idea of expiation has to do with reparation for a wrong, the satisfaction of the demands of justice through paying a penalty."

Certainly when it comes to the eternal effects of our sins, only Christ can make amends or reparation. Only he was able to pay the infinite price necessary to cover our sins. We are completely unable to do so, not only because we are finite creatures incapable of making an infinite satisfaction but because everything we have was given to us by God. For us to try to satisfy God's eternal justice would be like using money we had borrowed from someone to repay what we had stolen from him. No actual satisfaction would be made (cf. Ps. 49:7–9; Rom. 11:35). This does not mean we can't make amends or reparation for the temporal effects of our sins. If someone steals an item, he can return it. If someone damages another's reputation, he can publicly correct the slander. When someone destroys a piece of property, he can compensate the owner for its loss. All these are ways in which one can make at least partial amends (expiation) for what he has done.

An excellent biblical illustration of this principle is given in

Proverbs 16:6, which states: "By loyalty and faithfulness iniquity is atoned for, and by the fear of the Lord a man avoids evil" (cf. Lev. 6:1–7; Num. 5:5–8). Here we are told that a person makes temporal atonement (though never eternal atonement, which only Christ is capable of doing) for his sins through acts of loyalty and faithfulness.

27

Myths about Indulgences

Indulgences. The very word stirs up more misconceptions than perhaps any other teaching in Catholic theology. Those who attack the Church for its use of indulgences rely upon—and take advantage of—the ignorance of both Catholics and non-Catholics. What is an indulgence? The Church explains, "An indulgence is a remission before God of the temporal punishment due to sins whose guilt has already been forgiven, which the faithful Christian who is duly disposed gains under certain defined conditions through the Church's help when, as a minister of redemption, she dispenses and applies with authority the treasury of the satisfactions won by Christ and the saints" (*Indulgentiarum Doctrina* 1).

Step number one in explaining indulgences is to know what they are. Step number two is to clarify what they are not. Here are the seven most common myths about indulgences:

Myth 1: A person can buy his way out of hell with indulgences.

This charge is without foundation. Since indulgences remit only temporal penalties, they cannot remit the eternal penalty of hell. Once a person is in hell, no amount of indulgences will ever change that fact. The only way to avoid hell is by appealing to God's eternal mercy while still alive. After death, one's eternal fate is set (cf. Heb. 9:27).

Myth 2: A person can buy indulgences for sins not yet committed.

The Church has always taught that indulgences do not apply to sins not yet committed. The *Catholic Encyclopedia* notes, "[An indulgence] is not a permission to commit sin, nor a pardon of future sin; neither could be granted by any power."

Myth 3: A person can "buy forgiveness" with indulgences.

The definition of indulgences presupposes that forgiveness has already taken place: "An indulgence is a remission before God of the temporal punishment due to sins whose guilt has *already been forgiven*" (ID 1, emphasis added). Indulgences in no way forgive sins. They deal only with punishments left after sins have been forgiven.

Myth 4: Indulgences were invented as a means for the Church to raise money.

Indulgences developed from reflection on the sacrament of reconciliation. They are a way of shortening the penance of sacramental discipline and were in use centuries before money-related problems appeared.

Myth 5: An indulgence will shorten your time in purgatory by a fixed number of days.

The number of days that used to be attached to indulgences were references to the period of penance one might undergo during life on earth. The Catholic Church does not claim to know anything about how long or short purgatory is in general, much less in a specific person's case.

Myth 6: A person can buy indulgences.

The Council of Trent instituted severe reforms in the practice of granting indulgences, and, because of prior abuses, "in 1567 Pope Pius V canceled all grants of indulgences involving any fees or other financial transactions" (*Catholic Encyclopedia*). This act proved the Church's seriousness about removing abuses from indulgences.

Myth 7: A person used to be able to buy indulgences.

One never could "buy" indulgences. The financial scandal surrounding indulgences, the scandal that gave Martin Luther an excuse for his heterodoxy, involved alms—indulgences in which the giving of alms to some charitable fund or foundation was used as the occasion to grant the indulgence. There was no outright selling of indulgences. The *Catholic Encyclopedia* states: "It is easy to see how abuses crept in. Among the good works that might be encouraged by being made the condition of an indulgence, almsgiving would naturally hold a conspicuous place. . . . It is well to observe that in these purposes there is nothing essentially evil. To give money to God or to the poor is a praiseworthy act, and, when it is done from right motives, it will surely not go unrewarded."

Being able to explain these seven myths will be a large step in helping others to understand indulgences. But, there are still questions to be asked:

"How many of one's temporal penalties can be remitted?"

Potentially, all of them. The Church recognizes that Christ and the saints are interested in helping penitents deal with the aftermath of their sins, as indicated by the fact that they always pray for us (cf. Heb. 7:25; Rev. 5:8). Fulfilling its role in the administration of temporal penalties, the Church draws upon the rich supply of rewards God chose to bestow on the saints, who pleased him, and on his Son, who pleased him most of all.

The rewards on which the Church draws are infinite because Christ is God, so the rewards he accrued are infinite and can never be exhausted. His rewards alone, apart from the saints', could remove all temporal penalties from everyone, everywhere. The rewards of the saints are added to Christ's—not because anything is lacking in his, but because it is fitting that they be united with his rewards as the saints are united with him. Although immense, their rewards are finite, but his are infinite.

"If the Church has the resources to wipe out everyone's temporal penalties, why doesn't it do so?"

Because God does not wish this to be done. God himself instituted the pattern of temporal penalties being left behind. They fulfill valid functions, one of them disciplinary. If a child were never disciplined, he would never learn obedience. God disciplines us as his children—"the Lord disciplines him whom he loves, and chastises every son whom he receives" (Heb. 12:6)—so some temporal penalties must remain.

The Church cannot wipe out, with a stroke of the pen, everyone's temporal punishments, because their remission depends on the dispositions of the persons who suffer those temporal punishments. Just as repentance and faith are needed for the remission of eternal penalties, so they are needed for the remission of temporal penalties. Pope Paul VI stated, "Indulgences cannot be gained without a sincere conversion of outlook and unity with God" (ID 11). We might say that the degree of remission depends on how well the penitent has learned his lesson.

"How does one determine by what amount penalties have been lessened?"

Before Vatican II each indulgence was said to remove a certain number of "days" from one's discipline—for instance, an act might gain "300 days' indulgence"—but the use of the term *days* confused people, giving them the mistaken impression that in purgatory time as we know it still exists and that we can calculate our "good time" in a mechanical way. The number of days associated with indulgences actually never meant that that much "time" would be taken off one's stay in purgatory. Instead, it meant that an indefinite but partial (not complete) amount of remission would be granted, proportionate to what ancient Christians would have received for performing that many days' penance. So, someone gaining 300 days' indulgence gained roughly what an early Christian would have gained by, say, reciting a particular prayer on arising for 300 days.

To overcome the confusion Paul VI issued a revision of the handbook (*Enchiridion* is the formal name) of indulgences. Today, numbers of days are not associated with indulgences. They are either plenary or partial.

"What's the difference between a partial and a plenary indulgence?"

"An indulgence is partial or plenary according as it removes either part or all of the temporal punishment due to sin" (ID 2). Only God knows exactly how efficacious any particular partial indulgence is or whether a plenary indulgence was received at all.

"Don't indulgences duplicate or even negate the work of Christ?"

Despite the biblical underpinnings of indulgences, some are sharply critical of them and insist the doctrine supplants the work of Christ and turns us into our own saviors. This objection results from confusion about the nature of indulgences and how Christ's work is applied to us.

Indulgences apply only to temporal penalties, not to eternal ones. The Bible indicates that these penalties may remain after a sin has been forgiven and that God lessens these penalties as rewards to those who have pleased him. Since the Bible indicates this, Christ's work cannot be said to have been supplanted by indulgences.

The merits of Christ, since they are infinite, comprise most of those in the treasury of merits. By applying these to believers, the Church acts as Christ's servant in the application of what he has done for us, and we know from Scripture that Christ's work is applied to us over time and not in one big lump (cf. Phil. 2:12; 1 Pet. 1:9).

"Isn't it better to put all of the emphasis on Christ alone?"

If we ignore the fact of indulgences, we neglect what Christ does through us, and we fail to recognize the value of what he has done in us. Paul used this very sort of language: "Now I rejoice in my sufferings for your sake, and in my flesh I complete what is lacking in Christ's afflictions for the sake of his body, that is, the church" (Col. 1:24).

Even though Christ's sufferings were superabundant (far more than needed to pay for anything), Paul spoke of completing what was "lacking" in Christ's sufferings. If this mode of speech was permissible for Paul, it is permissible for us, even though the Catholic language about indulgences is far less shocking than was Paul's language about his own role in salvation.

Catholics should not be defensive about indulgences. They are based on principles straight from the Bible, and we can be confident not only that indulgences exist but that they are useful and worth obtaining.

Pope Paul VI declared, "The Church invites all its children to think over and weigh up in their minds as well as they can how the use of indulgences benefits their lives and all Christian society. . . . Supported by these truths, holy Mother Church again recommends the practice of indulgences to the faithful. It has been very dear to Christian people for many centuries as well as in our own day. Experience proves this" (ID 9).

How to Gain an Indulgence

To gain any indulgence you must be a Catholic in a state of grace. You must be a Catholic in order to be under the Church's jurisdiction, and you must be in a state of grace because apart from God's grace none of your actions are fundamentally pleasing to God (meritorious). You also must have at least the habitual intention of gaining an indulgence by the act performed.

To gain a partial indulgence, you must perform with a contrite heart the act to which the indulgence is attached.

To gain a plenary indulgence you must perform the act with a contrite heart, plus you must go to confession (one confession may suffice for several plenary indulgences), receive Holy Communion, and pray for the pope's intentions. (An Our Father and a Hail Mary said for the pope's intentions are sufficient, although you are free to substitute other prayers of your own choice.) The final condition is that you must be free from all attachment to sin, including venial sin.

If you attempt to receive a plenary indulgence but are unable to meet the last condition, a partial indulgence is received instead.

Below are indulgences listed in the *Handbook of Indulgences* (Catholic Book Publishing, 1991). Note that there is an indulgence for Bible reading. So, rather than discouraging Bible reading, the Catholic Church promotes it by giving indulgences for it! (This was the case long before Vatican II.)

- An act of spiritual communion, expressed in any devout formula whatsoever, is endowed with a partial indulgence.

- A partial indulgence is granted the Christian faithful who devoutly spend time in mental prayer.

- A plenary indulgence is granted when the rosary is recited in a church or oratory or when it is recited in a family, a religious community, or a pious association. A partial indulgence is granted for its recitation in all other circumstances.

- A partial indulgence is granted the Christian faithful who read Sacred Scripture with the veneration due God's word and as a form of spiritual reading. The indulgence will be a plenary one when such reading is done for at least one-half hour (provided the other conditions are met).

- A partial indulgence is granted to the Christian faithful who devoutly sign themselves with the cross while saying the customary formula: "In the name of the Father, and of the Son, and of the Holy Spirit. Amen."

In summary, the practice of indulgences neither takes away nor adds to the work of Christ. It is his work, through his body the Church, raising up children in his own likeness. "The Christian who seeks to purify himself of his sin and to become holy with the help of God's grace is not alone. 'The life of each of God's children is joined in Christ and through Christ in a wonderful way to the life of all the other Christian brethren in the supernatural unity of the mystical body of Christ, as in a single mystical person'" (*Catechism of the Catholic Church* 1474, cf. 1D 5).

28

Grace: What It Is
and What It Does

If you took your parish's catechism classes when you were growing up, you at least remember that there are two kinds of grace: sanctifying and actual. That may be all that you recall. The names being so similar, you might have the impression that sanctifying grace is nearly identical to actual grace. Not so.

Sanctifying grace stays in the soul. It's what makes the soul holy; it gives the soul supernatural life. More properly, it *is* supernatural life.

Actual grace, by contrast, is a supernatural push or encouragement. It's transient. It doesn't live in the soul but acts on the soul from the outside, so to speak. It's a supernatural kick in the pants. It gets the will and intellect moving so we can seek out and keep sanctifying grace.

Imagine yourself transported instantaneously to the bottom of the ocean. What's the very first thing you'll do? That's right: die. You'd die because you aren't equipped to live underwater. You don't have the right breathing apparatus.

If you want to live in the deep blue sea, you need equipment you aren't provided with naturally; you need something that will elevate you above your nature, something super- (that is, "above") natural, such as oxygen tanks.

It's much the same with your soul. In its natural state, it isn't fit for heaven. It doesn't have the right equipment, and if you die with your soul in its natural state, heaven won't be for you. What you need to live there is supernatural life, not just natural life. That supernatural life is called sanctifying grace. The reason you need sanctifying grace to be able to live in heaven is because you will be in perfect and absolute union with God, the source of all life (cf. Gal. 2:19; 1 Pet. 3:18).

If sanctifying grace dwells in your soul when you die, then you have the equipment you need, and you can live in heaven —though you may need to be purified first in purgatory (cf. 1 Cor. 3:12–16). If it doesn't dwell in your soul when you die— in other words, if your soul is spiritually dead by being in the state of mortal sin (cf. Gal. 5:19–21)—then you cannot live in heaven. You then have to face an eternity of spiritual death: the utter separation of your spirit from God (cf. Eph. 2:1, 5; 4:18). The worst part of this eternal separation will be that you yourself would have caused it to be that way.

Spiritual Suicide

You can obtain supernatural life by yielding to actual graces you receive. God keeps giving you these divine pushes, and all you have to do is go along.

For instance, he moves you to repentance, and if you take the hint you can find yourself in the confessional, where the guilt for your sins is remitted (cf. John 20:21–23). Through the sacrament of penance, through your reconciliation to God, you receive sanctifying grace. But you can lose it again by sinning mortally (cf. 1 John 5:16–17).

Keep that word in mind: mortal. It means death. Mortal sins are deadly sins because they kill off this supernatural life, this sanctifying grace. Mortal sins can't coexist with the supernatural life, because by their nature such sins are saying "No" to God, while sanctifying grace would be saying "Yes."

Venial sins don't destroy supernatural life, and they don't even lessen it. Mortal sins destroy it outright. But the trouble with venial sins is that they weaken us, making us more vulnerable to mortal sins.

When you lose supernatural life, there's nothing you can do on your own to regain it. You're reduced to the merely natural life again, and no natural act can merit a supernatural reward. You can merit a supernatural reward only by being made able to act above your nature, which you can do only if you have help—grace.

To regain supernatural life, you have to receive actual graces from God. Think of these as helping graces. Such graces differ from sanctifying grace in that they aren't a quality of the soul and don't abide in it. Rather, actual graces enable the soul to perform some supernatural act, such as an act of faith or repentance. If the soul responds to actual grace and makes the appropriate supernatural act, it again receives supernatural life.

Really Cleansed

Sanctifying grace implies a real transformation of the soul. Recall that most of the Protestant Reformers denied that a real transformation takes place. They said God doesn't actually wipe away our sins. Our souls don't become spotless and holy in themselves. Instead, they remain corrupted, sinful, full of sin. God merely throws a cloak over them and treats them as if they were spotless, knowing all the while that they're not.

But that isn't the Catholic view. We believe souls really are cleansed by an infusion of the supernatural life. Paul speaks of us as "a new creation" (2 Cor. 5:17), "created after the likeness of God in true righteousness and holiness" (Eph. 4:24). Of course, we're still subject to temptations to sin; we still suffer the effects of Adam's fall in that sense (what theologians call "concupiscence"), but God removes the guilt from our souls. We may still have a tendency to sin, but God has removed the sins we have, much like a mother might wash the dirt off of a child who has a tendency to get dirty again.

Our souls don't become something other than souls when God cleanses them and pours his grace into them; they don't cease to be what they were before. When grace elevates nature, our intellects are given the new power of faith, something they don't have at the merely natural level. Our wills are given the new powers of hope and charity, things also absent at the merely natural level.

Justification and Sanctification

We've mentioned that we need sanctifying grace in our souls if we're to be equipped for heaven. Another way of saying this is that we need to be justified. "But you were washed, you were sanctified, you were justified in the name of the Lord Jesus Christ and in the Spirit of our God" (1 Cor. 6:11).

The Protestant misunderstanding of justification lies in its claim that justification is merely a forensic (i.e., purely declaratory) legal declaration by God that the sinner is now "justified." If you "accept Christ as your personal Lord and Savior," then he *declares* you justified, though he doesn't really *make* you justified or sanctified. Your soul is in the same state as it was before, but you're eligible for heaven.

A person is expected thereafter to undergo sanctification (don't make the mistake of thinking Protestants say sanctification is unimportant), but the degree of sanctification achieved is, ultimately, immaterial to the question of whether you'll get to heaven. You will, since you're justified, and justification as a purely legal declaration is what counts. Unfortunately, this scheme is a legal fiction. It amounts to God telling an untruth by saying that the sinner has been justified, while all along he knows that the sinner is not really justified, but is only covered under the "cloak" of Christ's righteousness. But God does what he declares. "So shall my word be that goes forth from my mouth; it shall not return to me empty, but it shall accomplish that which I purpose, and prosper in the thing for which I sent it" (Is. 55:11). So, when God declares you justified, he makes you justified. Any justification that is not woven together with sanctification is no justification at all.

The Bible's teaching on justification is much more nuanced. Paul indicates that there is a real transformation that occurs in justification and that it is not just a change in legal status. This is seen, for example, in Romans 6:7, which every standard translation—Protestant ones included—renders as: "For he who has died is freed from sin" (or a close variant).

Paul is obviously speaking about being freed from sin in an experiential sense, for this is the passage where he is at pains to stress the fact that we have made a decisive break with sin that must be reflected in our behavior: "What shall we say then? Are we to continue in sin that grace may abound? By no means! How can we who died to sin still live in it?" (Rom. 6:1–2). "Let not sin therefore reign in your mortal bodies, to make you obey their passions. Do not yield your members to sin as instruments of wickedness, but yield yourselves to God as men who have been brought from death to life, and your members to God as instruments of righteousness" (Rom. 6:12–13).

The context here is what Protestants call *sanctification*, the process of being made holy. Sanctification is the sense in which we are said to be "freed from sin" in this passage. Yet in the Greek text, what is actually said is: "He who has died has been *justified* from sin." The term in Greek (*dikaioō*) is the word for being justified, yet the context indicates sanctification, which is why every standard translation renders the word *freed* rather than *justified*. This shows that, in Paul's mind, justification involves a real transformation: a real, experiential freeing from sin, not just a change of legal status. And it shows that, the way he uses terms, there is not the rigid wall between justification and sanctification that Protestants imagine.

According to Scripture, sanctification and justification aren't just one-time events but are ongoing processes in the life of the believer. Both can be spoken of as past events, as Paul mentions in 1 Corinthians 6:11: "But you were washed, you were sanctified, you were justified in the name of the Lord Jesus and in the Spirit of our God." Sanctification is also a present, ongoing process, as the author of Hebrews notes: "For by a single offering he has perfected for all time those who are sanctified" (Heb. 10:14). In regard to justification also being an ongoing process, compare Romans 4:3 and Genesis 15:6 with Hebrews 11:8, Genesis 12:1–4, James 2:21–23, and Genesis 22:1–18. In these passages, Abraham's justification is advanced.

Can Justification Be Lost?

Most Fundamentalists go on to say that losing ground in the sanc-tification battle won't jeopardize your justification. You might sin worse than you did before "getting saved," but you'll enter heaven anyway, because you can't undo your justification, which has nothing to do with whether you have supernatural life in your soul.

Calvin taught the absolute impossibility of losing justification. Luther said it could be lost only through the sin of unbelief—that is, by undoing the act of faith and rejecting Christ—but not by what Catholics call mortal sins.

Catholics see it differently. If you sin grievously, then the su-pernatural life in your soul disappears, since it can't coexist with serious sin. You then cease to be justified. If you were to die while unjustified, you'd go to hell. But you can become re-justified by having the supernatural life renewed in your soul, and you can do that by responding to the actual graces God sends you.

Acting on Actual Graces

He sends you an actual grace, say, in the form of a nagging voice that whispers, "You need to repent! Go to confession!" You do, your sins are forgiven, you're reconciled to God, and you have supernatural life again (cf. John 20:21–23). Or you say to yourself, "Maybe tomorrow," and that particular supernatural impulse, that actual grace, passes you by. But another is always on the way, God never abandoning us to our own stupidity (cf. 1 Tim. 2:4).

Once you have supernatural life—once sanctifying grace is in your soul—you can increase it by every supernaturally good ac-tion you do: receiving Communion, saying prayers, performing the corporal works of mercy. Is it worth increasing sanctifying grace once you have it? Isn't the minimum enough? Yes and no. It's enough to get you into heaven, but it may not be enough to sustain itself. It's easy to fall from grace, as you know. The more solidly you're wed to sanctifying grace, the more likely you can withstand temptations.

And if you do that, you maintain sanctifying grace. In other words, once you achieve the supernatural life, you don't want to take it easy. The minimum isn't good enough because it's easy to lose the minimum. We must continually seek God's grace, continually respond to the actual graces God is working within us, inclining us to turn to him and do good. This is what Paul discusses when he instructs us: "Therefore, my beloved, as you have always obeyed, so now, not only as in my presence but much more in my absence, work out your own salvation with fear and trembling; for God is at work in you, both to will and to work for his good pleasure. Do all things without grumbling or questioning, that you may be blameless and innocent, children of God without blemish in the midst of a crooked and perverse generation, among whom you shine as lights in the world, holding fast the word of life, so that in the day of Christ I may be proud that I did not run in vain or labor in vain" (Phil. 2:12–16).

29

Are Catholics Born Again?

Catholics and Protestants agree that to be saved, you have to be born again. Jesus said so: "Truly, truly, I say to you, unless one is born again, he cannot see the kingdom of God" (John 3:3)

When a Catholic says that he has been "born again," he refers to the transformation that God's grace accomplished in him during baptism. Evangelical Protestants typically mean something quite different when they talk about being "born again."

For an Evangelical, becoming "born again" often happens like this: He goes to a crusade or a revival where a minister delivers a sermon telling him of his need to be "born again."

"If you believe in the Lord Jesus Christ and believe he died for your sins, you'll be born again!" says the preacher. So the gentleman makes "a decision for Christ" and at the altar call goes forward to be led in "the sinner's prayer" by the minister. Then the minister tells all who prayed the sinner's prayer that they have been saved—"born again." But is the minister right? Not according to the Bible.

The Names of the New Birth

Regeneration (being "born again") is the transformation from death to life that occurs in our souls when we first come to God and are justified. He washes us clean of our sins and gives us a new nature, breaking the power of sin over us so that we will no longer be its slaves but its enemies who must fight it as part of the Christian life (cf. Rom. 6:1–22; Eph. 6:11–17). To understand the biblical teaching of being born again, we must understand the terms it uses to refer to this event.

The phrase "born again" may not appear in the Bible. The Greek phrase often translated "born again" (*gennāthā anōthen*) occurs twice in the Bible—John 3:3 and 3:7—and there is a question of how it should be translated. The Greek word *anothen* sometimes can be translated "again," but in the New Testament, it most often means "from above." In the King James Version, the *only* two times it is translated "again" are in John 3:3 and 3:7; every other time it is given a different rendering.

Another term is *regeneration*. When referring to something that occurs in the life of an individual believer, it appears in only Titus 3:5. In other passages, the new birth phenomenon is also described as receiving new life (Rom. 6:4), receiving the circumcision of the heart (Rom. 2:29; Col. 2:11–12), and becoming a "new creation" (2 Cor. 5:17; Gal. 6:15).

Regeneration in John 3

These different ways of talking about being "born again" describe effects of baptism, which Christ speaks of in John 3:5 as being "born of water and the Spirit." In Greek, this phrase is, literally, "born of water and Spirit," indicating one birth of water-and-Spirit, rather than "born of water *and of* the Spirit," as though it meant two different births—one birth of water and one birth of the Spirit.

In the water-and-Spirit rebirth that takes place at baptism, the repentant sinner is transformed from a state of sin to the state of grace. Peter mentioned this transformation from sin to grace when he exhorted people to "be baptized every one of you in the name of Jesus Christ for the forgiveness of your sins; and you shall receive the gift of the Holy Spirit" (Acts 2:38).

The context of Jesus' statements in John 3 makes it clear that he was referring to water baptism. Shortly before Jesus teaches Nicodemus about the necessity and regenerating effect of baptism, he himself was baptized by John the Baptist, and the circumstances are striking: Jesus goes down into the water, and as he is baptized, the heavens open, the Holy Spirit descends upon him in the form of a dove, and the voice of God the Father speaks from heaven, saying, "This is my beloved Son" (cf. Matt. 3:13–17; Mark 1:9–11; Luke 3:21–22; John 1:30–34). This scene gives us a graphic depiction of what happens at baptism: We are baptized with water, symbolizing our dying with Christ (cf. Rom. 6:3) and our rising with Christ to the newness of life (cf. Rom. 6:4–5); we receive the gift of sanctifying grace and the indwelling of the Holy Spirit (1 Cor. 12:13; Gal. 3:27); and we are adopted as God's sons (cf. Rom. 8:15–17).

After our Lord's teaching that it is necessary for salvation to be born from above by water and the Spirit (cf. John 3:1–21), "Jesus and his disciples went into the land of Judea; there he remained with them and baptized" (John 3:22).

Then we have the witness of the early Church that John 3:5 refers to baptismal regeneration. This was universally recognized by the early Christians. The Church Fathers were unanimous in teaching this:

In A.D. 151, Justin Martyr wrote, "As many as are persuaded and believe that what we [Christians] teach and say is true . . . are brought by us where there is water and are regenerated in the same manner in which we were ourselves regenerated. For, in the name of God the Father . . . and of our Savior Jesus Christ, and of the Holy Spirit [cf. Matt. 28:19], they then receive the washing with water. For Christ also said, 'Unless you are born again, you shall not enter into the kingdom of heaven' [John 3:3]" (*First Apology* 61).

Around 190, Irenaeus, the bishop of Lyons, wrote, " 'And [Naaman] dipped himself . . . seven times in the Jordan' [2 Kgs. 5:14]. It was not for nothing that Naaman of old, when suffering from leprosy, was purified upon his being baptized, but [this served] as an indication to us. For as we are lepers in sin, we are made clean, by means of the sacred water and the invocation of the Lord, from our old transgressions, being spiritually regenerated as newborn babes, even as the Lord has declared: 'Except a man be born again through water and the Spirit, he shall not enter into the kingdom of heaven' [John 3:5]" (*Fragment* 34).

In the year 252, Cyprian, the bishop of Carthage, said that

when those becoming Christians "receive also the baptism of the Church . . . then finally can they be fully sanctified and be the sons of God . . . since it is written, 'Except a man be born again of water and of the Spirit, he cannot enter into the kingdom of God' [John 3:5]" (*Letters* 71[72]:1).

In 419, Augustine wrote, "From the time he [Jesus] said, 'Except a man be born of water and the Spirit, he cannot enter into the kingdom of heaven' [John 3:5], and again, 'He that loses his life for my sake shall find it' [Matt. 10:39], no one becomes a member of Christ except it be either by baptism in Christ or death for Christ" (*On the Soul and Its Origin* 1:10).

Augustine also taught, "It is this one Spirit who makes it possible for an infant to be regenerated . . . when that infant is brought to baptism; and it is through this one Spirit that the infant so presented is reborn. For it is not written, 'Unless a man be born again by the will of his parents' or 'by the faith of those presenting him or ministering to him,' but, 'Unless a man be born again of water and the Holy Spirit' [John 3:5]. The water, therefore, manifesting exteriorly the sacrament of grace, and the Spirit effecting interiorly the benefit of grace, both regenerate in one Christ that man who was generated in Adam" (*Letters* 98:2).

Regeneration in the New Testament

The truth that regeneration comes through baptism is confirmed elsewhere in the Bible. Paul reminds us in Titus 3:5 that God "saved us, not because of deeds done by us in righteousness, but in virtue of his own mercy, by the washing of regeneration and renewal in the Holy Spirit."

Paul also said, "Do you not know that all of us who have been baptized into Christ Jesus were baptized into his death? We were buried therefore with him by baptism into death, so that as Christ was raised from the dead by the glory of the Father, we too might walk in newness of life" (Rom. 6:3–4).

This teaching—that baptism unites us with Christ's death and resurrection so that we might die to sin and receive new life—

is a key part of Paul's theology: "In [Christ] you were also circumcised, in the putting off of the sinful nature, not with a circumcision done by the hands of men but with the circumcision
[of] Christ, having been buried with him in baptism and raised
with him through your faith in the power of God, who raised
him from the dead. When you were dead in your sins and in the
uncircumcision of your sinful nature, God made you alive with
Christ" (Col. 2:11-13, NIV).

The Effects of Baptism

People often miss the fact that baptism gives us new life/new
birth because they have an impoverished view of the grace God
gives us through baptism, which they think is a mere symbol. But
Scripture is clear that baptism is much more than a mere symbol.

In Acts 2:38, Peter tells us, "Repent, and be baptized every one
of you in the name of Jesus Christ for the forgiveness of your sins;
and you shall receive the gift of the Holy Spirit." When Paul was
converted, he was told, "And now why do you wait? Rise and
be baptized, and wash away your sins, calling on his name" (Acts
22:16).

Peter also said, "God's patience waited in the days of Noah,
during the building of the ark, in which a few, that is, eight persons, were saved through water. Baptism, which corresponds to
this, now saves you, not as a removal of dirt from the body, but as
an appeal to God for a clear conscience, through the resurrection
of Jesus Christ" (1 Pet. 3:20-21). Peter says that, as in the time
of the flood, when eight people were "*saved through water*," so for
Christians, "*baptism . . . now saves you.*" It does not do so by the
water's physical action but through the power of Jesus Christ's
Resurrection, baptism's spiritual effects, and the appeal we make
to God to have our consciences cleansed.

These verses showing the supernatural grace God bestows through
baptism set the context for understanding the New Testament's
statements about receiving new life in the sacrament.

Protestants on Regeneration

Martin Luther wrote in his *Short Catechism* that baptism "works the forgiveness of sins, delivers from death and the devil, and grants eternal life to all who believe." His recognition that the Bible teaches baptismal regeneration has been preserved by Lutherans and a few other Protestant denominations. Even some Baptists recognize that the biblical evidence demands the historical Christian teaching of baptismal regeneration. Notable individuals who recognized that Scripture teaches baptismal regeneration include Baptist theologians George R. Beasley-Murray and Dale Moody.

Nevertheless, many Protestants have abandoned this biblical teaching, substituting man-made theories on regeneration. There are two main views held by those who deny the scriptural teaching that one is born again through baptism: the "Evangelical" view, common among Baptists, and the "Calvinist" view, common among Presbyterians.

Evangelicals claim that one is born again at the first moment of faith in Christ. According to this theory, faith in Christ produces regeneration. The Calvinist position is the reverse: Regeneration precedes and produces faith in Christ. Calvinists (some of whom also call themselves Evangelicals) suppose that God "secretly" regenerates people, without their being aware of it, and this *causes* them to place their faith in Christ.

To defend these theories, Evangelicals and Calvinists attempt to explain away the many unambiguous verses in the Bible that plainly teach baptismal regeneration. One strategy is to say that the water in John 3:5 refers not to baptism but to the amniotic fluid present at childbirth. The absurd implication of this view is that Jesus would have been saying, "You must be born of amniotic fluid and the Spirit." A check of the respected Protestant Greek lexicon *Kittel's Theological Dictionary of the New Testament* fails to turn up any instances in ancient, Septuagint or New Testament Greek where "water" (Greek: *hudor*) referred to "amniotic fluid" (cf. VIII:314–333).

Evangelicals and Calvinists try to deal with the other verses where new life is attributed to baptism either by ignoring them or by arguing that it is not actually water baptism that is being spoken of. The problem for them is that water is explicitly mentioned or implied in each of these verses.

In Acts 2:38, people are exhorted to take an action: "Be baptized . . . in the name of Jesus Christ," which does not refer to an internal baptism that is administered to people by themselves but the external baptism administered to them by others.

We are told that at Paul's conversion, "he rose and was baptized, and took food and was strengthened. For several days he was with the disciples at Damascus" (Acts 9:18–19). This was a water baptism. In Romans 6 and Colossians 2, Paul reminds his readers of their water baptisms, and he neither says nor implies anything about some sort of "invisible spiritual baptism."

In 1 Peter 3, water is mentioned twice, paralleling baptism with the flood, where eight were "saved through water," and noting that "*baptism now saves you*" by the power of Christ rather than by the physical action of water "removing . . . dirt from the body."

The anti-baptismal regeneration position is indefensible. It has no biblical basis whatsoever. So the answer to the question "Are Catholics born again?" is *yes!* Since all Catholics have been baptized, all Catholics have been born again.

Catholics should ask Protestants, "Are *you* born again—the way the *Bible* understands that concept?" If the Evangelical has not been properly water baptized, he has *not* been born again "the Bible way," regardless of what he may think.

30

Assurance of Salvation?

There are few more confusing topics than salvation. It goes beyond the standard question posed by Fundamentalists: "Have you been saved?" What the question also means is: "Don't you wish you had the *assurance* of salvation?" Evangelicals and Fundamentalists think they do have such an absolute assurance.

All they have to do is "accept Christ as their personal Lord and Savior," and it's done. They might well live exemplary lives thereafter, but living well is not crucial and definitely does not affect their salvation.

Kenneth E. Hagin, a well-known Pentecostal televangelist from the "Word Faith" wing of Protestantism, asserts that this assurance of salvation comes through being "born again": "Unless one is born anew, he cannot see the kingdom of God" (John 3:3). Though much of Hagin's theology is considered bizarre in many Protestant circles, his explanation of being born again could be endorsed by millions of Evangelical Protestants. In his booklet *The New Birth*, Hagin writes, "The new birth is a necessity to being saved. Through the new birth you come into the right relationship with God."

According to Hagin, there are many things that this new birth is not. "The new birth is not: confirmation, church membership, water baptism, the taking of sacraments, observing religious duties, an intellectual reception of Christianity, orthodoxy of faith, going to church, saying prayers, reading the Bible, being moral, being cultured or refined, doing good deeds, doing your best, nor any of the many other things some men are trusting in to save them." Those who have obtained the new birth "did the one thing necessary: they accepted Jesus Christ as personal Savior by repenting and turning to God with the whole heart as a little child."

That one act of the will, he explains, is all they needed to do. But is this true? Does the Bible support this concept?

Scripture teaches that one's final salvation depends on the state of the soul at death. As Jesus himself tells us, "He who endures to the end will be saved" (Matt. 24:13; cf. 25:31–46). One who dies in the state of friendship with God (the state of grace) will go to heaven. The one who dies in a state of enmity and rebellion against God (the state of mortal sin) will go to hell.

For many Fundamentalists and Evangelicals, it makes no difference as far as salvation is concerned—how you live or end your life. You can heed the altar call at church, announce that you've accepted Jesus as your personal Savior, and, so long as you really believe it, you're set. From that point on there is *nothing* you can do—no sin you can commit, no matter how heinous—that will forfeit your salvation. You can't undo your salvation, even if you wanted to.

Does this sound too good to be true? Yes, but nevertheless, it is something many Protestants claim. Take a look at what Wilson Ewin, the author of a booklet called *There Is Therefore Now No Condemnation*, says. He writes that "the person who places his faith in the Lord Jesus Christ and his blood shed at Calvary is eternally secure. He can never lose his salvation. No personal breaking of God's or man's laws or commandments can nullify that status.

"To deny the assurance of salvation would be to deny Christ's perfect redemption," argues Ewin, and this is something that he can say only because he confuses the redemption that Christ accomplished for us objectively with our individual appropriation of that redemption. The truth is that, in one sense, we are all redeemed by Christ's death on the cross—Christians, Jews, Muslims, even animists in the darkest forests (cf. 1 Tim. 2:6; 4:10; 1 John 2:2)—but our individual appropriation of what Christ provided is contingent on our response.

Certainly, Christ did die on the cross once for all and has entered into heaven to appear before God on our behalf. Christ has abundantly provided for our salvation, but that does not mean that there is no process by which this is applied to us as individuals. Obviously, there is a process, or we would have been saved and justified from all eternity, with no need to repent or have faith or anything else. We would have been born "saved," with no need to be born *again*. Since we were not, since it is necessary for those who hear the gospel to repent and embrace it, there is a time at which we come to be reconciled to God. And if so, then we, like Adam and Eve, can become unreconciled with God and, like the prodigal son, need to come back and be reconciled again with God, after having left his family.

You Can't Lose Heaven?

Ewin says that "no wrong act or sinful deed can ever affect the believer's salvation. The sinner did nothing to merit God's grace and likewise he can do nothing to demerit grace. True, sinful conduct always lessens one's fellowship with Christ, limits his contribution to God's work and can result in serious disciplinary action by the Holy Spirit."

One problem with this argument is that it is not even how things work in everyday life. If another person gives us something as a grace—as a gift—and even if we did nothing to deserve it, in no way does it follow that our actions are irrelevant to whether or not we keep the gift. We can lose it in all kinds of ways. We can misplace it, destroy it, give it to someone else, take it back to the store. We may even forfeit it by later displeasing the one who gave it—as when a person has been appointed to a special position but is later stripped of it because of mismanagement.

The argument fares no better when one turns to Scripture, for one finds that Adam and Eve, who received God's grace in a manner just as unmerited as anyone today, most definitely *did* demerit it—and lost grace not only for themselves but for us as well (cf. also Rom. 11:17–24). While the idea that what is received without merit cannot be demerited may have a kind of poetic charm for some, it does not stand up when compared with the way things really work—either in the everyday world or in the Bible.

Regarding the issue of whether Christians have an "absolute" assurance of salvation, regardless of their actions, consider this warning Paul gave: "Note then the kindness and the severity of God: severity toward those who have fallen, but God's kindness to you, provided you continue in his kindness; *otherwise you too will be cut off*" (Rom. 11:22; cf. Heb. 10:26–29; 2 Pet. 2:20–21).

Can You Know?

A related issue is the question of whether one can know with complete certainty that one is in a state of salvation. Even if a person could not lose his salvation, he still might not be sure if he ever had salvation. Similarly, even if he could be sure that he is *now* in a state of salvation, he might be able to fall from grace in the future. The "knowability" of salvation is different from the "loseability" of salvation.

From the Radio Bible Class, listeners can obtain a booklet called *Can Anyone Really Know for Sure?* The anonymous author says that the "Lord Jesus wanted his followers to be so sure of their salvation that they would rejoice more in the expectation of heaven than in victories on earth. 'These things I have written to you who believe in the name of the Son of God, that you may know that you have eternal life, and that you may continue to believe in the name of the Son of God' (1 John 5:13)."

Scripture verses that speak of our ability to know that we are abiding in grace are important and must be taken seriously. But they do not promise that we will be protected from self-deception on this matter. Even the author of *Can Anyone Really Know for Sure?* admits that there is a false assurance: "The New Testament teaches us that genuine assurance is possible and desirable, but it also warns us that we can be deceived through a false assurance. Jesus declared: 'Not everyone who says to me, "Lord, Lord" shall enter the kingdom of heaven' (Matt. 7:21)."

Sometimes Fundamentalists portray Catholics as if they must every moment be in terror of losing their salvation, since Catholics recognize that it is possible to lose salvation through mortal sin.

240 THE ESSENTIAL CATHOLIC SURVIVAL GUIDE

Fundamentalists then hold out the idea that, rather than living every moment in terror, they can have a calm, assured knowledge that they will, in fact, be saved, and that nothing can ever change this fact.

But this portrayal is erroneous. Catholics do not live in mortal terror concerning salvation. True, salvation can be lost through mortal sin, but such sins are by nature *grave* ones, and not the kind that a person living the Christian life is going to slip into on the spur of the moment, without deliberate thought and consent. Neither does the Catholic Church teach that one cannot have an assurance of salvation. This is true both of present and future salvation.

One can be confident of one's present salvation. This is one of the chief reasons that God gave us the sacraments—to provide visible assurances that he is invisibly providing us with his grace. And one can be confident that one has not thrown away that grace by simply examining one's life and seeing whether one has committed mortal sin. Indeed, the tests that John sets forth to help us know if we are abiding in grace are, in essence, tests of whether we are dwelling in grave sin. For example: "By this it may be seen who are the children of God, and who are the children of the devil: whoever does not do right is not of God, nor he who does not love his brother" (1 John 3:10); "if any one says, 'I love God,' and hates his brother, he is a liar; for he who does not love his brother whom he has seen, cannot love God whom he has not seen" (1 John 4:20); "for this is the love of God, that we keep his commandments. And his commandments are not burdensome" (1 John 5:3).

Likewise, by looking at the course of one's life in grace and the resolution of one's heart, one can also have an assurance of future salvation. It is this that Paul speaks of when he writes to the Philippians, "And I am sure that he who began a good work in you will bring it to completion at the day of Jesus Christ" (Phil. 1:6). This is not a promise for all Christians, or even necessarily all in the church at Philippi, but it does express confidence that the Philippian Christians in general would make it. The basis of this is their spiritual performance to date, and Paul explains to them that there is a basis for his confidence in them. Thus he says, "It is right for me to feel thus about you all, because I hold you in my heart, for you are all partakers with me of grace, both in my imprisonment and in the defense and confirmation of the gospel" (Phil. 1:7). The fact that the Philippians assisted Paul in his imprisonment and ministry showed that their hearts were with God and that it could be expected that they, at least in general, would persevere and remain with God.

There are many saintly men and women who have lived the Christian life and whose characters are marked with profound spiritual joy and peace. Such individuals can look forward with confidence to their reception in heaven.

Such an individual was Paul, writing at the end of his life: "I have fought the good fight, I have finished the race, I have kept the faith. Henceforth there is laid up for me the crown of righteousness, which the Lord, the righteous judge, will award to me on that Day" (2 Tim. 4:7-8). But earlier in life, even Paul did not claim an infallible assurance, either of his present justification or of his remaining in grace in the future. Concerning his present state, he wrote, "I am not aware of anything against myself, but I am not thereby acquitted [Greek: *dedikaiōmai*]. It is the Lord who judges me" (1 Cor. 4:4). Concerning his remaining life, Paul was frank in admitting that even he could fall away: "I pommel my body and subdue it, lest after preaching to others I myself should be disqualified" (1 Cor. 9:27). Of course, for a spiritual giant such as Paul, it would be quite unexpected and out of character for him to fall from God's grace. Nevertheless, he points out that, however much confidence he has in his own salvation, even he cannot be *infallibly* sure of either his own present state or his future course.

The same is true of us. We can, if our lives display a pattern of perseverance and spiritual fruit, have a confidence not only in our present state of grace but also of our future perseverance with God. Yet we cannot have an infallible certitude of our own salvation, as many Protestants will admit. There is the possibility of self-deception (cf. Matt. 7:22-23). As Jeremiah expressed it,

"The heart is deceitful above all things, and desperately corrupt; who can understand it?" (Jer. 17:9). There is also the possibility of falling from grace through mortal sin, and even of falling away from the faith entirely, for as Jesus told us, there are those who "believe for a while and in time of temptation fall away" (Luke 8:13). It is in light of these warnings and admonitions that we must understand Scripture's positive statements concerning our knowing and having confidence in our salvation. Assurance we may have; infallible certitude we may not.

For example, Philippians 2:12 says, "Therefore, my beloved, as you have always obeyed, so now, not only as in my presence but much more in my absence, *work out your own salvation* with fear and trembling" (emphasis added). This is not the language of self-confident assurance. Our salvation is something that remains to be worked out.

What to Say

"Are you saved?" asks the Fundamentalist. The Catholic should reply: "As the Bible says, I am already saved (cf. Rom. 8:24; Eph. 2:5–8), but I'm also *being* saved (cf. 1 Cor. 1:8; 2 Cor. 2:15; Phil. 2:12), and I have the hope that I *will be* saved (cf. Rom. 5:9–10; 1 Cor. 3:12–15). Like the apostle Paul, I am working out my salvation in fear and trembling (cf. Phil. 2:12), with hopeful confidence in the promises of Christ (cf. Rom. 5:2; 2 Tim. 2:11–13)."

31

How to Become a Catholic

Becoming Catholic is one of life's most profound and joyous experiences. Some are blessed enough to receive this great gift while they are infants, and, over time, they recognize the enormous grace that has been bestowed on them. Others enter the Catholic fold when they are older children or adults. This chapter examines the joyful process by which one becomes a Catholic.

A person is brought into full communion with the Catholic Church through reception of the three sacraments of Christian initiation—baptism, confirmation, and the Holy Eucharist—but the process by which one becomes a Catholic can take different forms.

A person who is baptized in the Catholic Church becomes a Catholic at that moment. One's initiation is deepened by confirmation and the Eucharist, but one becomes a Catholic at baptism. This is true for children who are baptized Catholic (and receive the other two sacraments later) and for adults who are baptized, confirmed, and receive the Eucharist at the same time.

Those who have been validly baptized outside the Church become Catholics by making a profession of the Catholic faith and being formally received into the Church. This is normally followed immediately by confirmation and the Eucharist.

Before a person is ready to be received into the Church, whether by baptism or by profession of faith, preparation is necessary. The amount and form of this preparation depends on the individual's circumstance. The most basic division in the kind of preparation needed is between those who are unbaptized and those who have already become Christian through baptism in another church.

For adults and children who have reached the age of reason (age seven), entrance into the Church is governed by the Rite of Christian Initiation for Adults (RCIA), sometimes called the Order of Christian Initiation for Adults (OCIA).

Preparation for the Unbaptized

Preparation for reception into the Church begins with the inquiry stage, in which the unbaptized person begins to learn about the Catholic faith and decide whether to embrace it.

The first formal step to Catholicism begins with the rite of reception into the *order of catechumens*, in which the unbaptized express their desire and intention to become Christians. *Catechumen* is a term the early Christians used to refer to those preparing to be baptized and become Christians.

The period of the catechumenate varies depending on how much the catechumen has learned and how ready he feels to take the step of becoming a Christian. However, the catechumenate often lasts less than a year.

The catechumenate's purpose is to provide the catechumens with a thorough background in Christian teaching. "A thoroughly comprehensive catechesis on the truths of Catholic doctrine and moral life, aided by approved catechetical texts, is to be provided during the period of the catechumenate" (U.S. Conference of Bishops, *National Statutes for the Catechumenate*, Nov. 11, 1986). The catechumenate is also intended to give the catechumens the opportunity to reflect upon and become firm in their desire to become Catholic and show that they are ready to take this serious and joyful step (cf. Luke 14:27–33; 2 Pet. 2:20–22).

The second formal step is taken with the *rite of election*, in which the catechumens' names are written in a book of those who will receive the sacraments of initiation. At the rite of election, the catechumen again expresses the desire and intention to become a Christian, and the Church judges that the catechumen is ready to take this step. Normally, the rite of election occurs on the first Sunday of Lent, the forty-day period of preparation for Easter.

After the rite of election, the candidates undergo a period of more intense reflection, purification, and enlightenment, in which they deepen their commitment to repentance and conversion. During this period the catechumens, now known as the elect, participate in several further rituals.

The three chief rituals, known as *scrutinies*, are normally celebrated at Mass on the third, fourth, and fifth Sundays of Lent. The scrutinies are rites for self-searching and repentance. They are meant to bring out the qualities of the catechumen's soul, heal those qualities that are weak or sinful, and strengthen those that are positive and good.

During this period, the catechumens are formally presented with the Apostles' Creed and the Lord's Prayer, which they will recite on the night they are initiated.

The *initiation* itself usually occurs on the Easter Vigil, the evening before Easter Sunday. That evening a special Mass is celebrated at which the catechumens are baptized, given confirmation, and receive the Holy Eucharist. At this point the catechumens become Catholics and are received into full communion with the Church.

Ideally the bishop oversees the Easter Vigil service and confers confirmation upon the catechumens, but often—due to large distances or numbers of catechumens a local parish priest will perform the rites.

The final state of Christian initiation is known as mystagogy, in which the new Christians are strengthened in the faith by further instruction and become more deeply rooted in the local Catholic community. The period of mystagogy normally lasts throughout the Easter season (the fifty days between Easter and Pentecost Sunday).

For the first year of their lives as Christians, those who have been received are known as *neophytes*, or "new Christians."

Preparation for Christians

The means by which those who have already been validly baptized become part of the Church differs considerably from that of the unbaptized.

Because they have already been baptized, they are already Christians; they are, therefore, not catechumens. Because of their status as Christians, the Church is concerned that they not be confused with those who are in the process of becoming Christians.

"Those who have already been baptized in another church or ecclesial community should not be treated as catechumens or so designated. Their doctrinal and spiritual preparation for reception into full Catholic communion should be determined according to the individual case, that is, it should depend on the extent to which the baptized person has led a Christian life within a community of faith and been appropriately catechized to deepen his or her inner adherence to the Church" (NSC 30).

For those who were baptized but who have never been instructed in the Christian faith or lived as Christians, it is appropriate for them to receive much of the same instruction in the faith as catechumens, but they are still not catechumens and are not to be referred to as such (NSC 3). As a result, they are not to participate in the rites intended for catechumens, such as the scrutinies. Even "the rites of presentation of the Creed, the Lord's Prayer, and the book of the Gospels are not proper except for those who have received no Christian instruction and formation" (NSC 31).

For those who have been instructed in the Christian faith and have lived as Christians, the situation is different. The U.S. Conference of Bishops states, "Those baptized persons who have lived as Christians and need only instruction in the Catholic tradition and a degree of probation within the Catholic community should not be asked to undergo a full program parallel to the catechumenate" (NSC 31). For this reason, they should not share in the same, full RCIA programs that catechumens do.

The timing of their reception into the Church is also different. "It is preferable that reception into full communion not take place at the Easter Vigil lest there be any confusion of such baptized Christians with the candidates for baptism, possible misunderstanding of or even reflection upon the sacrament of baptism celebrated in another church or ecclesial community" (NSC 33).

Rather than being received on Easter Vigil, "the reception of candidates into the communion of the Catholic Church should ordinarily take place at the Sunday Eucharist of the parish community, in such a way that it is understood that they are indeed Christian believers who have already shared in the sacramental life of the Church and are now welcomed into the Catholic eucharistic community" (NSC 32).

Christians coming into the Catholic Church must discuss with their pastor and/or bishop the amount of instruction needed and the time of their reception.

Peace with God

The sacrament of baptism removes all sins committed prior to it, but since Christians have already been baptized, it is necessary for them to confess mortal sins committed since baptism before receiving confirmation and the Eucharist.

In some cases, this can be difficult due to a large number of years between the Christian's baptism and reception into the Catholic Church. In such cases, the candidate should confess the mortal sins he can remember by kind and, to the extent possible, indicate how often such sins were committed. As always with the sacrament of reconciliation, the absolution covers any mortal sins that could not be remembered so long as the recipient intended to repent of all mortal sins.

Christians coming into the Church should receive the sacrament of reconciliation before their reception into the Church (there is no established point for when they should do this) to ensure that they are in a state of grace when they are received and confirmed. Their formation in the faith should stress that frequent confession is part of Catholic life: "The celebration of the sacrament of reconciliation with candidates for reception into full communion is to be carried out at a time prior to and distinct from the celebration of the rite of reception. As part of the formation of such candidates, they should be encouraged in the frequent celebration of this sacrament" (NSC 36).

The Christian fully enters the Church by profession of faith and formal reception. For the profession of faith, the candidate says, "I believe and profess all that the holy Catholic Church believes, teaches, and proclaims to be revealed by God."

The bishop or priest then formally receives the Christian into the Church by saying, "[Name], the Lord receives you into the Catholic Church. His loving kindness has led you here, so that in the unity of the Holy Spirit you may have full communion with us in the faith that you have professed in the presence of his family."

The bishop or priest then normally administers the sacrament of confirmation and celebrates the holy Eucharist, giving the new Catholic the Eucharist for the first time.

Reception in Special Cases

In some situations, there may be doubts whether a person's baptism was valid. All baptisms are assumed valid, *regardless of denomination*, unless after serious investigation there is reason to doubt that the candidate was baptized with water and the Trinitarian formula ("in the name of the Father and of the Son and of the Holy Spirit") or that the minister or recipient of baptism did not intend it to be an actual baptism.

If there are doubts about the validity of a person's baptism (or whether the person was baptized at all), then the candidate will be given a conditional baptism (one with the form "If you are not already baptized, I baptize you in the name of the Father and of the Son and of the Holy Spirit").

"If conditional baptism . . . seems necessary, this must be celebrated privately rather than at a public liturgical assembly of the community and with only those limited rites that the diocesan bishop determines. The reception into full communion should take place later at the Sunday Eucharist of the community" (NSC 37).

Another special case concerns those who have been baptized as

Catholics but who were not brought up in the faith or who have not received the sacraments of confirmation and the Eucharist. "Although baptized adult Catholics who have never received catechetical instruction or been admitted to the sacraments of confirmation and Eucharist are not catechumens, some elements of the usual catechumenal formation are appropriate to their preparation for the sacraments, in accord with the norms of the ritual *Preparation of Uncatechized Adults for Confirmation and Eucharist*" (NSC 25).

Waiting for the Day!

It can be a time of anxious longing while one waits to experience the warm embrace of membership in the Church and be immersed into Catholic society. This time of waiting and reflection is necessary, since becoming a Catholic is a momentous event. But waiting can be painful as one longs for the sacraments, especially the Eucharist, and the joys of Catholic life—the security that being a faithful Catholic bestows. Yet even before being received, those waiting to be fully incorporated already have a real relationship with the Church.

For those who are already Christians, their baptism itself forms a certain sacramental relationship with the Church (cf. *Unitatis Redintegratio* 3; *Catechism of the Catholic Church* 1271). They are also joined to the Church by their intention to enter it, as are the unbaptized who intend to do so: "Catechumens who, moved by the Holy Spirit, desire with an explicit intention to be incorporated into the Church are by that very intention joined to her. With love and solicitude mother Church already embraces them as her own" (*Lumen Gentium* 14:3; CCC 1249).

Thus, even before one is fully incorporated into the Church, one can enjoy the status of being recognized by the Church as one of her own, precious children.

32

Purgatory

The *Catechism of the Catholic Church* defines purgatory as a "purification, so as to achieve the holiness necessary to enter the joy of heaven," which is experienced by those "who die in God's grace and friendship, but still imperfectly purified" (CCC 1030). It notes that "this final purification of the elect . . . is entirely different from the punishment of the damned" (CCC 1031).

The purification is necessary because, as Scripture teaches, nothing unclean will enter the presence of God in heaven (cf. Rev. 21:27) and, while we may die with our mortal sins forgiven, there can still be many impurities in us, specifically venial sins and the temporal punishment due to sins already forgiven.

Two Judgments

When we die, we undergo what is called the particular, or individual, judgment. Scripture says that "it is appointed for men to die once, and after that comes judgment" (Heb. 9:27). We are judged instantly and receive our reward, for good or ill. We know at once what our final destiny will be. At the end of time, when Jesus returns, there will come the general judgment to which the Bible refers, for example, in Matthew 25:31–32: "When the Son of man comes in his glory, and all the angels with him, then he will sit on his glorious throne. Before him will be gathered all the nations, and he will separate them one from another as a shepherd separates the sheep from the goats." In this general judgment all our sins will be publicly revealed (cf. Luke 12:2–5).

Augustine said, in *The City of God*, that "temporary punishments are suffered by some in this life only, by others after death, by others both now and then; but all of them before that last and strictest judgment" (21:13). It is between the particular and general judgments, then, that the soul is purified of the remaining consequences of sin: "I tell you, you will never get out till you have paid the very last copper" (Luke 12.59).

Money, Money, Money

One argument anti-Catholics often use to attack purgatory is the idea that the Catholic Church makes money from promulgating the doctrine. Without purgatory, the claim asserts, the Church would go broke. A number of anti-Catholic books claim the Church owes the majority of its wealth to this doctrine. But the numbers just don't add up.

When a Catholic requests a memorial Mass for the dead—that is, a Mass said for the benefit of someone in purgatory—it is customary to give the parish priest a stipend, on the principles that the laborer is worth his hire (cf. Luke 10:7) and that those who preside at the altar share the altar's offerings (cf. 1 Cor. 9:13–14). In the United States, a stipend is commonly around five dollars; but the indigent do not have to pay anything. A few people, of course, freely offer more. This money goes to the parish priest, and priests are allowed to receive only one such stipend per day. No one gets rich on five dollars a day, and certainly not the Church, which does not receive the money anyway.

But look at what happens on a Sunday. There are often hundreds of people at Mass. In a crowded parish, there may be thousands. Many families and individuals deposit five dollars or more into the collection basket; others deposit less. A few give much more. A parish might have four or five or six Masses on a Sunday. The total from the Sunday collections far surpasses the paltry amount received from the memorial Masses.

A Catholic "Invention"?

Fundamentalists may be fond of saying the Catholic Church "invented" the doctrine of purgatory to make money, but they have difficulty saying just when. Most professional anti-Catholics—the ones who make their living attacking "Romanism"—seem to place the blame on Pope Gregory the Great, who reigned from A.D. 590–604.

But that hardly accounts for the request of Monica, mother of Augustine, who asked her son in the fourth century to remember her soul in his Masses. This would make no sense if she thought her soul would not benefit from prayers, as would be the case if she were in hell or in the full glory of heaven.

Nor does ascribing the doctrine to Gregory explain the graffiti in the catacombs, where Christians during the persecutions of the first three centuries recorded prayers for the dead. Indeed, some of the earliest Christian writings outside the New Testament, like the *Acts of Paul and Thecla* and the *Martyrdom of Perpetua and Felicity* (both written during the second century), refer to the Christian practice of praying for the dead. Such prayers would have been offered only if Christians believed in purgatory, even if they did not use that name for it.

Why No Protests?

Whenever a date is set for the "invention" of purgatory, you can point to historical evidence to show the doctrine was in existence before that date. Besides, if at some point the doctrine was pulled out of a clerical hat, why does ecclesiastical history record no protest against it?

A study of the history of doctrines indicates that Christians in the first centuries were up in arms (sometimes quite literally) if anyone suggested the least change in beliefs. They were extremely conservative people who tested a doctrine's truth by asking, "Was this believed by our ancestors? Was it handed on from the apostles?" Surely belief in purgatory would be considered a great change if it had not been believed from the first. So where are the records of protests?

They do not exist. There is no hint at all, in the oldest writings available to us (or in later ones, for that matter), that "true believers" in the immediate post-apostolic years spoke of purgatory as a novel doctrine. They must have understood that the oral teaching of the apostles—what Catholics call Tradition—and the Bible not only failed to contradict the doctrine but in fact confirmed it.

It is no wonder, then, that those who deny the existence of purgatory tend to touch upon the history of the belief only briefly. They prefer to claim that the Bible speaks only of heaven and hell. Wrong. It speaks plainly of a third condition, commonly called the limbo of the Fathers, where the just who had died before the Redemption were waiting for heaven to be opened to them. After his death and before his Resurrection, Christ visited those experiencing the limbo of the Fathers and preached to them the good news that heaven would now be opened to them (cf. 1 Pet. 3:19). These people thus were not in heaven, but neither were they experiencing the torments of hell.

Some have speculated that the limbo of the Fathers is the same as purgatory. This may or may not be the case. However, even if the limbo of the Fathers is not purgatory, its existence shows that a temporary, intermediate state is not contrary to Scripture. Look at it this way: If the limbo of the Fathers was purgatory, then this one verse directly teaches the existence of purgatory. If the limbo of the Fathers was a different temporary state, then the Bible says such a state can exist. It proves there can be more than just heaven and hell.

"Purgatory Not in Scripture"

Some Fundamentalists also charge, as though it actually proved something, "The word *purgatory* is found nowhere in Scripture."

THE ESSENTIAL CATHOLIC SURVIVAL GUIDE

This is true, and yet it does not disprove the existence of purgatory or the fact that belief in it has always been part of Church teaching. The words *Trinity* and *Incarnation* are not in Scripture either, yet those doctrines are clearly taught in it. Likewise, Scripture teaches that purgatory exists, even if it doesn't use that word and even if 1 Peter 3:19 refers to a place other than purgatory.

Christ refers to the sinner who "will not be forgiven, either in this age or in the age to come" (Matt. 12:32), suggesting that one can be freed after death of the consequences of one's sins. Similarly, Paul tells us that, when we are judged, each man's work will be tried. And what happens if a righteous man's work fails the test? "He will suffer loss, though he himself will be saved, but only as through fire" (1 Cor 3:15). Now this loss, this penalty, cannot refer to consignment to hell, since no one is saved there; and heaven cannot be meant, since there is no suffering ("fire") there. The Catholic doctrine of purgatory alone explains this passage.

Then, of course, there is the Bible's approval of prayers for the dead: "In doing this he acted very well and honorably, taking account of the resurrection. For if he were not expecting that those who had fallen would rise again, it would have been superfluous and foolish to pray for the dead. But if he was looking to the splendid reward that is laid up for those who fall asleep in godliness, it was a holy and pious thought. Therefore he made atonement for the dead, that they might be delivered from their sin" (2 Macc. 12:43–45). Prayers are not needed by those in heaven, and no one can help those in hell. That means some people must be in a third condition, at least temporarily. This verse so clearly illustrates the existence of purgatory that, at the time of the Reformation, Protestants had to cut the books of the Maccabees out of their Bibles in order to avoid accepting the doctrine.

Prayers for the dead and the consequent doctrine of purgatory have been part of the true religion since before the time of Christ. Not only can we show that it was practiced by the Jews of the time of the Maccabees, but it has been retained even by Orthodox Jews today, who recite a prayer known as the Mourner's *Kaddish* for eleven months after the death of a loved one so that the loved one may be purified. It was not the Catholic Church that added the doctrine of purgatory. Rather, any change in the original teaching has taken place in the Protestant churches, which rejected a doctrine that had always been believed by Jews and Christians.

Why Go to Purgatory?

Why would anyone go to purgatory? To be cleansed, for "nothing unclean shall enter it [heaven]" (Rev. 21:27). Anyone who has not been completely freed of sin and its effects is, to some extent, "unclean." Through repentance he may have gained the grace needed to be worthy of heaven, which is to say that he has been forgiven and his soul is spiritually alive. But that is not sufficient for gaining entrance into heaven. He needs to be cleansed completely.

Fundamentalists claim—as an article in Jimmy Swaggart's magazine, *The Evangelist*, put it—that "Scripture clearly reveals that all the demands of divine justice on the sinner have been completely fulfilled in Jesus Christ. It also reveals that Christ has totally redeemed, or purchased back, that which was lost. The advocates of a purgatory (and the necessity of prayer for the dead) say, in effect, that the redemption of Christ was incomplete. . . . It has all been done for us by Jesus Christ, there is nothing to be added or done by man."

It is entirely correct to say that Christ accomplished all of our salvation for us on the cross. But that does not settle the question of how this redemption is applied to us. Scripture reveals that it is applied to us over the course of time through, among other things, the process of sanctification through which the Christian is made holy. Sanctification involves suffering (cf. Rom. 5:3–5), and purgatory is the final stage of sanctification that some of us need to undergo before we enter heaven. Purgatory is the final phase of Christ's applying to us the purifying Redemption that he accomplished for us by his death on the cross.

No Contradiction

The Fundamentalist resistance to the biblical doctrine of purgatory presumes there is a contradiction between Christ's redeeming us on the cross and the process by which we are sanctified. There is not. And a Fundamentalist cannot say that suffering in the final stage of sanctification conflicts with the sufficiency of Christ's atonement without saying that suffering in the early stages of sanctification also presents a similar conflict. The Fundamentalist has it backward: Our suffering in sanctification does not take away from the cross. Rather, the cross produces our sanctification, which results in our suffering, because "for the moment all discipline seems painful rather than pleasant; later it yields the peaceful fruit of righteousness" (Heb. 12:11).

Nothing Unclean

Purgatory makes sense because there is a requirement that a soul not just be declared to be clean but actually be clean before a man may enter into eternal life. After all, if a guilty soul is merely "covered," if its sinful state still exists but is officially ignored, then it is still a guilty soul. It is still unclean.

Catholic theology takes seriously the notion that "nothing unclean shall enter heaven." From this it is inferred that a less than cleansed soul, even if "covered," remains a dirty soul and is not fit for heaven. It needs to be cleansed or "purged" of its remaining imperfections. The cleansing occurs in purgatory. Indeed, the necessity of the purging is taught in other passages of Scripture, such as 2 Thessalonians 2:13, which declares that God chose us "to be saved through sanctification by the Spirit." Sanctification is thus not an option, something that may or may not happen before one gets into heaven. It is an absolute requirement, as Hebrews 12:14 states that we must strive "for the holiness without which no one will see the Lord."

33

The Rapture

Are you Pre, Mid, or Post? If you don't know how to answer that question, you're probably a Catholic. Most Fundamentalists and Evangelicals know that these words are shorthand for *pre tribulation, mid-tribulation,* and *post tribulation.* The terms all refer to when the Rapture is supposed to occur.

The Millennium

In Revelation 20, we read, "Then I saw an angel coming down from heaven, holding in his hand the key of the bottomless pit and a great chain. And he seized the dragon, that ancient serpent, who is the Devil and Satan, and bound him for a thousand years, and threw him into the pit, and shut it and sealed it over him, that he should deceive the nations no more, till the thousand years were ended. After that he must be loosed for a little while. . . . And when the thousand years are ended, Satan will be loosed from his prison and will come out to deceive the nations which are at the four corners of the earth" (Rev. 20:1–3, 7–8).

The period of a thousand years, the writer tells us, is the reign of Christ, and the thousand-year period is popularly called the millennium. The millennium is a harbinger of the end of the world, and Revelation 20 is interpreted in three ways by conservative Protestants. The three schools of thought are called post-millennialism, amillennialism, and pre-millennialism. Let's take a look at them.

Post-Millennialism

According to Loraine Boettner in his book *The Millennium* (he also wrote the seriously defective anti-Catholic book *Roman Catholi-*

cism), post-millennialism is "that view of last things which holds that the kingdom of God is now being extended in the world through the preaching of the gospel and the saving work of the Holy Spirit, that the world eventually is to be Christianized and that the return of Christ will occur at the close of a long period of righteousness and peace, commonly called the millennium."

This view was popular with nineteenth-century Protestants when progress was expected even in religion and before twentieth-century horrors were tasted. Today few hold to it, except such groups as Christian Reconstructionists, an outgrowth of the conservative Presbyterian movement.

Commentators point out that post-millennialism is to be distinguished from the view of theological and secular liberals who envision social betterment and even the kingdom of God coming through purely natural (rather than supernatural) means. Post-millennialists, however, argue that man is incapable of building a paradise for himself; paradise will come about only by God's grace.

Post-millennialists also typically say that the millennium spoken of in Revelation 20 should be understood figuratively, and that the phrase "a thousand years" refers not to a fixed period of ten centuries but to an indefinitely long time. For example, Psalm 50:10 speaks of God's sovereignty over all that is and tells us that God owns "the cattle on a thousand hills." This is not meant to be taken literally.

At the millennium's end will come the Second Coming, the general resurrection of the dead, and the last judgment.

The problem with post-millennialism is that Scripture does not depict the world as experiencing a period of complete (or relatively complete) Christianization before the Second Coming. There are numerous passages that speak of the age between the First and Second Comings as a time of great sorrow and strife for Christians. One revealing passage is the parable of the wheat and the weeds (cf. Matt. 13:24–30, 36–43). In this parable, Christ declares that the righteous and the wicked will both be planted and grow alongside each other in God's field ("the field is the world") until the end of the world, when they will be separated, judged, and either be thrown into the fire of hell or inherit God's kingdom. There is no biblical evidence that the world will eventually become totally (or even almost totally) Christian, but rather that there will always be a parallel development of the righteous and the wicked until the final judgment.

Amillennialism

The amillennial view interprets Revelation 20 symbolically and sees the millennium not as an earthly golden age in which the world will be totally Christianized but as the present period of Christ's rule in heaven and on the earth through his Church. This was the view of the Protestant Reformers and is still the most common view among traditional Protestants, though not among most of the newer Evangelical and Fundamentalist groups.

Amillennialists also believe in the coexistence of good and evil on earth until the end. The tension that exists on earth between the righteous and the wicked will be resolved only by Christ's return at the end of time. The golden age of the millennium is instead the heavenly reign of Christ with the saints, in which the Church on earth participates to some degree, though not in the glorious way it will at the Second Coming.

Amillennialists point out that the thrones of the saints who reign with Christ during the millennium appear to be set in heaven (cf. Rev. 4:4; 11:16; 20:4) and that the text nowhere states that Christ is on earth during this reign with the saints.

They explain that, although the world will never be fully Christianized until the Second Coming, the millennium does have effects on earth in that Satan cannot deceive the nations by hindering the preaching of the gospel (cf. Rev. 20:3). They point out that Jesus spoke of "binding the strong man" (Satan) in order to plunder his house by rescuing people from his grip (cf. Matt. 12:29). When the disciples returned from a tour of preaching the gospel, rejoicing at how demons were subject to them, Jesus declared, "I saw Satan fall like lightning" (Luke 10:18). Thus for the gospel to move forward at all in the world, it is necessary for Satan to be bound in one sense, even if he may still be active in attacking individuals (cf. 1 Pet. 5:8).

The millennium is a golden age not when compared to the glories of the age to come but in comparison to all prior ages of human history, in which the world was swallowed in pagan darkness. Today, a third of the human race is Christian and even more than that have repudiated pagan idols and embraced the worship of the God of Abraham.

Pre-Millennialism

Third on the list is pre-millennialism, currently the most popular among Fundamentalists and Evangelicals (even though a century ago amillennialism was). Most of the books written about the end times, such as Hal Lindsey's *The Late Great Planet Earth*, are written from a pre-millennial perspective.

Like post-millennialists, pre-millennialists believe that the thousand years is an earthly golden age during which the world will be thoroughly Christianized. Unlike post-millennialists, they believe that it will occur after the Second Coming rather than before, so that Christ reigns physically on earth during the millennium. They believe that the Final Judgment will occur only after the millennium is over (which many interpret to be exactly one thousand years).

But Scripture does not support the idea of a thousand-year span between the Second Coming and the Final Judgment. Christ declares, "For the Son of man is to come with his angels in the glory of his Father, and then he will repay every man for what he has done" (Matt. 16:27), and "when the Son of man comes in his glory, and all the angels with him, then he will sit on his glorious throne. Before him will be gathered all the nations, and he will separate them one from another as a shepherd separates the sheep from the goats. . . . And they [the goats] will go away into eternal punishment, but the righteous into eternal life" (Matt. 25:31–32, 46).

The Rapture

Pre-millennialists often give much attention to the doctrine of the Rapture. According to this doctrine, when Christ returns, all of the elect who have died will be raised and transformed into a glorious state, along with the living elect, and then be caught up to be with Christ. The key text referring to the Rapture is 1 Thessalonians 4:16–17: "For the Lord himself will descend from heaven with a cry of command, with the archangel's call, and with the sound of the trumpet of God. And the dead in Christ will rise first; then we who are alive, who are left, shall be caught up together with them in the clouds to meet the Lord in the air; and so we shall always be with the Lord."

Pre-millennialists hold, as do virtually all Christians (except certain post-millennialists), that the Second Coming will be preceded by a time of great trouble and persecution of God's people (cf. 2 Thess. 2:1–4). This period is often called the tribulation. Until the nineteenth century, all Christians agreed that the Rapture—though it was not called that at the time—would occur immediately before the Second Coming, at the close of the period of persecution. This position is today called the "post-tribulational" view because it says the Rapture will come after the tribulation.

But in the 1800s, some began to claim that the Rapture would occur before the period of persecution. This position, now known as the "pre-tribulational" view, was embraced by John Nelson Darby, an early leader of a Fundamentalist movement that became known as Dispensationalism. Darby's pre-tribulational view of the Rapture was then picked up by a man named C. I. Scofield, who taught the view in the footnotes of his *Scofield Reference Bible*, which was widely distributed in England and America. Many Protestants who read the *Scofield Reference Bible* uncritically accepted what its footnotes said and adopted the pre-tribulational view, even though no Christian had heard of it in the previous 1,800 years of Church history.

Eventually, a third position developed, known as the "mid-tribulational" view, which claims that the Rapture will occur during the middle of the tribulation. Finally, a fourth view developed that claims that there will not be a single Rapture where all believers are gathered to Christ, but there will be a series of mini-raptures that occur at different times with respect to the tribulation.

This confusion has caused the movement to split into bitterly opposed camps.

The problem with all of the positions (except the historical, post-tribulational view, which was accepted by all Christians, including non-pre-millennialists) is that they split the Second Coming into different events. In the case of the pre-trib view, Christ is thought to have three comings—one when he was born in Bethlehem, one when he returns for the Rapture at the tribulation's beginning, and one at tribulation's end, when he establishes the millennium. This three-comings view is foreign to Scripture.

Problems with the pre-tribulational view are highlighted by Baptist (and pre-millennial) theologian Dale Moody, who wrote: "Belief in a pre-tribulational rapture . . . contradicts all three chapters in the New Testament that mention the tribulation and the Rapture together (Mark 13:24–27; Matt. 24:26–31; 2 Thess. 2:1–12). . . . The theory is so biblically bankrupt that the usual defense is made using three passages that do not even mention a tribulation (John 14:3; 1 Thess. 4:17; 1 Cor. 15:52). These are important passages, but they have not had one word to say about a pre-tribulational rapture. The score is 3 to 0, three passages for a post-tribulational rapture and three that say nothing on the subject. . . . Pre-tribulationism is biblically bankrupt and does not know it" (*The Word of Truth*, 556–7).

What's the Catholic Position?

As far as the millennium goes, we tend to agree with Augustine and, derivatively, with the amillennialists. The Catholic position has thus historically been "amillennial" (as has been the majority Christian position in general, including that of the Protestant Reformers), though Catholics do not typically use this term. The Church has rejected the pre-millennial position, sometimes called "millenarianism" (cf. *Catechism of the Catholic Church* 676). In the 1940s the Holy Office judged that pre-millennialism "cannot safely be taught," though the Church has not dogmatically defined this issue.

With respect to the Rapture, Catholics certainly believe that the event of our gathering together to be with Christ will take place, though they do not generally use the word *Rapture* to refer to this event (somewhat ironically, since the term is derived from the text of the Latin Vulgate of 1 Thessalonians 4:17—"we will be caught up" [Latin: *rapiemur*]).

Spinning Wheels?

Many spend much time looking for signs in the heavens and in the headlines. This is especially true of pre-millennialists, who anxiously await the tribulation because it will inaugurate the rapture and millennium.

A more balanced perspective is given by Peter, who writes, "But do not ignore this one fact, beloved, that with the Lord one day is as a thousand years, and a thousand years as one day. The Lord is not slow about his promise as some count slowness, but is forbearing toward you, not wishing that any should perish, but that all should reach repentance. . . . Since all these things are thus to be dissolved, what sort of persons ought you to be in lives of holiness and godliness, waiting for and hastening the coming of the day of God, because of which the heavens will be kindled and dissolved, and the elements will melt with fire! But according to his promise we wait for new heavens and a new earth in which righteousness dwells. Therefore, beloved, since you wait for these, be zealous to be found by him without spot or blemish, and at peace" (2 Pet. 3:8–14).

34

Hunting the Whore of Babylon

Some anti-Catholics claim the Catholic Church is the Whore of Babylon of Revelation 17 and 18. Dave Hunt, in his 1994 book *A Woman Rides the Beast*, presents nine arguments to try to prove this. His claims are a useful summary of those commonly used by Fundamentalists, and an examination of them shows why they don't work.

1. Seven Hills

Hunt argues that the Whore "is a city built on seven hills," which he identifies as the seven hills of ancient Rome. This argument is based on Revelation 17:9, which states that the woman sits on seven mountains.

The Greek word in this passage is *horos*. Of the sixty-five occurrences of this word in the New Testament, only three are rendered "hill" by the King James Version. The remaining sixty-two are translated as "mountain" or "mount." Modern Bibles have similar ratios. If the passage states that the Whore sits on "seven mountains," it could refer to anything. Mountains are common biblical symbols, often symbolizing whole kingdoms (cf. Ps. 68:15; Dan. 2:35; Amos 4:1; 6:1; Obad. 8–21). The Whore's seven mountains might be seven kingdoms she reigns over or seven kingdoms with which she has something in common.

The number seven may also be symbolic, for it often represents *completeness* in the Bible. If so, the seven mountains might signify that the Whore reigns over all earth's kingdoms.

Even if we accept that the word *horos* should be translated literally as "hill" in this passage, it still doesn't narrow us down to

Rome. Other cities are known for having been built on seven hills as well.

Even if we grant that the reference is to Rome, which Rome are we talking about—pagan Rome or Christian Rome? As we will see, ancient, pagan Rome fits all of Hunt's criteria as well, or better, than Rome during the Christian centuries.

Now bring in the distinction between Rome and Vatican City— the city where the Catholic Church is headquartered—and Hunt's claim becomes less plausible. Vatican City is not built on seven hills but only one: Vatican Hill, which is *not* one of the seven upon which ancient Rome was built. Those hills are on the east side of the Tiber river; Vatican Hill is on the west.

2. *"Babylon"—What's in a Name?*

Hunt notes that the Whore will be a city "known as Babylon." This is based on Revelation 17:5, which says that her name is "Babylon the Great."

The phrase "Babylon the great" (Greek: *Babulon ā megalā*) oc- curs five times in Revelation (14:8, 16:19, 17:5, 18:2, and 18:21). Light is shed on its meaning when one notices that Babylon is referred to as "the great city" seven times in the book (16:19; 17:18; 18:10, 16, 18, 19, 21). Other than these, there is only one reference to "the great city." That passage is 11:8, which states that the bodies of God's two witnesses "will lie in the street of the *great city*, which is allegorically called Sodom and Egypt, where their Lord was crucified."

"The great city" is symbolically called Sodom, a reference to Jerusalem, symbolically called "Sodom" in the Old Testament (cf. Is. 1:10; Ezek. 16:1–3, 46–56). We also know Jerusalem is the "the great city" of Revelation 11:8 because the verse says it was "where [the] Lord was crucified."

Revelation consistently speaks as if there were only one "great city" ("*the* great city"), suggesting that the great city of 11:8 is the same as the great city mentioned in the other seven texts—

Babylon. Additional evidence for the identity of the two is the fact that both are symbolically named after great Old Testament enemies of the faith: Sodom, Egypt, and Babylon.

This suggests that Babylon the great may be Jerusalem, not Rome. Many Protestant and Catholic commentators have adopted this interpretation. On the other hand, early Church Fathers often referred to Rome as "Babylon," but every reference was to *pagan* Rome, which martyred Christians.

3. Commits Fornication

Hunt tells us, "The woman is called a 'whore' (verse 1), with whom earthly kings 'have committed fornication' (verse 2). Against only two cities could such a charge be made: Jerusalem and Rome."

Here Hunt admits that the prophets often referred to Jerusalem as a spiritual whore, suggesting that the Whore might be apostate Jerusalem. Ancient, pagan Rome also fits the description, since through the cult of emperor worship it also committed spiritual fornication with "the kings of the earth" (those nations it conquered).

To identify the Whore as Vatican City, Hunt interprets the fornication as alleged "unholy alliances" forged between Vatican City and other nations, but he fails to cite any reasons that the Vatican's diplomatic relations with other nations are "unholy."

He also confuses Vatican City with the city of Rome, and he neglects the fact that pagan Rome had "unholy alliances" with the kingdoms it governed (unholy because they were built on paganism and emperor worship).

4. Clothed in Purple and Red

Hunt states, "She [the Whore] is clothed in 'purple and scarlet' (verse 4), the colors of the Catholic clergy." He then cites

THE ESSENTIAL CATHOLIC SURVIVAL GUIDE

the *Catholic Encyclopedia* to show that bishops wear certain purple vestments and cardinals wear certain red vestments.

Hunt ignores the obvious symbolic meaning of the colors— purple for royalty and red for the blood of Christian martyrs. Instead, he is suddenly literal in his interpretation. He understood well enough that the woman symbolizes a city and that the fornication symbolizes something other than literal sex, but now he wants to assign the colors a literal, earthly fulfillment in a few vestments of certain Catholic clergy.

Purple and red are not the dominant colors of Catholic clerical vestments. White is. All priests wear white (including bishops and cardinals when they are saying Mass)—even the pope does so.

The purple and scarlet of the Whore are contrasted with the white of the New Jerusalem, the Bride of Christ (Rev. 19:8). This is a problem for Hunt for three reasons: (a) we have already noted that the dominant color of Catholic clerical vestments is white, which would identify them with New Jerusalem if the color is taken literally; (b) the clothing of the Bride is given a symbolic interpretation ("the righteous acts of the saints," 19:8), implying that the clothing of the Whore should also be given a symbolic meaning; and (c) the identification of the Bride as *New* Jerusalem (Rev. 3:12; 21:2, 10) suggests that the Whore may be *old* (apostate) Jerusalem—a contrast used elsewhere in Scripture (e.g., Gal. 4:25–26).

It is appropriate for Catholic clerics to wear purple and scarlet, if for no other reason because they have been liturgical colors of the true religion since ancient Israel.

Hunt neglects to remind his readers that God commanded that scarlet yarn and wool be used in liturgical ceremonies (Lev. 14:4, 6, 49–52; Num. 19:6) and that God commanded that *the priests' vestments* be made with purple and scarlet yarn (Ex. 28:4–8, 15, 33; 39:1–8, 24, 29).

5. Possesses Great Wealth

Hunt states, "[The Whore's] incredible wealth next caught John's eye. She was 'decked with gold and precious stones and pearls' [Rev. 17:4]." The problem is that, regardless of what it had in the past, the modern Vatican is not fantastically wealthy. In fact, it has run a budget deficit in most recent years and has an annual budget comparable to that of the archdiocese of Chicago. Furthermore, wealth was much more in character with pagan Rome or apostate Jerusalem, both key economic centers.

6. A Golden Cup

Hunt states that the Whore "has 'a golden cup [chalice] in her hand, full of abominations and filthiness of her fornication.'" This is another reference to Revelation 17:4. Then he states that the "Church is known for its many thousands of gold chalices around the world."

To make the Whore's gold cup suggestive of the eucharistic chalice, Hunt inserts the word *chalice* in square brackets, though the Greek word here is the ordinary word for cup (*potārion*), which appears thirty-three times in the New Testament and is always translated "cup."

He ignores the fact that the Catholic chalice is used in the celebration of the Lord's Supper—a ritual commanded by Christ (Luke 22:19–20; 1 Cor. 11:24–25); he ignores the fact that the majority of eucharistic chalices Catholics use are not made out of gold but other materials, such as brass, silver, glass, and even earthenware; he ignores the fact that gold liturgical vessels and utensils have been part of the true religion ever since ancient Israel—again at the command of God (Ex. 25:38–40; 37:23–24; Num. 31:50–51; 2 Chr. 24:14); and he again uses a literal interpretation, according to which the Whore's cup is not a single symbol applying to the city of Rome but a collection of many literal cups used in cities throughout the world. But Revelation tells us that it's the cup of God's wrath that is given to the Whore (Rev. 14:10; cf. 18:6). This has nothing to do with eucharistic chalices.

7. The Mother of Harlots

Now for Hunt's most hilarious argument: "John's attention is next drawn to the inscription on the woman's forehead: 'THE MOTHER OF HARLOTS AND ABOMINATIONS OF THE EARTH' (verse 5, [Hunt's emphasis]). Sadly enough, the Roman Catholic Church fits that description as precisely as she fits the others. Much of the cause is due to the unbiblical doctrine of priestly celibacy," which has "made sinners of the clergy and harlots out of those with whom they secretly cohabit."

Priestly celibacy is not a doctrine but a discipline—a discipline in the Latin rite of the Church—and even this rite has not always been mandatory. This discipline can scarcely be unbiblical, since Hunt himself says, "The great apostle Paul was a celibate and recommended that life to others who wanted to devote themselves fully to serving Christ."

Hunt has again lurched to an absurdly literal interpretation. He should interpret the harlotry of the Whore's daughters as the same as their mother's, which is why she is called their mother in the first place. This would make it spiritual or political fornication or the persecution of Christian martyrs (cf. Rev. 17:2, 6, 18:6). Instead, Hunt gives the interpretation of the daughters as literal, earthly prostitutes committing literal, earthly fornication.

If Hunt did not have a fixation on the King James Version, he would notice another point that identifies the daughters' harlotries with that of their mother: The same Greek word (*pornā*) is used for both mother and daughters. The King James Version translates this word as "whore" whenever it refers to the mother but as "harlot" when it refers to the daughters. Modern translations render it consistently. John sees the "great harlot" (17:1, 15, 16; 19:2) who is "the mother of harlots" (17:5). The harlotries of the daughters must be the same as the mother's, which Hunt admits is not literal sex!

8. Sheds the Blood of Saints

Hunt states, "John next notices that the woman is drunk—not with alcohol but with the blood of the saints, and with the blood of the martyrs of Jesus [cf. verse 6]." He then advances charges of brutality and killing by the Inquisitions, supposed forced conversions of nations, and even the Nazi holocaust!

This section of the book abounds with historical errors, not the least of which is his implication that the Church endorses the forced conversion of nations. The Church emphatically does not do so. It has condemned forced conversions as early as the third century (before then they were scarcely even possible) and has formally condemned them on repeated occasions, as in the *Catechism of the Catholic Church* (CCC 160, 1738, 1782, 2106–7).

But pagan Rome and apostate Jerusalem do fit the description of a city drunk with the blood of saints and the martyrs of Jesus. And since they were notorious persecutors of Christians, the original audience would have automatically thought of one of these two as the city that persecutes Christians, not an undreamed-of Christian Rome that was centuries in the future.

9. Reigns over Kings

For his last argument, Hunt states, "Finally, the angel reveals that the woman 'is that great city, which reigneth over the kings of the earth' (verse 18). Is there such a city? Yes, and again only one: Vatican City."

This is a joke. Vatican City has no power over other nations; it certainly does not reign over them. In fact, the Vatican's very existence has been threatened in the past two centuries by Italian nationalism.

Hunt appeals to power the popes once had over Christian political rulers (neglecting the fact that this was always a limited authority, by the popes' own admission), but at that time there was no Vatican City. The Vatican became a separate city in 1929, when the Holy See and Italy signed the Lateran Treaty.

Hunt seems to understand this passage to be talking about Vatican City, since the modern city of Rome is only a very minor political force. If the reign is a literal, political one, then pagan Rome fulfills the requirement far better than Christian Rome ever did.

35

The Whore of Babylon

In "Hunting the Whore of Babylon," we looked at nine arguments given by fundamentalist Dave Hunt for his claim that the Catholic Church is the Whore of Babylon from Revelation 17–18. His arguments are typical of those used by fundamentalist anti-Catholics and are easily proven wrong.

But we can go beyond a mere critique of the shallow anti-Catholic arguments like Hunt's. There is irrefutable evidence in Revelation 17–18 (the chapters Fundamentalists love to quote *against* the Catholic Church) that proves that it is impossible for the Catholic Church to be the Whore.

A Vision in the Wilderness

When John introduces the Whore in Revelation 17, he tells us: "Then one of the seven angels who had the seven bowls came and said to me, 'Come, I will show you the judgment of the great harlot who is seated upon many waters, with whom the kings of the earth have committed fornication, and with the wine of whose fornication the dwellers on earth have become drunk.' And he carried me away in the Spirit into a wilderness, and I saw a woman sitting on a scarlet beast which was full of blasphemous names, and it had seven heads and ten horns. The woman was arrayed in purple and scarlet, and bedecked with gold and jewels and pearls, holding in her hand a golden cup full of abominations and the impurities of her fornication; and on her forehead was written a name of mystery: 'Babylon the great, mother of harlots and of earth's abominations.' And I saw the woman, drunk with the blood of the saints and the blood of the martyrs of Jesus. When I saw her I marveled greatly" (Rev. 17:1–6).

This passage tells us several things about the Whore: (1) She is an international power, since she "sits on many waters," representing different peoples (17:15), she has committed fornication with "the kings of the earth," and she has inflamed "the dwellers on earth" with her fornication. (2) She is connected with the seven-headed beast from Revelation 13:1–10. That beast was a major pagan empire, since its symbolism combined animal elements from four other major pagan empires (compare Rev. 13:1–2 with Dan. 7:1–8). (3) The woman is connected with royalty, since she is dressed in the royal color purple. (4) The woman is rich, for she is "bedecked with gold and jewels and pearls, holding in her hand a golden cup." (5) She has committed some kind of fornication, which in Scripture is often a symbol of false religion—lack of fidelity to the God who created heaven and earth. (6) She is symbolically known as Babylon. (7) She is a central cause of "abominations" in the land, abominations being a reference to practices—especially religious practices—that are offensive to God. (8) She persecutes Christians, "the saints and . . . martyrs of Jesus."

While the rest of her description could refer to a number of things, the symbolic designation of "Babylon" narrows it down to two: pagan Rome and apostate Jerusalem. It is well known that the early Church Fathers referred to pagan Rome as "Babylon"; however, there are also indications in Revelation that the Whore might be apostate Jerusalem. Historically, a number of commentators, both Protestant and Catholic, have adopted this interpretation.

The Seven Heads

Continuing in Revelation, the angel begins to explain to John the woman's symbolism: "This calls for a mind with wisdom: the seven heads are seven mountains on which the woman is seated; they are also seven kings, five of whom have fallen, one is, the other has not yet come, and when he comes he must remain only a little while" (Rev. 17:9–10).

Fundamentalists argue that these seven mountains must be the seven hills of ancient Rome. However the Greek word here, *horos*, is usually translated "mountain" in Scripture. Mountains are often symbols of kingdoms in Scripture (cf. Ps. 68:15; Dan. 2:35; Obad. 0 21, Amos 4.1, 6.1), which might be why the seven heads also symbolize seven kings. The mountains could stand for a series of seven kings, five of whom have already fallen.

This passage gives us a key rule of Bible interpretation that is often denied by Fundamentalists: A symbol does not have to refer to one and only one thing. Here Scripture itself tells us that the heads refer to *both* seven mountains *and* seven kings, meaning the symbol has multiple fulfillments. Thus there is not a one-to-one correspondence in the Bible between symbols and their referents.

Also, the mountains could be a reference to pagan Rome, yet the Whore could still be a reference to apostate Jerusalem. In this case, her sitting on the beast would not indicate a geographical location but an alliance between the two powers. The Whore (Jerusalem) would be allied with the beast (Rome) in persecuting "the saints and . . . martyrs of Jesus." (Note that the Whore also sits on many waters, which, we are told, are many peoples [cf. 17:15]. The context makes it clear that here her "sitting" on something does not refer to a geographical location.)

This passage gives us one reason that the Catholic Church cannot be the Whore. We are told that the heads "are also seven kings, five of whom have fallen, one is, the other has not yet come." If five of these kings had fallen in John's day and one of them was still in existence, then the Whore must have existed in John's day. Yet Christian Rome and Vatican City did not. However, pagan Rome *did* have a line of emperors, and the majority of commentators see this as the line of kings to which 17:10 refers. Five of these emperors are referred to as having already fallen, one as still reigning in John's time, and another yet to come. Since Jerusalem had no such line of kings in the first century, this gives us evidence that the beast (though not the Whore) is Rome.

The Ten Horns

The angel also interprets for John the meaning of the beast's ten horns: "And the ten horns that you saw are ten kings who have not yet received royal power, but they are to receive authority as kings for one hour, together with the beast. These are of one mind and give over their power and authority to the beast; they will make war on the Lamb, and the Lamb will conquer them, for he is Lord of lords and King of kings, and those with him are called and chosen and faithful" (17:12–14).

This shows us that the beast is allied with ten lower rulers and their own territories. Some Fundamentalists bent on making this apply to modern times and the Catholic Church have argued that the horns refer to the European Union and a revived Roman empire with the Catholic Church at its head. The problem is that there are *ten* kings, but there are now many *more than ten* nations in the European Union.

However, what we are told about the horns does fit one of the other candidates we have for the Whore—apostate Jerusalem. The angel tells John: "And the ten horns that you saw, they and the beast will hate the harlot; they will make her desolate and naked, and devour her flesh and burn her up with fire, for God has put it into their hearts to carry out his purpose by being of one mind and giving over their royal power to the beast, until the words of God shall be fulfilled" (17:16–17).

If the Whore is Jerusalem and the beast is Rome (with the ten horns as vassal states), then the prophecy makes perfect sense. The alliance between the two in persecuting Christians broke down in A.D. 66–70, when Rome and its allied forces conquered Israel and then destroyed, sacked, and burned Jerusalem, just as Jesus prophesied (Luke 21:5–24).

The Whore's Authority

Finally the angel tells John: "And the woman that you saw is the great city which has dominion over the kings of the earth" (17:18). This again points to pagan Rome or apostate Jerusalem. In the case of the former, the dominion would be political; in the case of the latter, it could be a number of things. It could be spiritual dominion in that Jerusalem held the religion of the true God. It could be a reference to the manipulation by certain Jews and Jewish leaders of gentiles into persecuting Christians.

It could even be political, since Jerusalem was the center of political power in Canaan and, under the authority of the Romans, it ruled a considerable amount of territory and less powerful peoples. On this thesis, "the kings of the earth" would be "the kings of the *land*" (the Greek phrase can be translated either way). Such local rulers of the land of Canaan would naturally resent Jerusalem and wish to cooperate with the Romans in its destruction—just as history records they did. Local non-Jewish peoples were used by the Romans in the capture of Jerusalem.

The Hub of World Commerce

Continuing in chapter 18, John sees the destruction of the Whore, and a number of facts are revealed that also show that she cannot be the Catholic Church. For one, she is depicted as a major center of international trade and commerce. When it is destroyed in chapter 18, we read that "the merchants of the earth [or land] weep and mourn for her, since no one buys their cargo any more" (18:11) and "all shipmasters and seafaring men, sailors and all whose trade is on the sea . . . wept and mourned, crying out, 'Alas, alas, for the great city where all who had ships at sea grew rich by her wealth!' " (18:17–19).

Pagan Rome was indeed the hub of world commerce in its day, supported by its maritime trading empire around the Mediterranean, but Christian Rome is *not* the hub of world commerce. After the Reformation, the economic center of power was located in Germany, Holland, England, and more recently, in the United States and Japan.

Persecuting Apostles and Prophets

When the Whore falls we read, " 'Rejoice over her, O heaven! O saints and apostles and prophets, for God has given judgment for you against her!' . . . In her was found the blood of prophets and of saints, and of all who have been slain on earth" (18:20, 24). This shows that the Whore persecuted not just Christians but apostles and prophets. Apostles existed only in the first century, since one of the requirements for being an apostle was seeing the risen Christ (cf. 1 Cor. 9:1). Prophets existed as a group only in the Old Testament and in the first century (cf. Acts 11:27–28; 13:1; 15:32; 21:10).

Since the Whore persecuted apostles and prophets, the Whore must have existed in the first century. This totally demolishes the claim that Christian Rome or Vatican City is the Whore. Rome was not a Christian city at that time, and Vatican City did not even exist, so neither of them could be the Whore. Furthermore, Fundamentalists continually (though wrongly) claim that Catholicism itself did not exist in the first century, meaning that *based on their very own argument* Catholicism could not be the Whore!

Fundamentalists are fond of conjecturing that in the last days there will be a "revived Roman empire," such as the one that persecuted Christians in the first century. Yet they never draw the inference that this empire would be headed by a revived *pagan* Rome, with the bishop of Rome leading the Christian underground, just as he did in the first century.

Still, Revelation 18:20 and 18:24 prove that the Whore had to be a creature of the first century, which, in the Fundamentalist view, the Catholic Church was not. Thus, on their own view, their identification of the Catholic Church with the Whore is completely impossible! Only ancient, pagan Rome or apostate Jerusalem could possibly be the Whore.

If Not the Whore, the Bride

The fact that the Catholic Church is singled out by Fundamentalists as the Whore reveals that they intuit the fact that it has an important role in God's plan. No other church gets accused of being the Whore—only the Catholic Church. And it is understandable why: The Catholic Church is the largest Christian body, larger than all other Christian bodies put together, suggesting a prominent place in God's plan. Fundamentalists assume, without objectively looking at the evidence, that the Catholic Church cannot be the Bride of Christ, so it must be the Whore of Babylon.

Yet the evidence for its true role is plain. The First Vatican Council taught that "the Church itself . . . because of its marvelous propagation, its exceptional holiness, and inexhaustible fruitfulness in all good works; because of its Catholic unity and invincible stability, is a very great and perpetual motive of credibility and an incontestable witness of its own divine mission" (*On the Catholic Faith* 3).

So why is the Bride maligned as the Whore? Jesus himself answered the question: "If they have called the master of the house Beelzebul, how much more will they malign those of his household" (Matt. 10:25). "If the world hates you, know that it has hated me before it hated you. If you were of the world, the world would love its own; but because you are not of the world . . . the world hates you. Remember the word that I said to you, 'A servant is not greater than his master.' If they persecuted me, they will persecute you" (John 15:18 20).

36

Birth Control

In 1968, Pope Paul VI issued his landmark encyclical letter *Humanae Vitae* (Latin: "Human Life"), which reemphasized the Church's constant teaching that it is always intrinsically wrong to use contraception to prevent new human beings from coming into existence.

Contraception is "any action that, either in anticipation of the conjugal act [sexual intercourse], or in its accomplishment, or in the development of its natural consequences, proposes, whether as an end or as a means, to render procreation impossible" (HV 14). This includes sterilization, condoms and other barrier methods, spermicides, *coitus interruptus* (withdrawal method), the pill, and all other such methods.

The Historical Christian Teaching

Few realize that up until 1930, *all* Protestant denominations agreed with the Catholic Church's teaching condemning contraception as sinful. At its 1930 Lambeth Conference, the Anglican church, swayed by growing social pressure, announced that contraception would be allowed in *some* circumstances. Soon the Anglican church completely caved in, allowing contraception across the board. Since then, all other Protestant denominations have followed suit. Today, the Catholic Church alone proclaims the historical Christian position on contraception.

Evidence that contraception is in conflict with God's laws comes from a variety of sources that will be examined in this chapter.

Nature

Contraception is wrong because it is a deliberate violation of the design that God built into the human race, often referred to as "natural law." The natural law purpose of sex is procreation. The pleasure that sexual intercourse provides is an additional blessing from God, intended to offer the possibility of new life while strengthening the bond of intimacy, respect, and love between husband and wife. The loving environment this bond creates is the perfect setting for nurturing children.

But sexual pleasure within marriage becomes unnatural and even harmful to the spouses—when it is used in a way that deliberately excludes the basic purpose of sex, which is procreation. God's gift of the sex act, along with its pleasure and intimacy, must not be abused by deliberately frustrating its natural end: procreation.

Scripture

Is contraception a modern invention? Hardly! Birth control has been around for millennia. Scrolls found in Egypt, dating to 1900 B.C., describe ancient methods of birth control that were later practiced in the Roman Empire during the apostolic age. Wool that absorbed sperm, poisons that fumigated the uterus, potions, and other methods were used to prevent conception. In some centuries, even condoms were used (though made out of animal skin rather than latex).

The Bible mentions at least one form of contraception specifically and condemns it. *Coitus interruptus*, was used by Onan to avoid fulfilling his duty according to the ancient Jewish law of fathering children for one's dead brother. "Then Judah said to Onan, 'Go in to your brother's wife, and perform the duty of a brother-in-law to her, and raise up offspring for your brother.' But Onan knew that the offspring would not be his; so when he went in to his brother's wife he spilled the semen on the ground, lest he should give offspring to his brother. And what he did was displeasing in the sight of the Lord, and he slew him also" (Gen. 38:8–10).

The biblical penalty for not giving your brother's widow children was public humiliation, not death (cf. Deut. 25:7–10). But Onan received death as punishment for his crime. This means that his crime was more than simply not fulfilling the duty of a brother-in-law. He lost his life because he violated natural law, as Jewish and Christian commentators have always understood. For this reason, certain forms of contraception have historically been known as "Onanism," after the man who practiced it, just as homosexuality has historically been known as "sodomy," after the men of Sodom, who practiced that vice (cf. Gen. 19).

Contraception was so far outside the biblical mindset and so obviously wrong that it did not need the frequent condemnations other sins did. Scripture condemns the practice when it mentions it. Once a moral principle has been established in the Bible, every possible application of it need not be mentioned. For example, the general principle that theft is wrong was clearly established in Scripture, but there's no need to provide an exhaustive list of every kind of theft. Similarly, since the principle that contraception is wrong has been established by being condemned when it's mentioned in the Bible, every particular form of contraception does not need to be dealt with in Scripture in order for us to see that it is condemned.

Apostolic Tradition

The biblical teaching that birth control is wrong is found even more explicitly among the Church Fathers, who recognized the biblical and natural law principles underlying the condemnation.

In A.D. 195, Clement of Alexandria wrote, "Because of its divine institution for the propagation of man, the seed is not to be vainly ejaculated, nor is it to be damaged, nor is it to be wasted" (*The Instructor of Children* 2:10:91:2).

Hippolytus of Rome wrote in 255 that "on account of their prominent ancestry and great property, the so-called faithful [certain Christian women who had affairs with male servants] want no children from slaves or lowborn commoners, [so] they use drugs of sterility or bind themselves tightly in order to expel a fetus that has already been engendered" (*Refutation of All Heresies* 9:12).

Around 307, Lactantius explained that some "complain of the scantiness of their means, and allege that they have not enough for bringing up more children, as though, in truth, their means were in [their] power . . . or God did not daily make the rich poor and the poor rich. Wherefore, if any man on any account of poverty shall be unable to bring up children, it is better to abstain from relations with his wife" (*Divine Institutes* 6:20).

The First Council of Nicaea, the first ecumenical council and the one that defined Christ's divinity, declared in 325, "If anyone in sound health has castrated himself, it behooves that such a one, if enrolled among the clergy, should cease [from his ministry], and that from henceforth no such person should be promoted. But, as it is evident that this is said of those who willfully do the thing and presume to castrate themselves, so if any have been made eunuchs by barbarians, or by their masters, and should otherwise be found worthy, such men this canon admits to the clergy" (canon 1).

Augustine wrote in 419, "I am supposing, then, although you are not lying [with your wife] for the sake of procreating offspring, you are not for the sake of lust obstructing their procreation by an evil prayer or an evil deed. Those who do this, although they are called husband and wife, are not; nor do they retain any reality of marriage, but with a respectable name cover a shame. Sometimes this lustful cruelty, or cruel lust, comes to this, that they even procure poisons of sterility [oral contraceptives]" (*Marriage and Concupiscence* 1:15:17).

Apostolic Tradition's condemnation of contraception is so great that it was followed by Protestants until 1930 and was upheld by all key Protestant Reformers. Martin Luther said, "The exceedingly foul deed of Onan, the basest of wretches . . . is a most disgraceful sin. It is far more atrocious than incest and adultery. We call it unchastity, yes, a sodomitic sin. For Onan goes in to her; that is, he lies with her and copulates, and when it comes to the point of insemination, spills the semen, lest the woman conceive. Surely at such a time the order of nature established by God in procreation should be followed. Accordingly, it was a most disgraceful crime. . . . Consequently, he deserved to be killed by God. He committed an evil deed. Therefore, God punished him."

John Calvin said, "The voluntary spilling of semen outside of intercourse between man and woman is a monstrous thing. Deliberately to withdraw from coitus in order that semen may fall on the ground is doubly monstrous. For this is to extinguish the hope of the race and to kill before he is born the hoped-for offspring."

John Wesley warned, "Those sins that dishonor the body are very displeasing to God, and the evidence of vile affections. Observe, the thing that he [Onan] did displeased the Lord—and it is to be feared; thousands, especially of single persons, by this very thing, still displease the Lord, and destroy their own souls." (These passages are quoted in Charles D. Provan, *The Bible and Birth Control*, which contains many quotes from Protestant figures who recognize contraception's evils.)

The Magisterium

The Church also, fulfilling the role given it by Christ as the identifier and interpreter of Scripture and apostolic Tradition, has constantly condemned contraception as gravely sinful.

In *Humanae Vitae*, Pope Paul VI stated, "We must once again declare that the direct interruption of the generative process already begun, and, above all, directly willed and procured abortion, even if for therapeutic reasons, are to be absolutely excluded as licit means of regulating birth. Equally to be excluded, as the teaching authority of the Church has frequently declared, is direct sterilization, whether perpetual or temporary, whether of the man or of the woman. Similarly excluded is every action that, either in anticipation of the conjugal act, or in its accomplishment, or in the development of its natural consequences, proposes, whether as an end or as a means, to render procreation impossible" (HV 14). This was reiterated in the *Catechism of the Catholic Church*: "Legitimate intentions on the part of the spouses do not justify re course to morally unacceptable means (for example, direct sterilization or contraception)" (CCC 2399).

The Church has also affirmed that the illicitness of contraception is an infallible doctrine: "The Church has always taught the intrinsic evil of contraception, that is, of every marital act intentionally rendered unfruitful. This teaching is to be held as definitive and irreformable. Contraception is gravely opposed to marital chastity, it is contrary to the good of the transmission of life (the procreative aspect of matrimony), and to the reciprocal self-giving of the spouses (the unitive aspect of matrimony); it harms true love and denies the sovereign role of God in the transmission of human life" (*Vademecum for Confessors* 2:4).

Human Experience

Pope Paul VI predicted grave consequences that would arise from the widespread and unrestrained use of contraception. He warned, "Upright men can even better convince themselves of the solid grounds on which the teaching of the Church in this field is based if they care to reflect upon the consequences of methods of artificially limiting the increase of children. Let them consider, first of all, how wide and easy a road would thus be opened up toward conjugal infidelity and the general lowering of morality. Not much experience is needed in order to know human weakness, and to understand that men—especially the young, who are so vulnerable on this point—have need of encouragement to be faithful to the moral law, so that they must not be offered some easy means of eluding its observance. It is also to be feared that the man, growing used to the employment of anti-conceptive practices, may finally lose respect for the woman and, no longer caring for her physical and psychological equilibrium, may come to the point of considering her as a mere instrument of selfish enjoyment, and no longer as his respected and beloved companion" (HV 17). No one can doubt the fulfillment of these prophetic words. They have all been more than fulfilled in this country as a result of the widespread availability of contraceptives, the "free love" movement that started in the 1960s, and the loose sexual morality that it spawned and that continues to pervade Western culture.

Indeed, recent studies reveal a far greater divorce rate in marriages in which contraception is regularly practiced than in those marriages in which it is not. Experience, natural law, Scripture, Tradition, and the magisterium all testify to the moral evil of contraception.

Wishful Thinking

Ignoring the mountain of evidence, some maintain that the Church considers the use of contraception a matter for each married couple to decide according to their "individual conscience." Yet nothing could be further from the truth. The Church has always maintained the historical Christian teaching that deliberate acts of contraception are always gravely sinful, which means that it is mortally sinful if done with full knowledge and deliberate consent (cf. CCC 1857). This teaching cannot be changed and has been infallibly taught by the Church.

There is no way to deny the fact that the Church has always and everywhere condemned contraception. The matter has already been infallibly decided. The so-called "individual conscience" argument amounts to "individual disobedience."

37

Homosexuality

Every human being is called to receive a gift of divine sonship, to become a child of God by grace. However, to receive this gift, we must reject sin, including homosexual behavior—that is, acts intended to arouse or stimulate a sexual response regarding a person of the same sex. The Catholic Church teaches that such acts are always violations of divine and natural law.

Homosexual desires, however, are not in themselves sinful. People are subject to a wide variety of sinful desires over which they have little direct control, but these do not become sinful until a person acts upon them, by either *acting out* the desire or *encouraging* the desire and deliberately engaging in fantasies about acting it out. People tempted by homosexual desires, like people tempted by improper heterosexual desires, are not sinning until they act upon those desires in some manner.

Divine Law

The rejection of homosexual behavior that is found in the Old Testament is well known. In Genesis 19, two angels in disguise visit the city of Sodom and are offered hospitality and shelter by Lot. During the night, the men of Sodom demand that Lot hand over his guests for homosexual intercourse. Lot refuses, and the angels blind the men of Sodom. Lot and his household escape, and the town is destroyed by fire "because the outcry against its people has become great before the Lord" (Gen. 19:13).

Throughout history, Jewish and Christian scholars have recognized that one of the chief sins involved in God's destruction of Sodom was its people's homosexual behavior. But today, certain homosexual activists promote the idea that the sin of Sodom was merely a lack of hospitality. Although inhospitality is a sin, it is clearly the homosexual behavior of the Sodomites that is singled out for special criticism in the account of their city's destruction. We must look to Scripture's own interpretation of the sin of Sodom.

Jude 7 records that Sodom and Gomorrah "acted immorally and indulged in unnatural lust." Ezekiel says that Sodom committed "abominable things" (Ezek. 16:50), which could refer to homosexual and heterosexual acts of sin. Lot even offered his two virgin daughters in place of his guests, but the men of Sodom rejected the offer, preferring homosexual sex over heterosexual sex (Gen. 19:8–9). Ezekiel does allude to a lack of hospitality in saying that Sodom "did not aid the poor and needy" (Ezek. 16:49). So homosexual acts and a lack of hospitality both contributed to the destruction of Sodom, with the former being the far greater sin, the "abominable thing" that set off God's wrath.

But the Sodom incident is not the only time the Old Testament deals with homosexuality. An explicit condemnation is found in the book of Leviticus: "You shall not lie with a male as with a woman; it is an abomination. . . . If a man lies with a male as with a woman, both of them have committed an abomination; they shall be put to death, their blood is upon them" (Lev. 18:22; 20:13).

Reinterpreting Scripture

To discount this, some homosexual activists have argued that moral imperatives from the Old Testament can be dismissed since there were certain ceremonial requirements at the time—such as not eating pork, or circumcising male babies—that are no longer binding.

While the Old Testament's *ceremonial* requirements are no longer binding, its *moral* requirements are. God may issue different ceremonies for use in different times and cultures, but his moral requirements are eternal and are binding on all cultures.

Confirming this fact is the New Testament's forceful rejection of homosexual behavior as well. In Romans 1, Paul attributes the homosexual desires of some to a refusal to acknowledge and worship God. He says, "For this reason God gave them up to dishonorable passions. Their women exchanged natural relations for unnatural, and the men likewise gave up natural relations with women and were consumed with passion for one another, men committing shameless acts with men and receiving in their own persons the due penalty for their error. And since they did not see fit to acknowledge God, God gave them up to a base mind and to improper conduct. . . . Though they know God's decree that those who do such things deserve to die, they not only do them but approve those who practice them" (Rom. 1:26-28, 32).

Elsewhere Paul again warns that homosexual behavior is one of the sins that will deprive one of heaven: "Do you not know that the wicked will not inherit the kingdom of God? Do not be deceived: Neither the sexually immoral nor idolaters nor adulterers nor male prostitutes nor homosexual offenders nor thieves nor the greedy nor drunkards nor slanderers nor swindlers will inherit the kingdom of God" (1 Cor. 6:9-10, NIV).

All of Scripture teaches the unacceptability of homosexual behavior. But the rejection of this behavior is not an arbitrary prohibition. It, like other moral imperatives, is rooted in natural law —the design that God has built into human nature.

Natural Law

People have a basic, ethical intuition that certain behaviors are wrong because they are unnatural. We perceive intuitively that the natural sex partner of a human is another human, not an animal.

The same reasoning applies to the case of homosexual behavior. The natural sex partner for a man is a woman, and the natural sex partner for a woman is a man. Thus, people have the corresponding intuition concerning homosexuality that they do about bestiality—that it is wrong because it is unnatural.

Natural law reasoning is the basis for almost all standard moral intuitions. For example, it is the dignity and value that each human being naturally possesses that makes the needless destruction of human life or infliction of physical and emotional pain immoral. This gives rise to a host of specific moral principles, such as the unacceptability of murder, kidnapping, mutilation, physical and emotional abuse, and so forth.

"I Was Born this Way"

Many homosexuals argue that they have not chosen their condition but were born that way, making homosexual behavior natural for them.

But because something was not chosen does not mean it was inborn. Some desires are acquired or strengthened by habituation and conditioning instead of by conscious choice. For example, no one chooses to be an alcoholic, but one can become habituated to alcohol. Just as one can acquire alcoholic desires (by repeatedly becoming intoxicated) without consciously choosing them, so one may acquire homosexual desires (by engaging in homosexual fantasies or behavior) without consciously choosing them.

Since sexual desire is subject to a high degree of cognitive conditioning in humans (there is no biological reason we find certain scents, forms of dress, or forms of underwear sexually stimulating), it would be most unusual if homosexual desires were not subject to a similar degree of cognitive conditioning.

Even if there is a genetic predisposition toward homosexuality (and studies on this point are inconclusive), the behavior remains unnatural because homosexuality is still not part of the natural design of humanity. It does not make homosexual behavior acceptable; other behaviors are not rendered acceptable simply because there may be a genetic predisposition toward them.

For example, scientific studies suggest some people are born with a hereditary disposition to alcoholism, but no one would argue someone ought to fulfill these inborn urges by becoming an alcoholic. Alcoholism is not an acceptable "lifestyle" any more than homosexuality is.

The 10 Percent Argument

Homosexual activists often justify homosexuality by claiming that 10 percent of the population is homosexual, meaning that it is a common and thus acceptable behavior.

But not all common behaviors are acceptable, and even if 10 percent of the population were born homosexual, this would prove nothing. One hundred percent of the population is born with original sin and the desires flowing from it. If those desires manifest themselves in a homosexual fashion in 10 percent of the population, all that does is give us information about the demographics of original sin.

But the fact is that the 10 percent figure is false. It stems from the 1948 report by Alfred Kinsey, *Sexual Behavior in the Human Male*. The study was profoundly flawed, as later psychologists studying sexual behavior have agreed. Kinsey's subjects were drawn heavily from convicted criminals; 1,400 of his 5,300 final subjects (26 percent) were convicted sex offenders—a group that by definition is not representative of normal sexual practices.

Furthermore, the 10 percent figure includes people who are not exclusively homosexual but engaged in *some* homosexual behavior for a period of time and then stopped—people who had gone through a fully or partially homosexual "phase" but were not long-term homosexuals. (For a critique of Kinsey's research methods, see *Kinsey, Sex, and Fraud* by Judith Reisman and Edward Eichel [Lafayette, Louisiana: Lochinvar & Huntington House, 1990].)

Recent and more scientifically accurate studies have shown that only around 1 to 2 percent of the population is homosexual.

"You're Just a Homophobe"

Those opposed to homosexual behavior are often charged with "homophobia"—that they hold the position they do because they are "afraid" of homosexuals. Sometimes the charge is even made that these same people are perhaps homosexuals themselves and are overcompensating to hide this fact, even from themselves, by condemning other homosexuals.

Both of these arguments attempt to stop rational discussion of an issue by shifting the focus to one of the participants. In doing so, they dismiss another person's arguments based on some real or supposed attribute of the person. In this case, the supposed attribute is a fear of homosexuals.

Like similar attempts to avoid rational discussion of an issue, the homophobia argument completely misses the point. Even if a person were afraid of homosexuals, that would not diminish his arguments against their behavior. The fact that a person is afraid of handguns would not nullify arguments against handguns, nor would the fact that a person might be afraid of handgun control diminish arguments against handgun control.

Furthermore, the homophobia charge rings false. The vast majority of those who oppose homosexual behavior are in no way "afraid" of homosexuals. A disagreement is not the same as a fear. One can disagree with something without fearing it, and the attempt to shut down rational discussion by crying "homophobe!" falls flat. It is an attempt to divert attention from the arguments against one's position by focusing attention on the one who made the arguments while trying to claim the moral high ground against him.

The Call to Chastity

The modern arguments in favor of homosexuality have thus been insufficient to overcome the evidence that homosexual behavior is against divine and natural law, as the Bible and the Church, as well as the wider circle of Jewish and Christian (not to mention Muslim) writers, have always held.

The Catholic Church thus teaches, "Basing itself on Sacred Scripture, which presents homosexual acts as acts of grave depravity, tradition has always declared that homosexual acts are intrinsically disordered. They are contrary to the natural law. They close the sexual act to the gift of life. They do not proceed from a genuine affective and sexual complementarity. Under no circumstances can they be approved" (*Catechism of the Catholic Church* 2357).

However, the Church also acknowledges that homosexuality's "psychological genesis remains largely unexplained. . . . The number of men and women who have deep-seated homosexual tendencies is not negligible. This inclination, which is objectively disordered, constitutes for most of them a trial. They must be accepted with respect, compassion, and sensitivity. Every sign of unjust discrimination in their regard should be avoided. These persons are called to fulfill God's will in their lives and, if they are Christians, to unite to the sacrifice of the Lord's cross the difficulties that they may encounter from their condition.

"Homosexual persons are called to chastity. By the virtues of self-mastery that teach them inner freedom, at times by the support of disinterested friendship, by prayer and sacramental grace, they can and should gradually and resolutely approach Christian perfection" (CCC 2357–2359).

Paul comfortingly reminds us, "No temptation has overtaken you that is not common to man. God is faithful, and he will not let you be tempted beyond your strength, but with the temptation will also provide the way of escape, that you may be able to endure it" (1 Cor. 10:13).

Homosexuals who want to live chastely can contact Courage, a national, Church-approved support group for help in deliverance from the homosexual lifestyle:

> Courage
> c/o Church of St. John the Baptist
> 210 West 31st Street
> New York, NY 10001
> (212) 268-1010
> Web: http://couragerc.net

38

Adam, Eve, and Evolution

The controversy surrounding evolution touches on our most central beliefs about ourselves and the world. Evolutionary theories have been used to answer questions about the origins of the universe, life, and man. These may be referred to as cosmological evolution, biological evolution, and human evolution. One's opinion concerning one of these areas does not dictate what one believes concerning others.

People usually take one of three basic positions on the origins of the cosmos, life, and man: (1) *special* or *instantaneous creation*, (2) *developmental creation* or *theistic evolution*, (3) and *atheistic evolution*. The first holds that a given thing did not develop but was instantaneously and directly created by God. The second position holds that a given thing did develop from a previous state or form but that this process was under God's guidance. The third position claims that a thing developed due to random forces *alone*.

Related to the question of *how* the universe, life, and man arose is the question of *when* they arose. Those who attribute the origin of all three to special creation often hold that they arose at about the same time, perhaps 6,000 to 10,000 years ago. Those who attribute all three to atheistic evolution have a much longer time scale. They generally hold the universe to be 10 billion to 20 billion years old, life on earth to be about 4 billion years old, and modern man (the subspecies *homo sapiens*) to be about 30,000 years old. Those who believe in varieties of developmental creation hold dates used by either or both of the other two positions.

The Catholic Position

What is the Catholic position concerning belief or unbelief in evolution? The question may never be finally settled, but there are definite parameters to what is acceptable Catholic belief.

Concerning cosmological evolution, the Church has infallibly defined that the universe was specially created out of nothing. Vatican I solemnly defined that everyone must "confess the world and all things which are contained in it, both spiritual and material, as regards their whole substance, have been produced by God from nothing" (*Canons on God the Creator of All Things*, canon 5).

The Church does not have an official position on whether the stars, nebulae, and planets we see today were created at that time or whether they developed over time (for example, in the aftermath of the Big Bang that modern cosmologists discuss). However, the Church would maintain that, if the stars and planets did develop over time, this must ultimately be attributed to God and his plan, for Scripture records: "By the word of the Lord the heavens were made, and all their host [stars, nebulae, planets] by the breath of his mouth" (Ps. 33:6).

Concerning biological evolution, the Church does not have an official position on whether various life forms developed over the course of time. However, it says that, if they did develop, then they did so under the impetus and guidance of God, and their ultimate creation must be ascribed to him.

Concerning human evolution, the Church has a more definite teaching. It allows for the possibility that man's *body* developed from previous biological forms, under God's guidance, but it insists on the *special creation* of his *soul*. Pope Pius XII declared that "the teaching authority of the Church does not forbid that, in conformity with the present state of human sciences and sacred theology, research and discussions . . . take place with regard to the doctrine of evolution, in as far as it inquires into the origin of the human body as coming from preexistent and living matter— [but] the Catholic faith obliges us to hold that souls are immediately created by God" (*Humani Generis* 36). So whether the human body was specially created or developed, we are required to hold as a matter of Catholic faith that the human soul is specially created; it did not evolve, and it is not inherited from our parents, as our bodies are.

While the Church permits belief in either special creation or developmental creation on certain questions, it in no circumstances permits belief in atheistic evolution.

The Time Question

Much less has been defined as to *when* the universe, life, and man appeared. The Church has infallibly determined that the universe is of finite age—that it has not existed from all eternity—but it has not infallibly defined whether the world was created only a few thousand years ago or several billion years ago.

Catholics should weigh the evidence for the universe's age by examining biblical and scientific evidence. "Though faith is above reason, there can never be any real discrepancy between faith and reason. Since the same God who reveals mysteries and infuses faith has bestowed the light of reason on the human mind, God cannot deny himself, nor can truth ever contradict truth" (*Catechism of the Catholic Church* 159).

The contribution made by the physical sciences to examining these questions is stressed by the *Catechism*, which states, "The question about the origins of the world and of man has been the object of many scientific studies that have splendidly enriched our knowledge of the age and dimensions of the cosmos, the development of life-forms and the appearance of man. These discoveries invite us to even greater admiration for the greatness of the Creator, prompting us to give him thanks for all his works and for the understanding and wisdom he gives to scholars and researchers" (CCC 283).

It is outside the scope of this chapter to look at the scientific evidence, but a few words need to be said about the interpretation of Genesis and its six days of creation. While there are many interpretations of these six days, they can be grouped into two basic methods of reading the account—a *chronological reading* and a *topical reading*.

The Chronological Reading

According to the chronological reading, the six days of creation should be understood to have followed each other in strict chronological order. This view is often coupled with the claim that the six days were standard twenty-four-hour periods.

Some have denied that they were standard days on the basis that the Hebrew word used in this passage for day (*yom*) can sometimes mean a longer-than-twenty-four-hour period (as it does in Genesis 2:4). However, it seems clear that Genesis 1 presents the days to us as standard days. At the end of each one is a formula like "And there was evening and there was morning, one day" (Gen. 1:5). Evening and morning are, of course, the transition points between day and night (this is the meaning of the Hebrew terms here), but periods of time longer than twenty-four hours are not composed of a day and a night. Genesis is presenting these days to us as twenty-four-hour, solar days. If we are not meant to understand them as twenty-four-hour days, it would most likely be because Genesis 1 is not meant to be understood as a literal chronological account.

That is a possibility. Pope Pius XII warned us, "What is the literal sense of a passage is not always as obvious in the speeches and writings of the ancient authors of the East, as it is in the works of our own time. For what they wished to express is not to be determined by the rules of grammar and philology alone, nor solely by the context; the interpreter must, as it were, go back wholly in spirit to those remote centuries of the East and with the aid of history, archaeology, ethnology, and other sciences, accurately determine what modes of writing, so to speak, the authors of that ancient period would be likely to use, and in fact did use. For the ancient peoples of the East, in order to express their ideas, did not always employ those forms or kinds of speech which we use today; but rather those used by the men of their times and countries. What those exactly were the commentator cannot determine as it were in advance, but only after a careful examination of the ancient literature of the East" (*Divino Afflante Spiritu* 35–36).

The Topical Reading

This leads us to the possibility that Genesis 1 is to be given a non-chronological, topical reading. Advocates of this view point out that, in ancient literature, it was common to sequence historical material by topic rather than in strict chronological order.

The argument for a topical ordering notes that at the time the world was created, it had two problems—it was "formless and empty" (1:2). In the first three days of creation, God solves the formlessness problem by structuring different aspects of the environment.

On day one he separates day from night; on day two he separates the waters below (oceans) from the waters above (clouds), with the sky in between; and on day three he separates the waters below from each other, creating dry land. Thus the world has been given form.

But it is still empty, so on the second three days God solves the world's emptiness problem by giving occupants to each of the three realms he ordered on the previous three days. Thus, having solved the problems of formlessness and emptiness, the task he set for himself, God's work is complete and he rests on the seventh day.

Real History

The argument is that all of this is *real* history, it is simply ordered topically rather than chronologically, and the ancient audience of Genesis, it is argued, would have understood it as such.

Even if Genesis 1 records God's work in a topical fashion, it still records his work—things he really did.

The *Catechism* explains that "Scripture presents the work of the Creator symbolically as a succession of six days of divine 'work,' concluded by the 'rest' of the seventh day" (CCC 337), but "nothing exists that does not owe its existence to God the Creator. The world began when God's word drew it out of nothingness; all existent beings, all of nature, and all human history is rooted in this primordial event, the very genesis by which the world was constituted and time begun" (CCC 338).

It is impossible to dismiss the events of Genesis 1 as a mere legend. They are accounts of *real* history, even if they are told in a style of historical writing that Westerners do not typically use.

Adam and Eve: Real People

It is equally impermissible to dismiss the story of Adam and Eve and the fall (Gen. 2–3) as a fiction. A question often raised in this context is whether the human race descended from an original pair of two human beings (a teaching known as monogenism) or a pool of early human couples (a teaching known as polygenism).

In this regard, Pope Pius XII stated: "When, however, there is question of another conjectural opinion, namely polygenism, the children of the Church by no means enjoy such liberty. For the faithful cannot embrace that opinion that maintains either that after Adam there existed on this earth true men who did not take their origin through natural generation from him as from the first parents of all, or that Adam represents a certain number of first parents. Now, it is in no way apparent how such an opinion can be reconciled with that which the sources of revealed truth and the documents of the teaching authority of the Church proposed with regard to original sin, which proceeds from a sin actually committed by an individual Adam in which through generation is passed onto all and is in everyone as his own" (*Humani Generis* 37).

The story of the creation and fall of man is a true one, even if not written entirely according to modern literary techniques. The *Catechism* states, "The account of the fall in Genesis 3 uses figurative language, but affirms a primeval event, a deed that took place at the beginning of the history of man. Revelation gives us the certainty of faith that the whole of human history is marked by the original fault freely committed by our first parents" (CCC 390).

Science and Religion

The Catholic Church has always taught that "no real disagreement can exist between the theologian and the scientist provided each keeps within his own limits. . . . If nevertheless there is a disagreement . . . it should be remembered that the sacred writers, or more truly 'the Spirit of God who spoke through them, did not wish to teach men such truths (as the inner structure of visible objects) which do not help anyone to salvation'; and that, for this reason, rather than trying to provide a scientific exposition of nature, they sometimes describe and treat these matters either in a somewhat figurative language or as the common manner of speech those times required, and indeed still requires nowadays in everyday life, even amongst most learned people" (*Providentissimus Deus* 18).

As the *Catechism* puts it, "Methodical research in all branches of knowledge, provided it is carried out in a truly scientific manner and does not override moral laws, can never conflict with the faith, because the things of the world and the things the of the faith derive from the same God. The humble and persevering investigator of the secrets of nature is being led, as it were, by the hand of God in spite of himself, for it is God, the conserver of all things, who made them what they are" (CCC 159). The Catholic Church has no fear of science or scientific discovery.

39

The Galileo Controversy

It is commonly believed that the Catholic Church persecuted Galileo for abandoning the geocentric (earth-at-the-center) view of the solar system for the heliocentric (sun-at-the-center) view.

The Galileo case, for many anti-Catholics, is thought to prove that the Church abhors science, refuses to abandon outdated teachings, and is not infallible. For Catholics, the episode is often an embarrassment. It shouldn't be.

This chapter provides a brief explanation of what really happened to Galileo.

Anti-Scientific?

The Church is not anti-scientific. It has supported scientific endeavors for centuries. During Galileo's time, the Jesuits had a highly respected group of astronomers and scientists in Rome. In addition, many notable scientists received encouragement and funding from the Church and from individual Church officials. Many of the scientific advances during this period were made either by clerics or as a result of Church funding.

Nicolaus Copernicus dedicated his most famous work, *On the Revolution of the Celestial Orbs*, in which he gave an excellent account of heliocentricity, to Pope Paul III. Copernicus entrusted this work to Andreas Osiander, a Lutheran clergyman who knew that Protestant reaction to it would be negative, since Martin Luther seemed to have condemned the new theory. Osiander wrote a preface to the book, in which heliocentrism was presented only as a theory that would account for the movements of the planets more simply than geocentrism did—something Copernicus did not intend.

Ten years prior to Galileo, Johannes Kepler published a heliocentric work that expanded on Copernicus' work. As a result, Kepler also found opposition among his fellow Protestants for his heliocentric views and found a welcome reception among some Jesuits who were known for their scientific achievements.

Clinging to Tradition?

Anti-Catholics often cite the Galileo case as an example of the Church refusing to abandon outdated or incorrect teaching and clinging to a "tradition." They fail to realize that the judges who presided over Galileo's case were not the only people who held to a geocentric view of the universe. It was the received view among *scientists* at the time.

Centuries earlier, Aristotle had refuted heliocentricity, and by Galileo's time, nearly every major thinker subscribed to a geocentric view. Copernicus refrained from publishing his heliocentric theory for some time, not out of fear of censure from the Church but out of fear of ridicule from his colleagues.

Many people wrongly believe Galileo proved heliocentricity. He could not answer the strongest argument against it, which had been made nearly two thousand years earlier by Aristotle: If heliocentrism were true, then there would be observable parallax shifts in the stars' positions as the earth moved in its orbit around the sun. However, given the technology of Galileo's time, no such shifts in their positions could be observed. It would require more sensitive measuring equipment than was available in Galileo's day to document the existence of these shifts, given the stars' great distance. Until then, the available evidence suggested that the stars were fixed in their positions relative to the earth, and, thus, that the earth and the stars were not moving in space—only the sun, moon, and planets were.

Thus Galileo did not prove the theory by the Aristotelian standards of science in his day. In his *Letter to the Grand Duchess Christina* and other documents, Galileo claimed that the Copernican theory had the "sensible demonstrations" needed according to Aristotelian science, but most knew that such demonstrations were not yet forthcoming. Most astronomers in that day were not convinced of the great distance of the stars that the Copernican theory required to account for the absence of observable parallax shifts. This is one of the main reasons the respected astronomer Tycho Brahe refused to adopt Copernicus fully.

Galileo could have safely proposed heliocentricity as a theory or a method to more simply account for the planets' motions. His problem arose when he stopped proposing it as a scientific theory and began proclaiming it as truth, though there was no conclusive proof of it at the time. Even so, Galileo would not have been in so much trouble if he had chosen to stay within the realm of science and out of the realm of theology. But, despite his friends' warnings, he insisted on moving the debate onto theological grounds.

In 1614, Galileo felt compelled to answer the charge that this "new science" was contrary to certain Scripture passages. His opponents pointed to Bible passages with statements like "And the sun stood still, and the moon stayed" (Josh. 10:13). This is not an isolated occurrence. Psalms 93 and 104 and Ecclesiastes 1:5 also speak of celestial motion and terrestrial stability. A literal reading of these passages would have to be abandoned if the heliocentric theory were adopted. Yet this should not have posed a problem. As Augustine put it, "One does *not* read in the Gospel that the Lord said: 'I will send you the Paraclete who will teach you about the course of the sun and moon.' For he willed to make them Christians, not mathematicians." Following Augustine's example, Galileo urged caution in not interpreting these biblical statements too literally.

Unfortunately, throughout Church history there have been those who insist on reading the Bible in a more literal sense than it was intended. They fail to appreciate, for example, instances in which Scripture uses what is called "phenomenological" language —that is, the language of appearances. Just as we today speak of the sun rising and setting to cause day and night, rather than the earth turning, so did the ancients. From an earthbound perspective, the sun does *appear* to rise and set, and the earth *appears* to be immobile. When we describe these things according to their appearances, we are using phenomenological language.

The phenomenological language concerning the motion of the heavens and the non-motion of the earth is obvious to us today but was less so in previous centuries. Scripture scholars of the past were willing to consider whether particular statements were to be taken literally or phenomenologically, but they did not like being *told* by a non-Scripture scholar, such as Galileo, that the words of the sacred page *must* be taken in a particular sense.

During this period, personal interpretation of Scripture was a sensitive subject. In the early 1600s, the Church had just been through the Reformation experience, and one of the chief quarrels with Protestants was over individual interpretation of the Bible.

Theologians were not prepared to entertain the heliocentric theory based on a layman's interpretation. Yet Galileo insisted on moving the debate into a theological realm. There is little question that if Galileo had kept the discussion within the accepted boundaries of astronomy (i.e., predicting planetary motions) and had not claimed physical truth for the heliocentric theory, the issue would not have escalated to the point it did. After all, he had not proved the new theory beyond reasonable doubt.

Galileo "Confronts" Rome

Galileo came to Rome to see Pope Paul V (1605–1621). The Pope, weary of controversy, turned the matter over to the Holy Office, which issued a condemnation of Galileo's theory in 1616. Things returned to relative quiet for a time, until Galileo forced another showdown.

At Galileo's request, Robert Cardinal Bellarmine, a Jesuit—one of the most important Catholic theologians of the day—issued a certificate that, although it forbade Galileo to hold or defend the heliocentric theory, did not prevent him from conjecturing it. When Galileo met with the new Pope, Urban VIII, in 1623, he received permission from his longtime friend to write a work on heliocentrism, but the new pontiff cautioned him to not advocate the new position but only present arguments for and against it. When Galileo wrote the *Dialogue on the Two World Systems*, he used an argument the Pope had offered and placed it in the mouth of his character Simplicio. Galileo, perhaps inadvertently, made fun of the Pope, a result that could have only disastrous consequences. Urban felt mocked and could not believe how his friend could disgrace him publicly. Galileo had mocked the very person he needed as a benefactor. He also alienated his long-time supporters, the Jesuits, with attacks on one of their astronomers. The result was the infamous trial, which is still heralded as the final separation of science and religion.

Tortured for His Beliefs?

In the end, Galileo recanted his heliocentric teachings, but it was not—as is commonly supposed—under torture nor after a harsh imprisonment. Galileo was, in fact, treated surprisingly well.

As historian Giorgio de Santillana (who is not overly fond of the Catholic Church) noted, "We must, if anything, admire the cautiousness and legal scruples of the Roman authorities." Galileo was offered every convenience possible to make his imprisonment in his home bearable.

Galileo's friend Nicolini, Tuscan ambassador to the Vatican, sent regular reports to the court regarding affairs in Rome. Many of his letters dealt with the ongoing controversy surrounding Galileo.

Nicolini revealed the circumstances surrounding Galileo's "imprisonment" when he reported to the Tuscan king: "The Pope told me that he had shown Galileo a favor never accorded to another" (Feb. 13, 1633); "he has a servant and every convenience" (April 16); and "in regard to the person of Galileo, he ought to be imprisoned for some time because he disobeyed the orders of 1616, but the Pope says that after the publication of the sentence he will consider with me as to what can be done to afflict him as little as possible" (June 18).

Had Galileo been tortured, Nicolini would have reported it to his king. While instruments of torture may have been present during Galileo's recantation (this was the custom of the legal system in Europe at that time), they definitely were not used. The records demonstrate that Galileo could not be tortured because of regulations laid down in the *Directory for Inquisitors* (Nicholas Eymeric, 1595). This was the official guide of the Holy Office, the Church office charged with dealing with such matters, and was followed to the letter.

As noted scientist and philosopher Alfred North Whitehead remarked, in an age that saw a large number of "witches" subjected to torture and execution by Protestants in New England, "the worst that happened to the men of science was that Galileo suffered an honorable detention and a mild reproof." Even so, the Catholic Church today acknowledges that Galileo's condemnation was wrong. The Vatican has even issued two stamps of Galileo as an expression of regret for his mistreatment.

Infallibility

Although three of the ten cardinals who judged Galileo refused to sign the verdict, his works were eventually condemned. Anti-Catholics often assert that his conviction and later rehabilitation somehow disproves the doctrine of papal infallibility, but this is not the case, for the Pope never *tried* to make an infallible ruling concerning Galileo's views.

The Church has never claimed ordinary tribunals, such as the one that judged Galileo, to be infallible. Church tribunals have disciplinary and juridical authority only; neither they nor their decisions are infallible.

No ecumenical council met concerning Galileo, and the Pope was not at the center of the discussions, which were handled by the Holy Office. When the Holy Office finished its work, Urban VIII ratified its verdict but did not attempt to engage infallibility.

Three conditions must be met for a pope to exercise the charism of infallibility: (1) he must speak in his official capacity as the successor of Peter; (2) he must speak on a matter of faith or morals; *and* (3) he must solemnly define the doctrine as one that must be held by all the faithful.

In Galileo's case, the second and third conditions were not present, and possibly not even the first. Catholic theology has never claimed that a mere papal ratification of a tribunal decree is an exercise of infallibility. It is a straw-man argument to represent the Catholic Church as having infallibly defined a scientific theory that turned out to be false. The strongest claim that can be made is that the Church of Galileo's day issued a non-infallible disciplinary ruling concerning a scientist who was advocating a new and still-unproved theory and demanding that the Church change its understanding of Scripture to fit his.

It is a good thing that the Church did not rush to embrace Galileo's views, because it turned out that his ideas were not entirely correct. Galileo believed that the sun was not just the fixed center of the solar system but the fixed center of the universe. We now know that the sun is not the center of the universe and that it *does* move—it simply orbits the center of the galaxy rather than the earth.

As more recent science has shown, both Galileo *and* his opponents were partly right and partly wrong. Galileo was right in asserting the mobility of the earth and wrong in asserting the immobility of the sun. His opponents were right in asserting the mobility of the sun and wrong in asserting the immobility of the earth.

Had the Catholic Church rushed to endorse Galileo's views—and there were many in the Church who were quite favorable to them—the Church would have embraced what modern science has disproved.

40

The Anti-Catholic Bible

Not so long ago people were saying that anti-Catholicism was going the way of the dinosaur. If so, it looks like the dinosaur has made an unexpected comeback, because anti-Catholicism is healthier and more widespread now than it has been for years. Since the late 1970s several new anti-Catholic organizations have been founded, and some older ones have been revitalized. A partial lineup includes Chick Publications, Mission to Catholics International, Lumen Productions, Research and Education Foundation, Osterhus Publishing House, Christians United for Reformation (CURE), Harvest House, and Bob Jones University Press. Combined they turn out more anti-Catholic tracts, magazines, and books than ever before—*millions* of copies each year.

When one reads enough of this material, one becomes aware that the same points tend to be made by different writers in the same way, even in the same words. Who is borrowing from whom? It doesn't seem that any of these groups relies very heavily on any other. Instead, they all fall back on one source, Loraine Boettner's work *Roman Catholicism*, a book first published in 1962 by Presbyterian and Reformed Publishing Company of Philadelphia and reprinted many times since.

This book is the origin of much of what professional anti-Catholics distribute. It can be called, to use a phrase that might rankle some, the "Bible" of the anti-Catholic movement.

At first glance *Roman Catholicism* seems impressive. Its 460 large pages of text are closely packed with quotations. The table of contents is broken down into dozens of categories, and the indices, though skimpy, are at least there. But a careful reading makes it clear that the author's antagonism to the Catholic Church has gravely compromised his intellectual objectivity.

He Swallows Them Whole

The book suffers from a serious lack of scholarly rigor. Boettner accepts at face value virtually any claim made by an opponent of the Church. Even when verification of a charge is easy, he does not bother to check it out. If he finds something unflattering to Catholicism, he prints it.

When the topic is the infallibility of the pope, Boettner quotes at length from a speech alleged to have been given in 1870 at the First Vatican Council, where papal infallibility was formally defined. The speech, attributed to "the scholarly archbishop [*sic*, bishop] Strossmeyer," claims that the "archbishop" read the New Testament for the first time shortly before he gave the speech and found no mention at all of the papacy. The speech then concludes that Peter was given no greater authority than the other apostles. The trouble is that the speech is a well-known forgery. Bishop Strossmeyer did not make that speech, and, in fact, when it was being circulated by a disgruntled former Catholic, the bishop repeatedly and publicly denied that it was his and demanded a retraction by the guilty party. A glance at the *Catholic Encyclopedia* or a work like Newman Eberhardt's *A Summary of Catholic History* would have clued in Boettner.

This gross error has been repeated by many of the anti-Catholic groups that rely on Boettner. None of them, apparently, became suspicious, though the speech reads as though it came from a stereotypical "Bible thumping" Protestant rather than a "scholarly" Catholic bishop.

Sometimes Boettner's mistakes are just juvenile. He calls All Souls' Day (November 2) "Purgatory Day," a term never used by Catholics because the feast is not in commemoration of purgatory but of the souls there.

He argues that the book of Tobit cannot be an inspired book of the Bible because its "stories are fantastic and incredible," and it includes an account of appearances of an angel disguised as a man. Boettner does not seem to realize that such an argument could be used against, say, the book of Jonah or Genesis. Is living in the belly of a great fish any more incredible than meeting an angel in disguise? And then there's the more basic problem that other books in Scripture—books Boettner and all Protestants accept as inspired—also contain references to angels appearing disguised as ꞁꞁꞁ ꞁꞁ (ꞁ ꞁꞁ , ꞁꞁ ꞁꞁ ꞁꞁꞁ, ꞁꞁ ꞁꞁ ꞁ ꞁ ꞁ)

When he writes about the definition of papal infallibility, Boettner says that a pope speaks infallibly only "when he is speaking *ex cathedra*, that is, seated in the papal chair." He then points out that what is venerated as Peter's chair in St. Peter's Basilica may be only a thousand years old, implying that since Peter's actual chair is not present, there is no place for the pope to sit, and thus, by the Church's own principles, the pope cannot make any infallible pronouncements.

Boettner entirely misunderstands the meaning of the Latin term *ex cathedra*. It does translate as "from the chair," but it does not mean that the pope has to be sitting in the literal chair Peter owned for his decree to be infallible and qualify as an *ex cathedra* pronouncement. To speak "from the chair of Peter" is what the pope does when he speaks with the fullness of his authority as the successor of Peter. It is a metaphor that refers to the pope's authority to teach, not where he sits when he teaches.

Notice, too, that the term *ex cathedra*, as a reference to teaching authority, was not invented by the Catholic Church. Jesus used it. In Matthew 23:2–3 Jesus said, "The scribes and the Pharisees sit on Moses' *seat* (Greek: *kathedras*, Latin: *cathedra*); so practice and observe whatever they tell you, but not what they do; for they preach, but do not practice." Even though these rabbis did not live according to the norms they taught, Jesus points out that they did have authority to teach and make rules binding on the Jewish community.

Where Did You Get That?

Boettner's *Roman Catholicism* contains a mere two dozen footnotes, all of them added to recent reprintings to reflect minor changes in the Catholic Church since the Second Vatican Council. Within the text, biblical passages are properly cited, but references to Catholic works are so vague as to discourage checking by making it difficult or impossible to locate the work or the reference. Many times there is no reference. A certain pope will be alleged to have said something, but there is no citation given to support the claim. A Catholic author of the seventeenth century is alleged to have claimed something, but again there is no reference that can be checked. Sometimes there may be mention of a Catholic book, but no page number or publication information given.

By contrast, when non-Catholic authors are cited, the reference usually includes title and page number. One suspects that Boettner took his alleged Catholic quotations and citations from Protestant works and then deliberately failed to reference them in order to conceal the extent to which he is dependent on secondary sources. This is a common tactic among writers who have not done primary source research and rely on secondary sources.

What is even worse, Boettner seems to have no appreciation of the Catholic Church from the inside. He seems to have made little effort to learn what the Catholic Church says about itself or how Catholics answer the objections he makes. His "inside information" comes from disaffected ex-priests such as Emmett McLoughlin and L. H. Lehmann or outright crackpots like the nineteenth-century sensationalist Charles Chiniquy.

The bibliography lists more books by ex-Catholics with grudges than by Catholics. Of the mere seven books he cites written by Catholics, one is an inspirational text (by Archbishop Fulton Sheen), one concerns Catholic principles of politics (a topic hardly touched on by Boettner), three are overviews of the Catholic faith written for laymen (one dates from 1876), and the last is a one-volume abridgment of Philip Hughes's three-volume work *A History of the Church*, from which Boettner takes a few lines (out of context) because, in isolation, they look compromising. These books are all fine in themselves, but they refer to only a fraction of the topics Boettner writes about, and none of them were written as a response to Protestant arguments. On most issues he provides only a statement of the Fundamentalist position, which he contrasts to a caricature of the Catholic position as set out by one of the ex-priests he cites.

It may be that a man leaving one religion for another can write fairly, without bitterness, about the one he left behind. John Henry Newman did so in his autobiography, *Apologia Pro Vita Sua*. But some people have an urge to write about their change of beliefs to vent their frustrations or justify their actions. Their books should be read and used with discretion, and if they show signs of rancor or bitterness, they shouldn't be regarded as trustworthy, unbiased explanations of the religion they abandoned. Alas, Boettner can't keep away from such books. He even uses works by the notorious anti-Catholic writer Paul Blanshard, whose writings were so contorted they were disavowed in the 1950s by other anti-Catholics.

Do Your Homework First

When writing about his own faith, Boettner remarks that the Evangelical or Fundamentalist position "came down through the ante-Nicene Fathers and Augustine," which suggests that he accepts as in some way authoritative Christian writings prior to 430, the year of Augustine's death. But Boettner shows virtually no familiarity with the patristic writings of the first several centuries of the Christian era. His book includes only six references to Augustine and nine to Augustine's contemporary, Jerome. There is one mention of Pope Gelasius I, who lived a century later, and the next oldest writers cited are from the Middle Ages.

Boettner could have examined *Patrology*, Johannes Quasten's four-volume work on the writings of the early Church, composed in the decade before *Roman Catholicism* was written; or Joseph Tixeront's *History of Dogmas*, an older but standard Catholic work on historical theology. Even a casual reading of these works would have demonstrated to him that from the earliest years distinctive Catholic doctrines were held and taught by the Church—belief in the Real Presence of Christ in the Eucharist; baptismal regeneration; a hierarchy of bishops, priests, and deacons; the Mass as a sacrifice; the special authority of the bishop of Rome; prayers for the dead—and he would have seen that the contrary Fundamentalist positions he espouses are not supported. He thinks he knows what Augustine and the other Fathers wrote, but he gives no impression that he is at all familiar with their writings.

In the chapter on Mary he claims, "The phrase 'Mother of God' originated in the Council of Ephesus, in the year 431." Boettner makes a score of blunders here. Does he expect his readers to believe that the phrase "Mother of God" was never used until the day it became a dogma? He presupposes that his readers trust him with a blind obedience, never bothering to do the homework that he failed to do.

By suggesting that a doctrine is not taught until it is infallibly defined, one could equally argue that no one believed that Jesus was God until the Council of Nicaea defined the matter in 325. The divinity of Christ was taught centuries before Nicaea, just as the phrase "Mother of God" permeated the writings of the Church Fathers long before Ephesus. Hippolytus, Clement of Alexandria, Cyril of Jerusalem, Athanasius, Ambrose, Jerome, and numerous others took for granted that Mary could rightly be given this title. Boettner curiously omits reference to these, as they would decimate his argument.

In his introduction, Boettner boasts: "Let Protestants challenge Rome to full and open debate regarding the distinctive doctrines that separate the two systems, and it will be seen that the one thing Rome does not want is public discussion." The curious thing is that many of the anti-Catholic groups that rely so heavily on Boettner are unwilling to engage in public debates.

Many representatives of such groups will give talks at Fundamentalist churches to stoke the fires of anti-Catholicism, and those in the audience will be sent to stand outside Catholic churches and distribute tracts. But challenge any to a debate and what happens? The people with the tracts will say they have to check with their pastors. Besides, they say, they aren't professional debaters and don't want to be set up. Their pastors refuse to sanction any public forums because they say they "don't see the need," or they worry about heat from their congregations for consorting with papists. Is this the "full and open debate" Boettner calls for?

Many Protestants—whether or not they realize how inaccurate and unscholarly Boettner's work is—look to *Roman Catholicism* for their arguments against the Catholic Church. Catholics should prepare themselves for discussions with Protestants by studying Scripture and Church history and by reading solid books on apologetics. That way they will be prepared to heed Peter's exhortation: "Always be prepared to make a defense to any one who calls you to account for the hope that is in you, yet do it with gentleness and reverence" (1 Pet. 3:15).

41

Anti-Catholic Whoppers

It is said that if a lie is repeated often enough and loudly enough, people will come to believe it. That isn't necessarily so.

A real whopper may never be fully believed by anyone, no matter how often or loudly it is proclaimed. But for a whopper to be effective, it does not need to be believed in every detail. It is enough that it leaves behind a bad impression. People will think that if anyone bothers to promote such a lie, there must be a kernel of truth in it.

The same goes for exaggeration and false implications. Distort the truth and people will think it has some basis in fact. Take a truth and phrase it in such a way that it looks suspicious, or juxtapose it with an acknowledged evil, and the mind will be tempted to draw all sorts of ill-founded conclusions.

The following are three examples of the whoppers, exaggerations, and false implications found in the writings of professional anti-Catholics. These are not isolated slips of the pen. They are the kinds of things that fill tracts to overflowing, and they demonstrate that anti-Catholic writers often use dishonest reporting to advance their cause.

The Joke's on Jones

Not long after Pope Paul VI died in 1978, Bob Jones, chancellor of Bob Jones University in Greenville, South Carolina, wrote an ill-tempered article in his school's magazine, *Faith for the Family* (not to be confused with Dr. James Dobson's magazine, *Focus on the Family*). The article was republished by the Fundamentalist organization Mission to Catholics, International (run by an ex-

Carmelite priest-turned-Fundamentalist minister) as a tract entitled *The Church of Rome in Perspective.*

No effort is made to be conciliatory, as the first line demonstrates: "Pope Paul VI, archpriest of Satan, a deceiver and an anti-
Christ, has, like Judas, gone to his own place." It goes downhill
from there. At one point, Jones attempts to raise the level of discussion, if only momentarily, by citing a diary kept by Bernard
Berenson, the famous art collector and critic (who was, by the
way, an Episcopalian). Here is what Jones says:

"A pope must be an opportunist, a tyrant, a hypocrite, and a
deceiver or he cannot be a pope. Bernard Berenson, in his *Rumor
and Reflection* (a sort of notebook which he kept while hiding from
the Germans in the hills above Florence during the Second World
War), tells about the death of an early twentieth-century pope as
described by his personal physician. When they came to give him
the last rites, the pope ordered the priest and acolytes from the
room, crying, 'Get out of here. The comedy is over.'"

The implication is that some unidentified pope, knowing his
end was at hand, acknowledged that his office and religion were
jokes and that he had lived a lie. That would be a damning indict-
ment if true—but was it? Compare what Jones gives with what
Berenson actually wrote. This is the entire entry for May 5, 1941,
and it is found on page 43 of *Rumor and Reflection*, which was published by Simon and Schuster in 1952:

"Yesterday a friend was here, a Roman of good family, closely
related to the late Cardinal Vannutelli and thus in touch with the
Vatican. He told me that soon after the death of Pope Benedict
XV, his own father was dying. A priest was called in, but the
father refused to see him.

"Thinking to comfort the son, the priest said: 'Don't take it
hard. Such things will happen nowadays. Why, the late Holy Father on his deathbed sent away the priests with: 'Off with you,
the play is over' (*la commedia e finita*). His Holiness surely meant
commedia as in the *Divine Comedy*, the title of Dante's masterpiece,"
Berenson states.

The problem is not just that Jones did not report the words accurately or that he attributed the story to the pope's physician or that he was repeating material that he got at least third-hand. The problem is that he did not know (or care) what the pope meant by *"la commedia e finita."*

The word *comedy* is used in a much older sense than the one having to do with humor. Throughout history, until very recently, a "comedy" was simply a play or story with a happy ending (the opposite of a tragedy). What we today refer to as a comedy was then called a farce, and the pope did not say, "Get out of here, the farce is over," which even itself does not mean, "Get out of here, the mockery that has been my life is over."

Berenson was right to translate *"la commedia e finita"* as "the play is over." Another way to put it might be "The drama of my life is over," which is hardly the confession of duplicity that Jones wishes us to think the pope made.

The drama of the pope's life had a happy ending, for he did not say, "The tragedy is over."

A Snare and a Delusion

The Conversion Center of Havertown, Pennsylvania, puts out some of the more amusing anti-Catholic leaflets, though none is supposed to be taken humorously. One is called *10 Reasons Why I Am Not a Roman Catholic*. Although written some years ago and never updated, it still makes the rounds. Here are a few of the reasons given by the anonymous author.

"1. The papacy is a hoax. Peter never claimed to be pope. He was never in Rome."

It is true that Peter could not have used the term *pope* to describe himself, since the title was not conferred on the bishops of Rome during the earliest years of the Church. (Neither does the Bible claim to be "the Bible," for that term had not been invented yet; it simply claimed to be God's inspired word.) But that is hardly the point, since the question is not the title used but the existence of the office of pope, which has been united to the office of the bishop of Rome on the basis that Peter went to Rome and died there. It follows that if Peter never went to Rome (this is the real question), then he could hardly have been its bishop, and the present bishop of Rome could hardly be his successor.

Although the Bible has no unmistakable evidence that he was there (though 1 Peter 5:13 does imply it), early Christian writers such as Tertullian, Clement of Alexandria, and Lactantius are unanimous in saying that he went to Rome, presided over the Church there, and was martyred during Emperor Nero's persecution.

There was no early writer who claimed that Peter never went to Rome and died elsewhere, and no other ancient city ever claimed to be the place of his death or to have his remains—which makes sense, since in this century it has been demonstrated that his bones lay beneath the high altar of St. Peter's Basilica.

A popular account of the archaeological excavations conducted from 1939 to 1968, at which time Pope Paul VI confirmed that Peter's bones had been scientifically and historically identified, may be found in John E. Walsh's book *The Bones of St. Peter*.

"2. Maryolatry [*sic*] is a hoax."

Quite true. "Mariolatry" means the worship of Mary, giving her the kind of honor due only to God (Greek: *latria*). Since Catholics justifiably give her greater honor than they give other saints but less than they give to God (and not just less, but a fundamentally different kind of honor), Mariolatry does not exist in Catholic piety. In fact, the Catholic Church forbids Mariolatry because it forbids us to worship anyone other than God himself: "Idolatry not only refers to false pagan worship. It remains a constant temptation to faith. Idolatry consists in divinizing what is not God.

Man commits idolatry whenever he honors and reveres a creature in place of God. . . . Idolatry rejects the unique Lordship of God; it is therefore incompatible with communion with God" (*Catechism of the Catholic Church* 2113, cf. 2110–2112, 2114).

But what the author means, of course, is that any honor given to Mary constitutes Mariolatry. He is unable to distinguish mere honor from adoration. One wonders if he thinks people adore as God the judges whom they call "Your Honor," or whether God decrees "parent-olatry" when he commands, "Honor your father and your mother" (Ex. 20:12).

"3. Purgatory is a hoax. It is a money-making scheme."

If it is, it is one of the least efficient schemes ever devised by man. It is indeed customary to give a priest a small stipend for celebrating a memorial Mass. The usual amount is five dollars, though there is no obligation to give anything, and many people, out of poverty or ignorance, give nothing. A priest clever enough to operate a scheme for making money would surely be clever enough to choose something that generated a better income, especially since nobody gets rich off of five dollars a day (priests are permitted to accept only one stipend per day). But as far as the Bible is concerned, it's entirely reasonable for a priest to receive some small stipend for guest preaching, baptisms, weddings, and other ministerial functions.

The practice of remunerating ministers for their services, which is certainly not unique to the Catholic Church, is thoroughly biblical. Paul said, "Let the presbyters [priests] who rule well be considered worthy of double honor, especially those who labor in preaching and teaching; for the Scripture says, 'You shall not muzzle an ox when it is treading out the grain,' and, 'The laborer deserves his wages'" (1 Tim. 5:17–18; cf. Matt. 10:10; Luke 10:7).

There is no point in examining all the reasons adduced by the writer, but one should not overlook the ninth one:

"9. I am an American citizen and refuse to be the subject of a deluded Italian prince."

He would also, one supposes, refuse to be the subject of any foreign prince. What would his attitude be if an American is someday elected pope?

On the Fringe

In the nineteenth century, there was the anti-Catholic controversialist Maria Monk, who claimed to have been a nun who "escaped" from a Montreal convent to "tell all" about the immoral escapades of the sisters in the cloister. Although she died in 1849, after having been proved a fraud, her venomous spirit still stalks the land, and her name arises whenever the topic is anti-Catholicism in its more virulent strains.

Those who miss her will be pleased to know that there is a modern replacement, the late Alberto Rivera, whose life was immortalized in the pages of several comic books published by Chick Publications of Chino, California.

Rivera claimed to have been a Jesuit priest assigned by the Vatican to infiltrate and subvert Protestant churches, particularly Fundamentalist ones such as the Plymouth Brethren, Pentecostal, Baptist, and United Evangelical churches. He was so effective, he said, that he was secretly made a bishop. But then he saw the light, abandoned Catholicism, and barely escaped with his life.

Although the Christian Research Institute and *Christianity Today* (both Protestant) demonstrated that Rivera was never a priest and never offered any proof for his allegations, the comic books keep popping up and people keep believing Rivera's charges, no matter how ridiculous they are.

One of the juiciest is straight from Maria Monk. Rivera claimed that in the 1930s, the Spanish government, then in the hands of anticlerical parliamentarians, discovered graves of newborn children beneath monasteries and convents. In the first comic book in the series, Rivera included a diagram showing a monastery and convent some distance apart, with steps descending from each into a connecting tunnel, along which are the graves. The diagram includes a little arrow pointing to the tunnel and captioned "bodies of babies." Rivera claimed that the children were the result of illicit unions between monks and nuns, and the remainder of the story is easy enough to guess.

The Case of the Missing Dirt

What Rivera did not tell us is why the monks and nuns would have gone to all the trouble to dig a tunnel. Why not just slip into regular clothes, leave the monastery or convent late at night, and proceed in the darkness to a rendezvous point? Furthermore, where was all the excavated dirt put, and why didn't the neighbors inquire what all the picks, shovels, and wheelbarrows were for? And so on. The story becomes more improbable as the questions multiply. Of course, Rivera spoke only in generalities. He made no reference to a specific monastery or convent or to corroborating sources, because there are none.

Despite the patent falsehoods of the comic books, Rivera and Chick Publications have not been disavowed by many "respectable" anti-Catholics. In its newsletter, for instance, Mission to Catholics, International, said that it could not verify Rivera's charges and so could not recommend the comic books—but it would not write off Rivera and his publisher either. As the old saying goes, "The enemy of my enemy is my friend."

These three examples are not important in themselves, but they illustrate the material professional anti-Catholics produce. Even a brief acquaintance with the literature from Bob Jones University, Mission to Catholics, International, the Conversion Center, and Chick Publications shows that grotesqueries like these are standard fare. These and all the other charges can be demonstrated to be nothing but a mixture of prejudice, ignorance, and faulty scholarship.

42

Catholic "Inventions"

There's a well-known story—probably untrue—about a U.S. Senate race in a southern state some years ago. One candidate realized that he would have difficulty winning if he took the high road, so he decided to employ the confusion factor.

In the cities, his campaigning was unobjectionable, but he thought he could fool the folks in the countryside. When he made a speech in a small town (and when he was sure no journalists were around), he would refer to his opponent and his opponent's family using words chosen to mislead—for example, saying his opponent's sister was a "thespian" (actress) and that his brother was an acknowledged *homo sapiens* (human being). To the inattentive ear he seemed to be accusing his opponent and his relatives of all sorts of perversions. Although everything the candidate said was accurate, the impression he gave was wrong.

Depending on which version of the story one hears, this man either won the election by a whisker or was revealed to be the scoundrel that he was.

The Confusion Factor Again

Similar posturing comes from the mouths and pens of some professional anti-Catholics. Much of what they accuse the Catholic Church of believing or doing is accurate but tainted by innuendo.

The impression is that there must be something seriously wrong with the Catholic Church if so many of its individual beliefs or practices are made to seem unusual. Of course, there are also accusations that simply misrepresent the Catholic Church's position, and when these are mixed with the true-but-misleading statements, the Church comes away looking quite strange.

Does this matter? Of course it does, because so much of this kind of thing has been going on over the last few years that many non-Catholics have come to believe it, and many anti-Catholics have become confirmed in their antagonism toward the Church. Further, Catholics who lack a good grounding in their own religion find that they cannot answer accusations to their own satisfaction and may fall away from the practice of the faith or abandon the Church entirely and sign up elsewhere. Non-Catholics who have always been uneasy about the Catholic Church find their doubts made stronger, even when they recognize that many of the anti-Catholic claims are made by people who are careless in their research and biased in their writing.

The Anti-Catholic Bible

Let's look at a few examples of misleading charges. These are taken from Loraine Boettner's book *Roman Catholicism*, which might be called the "Bible" of the anti-Catholic movement. First published in 1962 by the Presbyterian and Reformed Publishing Company of Philadelphia, and reprinted many times since, this fat book is the source most anti-Catholic organizations rely on for information about the Church. Most borrow uncritically from Boettner, seldom giving him credit and never checking his sources. It must be admitted, though, that Boettner lists almost no sources for his claims, so the lack of documentation is not completely the responsibility of the people who have picked up his words.

Early in the book Boettner lists what he terms "Some Roman Catholic Heresies and Inventions." These consist of beliefs that were supposedly made up centuries after the New Testament era and practices or customs that bear little similarity to those mentioned in the Bible. The reader of these several dozen charges is supposed to turn from them in such despair that he will abandon the Catholic Church (if he is a Catholic) or will actively fight it (if he is a non-Catholic). Here are a few of the "inventions."

Item: "The Latin language, used in prayer and worship, imposed by [Pope] Gregory I [A.D.] 600."

It is true that Latin was used in worship in the year 600. The Church spread from the Greek-speaking East to the Latin-speaking West (for example, to Rome) during apostolic times. One of Paul's letters was written to the Christians in Rome. More than one of his letters was written from Rome. And there were Christians in Caesar's household in Paul's day (cf. Phil. 4:22). Worship, not surprisingly, was undertaken in the vernacular language, which was Greek in much of the East and Latin in the West (though at the beginning, Greek was used even in the West because it was then the *lingua franca* of the Roman Empire).

Latin was used in worship far earlier than 600. So what is Boettner trying to say here? Since Latin became the Catholic Church's official language (and, in fact, it still is—all Vatican documents of any importance are issued in authoritative Latin versions), perhaps we are to conclude that there is some mystery about it? Well, there probably is, to people who do not read Latin, just as there is mystery in French to those who know only English. So what is Boettner trying to do with this "invention"? Perhaps he is attempting to heighten suspicion, even if it is directed at nothing in particular.

One can make any adoption of an official language sound sinister. All one has to do is say the language was "imposed"—implying that it was opposed or forced upon people against their will, no matter how untrue this may be. Boettner is simply using a cheap rhetorical device.

Item: "Baptism of bells instituted by Pope John XIII . . . [A.D.] 965."

What is the reader supposed to make of this? Most non-Catholics realize that Catholics baptize infants, but bells? If Catholics think they can baptize bells, why not baptize automobiles or any other inanimate object? The charge, if true, does make the Church look silly. But what happened was not what Boettner implies. There was indeed a "baptism of bells," but it was not a baptism in the sacramental sense of the word. When a church received new bells for its bell tower, the bells were blessed, usually by the local bishop. Any object can be blessed, a blessing being a dedication of a thing to a sacred purpose. The ceremony used in the blessing of the bells was reminiscent in some ways of the ceremony used in baptism, so in popular usage it came to be called the "baptism of bells," though no one thought the bells were actually receiving a sacrament. The phrase is innocent, but when anti-Catholics refer to it in just a few words, it looks particularly bad.

New Word, Old Belief

Item: "Transubstantiation proclaimed by Pope Innocent III . . . [A.D.] 1215."

The implication of this is that transubstantiation was not believed until 1215—that it was, indeed, an invention. The facts are otherwise. Transubstantiation is the technical term used to describe what happens when the bread and wine used at Mass are turned into Christ's actual body and blood. The belief that this occurs has been held from the earliest times. It stems from the sixth chapter of John's Gospel, the eleventh chapter of 1 Corinthians, and the biblical accounts of the Last Supper. As centuries passed, theologians exercised their reason on the belief to understand more completely how such a thing could happen and what its happening would imply. It was seen that more precise terminology was needed to insure the belief's integrity. The word *transubstantiation* was finally chosen because it eliminated certain unorthodox interpretations of the doctrine, and the term was formally defined at the Fourth Lateran Council in 1215. So the use of the technical term was new, but the doctrine was not.

Fundamentalists can't have a problem with using a new word for an old belief, since they use the term *Trinity* to express the belief that God is one being in three Persons, though this word is not found in the Bible. Theophilus of Antioch first used it in A.D. 181 (in his letter *Ad Autolycum*), though Christians believed in the doctrine from apostolic times.

In the three items mentioned, Boettner has ascribed the actions to popes. However, he has provided no sources showing that popes did these things, and at least one of them is demonstrably inaccurate. (It was the Fourth Lateran Council, not the pope reigning at the time, that for the first time made official, magisterial use of the theological term *transubstantiation*.) A suspicion is created that, in order to make these developments look like "inventions," Boettner wanted to name a particular "inventor" and looked up whoever was pope in the years he wanted to cite.

Not all items in his list refer to popes, however. Some do refer to councils:

Item: "Bible forbidden to laymen, placed on the Index of Forbidden Books by the Council of Valencia . . . [A.D.] 1229."

This looks rather damaging, but Boettner has his history completely wrong. The first thing to note is that the Index of Forbidden Books was established in 1559, so a council held in 1229 could hardly have listed a book on it.

The second point is that there apparently has never been any Church council in Valencia, Spain. If there had been one, it could not have taken place in 1229 because Muslim Moors then controlled the city. It is inconceivable that Muslims, who were at war with Spanish Christians, and had been off and on for five centuries, would allow Catholic bishops to hold a council in one of their cities. The Christian armies did not liberate Valencia from Moorish rule until nine years later, 1238. So Valencia is out.

But there is another possibility, and that is Toulouse, France, where a council was held in 1229. And, yes, that council dealt with the Bible. It was organized in reaction to the Albigensian or Catharist heresy, which held that there are two gods and that marriage is evil because all matter (and thus physical flesh) is evil. From this the heretics concluded that fornication could be no sin, and they even encouraged suicide among their members. In order to promulgate their sect, the Albigensians published an inaccurate translation of the Bible in the vernacular language (rather like the Jehovah's Witnesses of today publishing their severely flawed *New World Translation* of the Bible, which has been deliberately mistranslated to support the sect's claims). Had it been an accurate translation, the Church would not have been concerned. Vernacular versions had been appearing for centuries. But what came from the hands of the Albigensians was an adulterated Bible. The bishops at Toulouse forbade the reading of it because it was inaccurate. In this they were caring for their flocks, just as a Protestant minister of today might tell his flock not to read the Jehovah's Witnesses' *New World Translation*.

A Reasonable Reason

Item: "The cup forbidden to the people at Communion by Council of Constance [A.D.] 1414."

The implication here is that bishops and priests were trying to keep from laymen something they should have had by rights. But the real situation is not hard to understand. The Catholic position has always been that, after the consecration of the elements, the entire body and blood of Christ are contained in the smallest particle from the host and in the tiniest drop from the cup. One does not receive only the body in the host and only the blood from the cup. If that were so, then for a complete Communion one indeed *would* need to partake of both. But if the entire body and blood are contained in both, then the communicant needs to receive only one—if there are good reasons for such a restriction, and in 1414 there certainly seemed to be.

The first reason was that many people misunderstood the Eucharist and thought it had to be received under both forms for the Communion to be complete. By restricting communicants to the host only, the Church would emphasize the true doctrine.

The other reason was a practical one. In giving the cup to the laity, there was a chance the contents would be spilled, so out of respect for Christ, the restriction was imposed.

These five "inventions" are representative of the forty-five listed by Boettner. He refers to a few of them again later in *Roman Catholicism*, but most make one appearance here and then disappear. No effort is made to give sources, and little effort is made to say what the significance of them might be. He suggests that any belief or practice not explicitly found in the New Testament in plain words must be spurious and must have been instituted for some nefarious purpose.

What Boettner does not point out is that modern Fundamentalism has beliefs and customs that are not found in the Bible, either. Many Fundamentalist churches, for example, forbid the drinking of wine as sinful, yet Christ not only drank wine (he was accused of being a drunkard; cf. Luke 7:34), he transformed water into wine (this being a biblical example of a form of transubstantiation since the substance of water became the substance of wine, though the species changed, too, in this case) as his first public miracle, hardly something he would have done had he disapproved of wine (cf. John 2:1–11). Boettner also notes that priests came to dress differently from laymen, without noticing that Fundamentalist ministers, who may wear expensive three-piece business suits or choir robes while conducting services, also dress differently from their congregants.

The examples could be multiplied, but the fact is that no church looks exactly the same as that of the New Testament era. Since Christ founded a living Church, one should expect it, like any living thing, to grow and mature, changing in appearance while maintaining identity in substance, holding on to the original deposit of faith, while coming to understand it more deeply and to apply it to new cultural situations. The real question is why anyone would think that the Church should have arrested its development and fossilized in one, immutable form at the end of the first century.

43

More Catholic "Inventions"

One of the key points of Loraine Boettner's magnum opus, *Roman Catholicism* (the main sourcebook for professional anti-Catholics), is that Catholicism must be untrue because it differs in so many particulars from the Christianity of the New Testament. Over the centuries, Boettner says, the Catholic Church has added beliefs, rituals, and customs that contradict those in the Bible. He calls this "the melancholy evidence of Rome's steadily increasing departure from the simplicity of the gospel," and he claims that repeatedly "human inventions have been substituted for Bible truth and practice" (p. 9).

He argues that Catholicism cannot be the religion established by Christ because it has all these "extras," forty-five of which he lists under the title "Some Roman Catholic Heresies and Inventions" (pp. 7–9). A few of these he examines at length in the book, but most of them are only mentioned and then conveniently dropped.

Many anti-Catholic organizations have reprinted all or portions of Boettner's list of "inventions," usually in leaflets that are commonly distributed outside Catholic churches after Mass. Do they produce the intended results? Yes and no. It depends on the knowledge and sophistication of the reader. Some people laugh at the charges, knowing what the facts really are. Others are stumped for answers, but figure they can establish Catholicism's credentials if they have to prove the Church's legitimacy. Yet some people are taken in, thinking no one would go to the trouble of disseminating such information if it were false.

Catholics need to realize that professional anti-Catholics have dozens of charges like these up their sleeves, and they produce them whenever they think they can make an impression on people who know less than they. Bizarre allegations sow confusion in Catholic minds. After all, most Catholics are not conversant with the finer points of Church history and practice and are ripe targets for evangelistic Fundamentalists.

Item: "Making the sign of the cross   [A.D.] 300."

That's it. That's the whole charge: that the sign of the cross was not "invented" until well into the Christian era. In reality, we can show that Christians were making the sign of the cross at a *much* earlier date. The theologian Tertullian, writing in A.D. 211, said that "in all our travels and movements in all our coming in and going out, in putting of our shoes, at the bath, at the table, in lighting our candles, in lying down, in sitting down, whatever employment occupieth us, we [Christians] mark our foreheads with the sign [of the cross]" (*The Chaplet* [*Crown*] 3). Making the sign of the cross was already an old custom when he wrote. It may well have been common even while the apostles were alive.

But the mistake Boettner makes concerning the antiquity of the practice is not the important thing. The real question is: Why does he single out this practice at all? The answer: Because the sign of the cross is not mentioned in the New Testament. The reader is supposed to conclude that it must be contrary to Christian teaching. But that makes little sense and, in fact, this line of reasoning undermines Boettner's own Fundamentalism.

The Pot Calling the Kettle Black

If Catholicism has changed matters of practice or customs over the centuries, Fundamentalism has done the same. Indeed, there were no altar calls and church steeples in the first century.

But the proper question is not whether Christ's Church today looks exactly as it did then—if that's the criterion for discerning the true Church from false ones, his Church cannot be found anywhere. Rather, what matters is whether his Church has kept the same beliefs as the early Church (which Catholicism has, unlike Boettner and all Fundamentalists—not to mention Evangelicals).

Item: "Priests began to dress differently from laymen . . . [A.D.] 500."

So what? This charge can be brought against Fundamentalist preachers who conduct services while dressed in choir robes. Furthermore, Boettner's statement is only a half-truth. The main vestment worn by priests during Mass is the chasuble, which is really nothing more than a stylized Roman overcoat. In the sixth century, while fashions changed around them, priests kept the same clothing they had used for liturgical purposes for some time. They did not adopt special dress for Mass; they just kept to the old styles, while everyday fashions changed, and over time their dress began to stand out.

But It's in the Bible!

Item: "Extreme Unction . . . [A.D.] 526."

This single line is no doubt intended to make the reader believe the Catholic Church invented this sacrament (also known as the anointing of the sick) five centuries after Christ. But Boettner makes no effort to give the Church's explanation of its origin. Why? Because the origin is found in the New Testament itself: "Is any among you sick? Let him call for the elders of the church, and let them pray over him, anointing him with oil in the name of the Lord; and the prayer of faith will save the sick man, and the Lord will raise him up; and if he has committed sins, he will be forgiven" (Jas. 5:14-15). This scriptural practice dates from the very beginnings of the Church. If Boettner wants to say this sacrament was invented, he should have said it was invented while the apostles were still alive—but that would give the sacrament legitimacy.

Item: "Worship of the cross, images, and relics authorized in . . . [A.D.] 786."

What's this? Do Catholics give slivers of wood, carvings of marble, and pieces of bone the kind of adoration they give God? That is the implication. What if a Catholic were to say to Boettner, "I saw you kneeling with your Bible in your hands the other day. Why do you worship a book?" He would rightly answer that he does not worship a book. Rather, he uses the Bible as an aid to prayer. Likewise, Catholics do not worship the cross, images, or relics. They use these physical objects to help them focus their minds and hearts upon Christ and his friends, the saints in heaven.

The man who keeps a picture of his family in his wallet does not worship his wife and children; rather, he honors them. The woman who keeps her parents' picture on the mantle does not subscribe to ancestor worship; the picture just reminds her of them so that she may more readily honor them. (Remember Exodus 20.12. "Honor your father and your mother.") No one thinks these pictures are objects of worship.

The origin of Boettner's allegation is that in the Byzantine Empire there developed what was known as the Iconoclastic heresy, which held that all images (statues, paintings, mosaics) of saints and of Jesus must be destroyed because they would be worshiped. In 787, at the Second Council of Nicaea, this heresy was defeated, and the old custom (dating to the first century) of permitting artistic representations was again allowed. Boettner had this date almost right; he simply did not understand either the history or the doctrine.

Following Paul's Advice

Item: "Celibacy of the priesthood, decreed by pope Gregory VII (Hildebrand) . . . [A.D.] 1079."

Anti-Catholics take considerable delight in noting that some of the apostles, including Peter, were married and that for centuries Catholic priests were allowed to marry.

Catholics do not deny that some of the early popes were married or that celibacy, for priests in the Western (Latin) rite, did not become mandatory until the early Middle Ages. Anti-Catholic writers generally fail to note that even today many Catholic priests in the Eastern rites are married and that it has always been that way. Celibacy in the Latin rite is purely a matter of discipline. It came to be thought that priests could better fulfill their duties if they remained unmarried.

Nor is this an unbiblical notion; it is Paul's advice. After saying he wished those to whom he was writing were, like he, unmarried (1 Cor. 7:7–9), Paul said he thought celibacy was the more perfect state (1 Cor 7:28), noting that "the unmarried man is anxious about the affairs of the Lord, how to please the Lord; but the married man is anxious about worldly affairs, how to please his wife" (1 Cor. 7:32–33).

This applies specifically to ministers of the gospel. When Paul counseled Timothy about how to fulfill his ministry, he cautioned him: "Share in suffering as a good soldier of Christ Jesus. No soldier on service gets entangled in civilian pursuits, since his aim is to satisfy the one who enlisted him" (2 Tim. 2:3–4). And Paul refers applaudingly to an order of Christian celibate widows (first-century nuns), saying: "But refuse to enroll younger widows; for when they grow wanton against Christ they desire to marry, and so they incur condemnation for having violated their first pledge" (1 Tim. 5:11–12).

So, the practice of clerical celibacy, even taking vows of celibacy, is thoroughly biblical. When a man becomes a priest in the Latin rite, he knows that he will not be able to marry. Marriage is a good thing (in fact, Catholics acknowledge that Christ elevated it to a sacrament), but it is something that priests are willing to forgo for the sake of being better priests.

No one is forced to be a priest (or a nun for that matter), so no Catholic is forced to be celibate. Those who want to take the vows of the religious life should not object to following the rules. That does not mean that the rules, as found at any one time, are ideal or cannot be modified—after all, they are not doctrines but matters of discipline. However, it does mean that it is unfair to imply, as Boettner does, that the Catholic faith scorns marriage.

Christ's Own Instruction

Item: "Auricular confession of sins to a priest instead of to God, instituted by pope Innocent III in [the] Lateran Council   [A D] 1215."

Charges like this might make one doubt the good faith of professional anti-Catholics. It would have taken little effort to discover the antiquity of auricular confession—and even less to learn that Catholics do not tell their sins to a priest "instead" of to God but to God *through* a priest.

Origen, writing his *Homilies on Leviticus* around 244, refers to the repentant sinner as one who "does not shrink from declaring his sin to a priest of the Lord." Cyprian of Carthage, writing seven years later in *The Lapsed*, says, "Finally, of how much greater faith and more salutary fear are they who . . . confess to the priests of God in a straightforward manner and in sorrow, making an open declaration of conscience." In the 300s, Aphraates offers this advice to priests: "If anyone uncovers his wound before you, give him the remedy of repentance. And he that is ashamed to make known his weakness, encourage him so that he will not hide it from you. And when he has revealed it to you, do not make it public" (*Treatises* 7:4).

These men, writing almost a thousand years before the Lateran Council of 1215, refer to a practice that was already well established. In fact, it dates back to the time of Jesus, for Christ commissioned the apostles this way: "If you forgive the sins of any, they are forgiven; if you retain the sins of any, they are retained" (John 20:23). The Lateran Council did not "invent" the practice; it merely reaffirmed it.

Who Added What?

Item: "Apocryphal books added to the Bible by the Council of Trent . . . [A.D.] 1546."

This reminds one of a famous comment made by a writer who joked, in discussing the English Reformation, that "the pope and his minions then seceded from the Church of England." It was not the Council of Trent that "added" what Protestants call the apocryphal books to the Bible. Instead, the Protestant Reformers excised out of the Bible these books that had been in common use for centuries.

The Council of Trent, convened to reaffirm Catholic doctrines and to revitalize the Church, proclaimed that these books had always belonged to the Bible and had to remain in it. After all, it was the Catholic Church, in the fourth century, at the councils of Rome, Hippo, and Carthage (A.D. 382, 393, 397, respectively), that officially decided which books belonged to the Bible and which did not. This had been reaffirmed by many popes and councils later, including the ecumenical Council of Florence. When the Council of Trent was convened, it merely formally restated the constant teaching of the Church.

A Final Word

Bishop Fulton Sheen once said that few people in America hate the Catholic religion, but there are many who hate what they mistakenly believe is the Catholic religion—and that if what they hate really were the Catholic religion, Catholics would hate it too. Highly inaccurate and inflammatory lists, like the one published in Boettner's *Roman Catholicism*, have done much to foster this kind of hatred. Even worse, they have discouraged Fundamentalists from finding out what the Catholic religion really is, and that is a disservice to both Protestants and Catholics.

Like others before him, Loraine Boettner found an enemy of his own fashioning. He castigated it, misrepresented it, and ridiculed it. But it was not the Catholic religion as it truly is, and the "history" he presented is not the history of the Catholic Church. Fundamentalists who are curious about the Catholic religion do themselves no favor by allowing themselves to be hoodwinked by such lists of "inventions." If they want to know what really happened, how Catholic beliefs and practices really arose, they will have to turn to more careful and better-informed writers.

44

Is Catholicism Pagan?

If few Fundamentalists know the history of their religion—which distressingly few do—even fewer have an appreciation of the history of the Catholic Church. They become easy prey for purveyors of fanciful "histories" that claim to account for the origin and advance of Catholicism.

Anti-Catholics often suggest that Catholicism did not exist prior to the Edict of Milan, which was issued in A.D. 313 and made Christianity legal in the Roman Empire. With this, pagan influences began to contaminate the previously untainted Christian Church. In no time, various inventions adopted from paganism began to replace the gospel that had been once for all delivered to the saints. That is the theory, at least.

Pagan Influence Fallacy

Opponents of the Church often attempt to discredit Catholicism by attempting to show similarities between it and the beliefs or practices of ancient paganism. This fallacy is frequently committed by Fundamentalists, Seventh-day Adventists, Jehovah's Witnesses, Mormons, and others against both Protestants and Catholics, and by atheists and skeptics against both Christians and Jews.

The nineteenth century witnessed a flowering of this "pagan influence fallacy." Publications such as *The Two Babylons* by Alexander Hislop (the classic English text charging the Catholic Church with paganism) paved the way for generations of antagonism toward the Church. During this time, entire new sects were created (Seventh-day Adventists, Mormons, Jehovah's Witnesses)—all considering traditional Catholicism and Protestantism as polluted by paganism. This era also saw atheistic "freethinkers" such as Robert Ingersoll writing books attacking Christianity and Judaism as pagan.

The pagan influence fallacy has not gone away in the twentieth century, but newer archaeology and more mature scholarship have diminished its influence. Yet there are still many committing it. In Protestant circles, numerous works have continued to popularize the claims of Alexander Hislop, most notably the comic books of Jack Chick and the book *Babylon Mystery Religion* by the young Ralph Woodrow. (Woodrow later realized its flaws and wrote *The Babylon Connection?* repudiating it and refuting Hislop.) Other Christian and quasi-Christian sects have continued to charge mainstream Christianity with paganism, and many atheists have continued to repeat—unquestioned—the charges of paganism leveled by their forebears.

Use of a Round Wafer Implies Sun Worship?

Hislop and Chick argue that the wafers of Communion are round, just like the wafers of the sun worshipers of Baal. They don't bother to mention that the wafers used by the same pagans were also ovals, triangles, folded over, or shaped like leaves or animals, etc. The fact that a wafer is round does not make it immoral or pagan, since even the Jews had wafers and cakes offered in the Old Testament (cf. Gen. 18:1-8; Ex 29:1-2).

Unfortunately for Chick and other Fundamentalists, their arguments backfire. An atheist will take the pagan connection one step further, saying, "Christianity itself is simply a regurgitation of pagan myths: the incarnation of a divinity from a virgin, a venerated mother and child, just like Isis and Osiris, Isa and Iswara, Fortuna and Jupiter, and Semiramis and Tammuz. Beyond this, some pagans had a triune god, and pagan gods were often pictured with wings, as was your God in Psalms 91:4. The flames on the heads of the apostles were also seen as an omen from the gods in Roman poetry and heathen myths long before Pentecost. A rock is struck that brings forth water in the Old Testament, just like the pagan goddess Rhea did long before then. Also, Jesus is known as the 'fish,' just like the fish-god Dagon, etc." Unless the Fundamentalists are willing to honestly examine the logical fallacies and historical inaccuracies, they are left defenseless. Fortunately, like the attacks on Catholicism in particular, all of the supposed parallels mentioned above self-destruct when examined with any scholarly rigor. If not guilty of historical inaccuracies, they all are guilty of what can be called "pagan influence fallacies."

Anything Can Be Attacked Using Fallacy

The pagan influence fallacy is committed when one charges that a particular religion, belief, or practice is of pagan origin or has been influenced by paganism and is therefore false, wrong, tainted, or to be repudiated. In this minimal form, the pagan influence fallacy is a subcase of the genetic fallacy, which improperly judges a thing based on its history or origins rather than on its own merits (e.g., "No one should use this medicine because it was invented by a drunkard and adulterer").

Very frequently, the pagan influence fallacy is committed in connection with other fallacies, most notably the *post hoc ergo propter hoc* ("After this, therefore because of this") fallacy—e.g., "Some ancient pagans did or believed something millennia ago; therefore any parallel Christian practices and beliefs must be derived from that source." Frequently, a variant on this fallacy is committed in which, as soon as a parallel with something pagan is noted, it is assumed that the pagan counterpart is the more ancient. This variant might be called the *similis hoc ergo propter hoc* ("Similar to this, therefore because of this") fallacy.

When the pagan influence fallacy is encountered, it should be pointed out that it is, in fact, a fallacy. To help make this clear to a religious person committing it, it may be helpful to illustrate with cases where the pagan influence fallacy could be committed against his own position (e.g., the practice of circumcision was practiced in the ancient world by a number of peoples—including the Egyptians—but few Jews or Christians would say that its divinely authorized use in Israel was an example of "pagan corruption").

To help a secular person see the fallacy involved, one might point to a parallel case of the genetic fallacy involving those of his perspective (e.g., "Nobody should accept this particular scientific theory because it was developed by an atheist").

Whenever one encounters a proposed example of pagan influence from anti-Catholics, one should demand that its existence be properly documented, not just asserted. The danger of accepting an inaccurate claim is too great. The amount of misinformation in this area is great enough that it is advisable to never accept a reported parallel as true unless it can be demonstrated from primary source documents or through reliable, scholarly secondary sources. After receiving documentation supporting the claim of a pagan parallel, one should ask a number of questions:

1. Is there a parallel? Frequently, there is not. The claim of a parallel may be erroneous, especially when the documentation provided is based on an old or undisclosed source.

For example: "The Egyptians had a trinity. They worshiped Osiris, Isis, and Horus, thousands of years before the Father, Son, and Holy Ghost were known" (Robert Ingersoll, *Why I Am an Agnostic*). This is not true. The Egyptians had an Ennead—a pantheon of nine major gods and goddesses. Osiris, Isis, and Horus were simply three divinities in the pantheon who were closely related by marriage and blood (not surprising, since the Ennead itself was an extended family) and who figured in the same myth cycle. They did not represent the three persons of a single divine being (the Christian understanding of the Trinity). The claim of an Egyptian trinity is simply wrong. There is no parallel.

2. Is the parallel dependent or independent? Even if there is a pagan parallel, that does not mean that there is a causal relationship involved. Two groups may develop similar beliefs, practices, and artifacts totally independently of each other. The idea that similar forms are always the result of diffusion from a common source

has long been rejected by archaeology and anthropology, and for very good reason: Humans are similar to each other and live in similar (i.e., terrestrial) environments, leading them to have similar cultural artifacts and views.

For example, Fundamentalists have made much of the fact that Catholic art includes Madonna and Child images and that non-Christian art, all over the world, also frequently includes mother and child images. There is nothing sinister in this. The fact is that, in every culture, there are mothers who hold their children! Sometimes this gets represented in art, including religious art, and it is used especially when a work of art is being done to show the motherhood of an individual. Mother-with-child images do not need to be explained by a theory of diffusion from a common, pagan religious source (such as Hislop's suggestion that such images stem from representations of Semiramis holding Tammuz). One need look no further than the fact that mothers holding children is a universal feature of human experience and a convenient way for artists to represent motherhood.

3. Is the parallel antecedent or consequent? Even if there is a pagan parallel that is causally related to a non-pagan counterpart, this does not establish which gave rise to the other. It may be that the pagan parallel is a late borrowing from a non-pagan source. Frequently, the pagan sources we have are so late that they have been shaped in reaction to Jewish and Christian ideas. Sometimes it is possible to tell that pagans have been borrowing from non-pagans. Other times, it cannot be discerned who is borrowing from whom (or, indeed, if anyone is borrowing from anyone).

For example, the ideas expressed in the Norse *Elder Edda* about the end and regeneration of the world were probably influenced by the teachings of Christians with whom the Norse had been in contact for centuries (cf. H. A. Guerber, *The Norsemen*, 339f).

4. Is the parallel treated positively, neutrally, or negatively? Even if there is a pagan parallel to a non-pagan counterpart, that does not mean that the item or concept was enthusiastically or uncritically accepted by non-pagans. One must ask how they regarded it. Did they regard it as something positive, neutral, or negative?

For example, circumcision and the symbol of the cross might be termed "neutral" Jewish and Christian counterparts to pagan parallels. It is quite likely that the early Hebrews first encountered the idea of circumcision among neighboring non-Jewish peoples, but that does not mean they regarded it as a religiously good thing for non-Jews to do. Circumcision was regarded as a religiously good thing only for Jews because for them it symbolized a special covenant with the one true God (cf. Gen. 17). The Hebrew Scriptures are silent in a religious appraisal of non-Jewish circumcision; they seemed indifferent to the fact that some pagans circumcised.

Similarly, the early Christians who adopted the cross as a symbol did not do so because it was a pagan religious symbol (the pagan cultures that used it as a symbol, notably in East Asia and the Americas, had no influence on the early Christians). The cross was used as a Christian symbol because Christ died on a cross—his execution being regarded as a bad thing in itself, in fact, an infinite injustice—but one from which he brought life for the world. Christians did not adopt it because it was a pagan symbol they liked and wanted to copy.

Examples of negative parallels are often found in Genesis. For instance, the Flood narrative (cf. Gen. 6–9) has parallels to pagan flood stories, but is written so that it refutes ideas in them. Thus Genesis attributes the flood to human sin (cf. Gen. 6:5–7), not overpopulation, as Atrahasis's *Epic* and the Greek poem *Cypria* did (cf. I. Kikawada and A. Quinn). The presence of flood stories in cultures around the world does not undermine the validity of the biblical narrative but lends it more credence.

Criticism, refutation, and replacement are also the principles behind modern holidays being celebrated to a limited extent around the same time as former pagan holidays. In actuality, reports of Christian holidays coinciding with pagan ones are often inaccurate (Christmas does not occur on Saturnalia, for example). However, to the extent the phenomenon occurs at all, Christian holidays were introduced to provide a wholesome, non-pagan alternative celebration, which thus critiques and rejects the pagan holiday. This is the same process that leads Fundamentalists who are offended at the inaccurately alleged pagan derivation of Halloween to introduce alternative "Reformation Day" celebrations for their children. (This modern Protestant holiday is based on the fact that the Reformation began when Martin Luther nailed his Ninety-Five Theses to the church door in Wittenberg, Germany, on October 31, 1517.) Another Fundamentalist substitution for Halloween has been "harvest festivals" that celebrate the season of autumn and the gathering of crops. These fundamentalist substitutions are no more "pagan" than the celebrations of days or seasons that may have been introduced by earlier Christians.

Historical Truth Prevails

Ultimately, all attempts to prove Catholicism "pagan" fail. Catholic doctrines are neither borrowed from the mystery religions nor introduced from pagans after the conversion of Constantine. To make a charge of paganism stick, one must be able to show more than a similarity between something in the Church and something in the non-Christian world. One must be able to demonstrate a legitimate connection between the two, showing clearly that one is a result of the other, and that there is something wrong with the non-Christian item.

In the final analysis, nobody has been able to prove these things regarding a doctrine of the Catholic faith, or even its officially authorized practices. The charge of paganism just doesn't work.

45

The Inquisition

Sooner or later, any discussion of apologetics with Fundamentalists will address the Inquisition. To non-Catholics it is a scandal; to Catholics, an embarrassment; to both, a confusion. It is a
handy stick for Catholic-bashing simply because most Catholics
seem at a loss for a sensible reply. This chapter will set the record
straight.

There have actually been several different inquisitions. The first
was established in 1184 in southern France as a response to the
Catharist heresy. This was known as the Medieval Inquisition,
and it was phased out as Catharism disappeared.

Quite separate was the Roman Inquisition, begun in 1542. It
was the least active and most benign of the three variations.

Separate again was the infamous Spanish Inquisition, started
in 1478, a state institution used to identify *conversos*—Jews and
Moors (Muslims) who pretended to convert to Christianity for
purposes of political or social advantage and secretly practiced their
former religion. More importantly, its job was also to clear the
good names of many people who were falsely accused of being
heretics. It was the Spanish Inquisition that, at least in the popular
imagination, had the worst record of fulfilling these duties.

The various inquisitions stretched through the better part of a
millennia and can collectively be called "the Inquisition."

The Main Sources

Fundamentalists writing about the Inquisition rely on books by
Henry C. Lea (1825–1909) and G. G. Coulton (1858–1947). Each

man got most of the facts right, and each made progress in basic research, so proper credit should not be denied them. The problem is that they did not weigh facts well because they harbored fierce animosity toward the Church—animosity that had little to do with the Inquisition itself.

The contrary problem has not been unknown. A few Catholic writers, particularly those less interested in digging for truth than in diffusing a criticism of the Church, have glossed over incontrovertible facts and tried to whitewash the Inquisition. This is as much a disservice to the truth as an exaggeration of the Inquisition's bad points. These well-intentioned but misguided apologists are, in one respect, much like Lea, Coulton, and contemporary Fundamentalist writers. They fear, while the others hope, that the facts about the Inquisition might prove the illegitimacy of the Catholic Church.

Don't Fear the Facts

But the facts fail to do that. The Church has nothing to fear from the truth. No account of foolishness, misguided zeal, or cruelty by Catholics can undo the divine foundation of the Church, though, admittedly, these things are stumbling blocks to Catholics and non-Catholics alike.

What must be grasped is that the Church contains within itself all sorts of sinners and knaves, and some of them obtain positions of responsibility. Paul and Christ himself warned us that there would be a few ravenous wolves among Church leaders (cf. Acts 20:29; Matt. 7:15).

Fundamentalists suffer from the mistaken notion that the Church includes only the elect. For them, sinners are outside the doors. Locate sinners, and you locate another place where the Church is not.

Thinking that Fundamentalists might have a point in their attacks on the Inquisition, Catholics tend to be defensive. This is the wrong attitude; rather, we should learn what really happened, understand events in light of the times, and then explain to anti-Catholics why the sorry tale does not prove what they think it proves.

Phony Statistics

Many Fundamentalists believe, for instance, that more people died under the Inquisition than in any war or plague. But in this they rely on phony "statistics" generated by one-upmanship among anti-Catholics, each of whom, it seems, tries to come up with the largest number of casualties.

But trying to straighten out such historical confusions can take one only so far. As Ronald Knox put it, we should be cautious, "lest we should wander interminably in a wilderness of comparative atrocity statistics." In fact, no one knows exactly how many people perished through the various Inquisitions. We can determine for certain, though, one thing about numbers given by Fundamentalists: They are far too large. One book popular with Fundamentalists claims that 95 million people died under the Inquisition.

The figure is so grotesquely off that one immediately doubts the writer's sanity, or at least his grasp of demographics. Not until modern times did the population of those countries where the Inquisitions existed approach 95 million.

Inquisitions did not exist in northern Europe, eastern Europe, Scandinavia, or England, being confined mainly to southern France, Italy, Spain, and a few parts of the Holy Roman Empire. The Inquisition could not have killed that many people because those parts of Europe did not have that many people to kill!

Furthermore, the plague, which killed a third of Europe's population, is credited by historians with major changes in the social structure. The Inquisition is credited with few—precisely because the number of its victims was comparatively small. In fact, recent studies indicate that at most there were only a few thousand capital sentences carried out for heresy in Spain, and these were over the course of several centuries.

What's the Point?

Ultimately, it may be a waste of time arguing about statistics. Instead, ask Fundamentalists just what they think the existence of the Inquisition demonstrates. They would not bring it up in the first place unless they thought it proves something about the Catholic Church. And what is that something? That Catholics are sinners? Guilty as charged. That at times people in positions of authority have used poor judgment? Ditto. That otherwise good Catholics, afire with zeal, sometimes lose their balance? All true, but such charges could be made even if the Inquisition had never existed, and perhaps it could be made of some Fundamentalists.

Fundamentalist writers claim the existence of the Inquisition proves that the Catholic Church could not be the Church founded by our Lord. They use the Inquisition as a good—perhaps their best—bad example. They think this shows that the Catholic Church is illegitimate. At first blush it might seem so, but there is only so much mileage in a ploy like that. Most people see at once that the argument is weak. One reason Fundamentalists talk about the Inquisition is that they take it as a personal attack, imagining it was established to eliminate (yes, you guessed it) the Fundamentalists themselves.

Not "Bible Christians"

Fundamentalists identify themselves with the Catharists (also known as the Albigensians), or perhaps it is better to say they identify the Catharists with themselves. They think the Catharists were twelfth-century Fundamentalists and that Catholics did to them what they would do to Fundamentalists today if they had the political strength they once had.

This is a fantasy. Fundamentalist writers take one point—that Catharists used a vernacular version of the Bible—and conclude from it that these people were "Bible Christians." In fact, theirs was a curious religion that apparently (no one knows for certain) came to France from what is now Bulgaria. Catharism was a blend of Gnosticism, which claimed to have access to a secret source of religious knowledge, and of Manichaeism, which said that matter is evil. The Catharists believed in two gods: the "good" God of the New Testament, who sent Jesus to save our souls from being trapped in matter, and the "evil" God of the Old Testament, who created the material world in the first place. The Catharists' beliefs entailed serious—truly civilization-destroying—social consequences.

Marriage was scorned because it legitimizes sexual relations, which Catharists identified as the Original Sin. But fornication was permitted because it was temporary, secret, and was not generally approved of while marriage was permanent, open, and publicly sanctioned.

The ramifications of such theories are not hard to imagine. In addition, ritualistic suicide was encouraged (those who would not take their own lives were frequently "helped" along), and Catharists refused to take oaths, which, in a feudal society, meant they opposed all governmental authority. Thus, Catharism was both a moral and a political danger.

Even Lea, so strongly opposed to the Catholic Church, admitted: "The cause of orthodoxy was the cause of progress and civilization. Had Catharism become dominant, or even had it been allowed to exist on equal terms, its influence could not have failed to become disastrous." Whatever else might be said about Catharism, it was certainly not the same as modern Fundamentalism, and Fundamentalist sympathy for this destructive belief system is sadly misplaced.

The Real Point

Many discussions about the Inquisition get bogged down in numbers, and many Catholics fail to understand what Fundamentalists are really driving at. As a result, Catholics restrict themselves to secondary matters. Instead, they should force the Fundamentalists to say explicitly what they are trying to prove.

However, there is a certain utility—though a decidedly limited one—in demonstrating that the kinds and degrees of punishments inflicted by the Spanish Inquisition were similar to (actually, even lighter than) those meted out by secular courts. It is equally true that, despite what we consider the Spanish Inquisition's lamentable procedures, many people preferred to have their cases tried by ecclesiastical courts because the secular courts had even fewer safeguards. In fact, historians have found records of people blaspheming in secular courts of the period so they could have their case transferred to an ecclesiastical court, where they would get a better hearing.

The crucial thing for Catholics, once they have obtained some appreciation of the history of the Inquisition, is to explain how such an institution could have been associated with a divinely established Church and why it is not proper to conclude, from the existence of the Inquisition, that the Catholic Church is not the Church of Christ. This is the real point at issue, and this is where any discussion should focus.

To that end, it is helpful to point out that it is easy to see how those who led the Inquisitions could think their actions were justified. The Bible itself records instances where God commanded that formal, legal inquiries—that is, inquisitions—be carried out to expose secret believers in false religions. In Deuteronomy 17:2–5, God said: "If there is found among you, within any of your towns which the Lord your God gives you, a man or woman who does what is evil in the sight of the Lord your God, in transgressing his covenant, and has gone and served other gods and worshiped them, or the sun or the moon or any of the host of heaven, which I have forbidden, and it is told you and you hear of it; then you shall inquire diligently, and if it is true and certain that such an abominable thing has been done in Israel, then you shall bring forth to your gates that man or woman who has done this evil thing, and you shall stone that man or woman to death with stones."

It is clear that there were some Israelites who posed as believers in and keepers of the covenant with Yahweh, while inwardly they did not believe and secretly practiced false religions, and even tried to spread them (cf. Deut. 13:6–11). To protect the kingdom from such hidden heresy, these secret practitioners of false religions had to be rooted out and expelled from the community. This directive from the Lord applied even to whole cities that turned away from the true religion (cf. Deut. 13:12–18). Like Israel, medieval Europe was a society of Christian kingdoms that were formally consecrated to the Lord Jesus Christ. It is therefore quite understandable that these Catholics would read their Bibles and conclude that for the good of their Christian society, they, like the Israelites before them, "must purge the evil from the midst of you" (Deut. 13:5). Paul repeats this principle in 1 Corinthians 5:13.

These same texts were interpreted similarly by the first Protestants, who also tried to root out and punish those they regarded as heretics. Both Luther and Calvin endorsed the right of the state to protect society by purging false religion. In fact, Calvin not only banished from Geneva those who did not share his views; he permitted and in some cases ordered others to be executed for "heresy" (e.g., Jacques Gouet, tortured and beheaded in 1547, and Michael Servetus, burned at the stake in 1553). In England and Ireland, Reformers engaged in their own ruthless inquisitions and executions. Conservative estimates indicate that thousands of English and Irish Catholics were put to death—many by being hanged, drawn, and quartered—for practicing the Catholic faith and refusing to become Protestant. An even greater number were forced to flee to the continent for their safety. We point this out to show that the situation was a two-way street; and both sides easily understood the Bible to require the use of penal sanctions to root out false religion from Christian society.

The fact that the Protestant Reformers also created inquisitions to root out Catholics and others who did not fall into line with the doctrines of the local Protestant sect shows that the existence of an inquisition does not prove that a movement is not of God. Protestants cannot make this claim against Catholics without having it backfire on themselves. Neither can Catholics make such a charge against Protestants. The truth of a particular system of belief must be decided on other grounds.

46

Exposing *Catholicism: Crisis of Faith*

Fundamentalist critics of the Catholic Church no longer restrict themselves to books and tracts. Today's anti-Catholic polemicists use the latest media. An example is *Catholicism: Crisis of Faith*, a slick, fifty-four-minute video featuring interviews with former Catholics—several of whom were priests and nuns—who now claim that their one-time co-religionists are not Christian.

The group responsible for this anti-Catholic video is "Lumen Productions" of San Leandro, California, an organization run by James McCarthy, a disgruntled former Catholic who left the Church in 1977. Today he is a Fundamentalist minister who describes the Catholic Church and its teachings as "an insult to the finished work of Christ."

Catholicism: Crisis of Faith is cunningly packaged to look like a Catholic video—and for a good reason. Its producers want to get it into the hands of unsuspecting Catholics.

The front of the slipcase shows a stained glass window with an illustration of priestly hands raising a host and chalice, apparently at the moment of consecration during Mass.

On the back of the slipcase is a photograph of a giant statue of the Blessed Virgin Mary. The words surrounding the statue are deceptively neutral: "Follow the journey of devout Catholic clergy and laity who courageously faced the crisis of faith and emerged with a life changing experience of Jesus Christ." Sounds pretty good, doesn't it? Think again.

There is no hint in the text on the slipcase that the video is an *attack* on Catholicism and features interviews with some of the most sharp-tongued anti-Catholics in America.

Deceptive Producers

McCarthy interviewed a lot of people for his video. But as is typical of Protestant anti-Catholic tactics, more than a few of these interviews were manipulated and misrepresented. Among them is the interview with Fr. Richard Chilson, author of eight books, including *Catholic Christianity* (Paulist, 1987).

Chilson told Catholic Answers, "McCarthy approached me saying that they were doing a video to help Christians understand the Catholic Church. He was all sweetness and ecumenism. I spend a lot of my ministry fighting Fundamentalists, and I must admit to having been duped by this. I figured they were Evangelical Christians rather than Fundamentalists and so agreed to cooperate in the interview. There was no preparation for the interview other than that I knew they wanted me to speak about the current state of Catholicism."

Chilson explains that the interview lasted an hour and a half and covered a wide range of subjects, including "the crisis in the Church today, the shortage of priests, and dissent."

After the interview, Chilson asked to see the finished video. He was never sent a copy and never had a chance to review his edited interview. No theatrical release was given to him to sign, but some months later he received a check for $125.00. (McCarthy claims that all interviewees signed releases.) Chilson had forgotten about the video entirely until, when at a convention, "some women approached me and asked if I were the priest in this video. They told me that it was pretty biased and suggested I go down to Hayward [California] where they would show it to me."

Deceptive Editing

Much of what McCarthy used of the Chilson interview concerned the Mass as a sacrifice. "The first extended quote they have from me in the video is part of that explanation, but it is not easy to give the Catholic understanding of eucharistic sacrifice in a sound bite. That discussion went on for at least fifteen minutes, and Mc-Carthy kept coming back to the idea of sacrifice."

Then comes a blatantly deceptive piece of editing. In voice-over, the narrator says, "Other Christian denominations celebrate that the sacrifice is finished. We asked Fr. Chilson why the Catholic Church chooses to focus on it continuing. Why not leave it finished?" The visuals show Chilson leaning back in his chair and passing his hand across his head, as though searching for an answer. He looks weary and replies, "I don't know if I can answer that. I am sorry, I know that's—that's a real issue between Protestants and Catholics, but I don't know if I can answer it in any better way than I've already kind of stumbled on."

The video cuts to Frank Eberhardt, once a Catholic seminarian and now a Fundamentalist who's made anti-Catholicism his full-time business. He says, "The Catholic priest cannot really explain how the finished work of Christ on the cross is continued today in the Mass."

Chilson explains why the editing was deceptive: "They, of course, made it look like I had nothing to say, whereas I had been trying to explain the issue for a good quarter hour. I would stand by what I said in the first shot [they used], although, taken out of context, it does not stand well on its own. The second shot is dirty pool. Indeed, I was suspicious that my response there may not even have been to that exact question. But even if it was, this was not lack of an answer on my part but frustration and exhaustion at going over the same ground again and again."

Chilson notes wryly that in the interview, as much time was spent on salvation as on the Eucharist, but "none of that was used because I gave them the gospel answer of salvation through Jesus Christ. Certainly, biased sampling was at work. If you fit their stereotype of a Catholic, you were on the screen. If you presented the gospel, you were ignored. I have to deal with this continually from Fundamentalists. The response is invariably that you are an exceptional Catholic" if you present the Catholic understanding of salvation as it really is—not as Fundamentalists think it is. "You become an exception that proves the rule."

There was a very good reason that McCarthy did not want to show Chilson expounding on salvation by grace alone through Christ alone. McCarthy wanted to set the viewer up for another segment of the video in which a group of anonymous Catholics were interviewed outside St. Patrick's Cathedral in New York City. Having a Catholic priest give a biblical exposition of the doctrine of salvation would have destroyed the force of the upcoming "man on the street" video by showing that those who understand the Catholic position have a biblical view of salvation.

Neither the video nor the transcript indicates the total number of Catholics interviewed. Most likely only those giving the "juiciest" answers (for the Fundamentalists' purposes) ended up featured in the video. The goal was to make the Catholic Church look silly and to feature only Catholics who had a confused or insufficient understanding of the Church's teaching on salvation. The inference drawn is that *all* Catholics believe the things these folks were saying.

All the viewer sees is the narrator asking nine lay Catholics how they think they can get to heaven. Here are some responses:

"Well, you know, by being a good Catholic and being nice to one another," replies one woman.

"As a woman you have to follow Mary's way to go to Christ," says another passer-by. (Including this comment was no doubt calculated to confirm Protestant viewers' worst suspicions about Catholic "Mariolatry.")

One man answers that he will go to heaven "by treating people properly. Be fair to everyone."

"I don't know. Just behaving myself," says another fellow, who admits he doesn't have a good answer.

An equally confused man replies, "By trying to live a clean and decent life, I guess."

Not one of these is a good answer, though each contains a partial truth (see Matt. 19:16–17; 25:31–46; Rom. 2:5–8). These people are easy foils for Fundamentalists. What makes this sort of subterfuge all the more obvious and deceitful is that McCarthy did not balance it with a similar selection of "random" responses from Protestants on the street.

Deceptive Narration

Chilson, whose doctoral work has been in Mahayana Buddhism, with a specialty in Tibetan Buddhism, said he selected this area of study because Buddhism "seemed to be as contrary to Christianity as it was possible to be."

The video quotes him as saying that, although Buddhists do not believe in God or the soul, behind their myths is a reality that corresponds to the reality addressed by Christianity. In this, Chilson, properly understood, is correct. Since all people face the same reality around them, even those without access to authentic revelation are able to grasp certain elements of that reality accurately —while misconstruing others. Even Buddhists (not to mention Muslims, Mormons, and Protestants) get some things right, for, as Paul taught, creation itself teaches us about God (Rom. 1:20), and the laws of God are written on the hearts of men (Rom. 2:14–16).

But the narrator's comments before and after Chilson's brief remarks on Buddhism lead the viewer to believe that Chilson in particular and the Catholic Church in general are working toward some kind of syncretistic amalgamation of Catholicism and Buddhism, something not even remotely implied in Chilson's remarks.

Mary Crucified?

The original release of *Catholicism: Crisis of Faith* showed a statue depicting a woman on a crucifix. The statue was said to be located in the cathedral of Quito, Ecuador. The narrator explained that Catholics have so confused the role of Mary in redemption, equating her work with her Son's, that they believe she, too, suffered for their sins.

But the confusion resides not in the Catholic Church but in the minds of McCarthy and the video's producers. Antonio Arregui, auxiliary bishop of Quito, certified that the statue in question is not in the city's cathedral but in a monastery in Quito. More importantly, the woman depicted is not Mary but a young woman martyr, St. Liberata. She is said to have been the daughter of a Portuguese prince. "Her father wished to marry her to a non-Christian and corrupt prince," explains Bishop Arregui. "When she refused, her father ordered that she be crucified." McCarthy was made aware of this grotesque blunder, but he admits it was still in the video as late as twenty-one months after its initial release.

The fact that such an outlandish claim—that Mary, too, was crucified—appeared in the original version at all shows McCarthy's sloppy scholarship.

Deceptive Study Materials

To maximize his video's impact, McCarthy produced a transcript and study guide to go with it. This allows it to be used for "Bible studies" in Protestant churches. Unfortunately, McCarthy isn't confining his sloppy scholarship and deceptive tactics just to Catholics. He has put them in the study material for Fundamentalists, as an examination of the footnotes shows. Footnotes in the transcript flesh out the on-screen arguments, but often disingenuously. In one scene, the narrator claims that "Catholicism has continued to add new doctrines to the Catholic faith from the traditions of men. The belief that the nature of the bread changed at the Mass was not added to official doctrine until the Fourth Lateran Council in 1215. This was the first time the Church sanctioned the theory of transubstantiation."

The footnote to this part of the transcript gives a lengthy quotation (from the *New Catholic Encyclopedia*) that gives the reader the impression that the Real Presence was a doctrine "invented" shortly before the Fourth Lateran Council and that belief in the doctrine is identical with belief in transubstantiation.

But as one would expect, the footnote quotes the *New Catholic Encyclopedia* selectively. The encyclopedia does *not* say that the doctrine was "invented" at that time. If the footnote had quoted the second paragraph of the encyclopedia's article on transubstantiation, one would have read, "The *scriptural evidence* requires that the bread cease to exist and that Christ's body be made present" (emphasis added).

Further paragraphs in the encyclopedia demonstrate that the Church Fathers taught the Real Presence, even though the technical term *transubstantiation* was not used until the medieval period. The encyclopedia does not say or imply that the doctrine was invented in 1215. It simply says that at that council, the term *transubstantiation* became the *official* way to express the ancient Christian doctrine concerning Christ's presence in the Eucharist.

In the footnotes to his transcript, McCarthy implies that, since the term *transubstantiation* was not officially used until the Fourth Lateran Council, the doctrine must have been invented around then. This is the same tactic the Jehovah's Witnesses use when they argue that, since the word *homoousios* ("one in substance") was not used by an ecumenical council to describe Christ's relationship with the Father, Christ's divinity was not believed until then.

This fallacy is obvious. The fact that a belief is expressed using different terms at different times does not prove that it is not the same belief. Language changes over time, and new questions are raised that necessitate new theological terms to express more precisely "the faith which was once for all delivered to the saints" (Jude 3).

But if clear thinking and balanced presentations of the evidence were the norm, anti-Catholicism in the form shown in *Catholicism: Crisis of Faith* would have died out long ago, this video would never have been produced, and, if produced, it would have no impact whatsoever.

47

The Great Heresies

From Christianity's beginnings, the Church has been attacked by those introducing false teachings, or heresies.

The Bible warned us this would happen. Paul told his young protégé, Timothy, "For the time is coming when people will not endure sound teaching, but having itching ears they will accumulate for themselves teachers to suit their own likings, and will turn away from listening to the truth and wander into myths" (2 Tim. 4:3–4).

What Is Heresy?

Heresy is an emotionally loaded term that is often misused. It is not the same thing as incredulity, schism, apostasy, or other sins against faith. The *Catechism of the Catholic Church* states, "Incredulity is the neglect of revealed truth or the willful refusal to assent to it. Heresy is the obstinate post-baptismal denial of some truth that must be believed with divine and Catholic faith, or it is likewise an obstinate doubt concerning the same; apostasy is the total repudiation of the Christian faith; schism is the refusal of submission to the Roman pontiff or of communion with the members of the Church subject to him" (CCC 2089).

To commit heresy, one must refuse to be corrected. A person who is ready to be corrected or unaware that what he has been saying is against Church teaching is not a heretic.

A person must be baptized to commit heresy. This means that movements that have split off from or been influenced by Christianity but do not practice baptism (or do not practice valid baptism) are not heresies but rather separate religions. Examples include Muslims, who do not practice baptism, and Jehovah's Witnesses, who do not practice valid baptism.

Finally, the doubt or denial involved in heresy must concern a matter that has been revealed by God and solemnly defined by the Church (for example, the Trinity, the Incarnation, the Real Presence of Christ in the Eucharist, the sacrifice of the Mass, the pope's infallibility, or the Immaculate Conception and Assumption of Mary).

It is important to distinguish heresy from schism and apostasy. In schism, one separates from the Catholic Church without repudiating a defined doctrine. An example of a contemporary schism is the Society of St. Pius X—the followers of the late Archbishop Marcel Lefebvre—who separated from the Church in the late 1980s but have not denied Catholic doctrines. In apostasy, one totally repudiates the Christian faith and no longer even claims to be a Christian.

With this in mind, let's look at some of the major heresies of Church history and when they began.

The Circumcisers (First Century)

The Circumcision heresy may be summed up in the words of Acts 15:1: "But some men came down from Judea and were teaching the brethren, 'Unless you are circumcised according to the custom of Moses, you cannot be saved.'"

Many of the early Christians were Jews who brought to the Christian faith many of their former practices. They recognized in Jesus the Messiah predicted by the prophets and the fulfillment of the Old Testament. Because circumcision had been required in the Old Testament for membership in God's covenant, many thought it would also be required for membership in the New Covenant that Christ had come to inaugurate. They believed one must be circumcised and keep the Mosaic law to come to Christ. In other words, one had to become a Jew to become a Christian.

They were wrong. God made it clear to Peter in Acts 10 that Gentiles are acceptable to God and may be baptized and become

Christians without circumcision. The same teaching was vigorously defended by Paul in his epistles to the Romans and the Galatians—to areas where the Circumcision heresy had spread.

Gnosticism (First and Second Centuries)

"Matter is evil!" was the cry of the Gnostics. This idea was borrowed from certain Greek philosophers. It stood against Catholic teaching, not only because it contradicts Genesis 1:31 ("And God saw everything that he had made, and behold, it was very good") and other Scripture passages but because it denies the Incarnation. If matter is evil, then Jesus Christ could not be true God and true man, for Christ is in no way evil. Thus many Gnostics denied the Incarnation, claiming that Christ only *appeared* to be a man but his humanity was an illusion. Some Gnostics, recognizing that the Old Testament taught that God created matter, claimed that the God of the Jews was an evil deity who was distinct from the New Testament God of Jesus Christ. They also proposed belief in many divine beings, known as "aeons," who mediated between man and the ultimate, unreachable God. The lowest of these aeons, the one who had contact with men, was supposed to be Jesus Christ.

Montanism (Late Second Century)

Montanus began his career innocently enough through preaching a return to penance and fervor. His movement also emphasized the continuance of miraculous gifts, such as speaking in tongues and prophecy. However, he also claimed that his teachings were above those of the Church, and soon he began to teach Christ's imminent return in his home town in Phrygia. There were also statements that Montanus himself either was, or at least specially spoke for, the Paraclete that Jesus had promised would come (in reality, the Holy Spirit).

Sabellianism (Early Third Century)

The Sabellianists taught that Jesus Christ and God the Father were not distinct Persons but two aspects or offices of one Person. According to them, the three Persons of the Trinity exist only in God's relation to man, not in objective reality.

Arianism (Fourth Century)

Arius taught that Christ was a creature made by God. By disguising his heresy using orthodox or near-orthodox terminology, he was able to sow great confusion in the Church. He was able to muster the support of many bishops, while others excommunicated him.

Arianism was solemnly condemned in 325 at the First Council of Nicaea, which defined the divinity of Christ, and in 381 at the First Council of Constantinople, which defined the divinity of the Holy Spirit. These two councils gave us the Nicene Creed, which Catholics recite at Mass every Sunday.

Pelagianism (Fifth Century)

Pelagius denied that we inherit original sin from Adam's sin and claimed that we become sinful only through the bad example of the sinful community into which we are born. Conversely, he denied that we inherit righteousness as a result of Christ's death on the cross and said that we become personally righteous by instruction and imitation in the Christian community, following the example of Christ. Pelagius stated that man is born morally neutral and can achieve heaven under his own powers. According to him, God's grace is not truly necessary but merely makes easier an otherwise difficult task.

Semi-Pelagianism (Fifth Century)

After Augustine refuted the teachings of Pelagius, some tried a modified version of his system. This, too, ended in heresy by claiming that humans can reach out to God under their own power, without God's grace; that once a person has entered a state of grace, one can retain it through one's efforts, without further grace from God; and that natural human effort alone can give one some claim to receiving grace though not strictly merit it.

Nestorianism (Fifth Century)

This heresy about the person of Christ was initiated by Nestorius, bishop of Constantinople, who denied Mary the title of *Theotokos* (Greek: "God-bearer" or, less literally, "Mother of God"). Nestorius claimed that she only bore Christ's human nature in her womb and proposed the alternative title *Christotokos* ("Christ-bearer" or "Mother of Christ").

Orthodox Catholic theologians recognized that Nestorius's theory would fracture Christ into two separate persons (one human and one divine, joined in a sort of loose unity), only one of whom was in her womb. The Church reacted in 431 with the Council of Ephesus, defining that Mary can be properly referred to as the Mother of God, not in the sense that she is older than God or the source of God but in the sense that the person she carried in her womb was, in fact, God incarnate ("in the flesh").

There is some doubt whether Nestorius himself held the heresy his statements imply, and in this century, the Assyrian Church of the East, historically regarded as a Nestorian church, has signed a fully orthodox joint declaration on christology with the Catholic Church and rejects Nestorianism. It is now in the process of coming into full ecclesial communion with the Catholic Church.

Monophysitism (Fifth Century)

Monophysitism originated as a reaction to Nestorianism. The Monophysites (led by a man named Eutyches) were horrified by Nestorius's implication that Christ was two people with two different natures (human and divine). They went to the other extreme, claiming that Christ was one person with only one nature (a fusion of human and divine elements). They are thus known as Monophysites because of their claim that Christ had only one nature (Greek: *mono* = one; *physis* = nature).

Orthodox Catholic theologians recognized that Monophysitism was as bad as Nestorianism because it denied Christ's full humanity and full divinity. If Christ did not have a fully human nature, then he would not be fully human, and if he did not have a fully divine nature, then he was not fully divine.

Iconoclasm (Seventh and Eighth Centuries)

This heresy arose when a group of people known as iconoclasts (literally, "icon smashers") claimed that it was sinful to make pictures and statues of Christ and the saints, despite the fact that in the Bible, God had commanded the making of religious statues (Ex. 25:18–20; 1 Chr. 28:18–19), including symbolic representations of Christ (cf. Num. 21:8–9 with John 3:14).

Catharism (Eleventh Century)

Catharism was a complicated mix of non-Christian religions reworked with Christian terminology. The Cathars had many different sects; they had in common a teaching that the world was created by an evil deity (so matter was evil) and we must worship the good deity instead.

The Albigensians formed one of the largest Cathar sects. They taught that the spirit was created by God and was good, while the body was created by an evil god, and the spirit must be freed from the body. Having children was one of the greatest evils, since it entailed imprisoning another "spirit" in flesh. Logically, marriage was forbidden, though fornication was permitted. Tremendous fasts and severe mortifications of all kinds were practiced, and their leaders went about in voluntary poverty.

Protestantism (Sixteenth Century)

Protestant groups display a wide variety of different doctrines. However, virtually all claim to believe in the teachings of *sola scriptura* ("by Scripture alone"—the idea that we must use only the Bible when forming our theology) and *sola fide* ("by faith alone"—the idea that we are justified by faith only).

The great diversity of Protestant doctrines stems from the doctrine of private judgment, which denies the infallible authority of the Church and claims that each individual is to interpret Scripture for himself. This idea is rejected in 2 Peter 1:20, where we are told the first rule of Bible interpretation: "First of all you must understand this, that no prophecy of scripture is a matter of one's own interpretation." A significant feature of this heresy is the attempt to pit the Church "against" the Bible, denying that the magisterium has any infallible authority to teach and interpret Scripture.

The doctrine of private judgment has resulted in an enormous number of different denominations. According to the *Christian Sourcebook*, there are approximately 20–30,000 denominations, with 270 new ones being formed each year. Virtually all of these are Protestant.

Jansenism (Seventeenth Century)

Jansenius, bishop of Ypres, France, initiated this heresy with a paper he wrote on Augustine, which redefined the doctrine of grace. Among other doctrines, his followers claimed that Christ died not for all men but only those who will be finally saved (the elect). This and other Jansenist errors were officially condemned by Pope Innocent X in 1653.

Heresies have been with us from the Church's beginning. They even have been started by Church leaders, who were then corrected by councils and popes. Fortunately, we have Christ's promise that heresies will never prevail against the Church, for he told Peter, "You are Peter, and on this rock I will build my Church, and *the powers of death shall not prevail against it*" (Matt. 16:18). The Church is truly, in Paul's words, "the pillar and bulwark of the truth" (1 Tim. 3:15).

48

Eastern Orthodoxy

One of the most tragic divisions within Christianity is the one between the Catholic Church and the Orthodox churches. Both have valid holy orders and apostolic succession through the episcopacy, both celebrate the same sacraments, both believe almost exactly the same theology, and both proclaim the same faith in Christ. So, why the division? What caused the division?

Emperor vs. Patriarch

After the western Roman Empire collapsed in A.D. 476, the eastern half continued under the title of the Byzantine Empire and was headquartered in Constantinople. The patriarch of that city had jurisdiction over the patriarchates of Alexandria, Antioch, and Jerusalem and served under the emperor, who ruled those lands with military might. In the East, the emperor wielded tremendous influence in church affairs. Some emperors even claimed to be equal in authority to the twelve apostles and as such claimed to have the power to appoint the patriarch of Constantinople. Although the two offices were legally autonomous, in practice the patriarch served at the emperor's pleasure. Many patriarchs of Constantinople were good and holy bishops who ruled well and resisted imperial encroachments on church matters, but it is difficult to withstand the designs of power-hungry or meddlesome emperors with armed soldiers at their disposal.

The patriarch often attempted to bolster his position in the universal Church to give himself more leverage in dealing with the emperor, and this usually brought him into conflict with Rome.

During the years of conflict between East and West, the Roman pontiff remained firm, defending the Catholic faith against heresies and unruly or immoral secular powers, especially the Byzantine emperor. The first conflict came when Emperor Constantius appointed an Arian heretic as patriarch. Pope Julian excommunicated the patriarch in 343, and Constantinople remained in schism until John Chrysostom assumed the patriarchate in 398.

Ironically, in the Church's eighth-century struggle against the Iconoclastic heresy (which sought to eliminate all sacred images), it was the pope and the Western bishops mainly who fought for the Catholic practice of venerating icons, which is still very much a part of Orthodox liturgy and spirituality. The patriarch of Constantinople sided with the heretical, iconoclastic emperors.

1054 and All That

The Norman conquest of southern Italy helped touch off the Great Schism between Eastern and Western Christendom. When the Catholic Normans took over the Byzantine-rite Greek colonies in southern Italy, they compelled the Greek communities there to adopt the Latin-rite custom of using unleavened bread for the Eucharist. This caused great aggravation among the Greek Catholics because it went against their ancient custom of using leavened bread.

In response, Patriarch Cerularius ordered all of the Latin-rite communities in Constantinople to conform to the Eastern practice of using leavened bread. You can imagine the uproar that ensued. The Latins refused, so the patriarch closed their churches and sent a hostile letter to Pope Leo IX.

What followed next was a tragedy of errors. In an attempt to quell the disturbance, the Pope sent a three-man delegation, led by Cardinal Humbert, to visit Patriarch Cerularius, but matters worsened. The legates presented the patriarch with the Pope's reply to his charges. Both sides managed to infuriate each other over diplomatic courtesies, and when the smoke cleared, a serious rift had developed. This was not, however, the actual break between the two communions. It's a popular myth that the schism dates to the year 1054 and that the Pope and the patriarch excommunicated each other at that time, but they did not.

Orthodox bishop Kallistos Ware (formerly Timothy Ware) writes, "The choice of Cardinal Humbert was unfortunate, for both he and Cerularius were men of stiff and intransigent temper. . . . After [an initial, unfriendly encounter] the patriarch refused to have further dealings with the legates. Eventually Humbert lost patience, and laid a bull of excommunication against Cerularius on the altar of the Church of the Holy Wisdom. . . . Cerularius and his synod retaliated by anathematizing Humbert (but not the Roman Church as such)" (*The Orthodox Church*, 67).

The *New Catholic Encyclopedia* says, "The consummation of the schism is generally dated from the year 1054, when this unfortunate sequence of events took place. This conclusion, however, is not correct, because in the bull composed by Humbert, only Patriarch Cerularius was excommunicated. The validity of the bull is questioned because Pope Leo IX was already dead at that time. On the other side, the Byzantine synod excommunicated only the legates and abstained from any attack on the Pope or the Latin Church."

There was no single event that marked the schism but rather a sliding into and out of schism during a period of several centuries, punctuated with temporary reconciliations. The East's final break with Rome did not come until the 1450s.

Attempts at Reconciliation

"Even after 1054 friendly relations between East and West continued. The two parts of Christendom were not yet conscious of a great gulf of separation between them. . . . The dispute remained something of which ordinary Christians in East and West were largely unaware" (Ware, 67).

This changed when the Byzantine Empire collapsed suddenly in 1453. A soldier forgot to lock one of the gates of the fortified city of Constantinople, and the Turks sacked the city. With the Turks in control of the capital city, the rest of the empire crumbled quickly. Under pressure from Muslims, most of the Eastern churches repudiated their union with Rome, and this is the split that persists to this day. The current Eastern Orthodox communion dates from the 1450s, making it a mere six decades older than the Protestant Reformation.

Eastern Fragmentation

Two subsequent events—one external, the other internal—reduced the patriarch of Constantinople's status to nearly that of a figurehead. The sword of Islam gave military protection to the center of the Eastern Orthodox world, but at a high price. The Muslim sultan sold the office of patriarch to the highest bidder and changed the occupants often to keep the money rolling in. From 1453 to 1923, the Turkish sultans deposed 105 out of the 159 patriarchs. Six were murdered, and only twenty-one died of natural causes while in office.

Another blow that weakened the patriarch's authority came from Russia. Ivan the Great assumed the title of "Czar" (Russian for "Caesar"). Moscow was then called the "third Rome," and the Czar tried to assume the role of protector for Eastern Christianity.

With the collapse of the patriarchal system, the Eastern church lost its center and fragmented along national lines. Russia claimed independence from the patriarch of Constantinople in 1589, the first nation to do this. Other ethnic and regional splintering quickly followed, and today there are eleven independent Orthodox churches. The Russian Orthodox church dominates contemporary Eastern Orthodoxy, representing seven-eighths of the total number of Orthodox Christians.

The Filioque *Problem*

One theological disagreement has to do with the Latin compound word *filioque* ("and the Son") which was added to the Nicene Creed by Spanish Catholic bishops around the end of the sixth century. With this addition, the Creed says that the Spirit "proceeds from the Father and the Son." Without the addition, it says the Spirit proceeds from the Father.

Eastern Orthodox have traditionally challenged this, either saying that the doctrine is inaccurate or, for those who believe that it is accurate, that the Pope had no authority to insert this word into the Creed (though it was later affirmed by an ecumenical council).

Many today, both Orthodox and Catholics, believe this controversy was a tempest in a teapot. The doctrine that the Holy Spirit proceeds from the Son as well as the Father is intimated in Scripture and present in the earliest Church Fathers. Controversy over it arose again only after the Eastern churches repudiated their union with Rome under pressure from the Muslims.

Eastern Orthodox often refer to the Holy Spirit proceeding from "the Father *through* the Son," which can be equivalent to the Catholic formula "from the Father *and* the Son." Since everything the Son has is from the Father, if the Spirit proceeds from the Son, then the Son can be spoken of only as one through whom the Spirit received what he has from the Father, the ultimate principle of the Godhead. Because the formulas are equivalent, the *Catechism of the Catholic Church* notes: "This legitimate complementarity, provided it does not become rigid, does not affect the identity of faith in the reality of the same mystery confessed" (CCC 248).

Today there is every hope that the equivalence of the two formulas can be formally recognized by all parties and that the *filioque* controversy can be resolved.

The Councils

A more substantive disagreement between Catholics and the Eastern Orthodox concerns the role of the pope and the ecumenical councils in the Church. Both sides agree that ecumenical councils have the ability to infallibly define doctrines, but a question arises concerning which councils are ecumenical.

The Eastern Orthodox communion bases its teachings on Scripture and "the seven ecumenical councils": Nicaea I (325), Constantinople I (381), Ephesus (431), Chalcedon (451), Constantinople II (553), Constantinople III (680), and Nicaea II (787). Catholics recognize these as the *first* seven ecumenical councils but not the *only* seven.

While Catholics recognize an ensuing series of ecumenical councils, leading up to Vatican II, which closed in 1965, the Eastern Orthodox say there have been no ecumenical councils since 787, and no teaching after Nicaea II is accepted as of universal authority.

One of the reasons the Eastern Orthodox do not claim to have had any ecumenical councils since Nicaea II is that they have been unable to agree on which councils are ecumenical. In Orthodox circles, the test for whether a council is ecumenical is whether it is "accepted by the church" as such. But that test is unworkable: Any disputants who are unhappy with a council's result can point to their own disagreement with it as evidence that the church has not accepted it as ecumenical, and it therefore has no authority.

The Pope's Authority

Since the Eastern schism began, the Orthodox have generally claimed that the pope has only a primacy of honor among the bishops of the world, not a primacy of authority. But the concept of a primacy of honor without a corresponding authority cannot be derived from the Bible. At every juncture where Jesus speaks of

Peter's relation to the other apostles, he emphasizes Peter's special mission to them and not simply his place of honor among them. In Matthew 16:19, Jesus gives Peter "the keys of the kingdom" and the power to bind and loose. While the latter is later given to the other apostles (Matt 18:18) the former is not. In Luke 22:28–32, Jesus assures the apostles that they all have authority, but then he singles out Peter, conferring upon him a special pastoral authority over the other disciples that he is to exercise by strengthening their faith (22:31–32).

In John 21:15–17, with only the other disciples present (cf. John 21:2), Jesus asks Peter, "Simon, son of John, do you love me more than these?"—in other words, is Peter more devoted to him than to the other disciples? When Peter responds that he is, Jesus instructs him: "Feed my lambs" (22:17). Thus we see Jesus describing the other disciples—the only other people who are present, the ones whom Jesus refers to as "these"—as part of the lambs that he instructs Peter to feed, giving him the role of pastor (shepherd) over them. This is a reference to Peter having more than merely a primacy of honor with respect to the other apostles but a primacy of pastoral discipline as well.

Ecumenical Prospects

While Catholics and Eastern Orthodox are separate for the moment, what unites us is still far greater than what divides us, and there are abundant reasons for optimism regarding reconciliation in the future. Over the last several decades, there has been a marked lessening of tensions and overcoming of long-standing hostilities.

In 1965, Pope Paul VI and Patriarch Athenagoras I of Constantinople lifted mutual excommunications dating from the eleventh century, and in 1995, Pope John Paul II and Patriarch Bartholomew I of Constantinople concelebrated the Eucharist together. John Paul II, the first Slavic pope, made the reconciliation of Eastern and Western Christendom a special theme of his pontificate, and he released a large number of documents and addresses honoring the contributions of Eastern Christendom and seeking to promote unity between Catholics and Orthodox.

It is again becoming possible to envision a time when the two communions will be united and, by the power of the Holy Spirit, fulfill their duty in bringing about Christ's solemn desire and command "that they may be one" (John 17:11).

49

Fundamentalism

Fundamentalism is a relatively new brand of Protestantism started in America that has attracted a tremendous following, including many fallen-away Catholics. How did this popular movement originate? The history of Fundamentalism may be viewed as having three main phases. The first lasted a generation, from the 1890s to the Scopes "Monkey Trial" of 1925. In this period, Fundamentalism emerged as a reaction to liberalizing trends in American Protestantism; it broke off, but never completely, from Evangelicalism, of which it may be considered one wing. In its second phase, it passed from public view but never actually disappeared or even lost ground. Finally, Fundamentalism came to the nation's attention again around 1970, and it has enjoyed considerable growth.

What has been particularly surprising is that Catholics seem to constitute a disproportionate share of the new recruits. The Catholic Church in America includes about a quarter of the country's inhabitants, so one might expect about a quarter of new Fundamentalists to have been Catholics at one time. But in many Fundamentalist congregations, anywhere from one-third to one-half of the members once belonged to the Catholic Church. This varies around the country, depending on how large the native Catholic population is.

Fundamentalist churches in the South have few converts from Catholicism because there have never been many Catholics in most parts of the South. In the Northeast and Midwest, where Catholics are more common, one finds former Catholics making up a majority of some Fundamentalist congregations. And in the Southwest, with its substantial Hispanic population, former Catholics *are* the congregation. Indeed, it has been estimated that one out of six Hispanics in this country is now a Fundamentalist. Twenty years ago there were almost no Hispanic Fundamentalists.

Fundamentalism: Relatively New

While the origin of the term *Fundamentalist* has a fairly simple history, the movement itself has a more confused origin. There was no individual founder, nor was there a single event that precipitated its advent. Of course, Fundamentalist writers insist that Fundamentalism is nothing but a continuation of Christian orthodoxy. According to this theory, Fundamentalism flourished for three centuries after Christ, went underground for twelve hundred years, surfaced again with the Reformation, took its knocks from various sources, and was alternately prominent or diminished in its influence and visibility. In short, according to its partisans, Fundamentalism has always been the Christian remnant, the faithful who remain after the rest of Christianity (if it can even be granted the title) has fallen into apostasy.

Until almost 100 years ago, Fundamentalism as we know it was not a separate movement within Protestantism, and the word itself was virtually unknown. Those people who today would be called Fundamentalists were formerly either Baptists, Presbyterians, or members of some other specific sect. But in the last decade of the nineteenth century, issues came to the fore that made them start to withdraw from mainline Protestantism.

The issues were the Social Gospel (a liberalizing and secularizing trend within Protestantism that tried to weaken the Christian message, making it a merely social and political agenda), the embrace of Darwinism (which seemed to call into question the reliability of Scripture), and the higher criticism of the Bible that originated in Germany.

To meet the challenge presented by these developments, early Fundamentalist leaders united around several basic principles, but it was not until the publication of a series of volumes called *The Fundamentals* that the movement received its name.

The basic elements of Fundamentalism were formulated about a century ago at the Presbyterian theological seminary in Princeton, New Jersey, by B. B. Warfield and Charles Hodge, among others. What they produced became known as Princeton theology, and it appealed to conservative Protestants who were concerned about the liberalizing trends of the Social Gospel movement, which was gaining steam at about the same time.

In 1909 the brothers Milton and Lyman Stewart, whose wealth came from the oil industry, were responsible for underwriting a series of twelve volumes entitled *The Fundamentals*. There were sixty-four contributors, including scholars such as James Orr, W. J. Eerdman, H. C. G. Moule, James M. Gray, and Warfield himself, as well as Episcopalian bishops, Presbyterian ministers, Methodist evangelists, and even an Egyptologist. As Edward Dobson, an associate pastor at Jerry Falwell's Thomas Road Baptist Church, summarized the collaboration, "They were certainly not anti-intellectual, snake-handling, cultic, obscurantist fanatics."

The preface to the volumes explained their purpose: "In 1909 God moved two Christian laymen to set aside a large sum of money for issuing twelve volumes that would set forth the fundamentals of the Christian faith, and which were to be sent free of charge to ministers of the gospel, missionaries, Sunday school superintendents, and others engaged in aggressive Christian work throughout the English speaking world."

Three million copies of the series were distributed. Harry Fosdick, a theological liberal, wrote an article in *The Christian Century* called "Shall the Fundamentalists Win?" He used the title of the books to designate the people he was opposing, and the label he originated became commonly used to designate those who adhered to *The Fundamentals*.

The fundamental doctrines identified in the series can be reduced to five: (1) the inspiration and what the writers call infallibility of Scripture, (2) the deity of Christ (including his Virgin Birth), (3) the substitutionary atonement of his death, (4) his literal Resurrection from the dead, and (5) his literal return at the Second Coming.

The Five Fundamentals

Fundamentalists' attitude toward the Bible is the keystone of their faith. Their understanding of inspiration and inerrancy comes from Benjamin Warfield's notion of plenary-verbal inspiration, meaning that the original autographs (manuscripts) of the Bible are all inspired, and the inspiration extends not just to the message God wished to convey but to the very words chosen by the sacred writers.

Although the doctrine of the inspiration and inerrancy of the Bible is most commonly cited as the essential cornerstone of the Fundamentalist beliefs, the logically prior doctrine is the deity of Christ. For the Catholic, his deity is accepted either on the word of the authoritative and infallible Church or because a dispassionate examination of the Bible and early Christian history shows that he must have been just what he claimed to be—God.

Most Catholics, as a practical matter, accept his divinity based upon the former method; many—the apologist Arnold Lunn is a good example—use the latter. In either case, there is a certain reasoning involved in the Catholic's embrace of this teaching. For many Fundamentalists, the assurance of Christ's divinity comes not through reason, or even through faith in the Catholic meaning of the word, but through an inner, personal experience.

As Warfield put it, "The supreme proof to every Christian of the deity of his Lord is in his own inner experience of the transforming power of his Lord upon the heart and life." One consequence of this has become painfully clear to many Fundamentalists: When one falls into sin, when the ardor that was present at conversion fades, the transforming power of Christ seems to go, and so can one's faith in his deity. This accounts for many defections from Fundamentalism to agnosticism and secularism; the tenuous basis for the Fundamentalist's beliefs does not provide for the dark night of the soul. When that darkness comes, the Fundamentalist has no reasonable basis for hope or faith.

As an appendage to the doctrine of the deity of Christ, and con-

sidered equally important in *The Fundamentals*, is the Virgin Birth
—although some Fundamentalists list this separately, resulting in
six basic doctrines rather than five. One might expect the reality of
heaven and hell or the existence of the Trinity to be next, but the
Virgin Birth is considered an essential doctrine, since it protects
belief in Christ's deity. One should keep in mind, though, that
when Fundamentalists speak of Christ's birth from a virgin, they
mean that Mary was a virgin only until his birth. Their common
understanding is that Mary later had other children, citing the
scriptural passages that refer to Christ's "brethren."

In reaction to the Social Gospel advocates, who said that Christ
gave nothing more than a good moral example, the early Fundamentalists insisted on their third doctrine, namely, that he died
a substitutionary death. He not only took on our sins, but he
received the penalty that would have been ours. He was actually
punished by the Father in our stead.

On the matter of the Resurrection, Fundamentalists do not differ from orthodox Catholics. They believe that Christ rose from
the dead physically, not just spiritually. His Resurrection was not
a collective hallucination of his followers nor something invented
by pious writers of later years. It really happened, and to deny it
is to deny Scripture's reliability.

The most disputed topic, among Fundamentalists themselves,
concerns the fifth belief listed in *The Fundamentals*: the Second
Coming. There is unanimous agreement that Christ will physically return to Earth, but the exact date has been disputed. Some
say it will be before the millennium, a thousand-year golden age
with Christ physically reigning on earth. Others say it will be
after the millennium. Others say that the millennium is Christ's
heavenly reign and that there will be no golden age on earth before the last judgment. Some Fundamentalists also believe in the
Rapture, the bodily taking into heaven of true believers before
the tribulation or time of trouble that precedes the millennium.
Others find no scriptural basis for such a belief.

Such are the five (or six) main doctrines discussed in the books
that gave Fundamentalism its name. But they are not necessarily

the beliefs that most distinguish Fundamentalism today. For instance, you rarely hear much discussion about the Virgin Birth, although there is no question that Fundamentalists still believe this doctrine. Rather, to the general public, and to most Fundamentalists themselves, today Fundamentalism has a different focus.

Distinguishing Marks

The belief that is first and foremost the defining characteristic of Fundamentalists is their reliance on the Bible to the complete exclusion of any authority exercised by the Church. The second is their insistence on a faith in Christ as one's personal Lord and Savior.

"Do you accept Christ as your personal Lord and Savior?" they ask. "Have you been saved?" This is unmodified Christian individualism, which holds that the individual is saved, without ever considering his relationship to a church, a congregation, or anyone else. It is a one-to-one relationship, with no community, no sacraments—just the individual Christian and his Lord. And the Christian knows when he has been saved, down to the hour and minute of his salvation, because his salvation came when he "accepted" Christ. It came like a flash.

In that instant, many Fundamentalists believe, their salvation is assured. There is now nothing that can undo it. Without that instant, that moment of acceptance, a person would be doomed to eternal hell. And that is why the third most visible characteristic of Fundamentalism is the emphasis on evangelism. If sinners do not undergo the same kind of salvation experience Fundamentalists have undergone, they will go to hell. Fundamentalists perceive a duty to spread their faith—what can be more charitable than giving others a chance for escaping hell?—and they have often been successful.

Their success is partly due to their discipline. For all their talk about the Catholic Church being "rule-laden," there are perhaps no Christians who operate in a more regimented manner. Their rules—non-biblical rules, one might add—extend not just to religion and religious practices proper but to facets of everyday life. Most people are familiar with their strictures on drinking, gambling, dancing, and smoking. Fundamentalists are also intensely involved in their local congregations. Many people returning to the Catholic Church from Fundamentalism complain that as Fundamentalists they had no time or room for themselves; everything centered around the church. All their friends were members; all their social activities were staged by it. Not to attend Wednesday evening services (in addition to one or two services on Sunday), not to participate in the Bible studies and youth groups, not to dress and act like everyone else in the congregation—these immediately put one beyond the pale, and in a small church (few Fundamentalist churches have more than a hundred members) this meant being ostracized, a silent invitation to conform or worship elsewhere.

Nevertheless, despite the criticism Fundamentalists sometimes receive, they do undertake the praiseworthy task of adhering to certain key Christian tenets in a society that has all too often forgotten about Christ.

50

Fundamentalist or Catholic?

At times Fundamentalists talk as if no case can be made for the Catholic faith. That's understandable. After all, if you're a Fundamentalist instead of a Catholic, it is because you do not believe that Catholicism is true. You reject it because you think it is false. But make sure that what you're rejecting is Catholicism and not merely a caricature of it. If you think that Catholics worship Mary, pray to statues, and claim that the pope is equal to God, then you are rejecting not Catholicism but someone's misrepresentation of it. You deserve to have the facts before you make up your mind. This chapter states a brief case for Catholicism in a few important areas. Catholic Answers has available tracts that consider in detail these and other topics—including, perhaps, just the ones you are most interested in.

Christian History

Christ established one Church with one set of beliefs (cf. Eph. 4:4–5). He did not establish numerous churches with contradictory beliefs. To see which one is the true Church, we must look for the one that has an unbroken historical link to the Church of the New Testament. Catholics are able to show such a link. They trace their leaders—the bishops—back through time, bishop by bishop, all the way to the apostles, and they show that the pope is the lineal successor to Peter, who was the first bishop of Rome. The same thing is true of Catholic beliefs and practices. Take any one you wish, and you can trace it back. This is just what John Henry Newman did in his book *An Essay on the Development of Christian Doctrine*.

He looked at Christian beliefs through the ages. Starting with the nineteenth century (he was writing in 1844), he worked backward century by century, seeing if Catholic beliefs that existed at any particular time could be traced to beliefs existing a century before. Back and back he went, until he got to New Testament times. What he demonstrated is that there is a real continuity of beliefs, that the Catholic Church has existed from day one of Church history, that it is in fact the Church established by Christ.

Newman was not a Catholic when he started the book, but his research convinced him of the truth of the Catholic faith, and as the book was finished he converted. Fundamentalist leaders make no effort to trace their version of Christianity century by century. They just claim that the Christianity existing in New Testament times was like today's Protestant Fundamentalism in all essentials.

According to modern Fundamentalists, the original Christian Church was doctrinally the same as today's Fundamentalist churches. When Emperor Constantine legalized Christianity in A.D. 313, pagans flocked to the Church in hopes of secular preferment, but the Church could not assimilate so many. It soon compromised its principles and became paganized by adopting pagan beliefs and practices. It developed the doctrines with which the Catholic Church is identified today. Simply put, it apostatized and became the Catholic Church. Meanwhile, true Christians (Fundamentalists) did not change their beliefs but were forced to remain in hiding until the Reformation.

The trouble with this history is that there are no historical facts whatsoever to back it up. Distinctively Catholic beliefs—the papacy, priesthood, invocation of saints, sacraments, veneration of Mary, salvation by something besides "faith alone," purgatory—were evident long before the fourth century, before Constantine. They were believed by Christians before this supposed "paganization" took place. Another difficulty is that there are no historical records—none at all—that imply that an underground Fundamentalist church existed from the early fourth century to the Reformation. In those years there were many schisms and heresies, most now vanished, but present-day Fundamentalists cannot find among them their missing Fundamentalist church. There were no groups that believed in all (or even most) of the doctrines espoused by the Protestant Reformers (e.g. *sola scriptura*, salvation by "faith alone," and an invisible church). No wonder Fundamentalist writers dislike discussing Church history!

Since the Christian Church was to exist historically and be like a city set on a mountain for all to see (cf. Matt. 5:14), it had to be visible and easily identifiable. A church that exists only in the hearts of believers is not visible and is more like the candle hidden under the bushel basket (cf. Matt. 5:15). But any visible church would necessarily be an institutional church that would need an earthly head. It would need an authority to which Christians could turn for the final resolution of doctrinal and disciplinary disputes. Christ appointed Peter and his successors to that position.

Christ designated Peter head of the Church on earth when he said, "And I tell you, you are Peter, and on this rock I will build my church" (Matt. 16:18). Fundamentalists, desiring to avoid the natural sense of the passage, say that *rock* refers not to Peter but to his profession of faith or to Christ himself. But Peter's profession of faith is two sentences away and can't be what is meant. Similarly, the reference can't be to Christ. The fact that he is elsewhere (by a quite different metaphor) called the cornerstone (Eph. 2:20; 1 Pet. 2:4–8) does not mean that Peter was not appointed the earthly foundation. The apostles were also described as foundation stones in a sense (Eph. 2:20; Rev. 21:14), meaning that Christ is not the only person the Bible speaks of as being the Church's foundation. In one sense the foundation was Christ, in another it was the apostles, and in another it was Peter. In Matthew 16:18, Christ has Peter in mind. He himself would be the Church's invisible foundation since he was returning to heaven, from where he would invisibly rule the Church. He needed to leave behind a visible authority, one whom people could locate when searching for religious truth. That visible authority is the papacy.

The Bible

Since the Reformers rejected the papacy, they also rejected the teaching authority of the Church. They looked elsewhere for the rule of faith and thought they found it solely in the Bible. Its interpretation would be left to the individual reader, guided by the Holy Spirit. But reason and experience tell us that the Bible could not have been intended as each man's private guide to the truth. If individual guidance by the Holy Spirit were a reality, everyone would understand the same thing from the Bible—since God cannot teach error. But Christians have understood contradictory things from Scripture. Fundamentalists even differ among themselves in what they think the Bible says.

The Bible also tells us that private interpretation is not to be the rule for understanding the Bible. Peter declares this to be a matter of prime importance, saying, "First of all you must understand this, that no prophecy of scripture is a matter of one's own interpretation" (2 Pet. 1:20). Later he warns about what can happen if a person ignorantly approaches Scripture on his own or is unstable in clinging to the apostolic teachings he has received. He states of Paul's letters, "There are some things in them hard to understand, which the ignorant and unstable twist to their own destruction, as they do the other scriptures" (2 Pet. 3:16). Private interpretation and instability in clinging to the doctrines passed down from the apostles can thus result in one twisting Scripture to one's own destruction.

The Bible also denies that it is sufficient as the Church's rule of faith. Paul acknowledges that much Christian teaching is to be found in the tradition that is handed down by word of mouth (1 Cor. 11:2; 2 Tim. 2:2). He instructs us to "stand firm and hold to the traditions which you were taught by us, either by word of mouth or by letter" (2 Thess. 2:15). We are told that the first Christians "devoted themselves to the apostles' teaching" (Acts 2:42), which was the oral teaching that was given even before the New Testament was written.

Justification

The Reformers saw justification as a mere legal act by which God declares the sinner to be meriting heaven even though he remains in fact unjust and sinful. It is not a real eradication of sin but a covering or non-imputation. It is not an inner renewal and a real sanctification, but only an external application of Christ's righteousness.

Scripture understands justification differently. It is a true eradication of sin and a true sanctification and renewal of the inner man, for "there is therefore now no condemnation for those who are in Christ Jesus" (Rom. 8:1) and "if any one is in Christ, he is a new creation; the old has passed away, behold, the new has come" (2 Cor. 5:17). Thus God chose us "to be saved, through sanctification by the Spirit and belief in the truth" (2 Thess. 2:13).

Scripture conceives of forgiveness of sins as a real and complete removal of them. The words used are *wipe out* (Ps. 51:2[50:3]), *blot out* (Is. 43:25), *take away* (Mic. 7:18), *remove* (John 1:29), and *cleanse* (Ps. 103 [102]:12). Scripture shows justification as a rebirth, as a generation of the supernatural life in a former sinner (John 3:5; Titus 3:5), as a thorough inner renewal (Eph. 4:23), and as a sanctification (1 Cor. 6:11). The soul itself becomes beautiful and holy. It is not just an ugly soul hidden under a beautiful cloak.

The Sacraments

While on earth, Christ used his humanity as a medium of his power (cf. Mark 5:25–30). He uses sacraments to distribute his grace now (cf. John 6:53–58, 20:21–23; Acts 2:38; Jas. 5:14–15; 1 Pet. 3:21). Not mere symbols, sacraments derive their power from him, so they are his very actions. In them he uses material things—water, wine, oil, the laying on of hands—to be avenues of his grace. Although one can receive grace in other ways, a key way is through the sacraments, which were instituted by Christ.

A sacrament is a visible rite or ceremony that signifies and confers grace. Thus baptism is a visible rite, and the pouring of the water signifies the cleansing of the soul by the grace it bestows. There are six other sacraments: the Eucharist, penance (also known as reconciliation or confession), the anointing of the sick, confirmation, matrimony, and holy orders.

The Mass

The Old Testament predicted that Christ would offer a sacrifice in bread and wine. Melchizedek was a priest and offered sacrifice with those elements (Gen. 14:18), and Christ was to be a priest in the order of Melchizedek (cf. Ps. 110 [109]:4), that is, offering sacrifice under the forms of bread and wine. We must then look for a New Testament sacrifice distinct from that of Calvary, because the Crucifixion was not of bread and wine. We find it in the Mass. There, bread and wine become the actual body and blood of Christ, as promised by him (John 6:53–58) and as instituted at the Last Supper.

The Catholic Church teaches that the sacrifice of the cross was complete and perfect. The Mass is not a new sacrificing of Christ (he doesn't suffer and die again, cf. Heb. 9:26), but a new offering of the same sacrifice. While what happened on Calvary happened once, its effects continue through the ages. Christ wants his salvific work to be present to each generation of those who come to God "since he always lives to make intercession for them" (Heb. 7:25). He surely has not abandoned us. Through the instrumentality of the priest, he is present again, demonstrating how he accomplished our salvation: "For from the rising of the sun to its setting my name is great among the nations, and in every place incense is offered to my name, and a pure offering; for my name is great among the nations, says the Lord of hosts" (Mal. 1:11).

A Modest Proposal

You have heard any number of people speak against the Catholic Church. Some do it casually, while others have made it their profession. Some are blunt, while others are subtle. They all paint an uninviting picture of a Church that believes in the most peculiar things. But do you really think that a fourth of all Americans would be Catholic if their religion were as odd as its opponents claim? Isn't it rather likely that you haven't been told the whole story? To make an informed decision, you need to hear both sides. Why not write to Catholic Answers for additional information and tracts? Either your suspicions will be confirmed, or you will discover that there is more to Catholicism than you once thought.

51

How to Talk with Fundamentalists

You surely have been through it. There is a knock at the door. Outside is a man or woman with a big smile, an open Bible, and a bunch of questions designed to attack the Catholic faith. Or you are accosted on the street by someone who asks, "Have you been saved?" Or, outside church after Mass, you find people passing out leaflets opposing Catholic beliefs and arguing with any who object.

If you get into a discussion, it appears to go nowhere. You end up frustrated, and no one seems at all convinced by what you've said. The others walk away, apparently thinking even less of the Catholic faith than before. You didn't handle the situation well, and you sense it.

The moral is that knowing how to argue is just as important as knowing what to argue. If you have no appreciation of technique, all the knowledge in the world won't help you since you won't be able to pass it along. You can be a walking theological treatise, but if you antagonize opponents or talk past them, you've wasted your time and theirs. Similarly, it isn't enough to be a good conversationalist. That won't make up for doctrinal or historical ignorance. To be an effective apologist, you must marry delivery and content.

Scripture and Prayer

Know the Bible. No matter how fine your religious training, no matter how well you think you know doctrines or Church history, you need to be familiar with Scripture if you intend to make an impression on Fundamentalists. (Of course, you should be conversant with the Bible anyway, not just as preparation for dealing with non-Catholics.)

Concentrate on the New Testament, though not to the exclusion of the Old. There's no need to memorize multiple passages of the Bible the way Fundamentalists do, but you need to acquire a basic knowledge of the whole of Scripture. You should be especially familiar, though, with the Gospels—if you aren't at ease with the details of Christ's life, you're in trouble. Frank Sheed, the street-corner apologist, put it this way: "A Catholic apologist who is not soaked in the Gospels is an anomaly in himself, and his work is doomed to aridity."

The New Testament is short enough to be read during the evenings of a single week. Spend several weeks with it before doing anything else, and then read it regularly. You should not read the Bible to the exclusion of all other books (many Fundamentalists do this and thus lack perspective), but it has to be the ground on which your other reading rests.

You also will accomplish little unless you have a vibrant prayer life. A good way to pray is to meditate on biblical verses. Read slowly, sit back, think.

Prayer is essential in winning converts. In your heart, pray before a conversation, during the discussion, and after it. It is helpful to write down the person's name you spoke with so that you will not forget to pray for him. It is a human tendency to measure the success of the discussion based upon how much you think the other changed his mind. But, in reality, "the greatest things on earth are done interiorly in the hearts of faithful souls" (St. Louis DeMontfort).

Technique

In discussions, never be afraid to acknowledge ignorance. If you don't know the answer to a question, say so. You'll survive, and so will your ego. The answers you give on other points will be taken more seriously if people you speak with see you're not trying to bluster your way through a discussion.

But, don't leave the questions unanswered. Tell the person that his question was a good one and that you'll bring him the answer in one week. Then, go do your homework and follow up with him as promised. This method will be much more effective than shrugging your shoulders and giving a contrived response that does not even convince you.

You must be absolutely honest. Never pretend doctrines or facts are other than they really are. Don't avoid hard cases, and don't water-down doctrine just to please your listeners. There's no need to try to make hard truths palatable. Just state them as they are— but first *know* what they are. If you can give only a one-sentence explanation of the Real Presence, you don't know enough to be discussing it. Admit this (to yourself, at least), then do your homework. An embarrassment today can result in fuller understanding —and better apologetics—tomorrow. When talk turns to awkward points of Church history, don't misrepresent them. Don't hide blemishes. Don't falsify. There's no need to. Put things in context, and recall that Scripture teaches that, while the Church itself can never be overcome by evil (Matt. 16:18), its individual members include sinners as well as saints (cf. Acts 20:29).

Watch Your Tongue

Sarcasm always backfires. Avoid it, even when your opponents stoop to it. When they do, their consciences will annoy them later; don't allow them to justify their rudeness by exchanging wisecrack for wisecrack.

Remember that God opposes the proud, even if they are right. "The Lord's servant must not be quarrelsome but kindly to every one, an apt teacher, forbearing, correcting his opponents with gentleness. God may perhaps grant that they will repent and come to know the truth" (2 Tim. 2:24–25).

Familiarize yourself with anti-Catholic literature. See what topics are emphasized: the Bible as the sole rule of faith, justification by faith alone, the Mass, prayers to Mary and the saints, and many more. See how the arguments, weak as they may be, are handled. You'll at once perceive that anti-Catholic materials are skewed, but if you can't think of complete and ready rejoinders, make notes and study up.

When arguing, keep your expectations modest. Don't expect conversions; they aren't overnight occurrences. Count yourself successful if your opponents leave with the feeling that there is a sensible Catholic response (even if not acceptable to them) to each of their charges. It would be a great spiritual triumph just to have an active anti-Catholic withdraw from the fray and mull things over.

Avoid technical words. Even Catholics can misunderstand what is meant by *transubstantiation, Immaculate Conception, Mediatrix,* and *merit.* On the other hand, don't be monosyllabic. To oversimplify is to sidestep fine points; that's equally bad. Try to phrase doctrines in language your audience is likely to understand and be sympathetic to, but don't change what a doctrine means in order to win a sympathetic hearing.

Try to show a doctrine in relation to other doctrines. It's important to see the Church as a totality.

Avoid verse-slinging. It accomplishes little. You need to get some perspective—and you need to give your opponents some. Enter the discussion with a plan; know what the main points should be, then stick with them.

The most fundamental topic to discuss is that of authority: Whose do you trust, and why should I accept yours? Since there are tens of thousands of denominations all using only the Bible and claiming personal guidance by the Holy Spirit, what sets your church or pastor apart from the rest?

Fundamentalists concentrate on a few scriptural passages they hope are damaging to Catholicism. Take the initiative. Address their points, but don't allow them to ask all the questions. Ask your own. Point out the weaknesses of Fundamentalism.

Aim to Explain

Don't argue to win. You can "win" yet drive people further from the Church. Argue to explain. Show Fundamentalists the Catholic position from the inside. This means reorienting them, giving them a new perspective. Remember, they think they take their beliefs straight from the Bible; in fact, the Bible is used to substantiate already-held beliefs. They begin with their own "tradition," which is generally their pastor's interpretation of the Bible. (For many Fundamentalists, their pastor is their pope. When confronted with hard questions, they don't turn to the Bible to discover the answers; they say instead, "Let us ask the pastor.")

No matter how well they have memorized it, Fundamentalists know little other than the Bible, which they know only selectively. They know little Church history, little formal theology. They may never have seen a catechism (or even know what one is). You must provide the larger picture. If the topic is the interpretation of a scriptural passage, go to a good commentary and study up, but also go to the Fathers of the Church and learn what they wrote about the subject.

Tell your opponents you do this because it is unlikely that people who were writing when the Church was young and memories of Christ were vivid would erroneously report what beliefs the Church started with. If early Christian writers took it for granted that a sacrificial priesthood was set up by Christ (which they did), that fact is a powerful argument in support of the priesthood. If writers living a few years after Christ mentioned the Real Presence (which they did), that argues in favor of the Catholic interpretation of John 6. And so on.

Don't Confuse Terms

Know what Fundamentalists mean by particular terms. You can waste much time by discussing two different things while using the same terminology. Take *faith*. To Catholics, faith is the acceptance of revealed truths (doctrines) on God's word alone. This is called theological or confessional faith. But for Fundamentalists, faith is trust in Christ's promises. This is fiducial faith.

Tradition is another confusing term, as are *inspiration* and *infallibility*. See what Fundamentalist writers mean by the terms; compare them with Catholic definitions. If you don't define terms clearly, Fundamentalists will misunderstand your argument. And don't presume a question means what it seems to mean. Find out what your opponents are trying to say. Take your time. If the question refers to the Virgin Birth, make sure they don't mean the birth of the Virgin.

Fundamentalists may say, "Let's start by admitting that the Bible is the sole rule of faith." Translation: "Let's admit the Church has no authoritative role; all answers to religious questions are to be found on the face of Scripture only." Don't agree to it. It just begs the question, and it's untrue. As a counter, ask your opponents to try to prove that the Bible was intended to be the sole rule of faith. The Bible makes no such claim—in fact, it denies it (1 Cor. 11:2; 2 Thess. 2:15; 2 Tim. 2:2; 2 Pet. 1:20; 3:15–16)—but you have to know which verses to cite to prove it.

Discuss the history of the Bible. You need to make plain that it was the Church that formed the Bible, not the Bible that formed the Church. Note, too, that the New Testament wasn't designed as a catechism. It was written to people who were already Christians, so it couldn't have been intended as the sole source of religious teaching. In the early years, teaching was oral and was under the authority of the Church, which also decided which books belonged in the Bible and which did not.

Misunderstandings

Bishop Fulton Sheen once wrote that few Americans hate the Catholic Church, but millions hate what they mistakenly think is the Catholic Church. You need to show Fundamentalists what the Church really believes.

Take up a single topic at a time; look at it leisurely, from several angles; and, don't let the discussion wander to other topics or it will bog down and accomplish nothing. Never presume that Fundamentalists know what you mean even by what you think are simple terms like *soul, revelation,* or *Mass.* If they did, they wouldn't have such odd ideas of what the Church stands for. You have to speak with them the way you would speak with uninstructed Catholics.

Remember, their knowledge of the Church is based almost entirely on what they have heard from the pulpit or in anti-Catholic tracts They are working in good faith, but they have been misinformed. Perhaps they should have done more homework, but the fault isn't theirs completely. They trust the sources they've had, but now they should be shown there is more to consider.

Remember, too, that the faith to believe is a gift. Not a few converts to Catholicism have expressed that what drew them to the Church was not primarily the strength of argument, scriptural proof, or one's ability to articulate the faith, as important as those factors are. What drew them were Catholics whose lives gave irresistible witness to the faith they professed. "Reverence Christ as Lord. Always be prepared to make a defense to any one who calls you to account for the hope that is in you, yet do it with gentleness and reverence" (1 Pet. 3:15).

52

Seventh-Day Adventism

Most people know little about the Seventh-day Adventists beyond that they worship on Saturdays, not Sundays. But there's more to this unique sect.

Adventist History

The Seventh-day Adventist church traces its roots to American preacher William Miller (1782–1849), a Baptist who predicted that the Second Coming would occur between March 21, 1843, and March 21, 1844. Because he and his followers proclaimed Christ's imminent advent, they were known as "Adventists."

When Christ failed to appear, Miller reluctantly endorsed the position of a group of his followers known as the "seventh-month movement," who claimed that Christ would return on October 22, 1844 (in the seventh month of the Jewish calendar).

When this didn't happen either, Miller forswore predicting the date of the Second Coming, and his followers broke up into a number of competing factions. Miller would have nothing to do with the new theories his followers produced, including ones that attempted to save part of his 1844 doctrine. He rejected this and other teachings being generated by his former followers, including those of Ellen Gould White.

Miller had claimed, based on his interpretation of Daniel and Revelation, that Christ would return in 1843–1844 to cleanse "the sanctuary" (Dan. 8:11–14; 9:26), which he interpreted as the earth. After the disappointments of 1844, several of his followers proposed an alternative theory. While walking in a cornfield on the morning of October 23, 1844, the day after Christ failed to return, Hiram Edson felt he received a spiritual revelation that indicated that Miller had misidentified the sanctuary. It was not the earth but the Holy of Holies in God's heavenly temple. Instead of coming out of the heavenly temple to cleanse the sanctuary of the earth, in 1844 Christ, for the first time, went into the heavenly Holy of Holies to cleanse it instead

Another group of Millerites was influenced by Joseph Bates, a retired sea captain, who in 1846 and 1849 issued pamphlets insisting that Christians observe the Jewish Sabbath—Saturday —instead of worshiping on Sunday. This helped feed the intense anti-Catholicism of Seventh-day Adventism, since they blamed the Catholic Church for changing the day of worship from Saturday to Sunday.

These two streams of thought—Christ entering the heavenly sanctuary and the need to keep the Jewish Sabbath—were combined by White, who claimed to have received many visions confirming these doctrines. Together with Edson and Bates, she formed the Seventh-day Adventist denomination, which officially received its name in 1860.

Today the denomination reports that it has 780,000 members in the United States and 7.8 million members elsewhere, many in Catholic countries.

Adventist Propaganda

White claimed to receive the first of several hundred visions in December 1844. She gained recognition in Adventist circles as a prophetess and became the church's leader. Over the next few decades, she provided guidance on almost every aspect of belief and worship, writing over fifty books commenting on health, education, finance, and other topics. Her works are held by her followers to be inerrant on matters of doctrine, as is the Bible, though they are on a slightly lower plane of honor than the Bible.

Her most important books, especially *The Desire of the Ages* and *The Great Controversy*, are frequently reprinted by Seventh-day Adventist publishing houses in a variety of formats. They often appear with different covers and titles. For example, *The Great Controversy* is often marketed as *America in Prophecy*. They are printed whole or in excerpted form. Sometimes White's name appears on the cover, sometimes a less well-known form of her name appears (such as E. G. White), and sometimes her name does not appear on the outside of the book at all.

This allows Adventists to put White's works in the hands of non-Adventists without alerting them that they are reading an Adventist publication until they are well into the work.

Adventist publishing houses also keep the terms *Seventh-day* and *Adventist* out of their names. Typical Adventist and Adventist-related publishing houses have names including Inspiration Books, Amazing Truth Publications, Review and Herald Publishing Association, and Pilgrims' Press.

This is because Adventists have always been regarded suspiciously by Evangelicals and have often been viewed as a fanatical cult (as have some of their offshoots, such as the Branch Davidians). Many Evangelical leaders have even asserted—*incorrectly*—that Adventists are not Christians, even though they believe in Christ's divinity and use a valid Trinitarian form of baptism.

Adventist-related publishing houses often conduct mass mailings of their literature to every home and post office box in a community. This has been done regularly with Amazing Truth Publications' anti-Catholic volume *National Sunday Law*.

Adventist Beliefs

Seventh-day Adventists agree with many Catholic doctrines, including the Trinity, Christ's divinity, the Virgin Birth, the atonement, a physical resurrection of the dead, and Christ's Second Coming. They use a valid form of baptism. They believe in original sin and reject the Evangelical teaching that one can never lose one's salvation no matter what one does (i.e., they *correctly* reject "once saved, always saved").

Unfortunately, they also hold many false and strange doctrines.

Among these are the following: (a) the Catholic Church is the Whore of Babylon; (b) the pope is the Antichrist; (c) in the last days, Sunday worship will be "the mark of the beast"; (d) there is a future millennium in which the devil will roam the earth while Christians are with Christ in heaven; (e) the soul sleeps between death and resurrection; and (f) on the last day, after a limited period of punishment in hell, the wicked will be annihilated and cease to exist rather than be eternally damned.

Many Adventists insist that, as a matter of discipline (not doctrine), one must not eat meats considered unclean under the Mosaic law (many endorse total vegetarianism), and one must avoid "worldly entertainments" (card-playing, dancing, smoking, drinking, reading non-religious books, listening to non-religious music, watching non-religious television, going to the movies, etc.).

Adventists also subscribe to the two Protestant shibboleths, *sola scriptura* (the Bible is the *sole* rule of faith) and *sola fide* (justification is by faith alone). Other Protestants, especially conservative Evangelicals and Fundamentalists, often attack Adventists on these points, claiming they do not really hold them, which is often used as "proof" that they are a "cult." However, along the spectrum of Protestantism (from high-church Lutherans and Anglicans to low-church Pentecostals and Baptists), there is little agreement about the meaning of these two phrases or about the doctrines they are supposed to represent.

Adventist Anti-Catholicism

As is clear from some of the beliefs listed above, Adventist theology is intensely anti-Catholic. Many Catholics who do not frequently come in contact with Adventists or their literature do not realize just how hostile they can be toward the Church.

Trying to give others the benefit of the doubt, Catholics may suppose that anti-Catholicism is part of Adventism's radical fringe. Unfortunately, this is untrue. Adventists who are moderate on Catholicism are a minority. Anti-Catholicism characterizes the denomination because it is embraced in White's "divinely inspired" writings. A few illustrations help indicate the scope of the problem:

"Babylon the Great, the mother of harlots . . . is further declared to be 'that great city, which reigneth over the kings of the earth.' Revelation 17:4–6, 18. The power that for so many centuries maintained despotic sway over the monarchs of Christendom is Rome. The purple and scarlet color, the gold and precious stones and pearls, vividly picture the magnificence and more than kingly pomp affected by the haughty see of Rome" (*The Great Controversy*, 338).

"It is one of the leading doctrines of Romanism that the pope is the visible head of the universal Church of Christ . . . and has been declared infallible. He demands the homage of all men. The same claim urged by Satan in the wilderness of temptation is still urged by him [Satan] through the Church of Rome, and vast numbers are ready to yield him homage" (ibid., 48).

"Marvelous in her shrewdness and cunning is the Roman Church. She can read what is to be. She bides her time, seeing that the Protestant churches are paying her homage in their acceptance of the false Sabbath. . . . And let it be remembered, it is the boast of Rome that she never changes. The principles of Gregory VII and Innocent III are still the principles of the Roman Catholic Church. And has she but the power, she would put them in practice with as much vigor now as in past centuries. . . . Rome is aiming to reestablish her power, to recover her lost supremacy" (ibid., 507–8).

"God's word has given warning of the impending danger; let this be unheeded, and the Protestant world will learn what the purposes of Rome really are, only when it is too late to escape the snare. She is silently growing into power. Her doctrines are exerting their influence in legislative halls, in the churches, and in the hearts of men. She is piling up her lofty and massive structures, in the secret recesses of which her former persecutions will be repeated. Stealthily and unsuspectedly she is strengthening her forces to further her own ends when the time shall come for her to strike. All that she desires is vantage ground, and this is already being given her. We shall soon see and shall feel what the purpose of the Roman element is. Whoever believe and obey the word of God will thereby incur reproach and persecution" (ibid., 508–9).

Strong stuff! Unfortunately, most Adventists believe this. Bear in mind that these quotes are not taken from an obscure work of White's that nobody ever reads. They are from what is probably her single most popular volume, *The Great Controversy*.

Adventist Eschatology

Seventh-day Adventism is basically consumed with the concept of the last days. It was formed from the remnants of the Millerite movement, which was created to await the world's end. In White's end times view, the Jewish Sabbath and the Catholic Church play prominent roles.

According to her, the papacy is the seven-headed beast from the sea in Revelation 13:1–10. Accompanying this beast is a lamb-like beast from the earth (Rev. 13:11–18). The latter causes the world to worship the former and has an image made of it. White proclaimed that the second beast is the United States (*The Great Controversy*, 387–8) and that it will force people to worship the papacy by "enforcing some observance which shall be an act of homage to the papacy" (ibid., 389). This observance, she says, is Sunday worship rather than Saturday worship.

White claims that the papacy changed the day of worship from Saturday to Sunday, making this change a mark of its authority. In her view, there will come a time when the United States will establish a "national Sunday law" and compel its citizens to worship on Sunday and thus take the mark of the beast. It will not compel them to become Catholics but to join a Protestant state-church that is an "image" of the papacy and, thus, "the image of the beast" (ibid., 382–96).

Seventh-day Adventism cannot change its views on the Catholic Church being the Whore of Babylon without admitting that it was wrong on Sunday worship. It cannot admit that Sunday worship is not the mark of the beast without changing its views on the

402 THE ESSENTIAL CATHOLIC SURVIVAL GUIDE

Jewish Sabbath. Seventh-day Adventism cannot cease to be anti-Catholic without ceasing to be *Seventh-day* Adventism.

There is a "moderate" wing of Adventism that is more open to Catholics as individuals (though still retaining White's views concerning the papacy). In fact, White was willing to concede that —in the here and now (before the end times)—some Catholics are saved. She wrote that "there are now true Christians in every church, not excepting the Roman Catholic communion, who honestly believe that Sunday is the Sabbath of divine appointment. God accepts their sincerity of purpose and their integrity before him. But when Sunday observance shall be enforced by law, and the world shall be enlightened concerning the obligation of the true Sabbath, then whoever shall transgress the command of God, to obey a precept which has no higher authority than Rome, will thereby honor popery above God" (ibid., 395).

Unfortunately, this one tolerant statement is embedded in hundreds of hostile statements. While this aspect of her teaching can be played up by her more moderate followers, it is difficult for them to do so, because the whole Adventist milieu in which they exist is anti-Catholic. The group is an eschatology sect, and its central eschatological teaching, other than Christ's Second Coming, is that the Second Coming will be preceded by a period in which the papacy will enforce Sunday worship on the world. Everyone who does not accept the papacy's Sunday worship will be killed, and everyone who does accept the papacy's Sunday worship will be destroyed by God.

Even moderate Seventh-day Adventists still wish to lead Catholics out of the Church, and because they are moderate in their presentation, they have an increased chance of doing so. For this reason, it is important that Catholics realize at the outset how anti-Catholic Seventh-day Adventism is in the end.

By virtue of their valid baptism, and their belief in Christ's divinity and the doctrine of the Trinity, Seventh-day Adventists are both ontologically and theologically Christians. But Christians, once separated from the Church our Lord founded, are susceptible to being "tossed to and fro and carried about with every wind of doctrine" (Eph. 4:14).

53

History of the Jehovah's Witnesses

Fifty years ago the Jehovah's Witnesses numbered fewer than 100,000. Now there are several million of them around the world. They don't have churches; they have "Kingdom Halls" instead. Their congregations are uniformly small, usually numbering less than 200. Most Witnesses used to be Catholics or Protestants. Let's look a little at their history, because that will help us understand their unique doctrines.

The sect now known as the Jehovah's Witnesses was started by Charles Taze Russell, who was born in 1852 and worked in Pittsburgh as a haberdasher. He was raised a Congregationalist, but at the age of seventeen he tried to convert an atheist to Christianity and ended up being converted instead—not to outright atheism but to agnosticism. Some years later he went to an Adventist meeting, was told that Jesus would be back at any time, and got interested in the Bible.

The leading light of Adventism had been William Miller, a flamboyant preacher who predicted that the world would end in 1843. When it didn't, he "discovered" an arithmetical error in his eschatological calculations and said it would end in 1844. When his prediction again failed, many people became frustrated and withdrew from the Adventist movement, but a remnant, led by Ellen G. White, went on to form the Seventh-day Adventist Church.

It was this diminished Adventism that influenced Russell, who took the title "Pastor" even though he never got through high school. In 1879, he began the Watch Tower—what would later be known as the Watchtower Bible and Tract Society, the teaching organ of the Jehovah's Witnesses. In 1908 he moved its headquarters to Brooklyn, where it has remained ever since.

Before he got his religious career well underway, Russell promoted what he called "miracle wheat," which he sold at sixty dollars per bushel. He claimed it would grow five times as well as regular wheat. In fact, it grew slightly less well than regular wheat, as was established in court when Russell was sued. Later he marketed a fake cancer cure and what he termed a "millennial bean" (which a wag has said probably got that name because it took a thousand years to sprout).

Unusual Doctrines

Russell taught his followers the non-existence of hell and the annihilation of unsaved people (a doctrine he picked up from the Adventists), the non-existence of the Trinity (he said only the Father, Jehovah, is God), the identification of Jesus with Michael the archangel, the reduction of the Holy Spirit from a person to a force, the mortality (not immortality) of the soul, and the return of Jesus in 1914.

When 1914 had come and gone, with no Jesus in sight, Russell modified his teachings and claimed that Jesus had, in fact, returned to Earth but that his return was invisible. His visible return would come later, but still very soon. It would result in the final conflict between God and the devil—the forces of good and the forces of evil—in which God would be victorious. This conflict is known to Witnesses as the battle of Armageddon, and just about everything the Witnesses teach centers around this doctrine.

Russell died in 1916 and was succeeded by "Judge" Joseph R. Rutherford. Rutherford, born in 1869, had been brought up as a Baptist and became the legal adviser to the Watch Tower. He never was a real judge but took the title because, as an attorney, he substituted at least once for an absent judge.

At one time he claimed Russell was next to Paul as an expounder of the gospel, but later, in an effort to have his own writings supplant Russell's, he let Russell's books go out of print. It was Rutherford who coined the slogan "Millions now living will never die." By it he meant that some people alive in 1914 would still be alive when Armageddon came and the world was restored to a paradise state.

In 1931 he changed the name of the sect to the Jehovah's Witnesses, which he based on Isaiah 43:10 (" 'You are my witnesses,' is the utterance of Jehovah, 'even my servant whom I have chosen,' " *New World Translation*). As an organizer, he equipped missionaries with portable phonographs, which they took door to door along with records of Rutherford. They didn't have to say much when they came calling; all they had to do was put on Rutherford's record. He displayed a marked hatred for Catholicism on his radio program and in the pamphlets he wrote. Later his successors tempered the sect's anti-Catholicism, but *Awake!* and *The Watchtower* still carry anti-Catholic articles every few issues, though the tone tends to be more subtle than the overtly lurid style of Rutherford's day.

Rutherford said that in 1925, Abraham, Isaac, Jacob, and the prophets would return to Earth, and for them he prepared a mansion named Beth Sarim in San Diego, California. He moved into this mansion (where he died in 1942) and bought an automobile with which to drive the resurrected patriarchs around. The Watch Tower Society quietly sold Beth Sarim years later to cover up an embarrassing moment in their history, namely another failed prophecy.

Trained to Give Testimonies

Rutherford was succeeded by Nathan Homer Knorr, who was born in 1905 and died in 1977. Knorr joined the movement as a teenager, working his way up through the ranks. He got rid of the phonographs and insisted that the missionaries attend courses and be trained in door-to-door evangelism techniques. The Witnesses now have a reputation as skillful deliverers of "personal testimonies."

Since the Bible, as preserved through the centuries, did not support the peculiar doctrines of the Witnesses, Knorr chose an anonymous committee to produce the *New World Translation*, which is used by no sect other than the Witnesses. By means of former Witnesses, the names of the five members of the translation committee eventually came to light. Four of the five members completely lack credentials to qualify them as Bible translators, and the fifth member studied non-biblical Greek for only about two years.

The *New World Translation* was produced because it buttresses Witnesses' beliefs through obscure or inaccurate renderings. For example, to prove that Jesus was only a creature, not God, the *New World Translation's* rendering of John 1:1 concludes this way: "and the Word was *a god*" [italics added]. Every other translation, Catholic and Protestant—not to mention the Greek original—has "and the Word was God."

What Happened to Armageddon?

Knorr was succeeded as head of the Jehovah's Witnesses by Frederick Franz. He had been the Witnesses' leading theologian, and his services were often called upon. For some years the sect's magazines had been predicting that Armageddon would occur in 1975. When it didn't, Franz had to find an explanation.

Witnesses believe that Adam was created in 4026 B.C. and that human beings have been allotted 6,000 years of existence until Armageddon and the beginning of the millennium. This figure is based on a "creative week" in which each of six days is equal to 1,000 years, with the Sabbath or seventh day being the beginning of the millennium. Simple arithmetic gives 1975 as the year Armageddon would arrive. Franz explained that Armageddon would actually come 6,000 years after Eve's creation. But when 1975 came and went, the Witnesses had to "adjust" their chronology to cover up a failed prediction. They accomplished this by maintaining that no one knew exactly how long after Adam's creation Eve came on the scene. Franz said that it was months—even years. Hence he was able to "stretch" the 1975 date to some indeterminate time in the future. In any case, Franz said that Witnesses would just have to wait, knowing the end is right around the corner.

When the final battle does occur—remember, it will be during the lifetime of "millions" of people alive in 1914, which means it can't be too far off—Jehovah will defeat Satan and the elect will go to heaven to rule with Christ. But, following a literal interpretation of the number mentioned in Revelation, chapters 7 and 14, only 144,000 are among the elect. They will go to heaven as spirit persons (without resurrected bodies). The remaining faithful (Jehovah's Witnesses), who are known as Jonadabs, will live forever on a renewed, paradise Earth in resurrected bodies. The unsaved will cease to exist at all, having been annihilated by Jehovah.

Franz was succeeded as president of the Watchtower in 1993 by Milton Henschel, who has continued the aggressive evangelization tactics of his predecessors. In 1995 the Watchtower quietly changed one of its major prophetic doctrines. Until this point, they had maintained that the generation alive in 1914 would not pass from the scene until Armageddon occurred. Now that this generation has almost entirely died out—and Armageddon has not occurred and does not seem like it will happen immediately —they had to change their doctrine. Now, the Watchtower says that Armageddon will simply occur "soon," and it is no longer tied to a particular, literal generation of people.

How They Make Converts

Most religions welcome converts, and the Witnesses' very reason for existence is to make them. To accomplish this they follow several steps.

First they try to get a copy of one of their magazines into the hands of a prospective convert. They lead off with a question designed to tap into universal concerns, such as "How would you like to live in a world without sickness, war, poverty, or any other problem?" If the prospect is willing to speak with them, they arrange what's known as a "back call"—that is, they return in a week or so for more discussions. This can be kept up indefinitely.

At some point the missionaries invite the prospect to a Bible study. This is not the usual sort of Bible study, where passages are examined in light of context, original word meaning, relevance to other verses in Scripture, etc. Instead, this "Bible study" is really an exposition of Witness doctrine by means of Watchtower literature. Simple questions are presented in the literature that are derived directly from the text. The answers, therefore, are readily discernible, making the prospective convert feel spiritually astute, since he or she can answer all the questions "correctly." The Bible study is directed along lines mandated by the officials in Brooklyn, and the prospect is there to learn, not to teach. If he progresses well, he's invited to a larger Bible study, which may be held at a Kingdom Hall.

About this time he's invited to attend a Sunday service. At the Kingdom Hall, which resembles not so much a church but a small lecture hall, the prospect hears a Witness discuss a few verses of Scripture and how those verses can be explained to non-Witnesses or how to "refute" standard Christian doctrines such as the Trinity, hell, the immortality of the soul, etc. The service includes taped music to accompany the singing of hymns, and there is always time allotted for obtaining Watchtower literature and publications.

Sharing Techniques

The prospective convert gets still more of this if he proceeds to the next step, which consists of going to meetings on Wednesday or Thursday nights. At those meetings Witnesses trade stories, explaining how they've done that week in going door to door, giving advice to one another, figuring out better ways to get the message across, and logging their hours. (Every month each Kingdom Hall mails to the headquarters in Brooklyn a detailed log of activities, including hours spent "witnessing" door-to-door, the number of converts made, and the number of pieces of literature distributed.)

If the prospect goes through all these steps, he's ready for admission to the sect. That involves baptism by immersion and agreeing to work actively as a missionary. Many missionaries take only part-time jobs so they can devote more time to their evangelization. Witnesses will typically spend sixty to 100 hours each month in their evangelizing work. Some will even go so far as to work full time for the WTS, receiving little more than room and board for their efforts.

Life As a Witness

Although not every Witness can put in so many hours, every Witness is expected to do what he can by way of missionary work. There is no separate, ordained ministry as is found in Protestant churches. Their sect operates no hospitals, sanitariums, orphanages, schools, colleges, or social welfare agencies. From their perspective it will all disappear in a few years anyway, so they don't expend their energies in these areas.

Jehovah's Witnesses live under a strict regimen. They may be "disfellowshipped" for a variety of reasons, such as attending a Catholic or Protestant church or receiving a blood transfusion. Disfellowshipping is the sect's equivalent of excommunication, though somewhat more harsh. A disfellowshipped Witness may attend Kingdom Hall, but he is not allowed to speak to anyone, and no one may speak to him. The others are to act as though he no longer exists. This applies even to his family, who may communicate with him only as much as is absolutely necessary.

They recognize the legitimacy of no governmental authority, since they believe all earthly authority is of Satan. They will not serve in the military, salute the flag, say the Pledge of Allegiance, vote, run for office, or serve as officials of labor unions.

No matter how peculiar their doctrines, they deserve to be complimented on their determination and single-minded zeal. However, as Paul might have said concerning them, "I can testify about them that they are zealous for God, but their zeal is not based on knowledge" (Rom. 10:2, NIV).

54

Distinctive Beliefs of the Jehovah's Witnesses

The Jehovah's Witnesses are quite forthcoming about their religious beliefs. Their religion, unlike Mormonism, isn't an esoteric one with secret doctrines known only to an initiated few.

When Mormons come to your door, they don't tell you that they believe in many gods, that Jesus and Lucifer were "spirit brothers," and that dark skin (in the case of blacks, Indians, and Hispanics) is supposedly a curse from God in punishment for wickedness. If they told you such things up front, you'd close the door immediately. Such teachings are saved for initiates. Thus, Mormonism is an esoteric religion (Webster: "esoteric: designed for or understood by the specially initiated alone").

The religion of the Jehovah's Witnesses, on the other hand, is exoteric (Webster: "suitable to be imparted to the public"). They're happy to tell you up front exactly what they believe, and they tell you not just when at your door but in their publications.

In their booklet entitled *Jehovah's Witnesses in the Twentieth Century*, for example, may be found a chart entitled "What Jehovah's Witnesses Believe." This chart list beliefs and the supposed scriptural authority for them.

Let's examine some of the beliefs, which are peculiar to the Jehovah's Witnesses. (In this chapter we give scriptural passages from the Revised Standard Version, a sound Bible translation that is recognized by Catholics and Protestants alike as one of the most accurate and dignified English translations of Scripture. Bear in mind that the Witnesses' use their own "in-house" Bible called the *New World Translation* (NWT), though it is regarded by Greek and Hebrew scholars as an extraordinarily poor and highly inaccurate translation. There are many places where it is not faithful to the Hebrew and Greek, especially where the text fails to support and often openly contradicts the Witnesses' peculiar doctrines. In addition, the five members of the translation committee for the NWT completely lack credentials as Bible scholars. Four of them never studied the biblical languages, and the fifth studied non-biblical Greek for a short period.)

Is Christ God?

1. "Christ is God's Son and is inferior to him." Given in support of this position are these verses: "And lo, a voice from heaven, saying, 'This is my beloved Son, with whom I am well pleased'" (Matt. 3:17). "I proceeded and came forth from God" (John 8:42). "If you loved me, you would have rejoiced, because I go to the Father; for the Father is greater than I" (John 14:28). "I am ascending to my Father and your Father, to my God and your God" (John 20:17). "The head of every man is Christ, the head of a woman is her husband, and the head of Christ is God" (1 Cor. 11:3). "When all things are subjected to him, then the Son himself will also be subjected to him who put all things under him, that God may be everything to every one" (1 Cor. 15:28).

At first glance these citations seem imposing. It does seem that Christ is inferior to God the Father in some sense. But the New Testament also has verses that clearly show Christ and the Father to be equals: "I and the Father are one" (John 10:30). "He who has seen me has seen the Father" (John 14:9). "All that the Father has is mine" (John 16:15). "The Jews sought all the more to kill him, because he not only broke the Sabbath but also called God his Father, making himself equal with God" (John 5:18). "[Jesus], though he was in the form of God, did not count equality with God a thing to be grasped" (Phil. 2:6). These seem to contradict the other verses.

How do we make sense of all this? By keeping in mind that Jesus is both God and man. Some verses, such as these last five, refer exclusively to his Godhead. Others refer to his humanity. So far as he is God, Jesus is equal to the Father. Christ's human nature, though, is created and is therefore inferior to the Father. But to focus on this aspect of Christ to the exclusion of his divine nature is a gross misunderstanding of who and what the Bible says Jesus Christ is. Other verses cited by the Witnesses, such as Matthew 3:17, show merely that Christ is God's Son, not that he is inferior (in fact, John 5:18 shows that being God's Son is being equal to God).

Was Christ Created?

2. *"Christ was the first of God's creations."* Verses cited by Witnesses in support of this claim include: "He is the image of the invisible God, the first-born of all creation" (Col. 1:15). "And to the angel of the church in Laodicea write: 'The words of the Amen [Christ], the faithful and true witness, the beginning of God's creation'" (Rev. 3:14).

In the first of the two verses, Witnesses think that "first-born" implies succession and inferiority. But the title "first-born" refers to Christ's place as the chief and unique Son of God (cf. Rom. 8:29). Further, the Greek of this verse can also be translated as "the first-born *over* all creation," as in the New International Version of the Bible.

Regarding the second verse from Revelation, it's hard to see how it helps the Witnesses at all. It merely says Christ was the source of creation. This implies Christ is divine, since God created everything.

The fact that there was no time when the Son did not exist is indicated in John 1:1-3: "In the beginning was the Word, and the Word was with God, and the Word was God. He was in the beginning with God; all things were made through him, and without him was not anything made that was made." This passage also shows that the Son is not a creature because all created things were made through him, and no created things were made except through him.

Hell No, We Won't Go?

3. *"Wicked will be eternally destroyed"* (that is, no hell, just annihilation). Verses given in support: " 'Depart from me you cursed into the eternal fire prepared for the devil and his angels.' . . . And they will go away into eternal punishment, but the righteous into eternal life" (Matt. 25:41, 46). (The NWT renders Matthew 25:46 as "And these will depart into everlasting *cutting-off*, but the righteous ones into everlasting life." This is one example of many where the NWT distorts the text to suit the Witnesses' beliefs.) "They shall suffer the punishment of eternal destruction and exclusion from the presence of the Lord and from the glory of his might" (2 Thess. 1:9).

You can see for yourself that these verses actually prove the opposite of what the Witnesses teach. That is, they prove the existence of hell. This is compounded when Revelation says of the damned: "And the smoke of their torment goes up for ever and ever; and they have no rest, day or night, these worshipers of the beast and its image, and whoever receives the mark of its name" (Rev. 14:11). If they are not given any rest, day or night, then obviously they are still around to experience torment.

No Blood Transfusions!

4. *"Taking blood into the body through mouth or veins violates God's laws."* The Jehovah's Witnesses are perhaps best known to other Americans as people who won't allow themselves or their children to have blood transfusions. In fact, they will go so far as to allow a loved one to die rather than accept a transfusion, as they believe transfusions are a gross violation of God's law. They support this notion with these verses: "Only you shall not eat flesh with its life, that is, its blood" (Gen. 9:4). "You shall not eat the blood of any creature, for the life of every creature is its blood" (Lev. 17:14). "For it has seemed good to the Holy Spirit and to us to lay upon you no greater burden than these necessary things that you

abstain from what has been sacrificed to idols and from blood and from what is strangled and from unchastity" (Acts 15:28, 29).

There are several problems with interpreting these verses to mean that transfusions are forbidden, not the least of which is the fact that the context is referring to animal blood, not human blood. Moreover, there is a great difference between eating blood and receiving a life-giving blood transfusion. Eating blood was wrong because it profaned the life of the animal. But for a person to willingly share his blood intravenously in order to share life with someone does not profane anything. Indeed, even ultra-Orthodox Jews, who strictly observe the Old Testament kosher laws, recognize that blood transfusions are not prohibited by the command to not eat blood.

The Witnesses must avoid other problematic passages that deal with God's prohibition of eating blood because these passages include a prohibition against eating fat. Witnesses do not believe eating fat is wrong, and they would see no problem at all with someone munching on fried pork rinds (deep-fried pieces of pig fat) or sitting down to dinner and enjoying a nice fatty cut of prime rib. But their vehement opposition to eating blood, when contrasted with their approval of eating fat, presents a serious problem for them. Why? Because Leviticus, the book they go to in order to substantiate their prohibition of eating (and receiving transfusions of) blood, contains, in the same passages, prohibitions against eating fat.

Consider these examples: "It shall be a perpetual statute throughout your generations, in all your dwelling places, that you eat neither fat nor blood" (Lev. 3:17). "The Lord said to Moses, 'Say to the people of Israel, You shall eat no fat, of ox, or sheep, or goat. The fat of an animal that dies of itself, and the fat of one that is torn by beasts, may be put to any other use, but on no account shall you eat it. For every person who eats of the fat of an animal of which an offering by fire is made to the Lord shall be cut off from his people. Moreover you shall eat no blood whatever, whether of fowl or of animal, in any of your dwellings. Whoever eats any blood, that person shall be cut off from his people'" (Lev 7:22–27).

These verses and others like them are difficult for Witnesses to explain, given that they lean heavily on the prohibitions against eating blood. It's totally inconsistent to maintain that God's "perpetual statute" against eating blood must be observed, while his "perpetual statute" (that appears in the very same context) against eating fat can be safely ignored. On this subject, as on many others, the Witnesses are highly selective and must ignore much of the Bible in order to make their beliefs seem "biblical."

Also, the Old Testament dietary laws simply don't apply to Christians today (cf. Col. 2.16–17, 22), and the ones given at the Council of Jerusalem passed into disuse as Jewish conversions to Christianity became uncommon toward the end of the first century and the Church became mainly Gentile. They weren't immutable doctrines but disciplinary rules.

No Clergy!

5. "A clergy class and special titles are improper." In support of this position, Witnesses refer to these verses: "I will not show partiality to any person or use flattery toward any man" (Job 32:21). "But you are not to be called rabbi, for you have one teacher, and you are all brethren. And call no man your father on earth, for you have one Father, who is in heaven. Neither be called masters, for you have one master, the Christ" (Matt. 23:8–10). "You know that the rulers of the Gentiles lord it over them, and their great men exercise authority over them. It shall not be so among you; but whoever would be great among you must be your servant, and whoever would be first among you must be your slave" (Matt. 20:25–27).

These verses simply show that our Lord was saying we shouldn't give to men credit for what really comes to us from God the Father and that his followers should be willing to serve. But Jesus shouldn't be understood in a crassly literal way. If Matthew 23:9 were taken that way, you'd have trouble finding a title for the man who married your mother.

Furthermore, writing under the inspiration of the Holy Spirit,

Paul called himself the father of the church he founded in Corinth: "For though you have countless guides in Christ, you do not have many fathers. For I became your father in Christ Jesus through the gospel" (1 Cor. 4:15). He also referred, under divine inspiration, to Timothy as "my son" (1 Tim. 1:18; 2 Tim. 2:1), but if he could call Timothy "my son," then Timothy could call him "my father," so long as he didn't confuse Paul's fatherhood with the kind of fatherhood that God has (cf. Matt. 23:9).

The Witnesses also ignore Scripture's teaching concerning the authority of Church leaders and the appropriate honor that is due them because of their office: "Respect those who labor among you and are over you in the Lord and admonish you, and . . . esteem them very highly in love because of their work" (1 Thess. 5:12–13), "let the elders who rule well be considered worthy of double honor" (1 Tim. 5:17), and "obey your leaders and submit to them; for they are keeping watch over your souls, as men who will have to give account. Let them do this joyfully, and not sadly, for that would be of no advantage to you" (Heb. 13:17).

In summary, then, understand that the Witnesses' use of the Bible typically involves two main problems. First, they quote passages out of context, highlighting only those verses that appear to support their beliefs, while ignoring others that contradict those beliefs. Second, their own NWT often distorts the text so as to support their beliefs. Be wary, then, when the Witnesses come to your door.

55

The God of the Jehovah's Witnesses

One of the most unique doctrines the Jehovah's Witnesses teach
is that Christ, both before he came to Earth and since he has returned to heaven, was and is Michael the archangel. To argue this,
the Witnesses use 1 Thessalonians 4:16: "The Lord himself will
descend from heaven with a commanding call, with an archangel's
voice and with God's trumpet." (Unless otherwise noted, all quotations are from the *New World Translation* [NWT] of the Bible,
published by the Watchtower Bible and Tract Society, the parent organization for the Jehovah's Witnesses.) From this verse the
Witnesses conclude that the Lord Jesus Christ is an archangel because he has "an archangel's voice." No other denomination has
ever come up with such a conclusion, because every other denomination has concluded that the return of the Lord will simply be
heralded by an archangel. But let's continue with the Witnesses'
argument.

They identify the archangel as Michael from Jude 9: "But when
Michael the archangel had a difference with the devil and was dis-
puting about Moses' body, he did not dare to bring a judgment
against him in abusive terms, but said: 'May Jehovah rebuke you.' "
How does this identification work? According to *Reasoning from
the Scriptures*, one of the manuals Witnesses use in door-to-door
evangelization, "the expression 'archangel' is never found in the
plural in the scriptures, thus implying there is only one" (218).

Actually, 1 Thessalonians 4:16 refers to *an* archangel's voice, not
to *the* archangel's voice, implying there is more than one archangel.
If there were only one, the Greek definite article (Greek's equivalent of "the") would be used, but it isn't. (The definite article
is used in Jude 9, but there it serves to identify which Michael
is being talked about—the Michael who is an archangel. In that

context, it no more implies that there is only one archangel than talking about Smokey the Bear implies that there is only one bear.)

Reasoning from the Scriptures claims that "the evidence indicates that the Son of God was known as Michael before he came to earth and is known by that name since his return to heaven where he resides as the glorified spirit Son of God" (218). The Bible contains little evidence concerning such a strange claim, but what little evidence there is argues against the Witnesses' position.

Look at Hebrews 1:5: "To which one of the angels did he [God] ever say: 'You are my son; I, today, I have become your father'?" This suggests the Son of God can't be an angel (or an archangel, since *archangel* simply means "high ranking angel"), because it was to the Son that the Father said, "I have become your father."

Even the Jehovah's Witnesses, in their own, backhanded way, recognize this. Look at their translation of verse 6: "Let all God's angels do obeisance to him," referring to the Son. The Witnesses want you to think the angels do obeisance to the (sole) archangel, but they know this isn't what the verse really says. Before 1970 the NWT didn't use the word *obeisance*. Until then verse 6 read this way: "Let all God's angels *worship* him" (italics added). Angels don't worship an archangel, who, after all, is just another creature. They worship God (cf. Rev. 19:9–10; 22:8–9). When the NWT was first made, this verse slipped by the translating committee and effectively undercut the Witnesses' assertion that Christ is really Michael.

Is Jesus Only a Man?

It will come as no surprise to learn that the Witnesses do not believe Jesus Christ is divine. He isn't God in their view. To support this theory, they appeal to their own rendering of John 1:1: "In the beginning the Word was, and the Word was with God, and the Word was a god." They use the lower-case *g* to show that Christ is merely a creature, even if the most exalted creature. In the book of Judges certain magistrates are called "gods," but it is clear from the context they're merely human beings. In that context the use of the word *god* refers to the significance of the responsibility and authority they had. No divinity is implied in the usage of Judges, and the Witnesses imply none when they call Christ "a god."

In every Catholic and Protestant translation, the final clause of John 1:1 is given this way: "and the Word was God." The translation given by the Witnesses simply isn't supported by the Greek. When missionaries come to your door and argue that Jesus is just a creature, point out the illegitimate translation of John 1:1. (If they insist their translation is correct, ask them whether Christ is true God or a false god by nature. Point out that only by Christ being true God do the opening verses to John's Gospel make any sense at all.) Then turn to John 20:28, where Thomas says, as he probes Jesus' wounds, "My Lord and my God!" Note that Jesus didn't correct Thomas's identification of him as God, because no correction was needed. Thomas, previously doubting, knew exactly what he was saying, and what he was saying was true.

The Jehovah's Witnesses deny the Incarnation. According to them, Jesus isn't God, so there's no question about God taking flesh. But they also deny it in a second sense. In the Incarnation, the Son's divine nature became united with a human nature, so his two natures co-existed. But the Witnesses say that even after Jesus' appearance on Earth there was only one nature—the human.

This is how they see it: In heaven, Jesus was the Son of God, a creature, and was known as Michael the archangel, a pure spirit. Upon coming to Earth he ceased to be a spirit at all. His spiritness entirely disappeared. On Earth the Son of God was purely human. This man Jesus was killed at Calvary. At his resurrection, his human body was not resuscitated. It remained in the tomb and God disintegrated it. There was no real, physical resurrection in the traditional Christian sense. Instead, what was resurrected was Michael's angelic spirit-body.

Keep in mind the sequence. In heaven: angel only. On Earth: human only. Back in heaven: angel only, again. There is no continuity here. The creature called Michael entirely ceased to exist!

The creature called Jesus (while here on Earth) began to exist, then, at death, he ceased to exist also. Then a creature identical to the original Michael began to exist again. (Witnesses believe that at death a person ceases to exist altogether and that the resurrection consists of God recreating an exact copy of that person from his memory.)

The Resurrection Was Real

None of that squares with the Bible. The Resurrection accounts in the Gospels are accounts of a revivified and glorified body, a body no longer in the tomb. There isn't a shred of evidence in the Gospels to indicate that anyone thought the body remained in the tomb. After the Resurrection, Jesus appeared to the apostles and said, " 'See my hands and my feet, that it is I myself; feel me and see, because a spirit does not have flesh and bones just as you behold that I have.' Then he said, 'Do you have something there to eat?' And they handed him a piece of broiled fish; and he took it and ate it before their eyes" (Luke 24:39–43). Here Jesus himself points out that he is more than just a spirit—he has a body, too.

"The Force Be with You"?

All this is about Christ. What about the Holy Spirit? The Jehovah's Witnesses are actually Unitarians, not Trinitarians. They don't believe in three divine Persons but in one, Jehovah (the Father). The Son isn't God but a creature. The Holy Spirit isn't God either—in fact, he isn't a person at all but "Jehovah's active force," something comparable to electricity. In the NWT we find his name given in lowercase: "the holy spirit."

To support this belief, the Witnesses rely on their rendering of passages such as Acts 2:1–4: "Now while the day of the [festival of] Pentecost was in progress . . . they all became filled with holy spirit." Written this way, it almost makes sense. But Christ spoke of the Holy Spirit as a person in several places, such as John 14:26: "But the helper, the holy spirit, which the Father will send in my name, that one will teach you all things and bring back to your minds all the things I have told you." How can an impersonal force teach anyone anything? Does the wind teach? Do gravity or electromagnetism teach? Of course not. This verse makes sense only if "the holy spirit" is really "the Holy Spirit," a divine Person. Moreover, the New Testament is replete with examples of the Spirit's personal attributes, such as thinking, speaking, guiding, hearing, loving, and willing, to name a few.

When speaking with a Witness about this passage, turn to Acts 5:1-11, the story of Ananias and Sapphira. In verse 3, Peter asks, "Why has Satan emboldened you to play false to the holy spirit and to hold back secretly some of the price of the field?" The one that was defrauded was "the holy spirit." In verse 4, Peter says, "You have played false, not to men, but to God." So it was God that was defrauded. The conclusion? That "the holy spirit" must be God, a conclusion drawn from the Witnesses' own NWT.

Is Christ Inferior?

The Witnesses argue that the Son is inferior in nature to the Father from verses such as these: "The Son cannot do a single thing of his own initiative, but only what he beholds the Father doing" (John 5:19). "I have not come of my own initiative, but he that sent me is real, and you do not know him. I know him because I am a representative from him, and that one sent me forth" (John 7:28-29). "I am going my way to the Father, because the Father is greater than I am" (John 14:28).

What can be said about these verses? First, they may be referring to Christ's human nature, as distinguished from his divine nature. His human nature, being created, is clearly subordinate to the Father's divine nature.

Second, they may also refer to Christ's Person insofar as the Person of the Son is generated or begotten by the Person of the

Father. This doesn't mean he is unequal in his divine nature and therefore not divine; rather, it means there is a certain logical relationship between the two Persons of the Father and the Son (who are both equally divine) in which it may be said, rightly, that "the Father is greater than I"—greater in the order of the three divine Persons, not greater in the order of nature or being.

Third, they may refer to the Son's role in the economy of redemption. He came to fulfill the Father's will in redeeming us and to reveal the Father to us, thus serving the Father. Hence, the Father holds a position in some sense superior to his. Thus the Son might be said to be inferior to the Father in the role he plays but not in his essential nature.

Are there verses that argue against the Witnesses' position? Sure. One example is John 5:1–18, where Jesus cures a man on the Sabbath. The Jews became angry because Jesus "worked" on the Sabbath, and in response Jesus said, " 'My Father has kept working until now, and I keep working.' On this account indeed, the Jews began seeking all the more to kill him, because not only was he breaking the Sabbath but he was also calling God his own Father, making himself equal to God" (5:17–18). Only God can be equal to himself, and this passage therefore shows that Jesus is God.

The Witnesses also ignore the import of Matthew 28:19: "Go therefore and make disciples of people of all the nations, baptizing them in the name of the Father and of the Son and of the holy spirit." Another translator's slip here? Note the singular "name." If the Father, Son, and "holy spirit" were three different entities —God, exalted creature, and impersonal force—then they'd have three names, not one name. The fact that the singular is used implies a unity of being.

What is that one name that the Father, the Son, and the Holy Spirit share? Jehovah. There can be no question that the Father is referred to in the Old Testament as Jehovah (or, more consistently rendered, Yahweh), but this name applies to the Son as well. For example, Jesus speaking in John 8:24 says, "Therefore I said to you, You will die in your sins. For if you do not believe that I am [he], you will die in your sins." Notice that the NWT has added "he" in brackets to obscure the fact that the Greek words here are the words for "I AM." An identical situation occurs at John 8:28.

As any Bible student knows, "I AM" is the literal translation of Jehovah or Yahweh (cf. Ex. 3:14: "God said to Moses . . . 'Say this to the people of Israel, 'I AM has sent me to you,'" RSV; note that the NWT mistranslates the Greek here). Thus Jesus claimed to be Jehovah. But if the Father is Jehovah and if Jesus is Jehovah, then the Holy Spirit is Jehovah, and thus the three divine Persons share one name.

Go over these verses carefully with the next Witness who comes to your door. Show him, always, the context of what is being said, whether on this topic or on any other. Remember, the Witnesses take verses out of context. They are the preeminent proof-texters. Often the very next verse will undercut their interpretation of the single verse they're expounding to you. Never accept their interpretations or their NWT at face value. Always have on hand Catholic and Protestant translations with which to compare the NWT. Read everything in context, always showing the Witnesses the context.

56

Strategies of the Jehovah's Witnesses

There may be no religious organization that engages in more publishing—proportionate to its membership—than the Watch Tower Bible and Tract Society (Watch Tower Society or WTS for short), the publishing arm of the Jehovah's Witnesses.

Each month Jehovah's Witnesses (JWs) distribute millions of books, magazines, and pamphlets, in dozens of languages. Many of these are intended for non-Witnesses to try to convert them, but others are intended for Witnesses themselves.

One of the handbooks used by missionaries in the field is entitled *Reasoning from the Scriptures*, which first came out in 1985. The handbook covers seventy-six topics, ranging from abortion and ancestor worship to paradise and philosophy to women and the world. Each topic is devoted a few pages, and several questions are devoted to each topic. The book clearly centers around WTS theology, and this point is evident in part from the fact that some of the specific subjects treated in the book are identified as "Not a Bible teaching" (e.g., apostolic succession, the Trinity) or "Not a Biblical practice" (e.g., birthdays).

The publication is intended to enable the average Witness going door-to-door to accomplish two basic purposes. First, the *Reasoning* book provides many Scripture references that seemingly support the WTS's belief system. Second, the book "arms" the JW with a variety of responses to statements and questions that are likely to surface in nearly any typical encounter at the home of a non-Witness.

Some topics have clearly been selected because they concern beliefs peculiar to Witnesses. Others have been included because they are held by those of other faiths, mostly mainline Christian denominations. This is especially true of Catholic doctrines.

(A side note here: The Witnesses believe that all Christian denominations are demonic in origin, and they maintain Christianity as a whole went apostate—that is, entirely abandoned the true faith—starting all the way back in the latter portion of the first century A.D. From their perspective, this alleged apostasy actually fulfills predictions in the New Testament that a mass falling away will occur. The main problem with this reasoning is that while the New Testament does speak of an apostasy, it refers to the falling away of large number of believers near the end times, *not* the defection of the Church *as an institution* at any time.)

Catholic doctrines discussed include apostolic succession, baptism as a sacrament bestowing grace (as opposed to a merely symbolic ordinance), confession, holidays and holy days (such as Christmas, Easter, and St. Valentine's Day), the use of images, Marian doctrines, the Mass, and purgatory. These alone constitute more than a tenth of the book and—coupled with the fact that the book attempts in a number of cases to specifically refute Catholic doctrine—give an indication that the Witnesses see the Catholic Church as a main target.

Reasoning from the Scriptures begins with two how-to chapters, "Introductions for Use in the Field Ministry" and "How You Might Respond to Potential Conversation Stoppers." The first of these gives suggested opening lines. "If the introductions you are now using seldom open the way for conversations, try some of these suggestions. When you do so, you will no doubt want to put them in your own words."

Sample Openings

Five openings are given under the heading "Bible/God." The first reads this way: "Hello. I'm making just a brief call to share an important message with you. Please note what it says here in the Bible. (Read Scripture, such as Revelation 21:3–4.) What do you think about that? Does it sound good to you?"

Notice the hook: "an important message." It works for the advertising industry; why not in this context? Then come the Bible verses, followed by questions. The missionaries don't tell their listener what to think—at least not at this point. Instead, they elicit his views. Once he gives them, it's awkward for him to back out of the conversation. They can toss out a few more questions and then make their point.

Notice also in this example that JWs typically ask prospective converts for their own opinion or feeling on a theological matter. The advantage this approach has for JWs is that virtually everyone has *some* kind of opinion on the subject matter presented, so this approach practically guarantees that JWs can successfully engage a person in a dialogue. Once the dialogue has been established, the JW is then on his way to potentially making a convert. Fortunately for the JW, the average person fails to realize that theological or religious truth does not depend on one's mere opinion or feeling.

Another opening line under this section is this one: "We're encouraging folks to read their Bible. The answers that it gives to important questions often surprise people. For example: . . . (Ps. 104:5; or Dan. 2:44; or some other)." Again, here the listener is told he'll be let in on a secret. He reads the passages, is asked his opinion, and then the Witnesses steer the conversation their way.

The leads given under the heading "Employment/Housing" are more down-to-earth: "We've been talking with your neighbors about what can be done to assure that there will be employment and housing for everyone. Do you believe that it is reasonable to expect that human governments will accomplish this? . . . But there is someone who knows how to solve these problems; that is mankind's Creator (Is. 65:21–23)."

This sounds rather compelling, doesn't it? Another approach is: "We are sharing with our neighbors a thought about good government. Most people would like to have the kind of government that is free from corruption, one that provides employment and good housing for everyone. What kind of government do you think can do all of that? . . . (Ps. 97:1–2; Is. 65:21–23)."

These last two examples show another typical approach for Witnesses: they often target universal needs and concerns. Who, for instance, is not worried about the future? Or about raising his family? Or about providing for his children? Or living in a world free from pollution, poverty, and crime? After all, no sane person would deny being concerned about these issues. So the "opening" for Witnesses often begins by focusing on these universal concerns, then continues by establishing a certain level of rapport, and finally turns to conversation that is more specifically religious or theological in nature.

Other introductions are grouped under headings such as "Crime/ Safety," "Current Events," "Family/Children," "Love/Kindness." At the end of these introductions are what might be called introduction continuers, lines to use when a missionary is about to have a door slammed in his face.

When many people in the area say, "I have my own religion," it is recommended the missionaries use this opening: "Good morning. We are visiting all the families on your block (or, in this area), and we find that most of them have their own religion. No doubt you do too. . . . But, regardless of our religion, we are affected by many of the same problems—high cost of living, crime, illness —is that not so? . . . Do you feel that there is any real solution to these things? . . . (2 Pet. 3:13; etc.)."

Taking Cues

When many people say, "I'm busy," this opening is used: "Hello. We're visiting everyone in this neighborhood with an important message. No doubt you are a busy person, so I'll be brief." If the missionaries find themselves in a territory that is often worked by other JWs, they begin this way: "I'm glad to find you at home. We're making our weekly visit in the neighborhood, and we have something more to share with you about the wonderful things that God's Kingdom will do for mankind."

The second chapter of the *Reasoning* book instructs missionaries in how to "respond to potential conversation stoppers." The reader is told that "not everyone is willing to listen, and we do not try to force them. But with discernment it is often possible to turn potential conversation stoppers into opportunities for further discussion. Here are examples of what some experienced Witnesses have used in their efforts to search out deserving ones (Matt. 10:11)."

Missionaries are told not to memorize these lines but to master them and put them in their own words. The key is sincerity. If the person who answers the door says, "I'm not interested," the JW is to follow up with this: "May I ask, Do you mean that you are not interested in the Bible, or is it religion in general that does not interest you? I ask that because we have met many who at one time were religious but no longer go to church because they see much hypocrisy in the churches (or, they feel that religion is just another money-making business; or, they do not approve of religion's involvement in politics; etc.). The Bible does not approve of such practices either and it provides the only basis on which we can look to the future with confidence." Six other responses to the "I'm not interested" line are given.

Keep in mind that the JW has been well-trained and is well-versed in the "pre-packaged" responses he has been taught. This fact adds to the *appearance* of the JW's credibility and even his biblical "knowledge." The reality, however, is that a given Witness has merely become adept at repeating select Bible verses and responses that he uses time and time again.

"Not Interested in Witnesses"

If the person is more specific still and says, "I'm not interested in the Jehovah's Witnesses," the missionaries give this kind of response: "Many folks tell us that. Have you ever wondered why people like me volunteer to make these calls even though we know that the majority of householders may not welcome us? (Give the gist of Matt. 25:31–33, explaining that a separating of people of all nations is taking place and that their response to the Kingdom message is an important factor in this. Or state the gist of Ezekiel

9:1–11, explaining that, on the basis of people's reaction to the Kingdom message, everyone is being 'marked' either for preservation through the great tribulation or for destruction by God.)"

Here you see peeping out one of the Witnesses' peculiar doctrines—they don't believe in hell. They think the unsaved are annihilated and simply cease to exist. Only the saved will live eternally. If the person at the door says, "I have my own religion," he should be asked, "Would you mind telling me, Does your religion teach that the time will come when people who love what is right will live on earth forever? . . . That is an appealing thought, isn't it? . . . It is right here in the Bible (Ps. 37:29; Matt. 5:5; Rev. 21:4)."

Notice again the approach: the Witness ultimately gets to a theological matter ("It is right here in the Bible") by means of an attraction to the emotions or one's opinions ("That is an appealing thought, isn't it?") and not to revealed religious truth.

Also, this belief that the majority of believers will reside on a paradise Earth is another doctrine peculiar to the Witnesses. They think the saved will live forever on a regenerated Earth sometime in the future, after the wicked have been destroyed by Jehovah God at the battle of Armageddon. But the "hook" they use is not peculiar to them.

Like Fundamentalists

Fundamentalists, though their theology is vastly better than that of the JWs, use a similar technique. On one hand, JWs argue to the truth of their position by asking, "That is an appealing thought, isn't it?" Many people will conclude, "Yes, it is, and therefore it must be true"—illogical, perhaps, but that's how many people think.

On the other hand, Fundamentalists will ask, "Wouldn't you like an absolute assurance of salvation?" "Who wouldn't?" is the reply, and, having given that reply, many people will find themselves accepting the Fundamentalists' notion that one can have an absolute assurance of salvation (a doctrine that arises from their belief that all one needs to do to be saved is to "accept" Jesus as one's "personal Lord and Savior").

If the person answering the door says, "I am already well acquainted with your work" (a polite way of saying, "Get lost"), the missionaries should say: "I am very glad to hear that. Do you have a close relative or friend that is a Witness? . . . May I ask, Do you believe what we teach from the Bible, namely, that we are living in 'the last days,' that soon God is going to destroy the wicked, and that this earth will become a paradise in which people can live forever in perfect health among neighbors who really love one another?" Notice that once again the Witness has managed to turn around the conversation with this response and thus at least "plant seeds" in the mind of the person at the door.

The *Reasoning* book next provides sample responses to Buddhists, Hindus, Jews, and Muslims, and then ends this section.

The above examples show how JWs typically work when they come knocking at your door. It is evident from the *Reasoning* book that they are quite prepared for virtually every kind of response they may face when going door-to-door. This preparation makes them relatively effective at what they do. But while their "gospel" is false and their presentation is carefully "pre-packaged," Catholics should at least take note of the JWs' willingness to promote what they believe. This is perhaps one lesson we can learn from them.

57

Are They Awake on the Watchtower?

They travel in pairs, carrying copies of their magazines. They're Jehovah's Witnesses, part of a non-Christian religion. Their publishing house—the Watchtower Bible and Tract Society—is headquartered in Brooklyn, New York, and publishes two magazines that appear twice each month: *Awake!*, which is a general interest magazine with occasional religious content, and *The Watchtower*, which more formally presents the doctrines and beliefs of the WTS and is usually intended for initiates or those who have at least expressed an interest in knowing more about the Jehovah's Witnesses.

It doesn't take long, after browsing through a few issues, to learn that the Witnesses have a fixation with Catholicism. They devote an inordinate amount of space in their magazines to attacks on Catholic beliefs. On the whole, the debunking is done in a relatively inoffensive manner, but nonetheless it's obvious which ecclesiastical organization is seen as the great enemy. (In the 1920s and 1930s—the era of "Judge" Rutherford, the second president of the WTS—the attacks on the Catholic Church were more virulent and direct, but the WTS has since toned down its approach.) Let's look at representative issues, but first it's necessary to understand the WTS's use of anonymity in its articles and publications.

Privacy at All Costs

The officials in Brooklyn value anonymity highly. The Jehovah's Witnesses publish their own translation of the Bible—the so-called *New World Translation*—which was produced by committee, but the names of the committee members have not been revealed by the WTS. This version is used routinely—but not exclusively—in their publications. It should be noted that JWs will use other Bible translations, but only when it suits their purposes to do so. The NWT is universally rejected by non-Witnesses, including secular Greek and Hebrew scholars. These scholars, and informed critics of the Watchtower, speculate that few of the members who served on the committee were experienced as translators or even knew the rudiments of Hebrew or Greek; the NWT appears to be little more than a modification of already-existing English versions. It was by means of two former Witnesses, Bill Cetnar (who worked in the Brooklyn headquarters) and Raymond Franz (a former member of the WTS's Governing Body) that the identity of the committee members became known and therefore that the scholars' suspicions were confirmed. According to Cetnar and Franz, only one member of the committee (Frederick Franz, fourth WTS president and Raymond Franz's uncle) studied biblical languages *at all*, and he studied non-biblical Greek for only two years.

Also, with the exception of some personal testimony stories, readers of both magazines will fail to find the names of people who authored the various articles contained in them. The WTS does this partly because it suppresses individuality within the organization and partly because it prevents the reader from examining an author's requisite credentials to teach on the given subject matter. Witnesses are taught to *submit* to the WTS, not to question its publications. Consequently, the anonymity is understandable.

Awake!

The November 8, 1988, issue of *Awake!* features on its cover a painting of the Virgin Mary and the title "Mary: The Answer to World Crisis?" Inside are seven short articles about Mary and Marian devotion. All but one, a personal conversion story, are anonymous. The byline for the first, for instance, is this: "By *Awake!* correspondent in Italy."

The first article in *Awake!* is about a recent Marian year. Like other pieces *Awake!* has run about things Catholic, it takes swipes at the Church of Rome. The reader is told that "traditionalist Catholics" were pleased with the televised proclamation of the Marian Year, but "for others, both Catholics and non-Catholics, it was a useless waste of money, a 'cosmic show' of doubtful taste."

Why did Pope John Paul II proclaim a Marian year in the first place? Because, "for quite some time, in the more conservative Catholic spheres, there has been concern over the fact that Marian worship seems to have been obscured." (Notice that Catholic doctrine has been subtly misrepresented. Catholics do not "worship" Mary, but they do honor and venerate her. Such misrepresentation is not an uncommon occurrence in the pages of WTS publications.) The writer says there were other motives—for instance, it was hoped that increased pilgrimages to Marian shrines would result in increased priestly vocations.

Not all Catholics were pleased that a Marian year had been proclaimed. "Catholic priest Franco Barbero [otherwise unidentified] caused a stir when he publicly declared that he never prayed to Mary. In his 'Letter to Mary,' Barbero states that she has been crushed 'under a mountain of dogmas, relics, devotionalisms, legends, superstition.' The same priest has also stated that even 'speaking of a "year of Mary" could raise legitimate perplexities.' "

Madonna Worshipers?

So far, these complaints sound as though they could come from any "Bible Christian" or even any secularist. But the Witnesses have twists of their own. The *Awake!* author asks why so many Catholics have become "Madonna worshipers." He answers, "There are many reasons. Some of them stem directly from doctrines taught by the Catholic Church. For example, since the Church teaches that Jesus is equal to God, this leaves no independent intermediary between man and God. God and Christ, surrounded by an aura of Trinitarian mystery, are no longer approach-

434   THE ESSENTIAL CATHOLIC SURVIVAL GUIDE

able, and for this reason the role of 'intermediary' between the Divinity and humankind has been delegated to the 'Madonna.' "

These lines might be confusing to those who don't realize that the Jehovah's Witnesses don't believe in the Trinity. They believe that Jesus is not divine, is not the second Person of the Trinity—in fact, that there is no second Person, because there is no Trinity in their view. If Jesus is not divine, what is he? A creature, though the best of creatures. He was the first thing created by God and had a prehuman existence, and it was through him, as an agent, that God created everything else.

Jesus Only an Archangel

Still, he's only a creature. The miracles he performed attested not to his own divinity but to approval of him by God. In heaven, Jesus is now known as Michael. (This identification of Jesus and Michael the archangel relies on Jude 9, Daniel 10:13 and 12:1, and Revelation 12:7–8. Read them for yourself and see how far-fetched this is.)

What these beliefs of the Witnesses amount to is the ancient heresy of Arianism, which is nothing new. Athanasius battled it a millennium and a half ago. The Witnesses, in condemning Marian doctrines, often come up with reasons of their own, quite distinct from those given by Fundamentalists. Like Fundamentalists, they oppose giving Mary the title *Theotokos* (Greek for "One who bore God" or, less literally, "Mother of God"). "It does not appear in the Bible," writes the anonymous author. Worse, "she cannot be described as the 'Mother of God' for the simple reason that Jesus was not 'God the Son,' but 'the Son of God.' The Trinity doctrine was no part of ancient Hebrew belief and is not taught in the Bible."

No Fundamentalist would argue like this. He would agree that the notion of Mary as *Theotokos* does not appear in the Bible (and he'd be wrong), but he'd never argue that Mary isn't the Mother of God on the grounds that Jesus isn't God. The Fundamentalist fully accepts our Lord's divinity.

Twisting Words

Awake! is not adverse to misquoting and twisting the words of Catholic writers when doing so can help them slam the Church. Referring to Mary, the anonymous writer says, "The [Catholic] Church claims she was always virgin. While the Bible itself specifically states that Mary was 'a virgin' before giving birth to Jesus, 'virginity after childbirth is not indicated in the New Testament,' writes Catholic theologian [René] Laurentin." This makes it seem that Laurentin, an expert in Mariology, disbelieves in the perpetual virginity of Mary. Quite the opposite. What he was saying is that the New Testament doesn't say, in so many words, that Mary remained a virgin after Jesus' birth—and it also doesn't say she didn't. But this quote is a typical example of how the WTS will cite sources in a selective and slanted manner: First, readers of WTS publications are never given the context of the sources cited. Second, the WTS will quote only a portion of relevant passages, giving the appearance that the author holds a view directly opposite of what he actually believes—and this opposite view conveniently supports WTS beliefs. Third, the WTS rarely provides sufficient references for their sources, leaving readers unable to check the sources for themselves.

Perfectly good arguments can be made that the New Testament does, indeed, establish Mary's perpetual virginity, but Laurentin was only acknowledging that we won't find in the text a line that says, "And Mary never had any other children." We are left to infer that from other facts given to us in the text.

The Watchtower

The Jehovah's Witnesses' other magazine is *The Watchtower*. Twenty-two million copies of each issue are printed in well over 100 languages, and about a third of those copies are in English. (*Awake!* has a somewhat smaller circulation.)

The December 1, 1988, issue of *The Watchtower* features a photograph of a cathedral on its cover. Superimposed is the question "What Traditions Please God?" Apparently not something like All Souls' Day, which "seems strange or even bizarre to an outside observer." And well it might, since we're told that it and many other "religious traditions are plainly derived from, or at least astonishingly similar to, non-Christian religious rites. For example, All Souls' Day virtually parallels the Buddhist festival of 'Ullambana,' a day set aside for 'the expression of filial piety to deceased ancestors and the release of spirits from bondage to this world.' " The *New Encyclopedia Britannica* is cited as the source of the last quotation. The (again) anonymous author asks, "Are followers of such traditions really worshipping in truth?" He refers the reader to John 4:23, "The true worshipers will worship the Father in spirit and truth."

The Give-Away

The next paragraph is a give-away. It throws a bright light on the author's confusion. It says: "Some argue that the mere acceptance of traditions into the Church justifies them. Said the Second Vatican Council in 1965: 'It is not from sacred Scripture alone that the Church draws her certainty about everything which has been revealed. Therefore both sacred Tradition and sacred Scripture are to be accepted and venerated with the same sense of devotion and reverence.' "

The confusion here is equating mere traditions—customs or ways of doing things—with Tradition, the oral teaching given by Jesus to the apostles and passed through their successors, the bishops. Vatican II, in this passage, was talking about "uppercase" Tradition, not "lowercase" tradition. The writer for *The Watchtower* was either grossly ignorant of the meaning of Catholic terms, or he tried to pull a fast one here, knowing that the word *Tradition* —also called "Sacred Tradition"—implies something other than mere "tradition"—or "human tradition."

Such an approach is not unusual for the WTS, which often misrepresents or confuses official Catholic doctrine and then refutes the mistaken notion rather than the actual teaching. This approach is called the "straw man" tactic. The misrepresented belief, which is essentially "made of nothing" and thus called a "straw man," is set up and then easily refuted or "knocked down." To the unsuspecting person, this tactic makes the WTS *appear* quite scholarly and biblically astute. The danger, however, lies in the fact that the WTS is refuting beliefs and teachings that are not legitimate Catholic doctrine.

All Souls' Day is a custom the Church developed centuries after the apostles, not a doctrine. Yet when Vatican II speaks of Tradition, it refers only to those doctrines and practices that have been handed down from the apostles, either implicitly or explicitly. It is only the latter—those that have come down to us from the apostles—that are automatically accepted. Those invented later can be changed, modified, or even abandoned as needed.

In any event, there is nothing wrong with All Souls' Day. The Bible teaches that we should pray for the dead (2 Macc. 12:44–45—though Witnesses rely on the Protestant canon of Scripture, which cut this book out of the Bible). And no serious historian would claim that All Souls' Day is in any way derived from the Buddhist festival Ullambana—though this is precisely the conclusion suggested from the way the WTS presents its sources.

These are but a few examples of how the WTS distorts Catholic beliefs and presents "scholarship" in support of its views. These examples provide a "representative slice" of the thinking and *modus operandi* of the WTS, and they should serve as a warning signal for those unsuspecting people who open their doors to JWs and welcome their message. When dealing with WTS publications, be forewarned that the material exhibited there is distorted in such a way so as to present what appears to be a rather compelling case for WTS theology. But all that glitters is not gold.

58

Stumpers for Jehovah's Witnesses

The sect known as Jehovah's Witnesses began with Charles Taze Russell in the 1870s. Russell was raised a Presbyterian, then joined the Congregational church, and was finally influenced by Adventist teachings. By his own admission, he had a hard time accepting the existence of hell. He sought out the Bible, and as his "studies" continued, he systematically began to reject the major doctrines of historical Christianity. He ultimately established his own belief system, and in 1879 he started publishing a magazine to promote his beliefs. This magazine was the precursor to today's *Watchtower* magazine, by which Jehovah's Witnesses are typically known.

In this chapter we will examine five topics relating to Russell, the JWs, and their parent organization, the Watch Tower Society. We will show that the beliefs of JWs are unscriptural, and that both Russell and the WTS are completely unreliable as spiritual guides.

Is the Watch Tower Society Reliable?

In 1910, Russell wrote, "If anyone lays the *Scripture Studies* [short for a seven-volume WTS publication entitled *Studies in the Scriptures*, hereafter abbreviated as *Studies*] aside, even after he has used them, after he has become familiar with them, after he has read them for ten years—if he lays them aside and ignores them and goes to the Bible alone, though he has understood the Bible for ten years, our experience shows that within two years he goes into darkness. On the other hand, if he had merely read the *Scripture Studies* with their references and had not read a page of the Bible, as such, he will be in the light at the end of two years" (*WT Reprints*, Sep. 15, 1910, 4685). The WTS maintains that it is God's reliable mouthpiece to the nations, and it claims to be God's inspired prophet (cf. WT, Apr. 1, 1972, 197)—and yet its prophecies have repeatedly proven to be false. The only conclusion to be drawn is that the WTS is to be rejected as a false prophet.

Among other things, the WTS predicted the following:

1889—"The 'battle of the great day of God almighty' (Rev. 16:14) which will end in AD 1914" (*Studies*, vol. 2, 1908 edition, 101).

1891—"With the end of AD 1914, what God calls Babylon, and what men call Christendom, will have passed away, as already shown from prophecy" (*Studies*, vol. 3, 153).

1894—"The end of 1914 is not the date for the beginning, but for the end of the time of trouble" (*WT Reprints*, Jan. 1, 1894, 1605 and 1677).

1897—"Our Lord is now present, since October 1874 AD" (*Studies*, vol. 4, 1897 edition, 621).

1916—"The six great 1000 year days beginning with Adam are ended, and that the great 7th day, the 1000 years of Christ's reign began in 1873" (*Studies*, vol. 2, p. 2 of foreword).

1917—"Scriptures . . . prove that the Lord's Second Advent occurred in the fall of 1874" (*Studies*, vol. 7, 68).

1918—"Therefore, we may confidently expect that 1925 will mark the return of Abraham, Isaac, Jacob, and the faithful prophets of old" (*Millions Now Living Will Never Die*, 89).

1922—"The date 1925 is even more distinctly indicated by the scriptures than 1914" (WT, Sep. 1, 1922, 262).

1923—"1925 is definitely settled by the scriptures. As to Noah, the Christian now has much more upon which to base his faith than Noah had upon which to base his faith in a coming deluge" (WT, Apr. 1, 1923, 106).

1925—"The year of 1925 is here. . . . Christians should not be so deeply concerned about what may transpire this year" (WT, Jan. 1, 1925, 3).

1931—"There was a measure of disappointment on the part of Jehovah's faithful ones on earth concerning the dates 1914, 1918,

& 1925 . . . and they also learned to quit fixing dates" (*Vindication*, 388, 389).

1939—"The disaster of Armageddon is just ahead" (*Salvation*, 361).

1941—"Armageddon is surely near . . . soon . . . within a few years" (*Children*, 10).

1946—"Armageddon . . . should come sometime before 1972" (*They Have Found a Faith*, 44).

1966—"Six thousand years from man's creation will end in 1975, and the seventh period of a thousand years of human history will begin in the fall of 1975 C.E." (*Life Everlasting in Freedom of the Sons of God*, 29).

1968—"The end of the six thousand years of man's history in the fall of 1975 is not tentative, but is accepted as a certain date" (WT, Jan. 1, 1968, 271).

Besides false prophecies, the WTS has misled its members through countless changes in doctrine and practice:

"To worship Christ in any form cannot be wrong" (WT, Mar. 1880, 83). "It is unscriptural for worshippers of the living and true God to render worship to the Son of God, Jesus Christ" (WT, Nov. 1, 1964, 671).

The men of Sodom will be resurrected (WT, July 1879, 7–8). The men of Sodom will not be resurrected (WT, June 1, 1952, 338). The men of Sodom will be resurrected (WT, Aug. 1, 1965, 479). The men of Sodom will not be resurrected (WT, June 1, 1988, 31). The men of Sodom will be resurrected (*Live Forever*, early ed., 179). The men of Sodom will not be resurrected (*Live Forever*, later ed., 179). The men of Sodom will be resurrected (*Insight on the Scriptures*, vol. 2, 985). The men of Sodom will not be resurrected (*Revelation: Its Grand Climax at Hand!* 273).

"There could be nothing against our consciences in going into the army" (WT, Apr. 15, 1903, 120). "Due to conscience, Jehovah's Witnesses must refuse military service" (WT, Feb. 1, 1951, 73).

"We may as well join in with the civilized world in celebrating the grand event [Christmas]" (*WT Reprints*, Dec. 1, 1904, 3468).

"Christmas and its music are not from Jehovah. . . . What is their source? . . . Satan the devil" (WT, Dec. 15, 1983, 7).

"Everyone in America should take pleasure in displaying the American flag" (*WT Reprints*, May 15, 1917, 6068). The flag is "an idolatrous symbol" (*Awake!* Sep. 8, 1971, 14).

A much longer list of such contradictions and doctrinal twists by the WTS could be formed, but this suffices to remove any reason one might have to believe that "it is through the columns of *The Watchtower* that Jehovah provides direction and constant scriptural counsel to his people" (WT, May 1, 1964, 277). If that is the case, then who is to say what will be taught tomorrow?

Can You Trust the New World Translation?

The *New World Translation*, the JWs' own Bible version, was created between 1950 and 1961 in several parts, beginning with the New Testament. The translation was made by an "anonymous" committee, which transliterated and altered passages that were problematic for earlier JWs. Nathan Knorr, Fred Franz, Albert Schroeder, George Gangas, and Milton Henschel were later identified as the men who created the text, which is used by no other sect. Franz studied non-biblical Greek for two years and taught himself Hebrew. The rest had no formal training in any biblical language. The text of the NWT is more of a transliteration to fit theological presumptions than it is a true translation. This can be seen in key verses that the Watch Tower Society changed in order to fit its doctrines.

To undermine the divinity of Christ in John 1:1, the NWT reads, "The word was a god." Non-JW Greek scholars call this "a shocking mistranslation," "incorrect," "monstrous," and "evidence of abysmal ignorance of the basic tenets of Greek grammar." Furthermore, Colossians 1:15–17 has been changed to read: "By means of him all [other] things were created." If the text were left as the original Greek reads, it would clearly state that Jesus created all things. However, the WTS cannot afford to say that anyone but Jehovah created all things, so it inserted the word *other* four times into the text.

The 1950, 1961, and 1970 editions of the NWT said that Jesus was to be worshiped (cf. Heb. 1:6), but the WTS changed the NWT so that later editions would support its doctrines. The translators now decided to render the Greek word for "worship" (*proskuneo*) as "do obeisance" every time it is applied to Jesus, but as "worship" when referring to Jehovah. If the translators were consistent, then Jesus would be given the worship due to God in Matthew 14:33, 28:9, 28:17, Luke 24:52, John 9:38, and Hebrews 1:6.

At the time of the Last Supper, there were over three dozen Aramaic words to say "this means," "represents," or "signifies," but Jesus used none of them in his statement. Since the WTS denies the Catholic teaching on the Eucharist, they have taken the liberty to change our Lord's words to "This *means* my body" in Matthew 26:26.

The NWT also translates the Greek word *kyrios* ("Lord") as "Jehovah" dozens of times in the New Testament, despite the fact that the word *Jehovah* is never used by any New Testament author. It should also be asked why the NWT does not translate *kurios* as "Jehovah" in Romans 10:9, 1 Corinthians 12:3, Philippians 2:11, 2 Thessalonians 2:1, and Revelation 22:21. If it did translate *kyrios* consistently, then Jesus would be Jehovah!

3. Is "Jehovah" God's Name?

In *Reasoning from the Scriptures*, the WTS teaches that "Jehovah" is the proper pronunciation of God's name, and so "everyone who calls on the name of Jehovah will be saved" (Rom. 10:13). They continue, "Many scholars favor the spelling 'Yahweh,' but it is uncertain and there is not agreement among them. On the other hand, 'Jehovah' is the form of the name that is most readily recognized, because it has been used in English for centuries" (195).

However, the Witnesses' own *Aid to Bible Understanding* says, "The first recorded use of this form [Jehovah] dates from the

13th century C.E. [after Christ]. Raymundus Martini, a Spanish monk of the Dominican order, used it in his book *Pugeo Fidei* of the year 1270. Hebrew scholars generally favor 'Yahweh' as the most likely pronunciation" (884–885).

New Testament Greek always uses the word *Lord* and never *Jehovah*, even in quotes from the Old Testament. *Encyclopedia Judaica, Webster's Encyclopedia, Jewish Encyclopedia, Encyclopedia Britannica, Universal Jewish Encyclopedia* and countless others agree that the title "Jehovah" is erroneous and was never used by the Jews.

4. Do Humans Possess an Immortal Soul?

Another mistake made by JWs is their denial of the immortality of the soul. The Bible mentions the soul approximately 200 times, and it can be seen to have very different meanings according to the context of each passage. This chapter will simply demonstrate that the soul is immortal according to Scripture.

Perhaps the strongest contradiction of the WTS doctrine is seen in Christ's descent to Hades. In 1 Peter 3:19, the apostle tells his audience how Jesus "preached to the spirits in prison." If the dead were aware of nothing, then his preaching would have been futile. In the Old Testament, the prophet Isaiah speaks of the condition of the dead: "Sheol beneath is stirred up to meet you when you come . . . All of them will speak and say to you . . . " (Is. 14:9–10). These verses indicate clearly that the dead are conscious, and the New Testament tells the same story. To be absent from the body is not to be unconscious, but rather it enables one to be home with the Lord, according to Paul (cf. 2 Cor. 5:8; Phil. 1:23). The body is just a tent, or tabernacle that does not last (cf. 2 Cor. 5:1–4; 2 Pet. 1:13), while man cannot kill the soul (cf. Matt. 10:28). In fact, the souls live past the death of the bodies, since John "saw . . . the souls of those who had been slain; . . . they cried with a loud voice" (Rev. 6:9–10). Because the soul does not die with the flesh, those in heaven are able to offer our prayers to God (cf. Rev. 5:8), and live in happiness (cf. Rev. 14:13).

5. Is Hell Real or Not?

The WTS also maintains that everlasting punishment is a myth and a lie invented by Satan. According to them, hell is merely mankind's common grave and is definitely not a fiery torture.

In Scripture, if one is in hell, "he shall be tormented with fire and sulphur. . . . And the smoke of their torment goes up for ever and ever, and they have no rest, day or night" (Rev. 14:10–11). This is an "eternal fire prepared for the devil and his angels" (Matt. 25:41). Jesus tells his listeners the parable of Lazarus and the rich man, in which the rich man dies and, "being in torment, he lifted up his eyes. . . . And he called out . . . 'I am in anguish in this flame'" (Luke 16:23–24). As a further illustration, Jesus states that hell is likened to Gehenna. This "Valley of Hinnom" was located southeast of Jerusalem, and was used as a garbage dump where trash and waste were continuously burned day and night in a large fire. Jesus informs his listeners that hell is like this, "where their worm does not die, and fire is not quenched" (Mark 9:48). It is the place where the wicked are sent, and from this "eternal fire" (Matt. 18:8) people will "weep and gnash their teeth" (Matt. 8:12). Now if hell were "a place of rest in hope" as the WTS teaches, then it is odd that Jesus would choose such contradictory illustrations to convey this. Lastly, Revelation 20 calls hell a "lake of fire" where all who are not in the book of life "will be tormented day and night for ever and ever" (Rev. 20:10). So, if one's name is in the book of life, one enters heaven (cf. Rev. 21:27). If it is not in the book, then a literal hell awaits.

59

More Stumpers for Jehovah's Witnesses

Some core beliefs of the Jehovah's Witnesses were examined in "Stumpers for Jehovah's Witnesses." In this sequel, we will examine some additional beliefs and teachings of the Watchtower Society, the parent organization of the JWs.

1. Are Jesus and Michael the Archangel Really the Same Person?

One of the most peculiar of the WTS's teachings is their assertion that Jesus is actually Michael the archangel. If the JW has difficulty explaining any particular doctrine, it will be this one. Even JWs will admit that if one were to have walked up to any of the apostles or disciples of Christ and asked them who Jesus was, they would not have said, "Well, he's Michael the archangel!" Not only was the very idea was unheard of before Charles Taze Russell (the founder of the WTS), but the Bible explicitly rejects the possibility of it.

For example, the author of Hebrews states, "To what angel did God ever say, 'Thou art my Son, today I have begotten thee'? . . . 'Let all God's angels worship him. . . . Thy throne, O God, is for ever and ever . . . Thou, Lord, didst found the earth in the beginning, and the heavens are the work of thy hands.' . . . To what angel has he ever said, 'Sit at my right hand'?" (Heb. 1:5–6, 8, 10, 13). Here, the author of Hebrews separates Jesus from angels and commands the angels to worship him (cf. Rev. 5:13–14; 14:6–7). The obvious problem is this: Archangels are creatures, but the

Bible forbids any creature to worship another creature. Thus, either the Bible is in error—by commanding the angels to worship an archangel—or Jesus is uncreated and cannot be an archangel. Since this gave the JWs a tremendous problem, they even had to change their own Bible translation, the *New World Translation*, to eliminate the references to worshiping Christ. (The 1950, 1961, and 1970 editions of the NWT read "worship" in Hebrews 1:6.) Beyond this, Jesus has the power to forgive sins and give eternal life, but no angel has this capacity.

2. Jesus: Creature or Creator?

The doctrine that most clearly sets the WTS apart from Christianity is its denial of the divinity of Christ. JWs maintain that Jesus is actually a creature—a highly exalted one at that—but not God himself. Scripturally, the evidence is not in their favor.

John 1:1 states unequivocally, "In the beginning was the Word, and the Word was with God, and the Word was God." This verse gave the JWs tremendous difficulty, and so in their own NWT they render the end of this verse as "And the word was a god." One great difficulty with this translation is how it contradicts passages such as Deuteronomy 32:39, which says, "There is no god beside me." Further contradictions can be seen in Exodus 20:3 ("You shall have no other gods besides me") and Isaiah 43:10 ("Before me no god was formed, nor shall there be any after me"). When a particular translation so clearly opposes other verses in Scripture, one can know immediately that it is inaccurate.

In John 20:28 Thomas says to Jesus, "My Lord and my God." In the original Greek it literally reads, "The Lord of me and the God of me." It would be nothing short of blasphemy for Jesus not to rebuke Thomas if he was wrong. Jesus does nothing of the sort; he instead accepts Thomas's profession of his identity as God.

The Bible indicates that God alone created the universe (Is. 44:24), and "the builder of all things is God" (Heb. 3:4). However, Jesus created the heavens and the earth (Heb. 1:10). This passage by itself proves that Jesus is God, since an Old Testament reference to God (Ps. 102:25–28) is now given to him.

In John 8:58, Jesus takes the name of God, "I Am" (Ex. 3:15–18), and applies it to himself. Only God may use this title without blaspheming (Ex. 20:7; Deut. 5:11), and the punishment for someone other than God to use the sacred "I Am" is stoning (Lev. 24:16). Thus in verse 59, Jesus' audience picked up stones to kill him, because they correctly understood his use of "I Am" as his claim to being God and hence thought he was guilty of blasphemy. This verse also proved to be difficult for the JWs to combat, and so they changed "I Am" to "I have been." The Greek here is *egō eimi*, which any first-semester Greek student can tell you means "I am." It should also be noted that it would be rather strange for people to stone Jesus for saying that he "had been."

JWs maintain that only Jehovah God may be prayed to. But Stephen prayed to Jesus in Acts 7:59, and so one must conclude that Jesus is God. Otherwise, Stephen blasphemed while filled with the Holy Spirit (7:55). Now the JWs will assert that Stephen was praying as a result of the vision he originally beheld, where he saw God and Jesus in heaven. However, verse 58 says that Stephen was dragged out of the city to be stoned, so clearly the vision had ended, for his stoning took place in a different location and at a later time. It is in the context of this later setting when Stephen clearly prays to Jesus that he might "receive [Stephen's] spirit."

The WTS would have their followers believe that Jehovah and Jesus are necessarily different beings, though the Bible tells another story. Jesus is called "Mighty God" in Isaiah 9:6, and in the very next chapter the same title is given to Jehovah in verse 21. Other shared titles include King of Kings (compare with Rev. 17:14), Lord of Lords (Deut. 10:17; Rev. 17:14), the only Savior (Is. 43:10–11; Acts 4:12), the First and the Last (Is. 44:6; 22:13), the Alpha and the Omega (Rev. 1:8; 22:13–16), Rock (Is. 8:14; 1 Pet. 2:7–8), and Shepherd (Ps. 23:1; Heb. 13:20–21).

Jesus and Jehovah have much more in common than titles, though. They are both worshiped by angels (Heb. 1:6; Neh. 9:6).

They are both unchanging (Heb. 13:8; Mal. 3:6). They both created the heavens and the earth (Heb. 1:10; Neh. 9:6) and are all-knowing (John 21:17; 1 John 3:20). Both give eternal life (John 10:28; 1 John 5:11) and judge the world (John 5:22; Ps. 96:13). To them every knee will bend and every tongue confess (Phil. 2:9–11; Is. 45:23).

3. Is the Holy Spirit a Force or God?

Since the WTS insists that the Trinity is unbiblical and false, they relegate the Holy Spirit to the role of God's impersonal active force that compels believers to do his will. In fact, they compare the Holy Spirit (which they render as "holy spirit") to electricity.

The Bible begs to differ, though. There are numerous verses in the New Testament that clearly demonstrate both the personality and divinity of the Holy Spirit. For example, in Acts 13:2, the Holy Spirit says, "Set apart for me Barnabas and Saul for the work to which I have called them." In Acts 10:19–20, this "impersonal force" considers himself to be a person. John 16 supports this idea by referring to the Holy Spirit as a "he" ten times in the same chapter. First Corinthians 12:11 states that the Holy Spirit "wills," which is an irrefutable attribute of personhood, as is the capacity to love we see demonstrated by the Spirit in Romans 15:30. Scripture also states that the Holy Spirit can be lied to (Acts 5:3), speak (Acts 10:19–20), hear (John 16:13–15), know the future (Acts 21:11), testify (John 15:26), teach (John 14:26), reprove (John 16:8–11), pray and intercede (Rom. 8:26), guide (John 16:13), call (Acts 13:2), be grieved (Eph. 4:30), feel hurt (Is. 63:10), be outraged (Heb. 10:29), desire (Gal. 5:17) and be blasphemed (Mark 3:29). Only a person is capable of these.

These examples demonstrate sufficiently that the Holy Spirit is a personal being, and so now one must demonstrate that he is God. Acts 5:1–4 teaches that a lie to the Holy Spirit is a lie to God himself. Isaiah 44:24 insists that God alone created the heavens and the earth, but Job 33:4 and Psalms 104:30 explain that the Holy Spirit created them. Only God is everlasting, and this is likewise an attribute Scripture gives the Holy Spirit (Heb. 9:14). The Jews put Jehovah to the test (Ex. 17:2), and the Holy Spirit takes the words of God and claims they "tested and tried me" (Heb. 3:9). Unless the Holy Spirit is God, he is an impostor. Again, in Hebrews 10:16, he claims to have placed his law in man's hearts, though this was God's work in Jeremiah 31:33. There is but one Lord (Eph. 4:5) and one Creator (Mal. 2:10), yet both the Father and the Spirit claim that they are him (Matt. 11:25 and 2 Cor. 3:17; 1 Cor. 8:6 and Ps. 104:30). Only the Catholic understanding of the Trinity reconciles these passages.

4. Was Christ Bodily Resurrected?

According to the WTS, "The man Jesus is dead, forever dead" (*Studies in the Scriptures*, vol. 5, p. 454). "We deny that he was raised in the flesh, and challenge any statement to that effect as being unscriptural" (*Studies*, vol. 7, p. 57). Jesus' fleshly body "was disposed of by Jehovah God, dissolved into its constitutive elements or atoms" (*The Watchtower*, September 1, 1953, 518). "In order to convince Thomas of who he was, he used a body with wound holes" (*You Can Live Forever in Paradise on Earth*, 145). "He was raised as an invisible spirit creature, with no physical body" (*Reasoning from the Scriptures*, 214–215).

However, according to Scripture, "If Christ has not been raised, your faith is futile and you are still in your sins" (1 Cor. 15:17). Jesus makes clear, even before death, that it is his body that will be raised up. He promises to raise up the temple once it is destroyed. "He spoke of the temple of his body" (John 2:21). After he had risen, he gives the same testimony, "See my hands and my feet, that it is I myself; handle me, and see, for a spirit has not flesh and bones as you see that I have. . . . Have you anything here to eat?" (Luke 24:39, 41). Jesus insists that Thomas place his finger into his wounded side, so as to prove that he had indeed risen from the dead (John 20:27). There is no question that Jesus had truly risen from the dead. No Christian was under the impression that he was invisibly raised as Michael the archangel, while God the Father dissolved his natural body. Such a presumption is without historical or scriptural warrant, and the "proof is in the pudding": Ask the JW to show you a Scripture verse that backs up the WTS's assertion about God disposing of Jesus' body. He can't, because there isn't one.

5. Is Heaven Just for the "Anointed Class"?

The WTS teaches that only the anointed 144,000 seen in Revelation 7 will enter heaven (the "anointed class"), while the remainder that are not annihilated (the "other sheep") will live forever on earth in paradise. However, the Bible poses some irreconcilable difficulties with this idea.

If Revelation 7 is to be taken literally, there would be only 144,000 Jewish male virgins taken from a square-shaped earth who are now in heaven worshiping a sheep. This would mean that Peter (not a virgin), the Blessed Mother (not a male), and Charles Taze Russell (not a Jew) could not be in heaven. Reading one number literally while taking the rest of a book symbolically is not sound exegesis. Beyond this, we see in Revelation 14 that the 144,000 stand before the twenty-four elders from Revelation 4:4. This at least brings the grand total to 144,024 people. But Scripture indicates that there are still more to come. Revelation 7:9 speaks of a countless multitude before the throne, which is in heaven (Rev. 14:2–3). Still in the book of Revelation, we read that all those with their name in the book of life are in heaven (21:27), while all whose names are not in the book of life are thrown into the pool of fire (20:15). There is no third "earthly" class. Jesus reiterates this and never speaks of two flocks. He has one bride, whose "reward is great in heaven" (Luke 6:23). Paul even exhorts the Christian community, calling them to remember that "our commonwealth is in heaven" (Phil. 3:20).

The JWs attempt to use verses such as Psalms 37:29 as evidence that the just are to inherit the land forever, which is earth. In context, this refers to inheriting the Promised Land as a sign of God's blessing in the Old Testament. But Hebrews 11:8–16 indicates that there is a homeland better than the Promised Land on earth, and this is the heavenly one for those who die in faith. The Old Testament patriarchs "acknowledged that they were strangers and exiles on the earth. . . . They are seeking a homeland. . . . But as it is, they desire a better country, that is, a heavenly one. . . . [God] has prepared for them a city. . . . And all these [Old Testament men and women], though well attested by their faith, did not receive what was promised . . . since God had foreseen something better for us" (Heb. 11:13–16, 39–40). Even the footnote of the NWT makes clear that the "city" spoken of in these verses is the *heavenly* Jerusalem mentioned in Hebrews 12:22 and Revelation 21:2. But the Watchtower still maintains that no one who lived before Christ will ever enter heaven. "The apostle Paul in the eleventh chapter of Hebrews names a long list of faithful men who died before the crucifixion of the Lord. . . . These can never be a part of the heavenly class" (*Millions Now Living,* 89). Only the 144,000 elite that all lived after the death of Christ will supposedly go to heaven. Matthew 8:11–12 provides severe difficulties for this idea, since Jesus proclaims, "many will come from east and west and sit at table with Abraham, Isaac, and Jacob in the kingdom of heaven, while the sons of the kingdom will be thrown into the outer darkness; there men will weep and gnash their teeth." No verse could be clearer in declaring that the patriarchs are in heaven. The following verses all demonstrate that Christians go to heaven and do not remain on earth: 2 Corinthians 5:1, Hebrews 3:1, Ephesians 2:6, Colossians 1:4–5, 1 Peter 1:4.

60

Distinctive Beliefs of
the Mormon Church

Are Mormons Protestants? No, but their founder, Joseph Smith, came from a Protestant background, and Protestant presuppositions form part of the basis of Mormonism.

Still, it isn't correct to call Mormons Protestants, because doing so implies they hold to the essentials of Christianity—what C. S. Lewis termed "mere Christianity." The fact is that they don't. Gordon B. Hinckley, the current president and prophet of the Mormon church, says (in a booklet called *What of the Mormons?*) that he and his co-religionists "are no closer to Protestantism than they are to Catholicism."

That isn't quite right—it would be better to say Mormons are even further from Catholicism than from Protestantism. But Hinckley is right in saying that Mormons are very different from Catholics and Protestants. Let's examine some of these differences. We can start by considering the young men who come to your door.

They always come in pairs and are dressed conservatively, usually in white shirts and ties. As often as not, they get from place to place by bicycle. They introduce themselves to you as Elder This and Elder That. The title "Elder" does not refer to their age (many are not even shaving regularly yet) but means they hold the higher of the two Mormon priesthoods, the "Melchizedek" order. This priesthood is something every practicing Mormon male is supposed to receive at about age eighteen, provided he conforms to the standards of the church.

The other priesthood—the Aaronic—is the lesser of the two and is concerned with the temporal affairs of the church, and its ranks are known as deacon, teacher, and priest. At age twelve boys become deacons and thus enter the "Aaronic priesthood."

The Melchizedek priesthood is concerned mainly with spiritual affairs, and it "embrac[es] all of the authority of the Aaronic," explains Hinckley. The Melchizedek ranks are elder, seventy, and high priest.

If the terms for the various levels of the Mormon priesthood are confusing, still more confusing is Mormonism's ecclesiastical structure. The basic unit, equivalent to a very small parish, is the ward. Several wards within a single geographical area form a stake, which corresponds to a large Catholic parish. The head of each ward isn't called a priest, as you might expect, but a bishop. A Mormon bishop can officiate at a civil marriage but not at a "temple marriage," which can be performed only by a "sealer" in one of Mormonism's temples.

Polygamy

Mormons try to attract new members by projecting an image of wholesome family life in their circles. This is an illusion— Mormon Utah has higher than average rates for suicide, divorce, and other domestic problems than the rest of the country. And if Mormonism's public image of large happy families and marriage bring to mind anything, it is polygamy.

Hinckley explains that "Mormonism claims to be a restoration of God's work in all previous dispensations. The Old Testament teaches that the patriarchs . . . had more than one wife under divine sanction. In the course of the development of the church in the nineteenth century, it was revealed to the leader of the church that such a practice should be entered into again." Although polygamy was permitted to Mormons, few practiced it. But enough did so to make polygamy the characteristic that most caught the attention of other Americans.

Mormonism, you should understand, is one of those religions that are peculiarly American. (A few others come to mind immediately, such as the Jehovah's Witnesses and Christian Science.) Although now spread beyond the borders of the United States, Mormonism is so tied to a certain brand of American nationalism that you couldn't imagine the religion starting anywhere else.

Mormonism: Made in America

If many of today's Fundamentalists are known for their belief that America is destined to play a key role in the events of the Last Days, Mormons are identified even more closely with America. The Mormons' theory is that Christ also established his Church here, among the Indians, where it eventually flopped, as did his original effort in Palestine.

The situation is somewhat similar to that of the Anglican church. In England, the Anglican church is not just the church of Englishmen; it is the established church. In theory, and even at times in practice, Parliament can decide what Anglicans are to believe officially and can make and unmake clerics of all grades, from the lowliest curate to the archbishop of Canterbury. Just as Anglicanism is tied to England, so Mormonism is tied to the United States. Although it is not the established religion of this country, Mormonism has allowed itself to be modified by Congress.

"In the late 1880s," says Hinckley, "Congress passed various measures prohibiting [polygamy]. When the Supreme Court declared these laws constitutional, the church indicated its willingness to comply. It could do nothing else in view of its basic teachings on the necessity for obedience to the law of the land. That was in 1890. Since then officers of the church have not performed plural marriages, and members who have entered into such relationships have been excommunicated."

Before Congress acted, Mormons were convinced polygamy was not merely permissible but positively good, for those "of the highest character who had proved themselves capable of maintaining more than one family." (Section 132 of *Doctrine and Covenants* is officially subtitled this way: "Revelation given through Joseph

Smith the Prophet, at Nauvoo, Illinois, recorded July 12, 1843, relating to the new and everlasting covenant, including the eternity of the marriage covenant, as also plurality of wives.")

Yet this position was dropped when Washington, D.C., threatened to deny statehood to Utah. Similarly, and more recently, a "revelation" saying blacks would no longer be denied the Mormon priesthood was given to Mormon leaders when the federal government became involved.

Continuing Revelation

Continuing revelations are not exceptions to Mormon practice. "We believe all that God has revealed, all that he does now reveal, and we believe that he will yet reveal many great and important things"—this is the ninth article of faith for Mormons and is an official statement of doctrine.

Mormon president and prophet Gordon B. Hinckley notes that "Christians and Jews generally maintain that God revealed himself and directed chosen men in ancient times. Mormons maintain that the need for divine guidance is as great or greater in our modern, complex world as it was in the comparatively simple times of the Hebrews." Thus, revelation continues.

It might be added: public revelation continues. Catholics hold that public or "general" revelation ended at the death of the last apostle (cf. *Catechism of the Catholic Church* 66, 73), but private revelations can be given still—and have been, as Marian apparitions at such places as Fatima and Lourdes testify (cf. CCC 67). Such revelations can never correct, supplement, or complete the Christian faith, which is precisely what Mormon "revelations" claim to do.

Mormonism's Debt to Puritanism

"Mormon theology," says Hinckley, "deals with such widely diversified subjects as the nature of heaven and the evils of alcohol.

Actually, in this philosophy the two are closely related. Since man is created in the image of God, his body is sacred. . . . As such, it ill becomes any man or women to injure or dissipate his or her health." So alcohol (as well as tobacco, tea, and caffeine) is out for the believing Mormon.

Here we have an example of Mormonism borrowing from Puritanism. The religion Joseph Smith developed uses elements of various forms of Protestantism. The emphasis on "temperance" —which, to the old-line Protestants, meant not the moderate use of alcohol but outright abstinence—is one such borrowing.

The curious thing is that this attitude is contrary to the Bible. It is one of those doctrines, shared by Fundamentalists and Mormons, that is believed independently of the Bible, though the Bible has been searched unsuccessfully for verses that seem to back it.

Jesus Wasn't a Teetotaler

The ancient Jews were a temperate people—temperate used in the right sense. They used light wine as part of the regular diet (cf. 1 Tim. 3:8). Jesus, you will recall, was called a wine-drinker (cf. Matt. 11:19), the charge being not that he drank but that he drank too much (that, of course, was false, but the charge itself reflects the fact that he did drink alcoholic beverages, such as the wine that was required for use in the Jewish Passover seder).

The New Testament nowhere says the Jews claimed Jesus should have been a teetotaler. Wine was used also at weddings, and our Lord clearly approved of the practice of wine drinking since he made wine from water when the wine was depleted at Cana (John 2:1–11).

Something Mormons seldom refer to is wine's medicinal uses (cf. Luke 10:34). You will recall that Paul advised Timothy to take wine to ease stomach pains (1 Tim. 5:23). Such apostolic admonitions co-exist uneasily with Mormonism's strictures against wine.

Mormons practice tithing (the practice of donating 10 percent of one's income for religious use) but would be shocked to learn that in a key Old Testament passage where tithing is discussed, God says: "You shall turn [your tithe] into money, and bind up the money in your hand, and go to the place which the Lord your God chooses, and spend the money for whatever you desire, oxen, or sheep, or wine or strong drink, whatever your appetite craves; and you shall eat there before the Lord your God and rejoice, you and your household" (Deut. 14:25–26). We're also told, "Give strong drink to him who is perishing, and wine to those in bitter distress; let them drink and forget their poverty, and remember their misery no more" (Prov. 31:6–7).

Often when founders of new religions get an idea, they take it to an extreme. So Joseph Smith confused the misuse of wine with its legitimate use. The Bible does condemn excessive drinking (1 Cor. 5:11; Gal. 5:21; Eph. 5:18; 1 Pet. 4:3), but the key here is the adjective *excessive*. This is why Paul says Church leaders must not be addicted to wine (1 Tim. 3:8).

When Hinckley refers to the "evils of alcohol," he gets it wrong. Alcohol itself is not evil, but the misuse of it is, just as a hammer, which can be used to pound in nails, can be misused to pound in skulls.

Plural Heavens

Polygamy was a doctrine some Mormons found hard to accept. Abstinence from alcohol is a teaching many find difficult. But one unique Mormon belief has supposedly brought blessing and relief to many souls, particularly potential converts.

Mormonism teaches that practically no one is forever damned to hell. Aside from Satan, his spirit followers, and perhaps a half-dozen notorious sinners, all people who have ever existed will share in heavenly "glory." Not, mind you, all in the same heaven. There are, in fact, three heavens.

The lowest heaven is populated by adulterers, murderers, thieves, liars and other evil-doers. These share in a glory and delight impossible to imagine. Their sins have been forgiven, and they now enjoy the eternal presence of the Holy Ghost.

The middle heaven contains the souls and bodies of good non-

Mormons and those Mormons who were in some way deficient in their obedience to church commandments. They will glory in the presence of Jesus Christ forever.

The top heaven is reserved for devout Mormons, who go on to become gods and rulers of their own universes. By having their wives and children "sealed" to them during an earthly, temple ceremony, these men-gods will procreate billions of spirits and place them into future, physical bodies. These future children will then worship their father-gods, obeying Mormon commandments, and eventually take their place in the eternal progression to their own godhood.

Mormons think this doctrine is a strong selling point. They point out (erroneously) that only their church offers families the chance to be together forever in eternity. But read the fine print: The only way you can have your family with you is if each one of them has lived a sterling Mormon life. Otherwise, a spouse, parent, or child may be locked forever in a lower heaven. Indeed, the faithful Mormon wife of a lukewarm Mormon man will leave him behind in an inferior place while she goes on and is sealed to a more devout Mormon gentleman. These two will then beget and raise their own, new family.

The LDS slogan, "Families are forever," means fractured families.

61

The Gods of the Mormon Church

George Orwell, in his novel *1984*, did Catholic apologists a great favor by coining the term "doublethink," which he defined as "the power of holding two contradictory beliefs in one's mind simultaneously, and accepting both of them." It's the most succinct way of describing certain religious beliefs. For an illustration of doublethink one need look no further than the Mormon church's doctrines about God.

Joseph Smith, Mormonism's founder, taught the doctrine of a "plurality of gods"—polytheism—as the bedrock belief of his church. He developed this doctrine over a period of years to reflect his belief that not only are there many gods, but they once were mortal men who had developed in righteousness until they had learned enough and merited godhood.

The Mormon church uses the term "eternal progression" for this process, and it refers to godhood as "exaltation." Such euphemisms are used because the idea of men becoming gods is blasphemous to orthodox Christians. Needless to say, Smith encountered much hostility to these doctrines and so thought it wise to disguise them with unfamiliar terminology.

Although he softened his terms, Smith minced no words in explaining his beliefs. "I will preach on the plurality of gods. I am going to tell you how God came to be God. We have imagined and supposed that God was God from all eternity. I will refute that idea, and take away the veil, so that you may see" (*King Follett Discourse*).

Mormonism's founder concluded that his flock didn't understand the nature of God. No mortal entirely does, of course, but this particular group was handicapped, not helped, by the strange theories expounded by Smith.

True to his word, Smith took away the veil of misunderstanding, only to replace it with a monolithic wall of doublethink. After all, to teach that the all-sovereign God, the infinite and supreme being, the Creator and Master of the universe, is merely an exalted man is a fine example of what Orwell had in mind.

Progressive Revelation to Smith

In 1844, shortly before his death in a gun battle at a jail in Carthage, Illinois, Joseph Smith delivered a sermon at the funeral of a Mormon named King Follett. The *King Follett Discourse* has become a key source for the Mormon church's beliefs on polytheism and eternal progression. It's short and can be purchased at any LDS bookstore for about a dollar. You can read it in half an hour.

To appreciate the extent of Smith's departure from traditional Christian thought, it's important to realize that his doctrines weren't "revealed" to his church all at once or in their present state. From his first vision in 1820 until his death in 1844, Joseph Smith crafted and modified his doctrines, often altering them so drastically that they became something else entirely as years passed.

Early in his career as "prophet, seer, and revelator" of the Church of Jesus Christ of Latter-day Saints, Smith wrote the *Book of Mormon*, which he claimed to be the "fullness of the everlasting gospel." In it are passages that proclaim that there is only one God and that God can't change.

The next time you speak with Mormon missionaries, cite these verses:

"I know that God is not a partial God, neither a changeable being; but he is unchangeable from all eternity to all eternity" (Moroni 8:18).

"For do we not read that God is the same yesterday, today and forever, and in him there is no variableness, neither shadow of changing? And now, if ye have imagined up unto yourselves a god who doth vary, and in whom there is shadow of changing, then ye have imagined up unto yourselves a god who is not a God of miracles" (Mormon 9:9–10).

It's hard to be more explicit than that. In his early years Smith did not believe in the "law of eternal progression." He had an orthodox understanding of God's immutable nature. But at some point in his theological odyssey, he changed his teaching completely.

Contradictory Views

Remember, Smith maintained the inspiration and truth of the *Book of Mormon* at the same time he believed the following: "God himself was once as we are now, and is an exalted man, and sits enthroned in yonder heavens! That is the great secret. If the veil were rent today, and the great God who upholds all worlds and all things by his power, was to make himself visible—I say, if you were to see him today, you would see him like a man in form—like yourselves in all the person, image, and very form as a man; for Adam was created in the very fashion, image, and likeness of God, and received instruction from, and walked, talked and conversed with him, as one man talks and communes with another" (*King Follett Discourse*).

This is one of Smith's more amazing displays of doublethink. Fourteen years after penning the *Book of Mormon*, he contradicts his earlier writings with this sermon—but he doesn't throw aside his earlier teaching. Both are to be accepted.

The Missionary's "Testimony"

If you question a Mormon missionary, he'll be familiar with the *King Follett Discourse* (or should be), and he'll have a "testimony" about the truth of the doctrine of eternal progression. If you have both the *Discourse* and the *Book of Mormon* on hand, read these passages to the missionary. Watch his reaction and press for an explanation. Ask him how it's possible to hold both positions. Mormons revere Joseph Smith as the highest authority in their church. What he said is scripture, and they're stuck when it comes to this topic. These two teachings from the prophet obviously don't agree with each other. This is where doublethink kicks in.

They can't believe that God is at once immutable and changing, that from all eternity he was as he now is, yet he evolved from a mere man. To Mormons this theological contradiction poses no problem because they don't think through the ramifications of such a position. Your job as an apologist is to show them there is a problem and then to offer a solution to it.

It's not enough to say God is eternal and to leave it at that. We need to take his infinite perfection into account. This is where the Mormons falter. They believe that although God is perfect now, he wasn't always so. Once he was imperfect, as a mortal, and he had to arrive at perfection through his own labor. (You might call it a sort of "hyper-Pelagianism.")

Jesus Christ

According to Mormon teaching, at one point in the eternities past, this man-become-God, or "Heavenly Father," begat the spirit body of his first son. Together with his heavenly wife, the Father raised his son in the council of the gods.

Before the creation of this world, Jesus Christ presented to his father a plan of salvation that would enable the billions of future human beings the opportunity of passing through mortality and returning to heaven, there to become gods of their own worlds. At the same time, another son of the Heavenly Father and brother of Christ offered a competing plan. When Christ's was chosen, the rejected Lucifer led a rebellion of one-third of the population of the heavens and was cast out.

In time, Mormons believe, the Heavenly Father came to earth and had physical, sexual intercourse with the Virgin Mary. Rejecting both the testimony of Scripture (cf. Luke 1:34–35) and the constant teaching of the Christian Church, Mormons believe Christ was conceived by the Father, and not by the Holy Spirit (*Journal of Discourses* 2:268).

Moreover, Mormons teach that Christ is a secondary, inferior god. He does not exist from all eternity. (Nor, for that matter, does his Father.) He was first made by a union of his heavenly parents. After having been reared and taught in the heavens, he achieved a certain divine stature. Through carnal relations with her Heavenly Father, the Virgin became pregnant with this lesser god.

Mormons now believe that Christ's divinity is virtually equal to that of his Father's. As we have seen, this is a compromised godhood: Jesus Christ merely joins the end of a long line of gods who have preceded him, an infinite "regression" of divine beings whose origin Mormons cannot explain. (Nor, for that matter, can they explain its end, as we will see when we discuss the doctrine of men becoming gods.)

The Holy Ghost

The LDS church teaches that all men must pass through mortality in human bodies before they can reach godhood. Yet their third, separate god, called the Holy Ghost, has not yet received a mortal body, even though he is considered to be another god. Mormon theology typically does not address this contradiction.

However, that's not to say that the Holy Ghost is without any body. In fact, he has a "spiritual body," in the actual shape of a man, with head, torso, and limbs. He can be in only one place at once. (In this he's no different from his two superiors in the Mormon "Godhead.")

Though to the Holy Ghost is now ascribed the power of each Mormon's individual "testimony" or feeling concerning the truth of Mormon doctrines, he was not always so honored. In fact, Joseph Smith originally acknowledged only two divine personages, referring to the Holy Ghost merely as the "mind" of the two (*Lectures on Faith*, 48-9).

Latter-day Saints do not believe that the Father, the Son, and the Holy Ghost are the only three gods there are. Rather, they believe in (though do not worship) a "plurality" of gods, gods without number, each one ruling his own creation. Thus, the three separate gods who rule our universe are finite in power—they sustain and govern only a tiny portion of all that exists.

The other gods have either preceded or followed the Heavenly Father who organized our world. In fact, men living today on this planet will one day become gods of their own universes. As such, they will mate with heavenly wives, beget spirit children, populate new worlds, and receive the worship and obedience we are now expected to give to our particular, current God.

Smith—and All Men—to Be Gods

The Mormon founder taught that faithful Mormon men can ascend to divinity. In the *King Follett Discourse*, Joseph Smith said, "My Father worked out his kingdom with fear and trembling, and I must do the same. And when I get to my kingdom [godhood], I shall present it to my Father, so that he may obtain kingdom upon kingdom, and it will exalt him in glory. He will then take a higher exaltation, and I will take his place, and thereby become exalted myself."

In any discussion with a Mormon about Mormonism's conflicting teachings on the nature of God, you have to cut away the camouflage. You have to get to the central facts. It's simple, really. Just show them how the *Book of Mormon* conflicts with Smith's later teachings. If he was right about God, when was he right? Take your pick, but you can't pick both, and neither can a Mormon, except if he uses doublethink. If a Mormon chooses either teaching as correct and admits the other must be wrong, Smith's credibility as a prophet collapses.

Don't Aim to Win an Argument

Be forewarned that your first discussion about the nature of God won't produce any visible change in your Mormon acquaintance. He's unlikely to admit the cogency and simplicity of your argument. He's probably working in good faith, and he's sincere in his beliefs. But psychologically you're at a disadvantage, since he wants to maintain his faith as he's known it. Be patient as you help him see these theological "black holes."

Keep in mind your ultimate goal isn't to win an argument, but to win a soul for Christ. What the Catholic apologist offers isn't just sound logic, or a preponderance of Bible quotations, or even the blunders Joseph Smith made. No, what he offers is the truth of the Catholic faith.

But you do need sound logic, buttressed by thorough homework, and you need patience that's sustained by charity. Above all, you need to pray that God will use your efforts to prepare your acquaintance's soul for the gift of faith. Doublethink isn't invincible. It's just an intellectual impediment, and it can be overcome.

You need to do some homework first, of course. You need a solid understanding of God's nature. We recommend reading the appropriate passages in the *Catechism of the Catholic Church,* Fr. John Hardon's *Catholic Catechism,* and Frank Sheed's *Theology and Sanity.*

These books are available in inexpensive paperbacks, and they should be a part of every Catholic's library. You should also have on hand a copy of the *Book of Mormon* and of the *King Follett Discourse.* If you have your references already marked in these books, you'll be ready the next time a Mormon missionary comes to your door.

62

Problems with the *Book of Mormon*

In these "latter days," there are few people who haven't been visited at least once by Mormon missionaries. At some point in your doorstep dialogue, these earnest young men will ask you to accept a copy of the *Book of Mormon*, read it, and pray about it, asking the Lord to "send the Holy Ghost to witness that it is true." Then, very solemnly, they'll "testify" to you that they know that the *Book of Mormon* is true, that it's God's inspired word, and that it contains the "fullness of the everlasting gospel."

They'll assure you that if you read their text in a spirit of prayerful inquiry, you, too, will receive the testimony of the Holy Ghost. That testimony will supposedly convince you beyond doubt that the *Book of Mormon* is exactly what they claim it to be.

Keep in mind that the missionaries want you to have a feeling about the *Book of Mormon* after reading it. They'll tell you that you'll receive the witness of the Holy Ghost in the form of a "burning in the bosom"—a warm, fuzzy feeling—after reading and praying about it. This feeling is the clincher for them. It's the real "proof" that the *Book of Mormon* is inspired Scripture, and everything else follows from that conclusion.

But think about it. How often have you felt strongly about something or someone only to learn that your feelings were misguided? Feelings, although a part of our human makeup, can't be a yardstick in matters like this.

After all, some people might get a warm, fuzzy feeling after reading anything from the *Communist Manifesto* to the Yellow Pages. They could pray about such a feeling, and they could take the lingering of the feeling as some kind of divine approbation, but no such sensation will prove the inspiration of Marx's or Ma Bell's writings.

When you tell the missionaries you don't need to pray about

the *Book of Mormon*, they'll think you're copping out, that you're afraid to learn the truth. Admittedly, you'll seem like a cad if you simply refuse and leave it at that. You need to provide them with an explanation for refusing.

The devout Mormon believes this text is inspired because Joseph Smith said it is. He believes Smith had the authority to claim divine inspiration for the *Book of Mormon* because the book itself says Smith was a prophet and had such authority.

Jesus Visited America?

Let's take a closer look at the text the missionaries offer. At first glance the *Book of Mormon* appears to be biblical in heft and style. It's couched in tedious "King James" English, and it features color renderings of Mormon scenes made to look like Bible illustrations.

The introduction tells you that the "*Book of Mormon* is a volume of holy scripture comparable to the Bible. It is a record of God's dealings with the ancient inhabitants of the Americas and contains, as does the Bible, the fullness of the everlasting gospel." There it is again—the "fullness of the everlasting gospel." Naturally, you ask yourself just what that phrase means.

According to the Mormon church, authentic Christianity can't be found in any of the so-called Christian churches—only, of course, in the Mormon church.

Mormons teach that, after Jesus ascended into heaven, the apostles taught the true doctrines of Christ and administered his sacred ordinances (roughly the equivalent of Catholic sacraments). After the death of the apostles, their successors continued the work of the gospel but with rapidly declining success. Within a few generations, the great apostasy foretold in the Bible had destroyed Christ's Church (contrary to Jesus' own promise in Matthew 16:18).

The Mormon church asserts that the Church Christ founded became increasingly corrupted by pagan ideas introduced by nefarious members. (Sound familiar?) Over a period of years, the Church lost all relationship with the Church Christ established.

Consequently, the keys of authority of the holy priesthood were withdrawn from the earth, and no man any longer had authorization to act in God's name.

From that time onward there were no valid baptisms, no laying on of hands for the receipt of the Holy Ghost, no blessings of any kind, and no administration of sacred ordinances. Confusions and heretical doctrines increased and led to the plethora of Christian sects seen today.

Mormons claim that, in order to restore the true Church and true gospel to the earth, in 1820 God the Father and Jesus Christ appeared to Joseph Smith in a grove of trees near his home. They told him that all professing Christians on the face of the earth were abominable and corrupt and that the true Church, having died out completely shortly after it began, was to be restored by Smith.

Mormons run into no small difficulty in reconciling the great apostasy theory with Christ's promise in Matthew 16:18: "You are Peter, and on this rock I will build my church, and the powers of death shall not prevail against it."

How could it be that Christ, who should have known better, would promise that his Church wouldn't be overcome if he knew full well a great apostasy would make short shrift of it in a matter of decades? Was Christ lying? Obviously not. Was he mistaken? No. Did he miscalculate things? No, again. Christ's divinity precluded such things.

What are we left with then? Could it be that Mormons are mistaken in their interpretation of such a crucial passage? This is the only tenable conclusion. If there were no great apostasy, then there could have been no need for a restoration of religious authority on the earth. There would be no "restored gospel," and the entire premise of the Mormon church would be undercut.

The fact is that the only church with an unbroken historical line to apostolic days is the Catholic Church. Even many Protestants acknowledge this, though they argue that there was a need for the Protestant Reformation in the sixteenth century.

As non-Catholic historians admit, it can be demonstrated easily that early Church writers, such as Ignatius of Antioch, Eusebius,

Clement of Rome, and Polycarp, had no conception of Mormon doctrine, and they knew nothing of a "great apostasy."

Nowhere in their writings can one find references to Christians embracing any of the peculiarly Mormon doctrines, such as polytheism, polygamy, celestial marriage, and temple ceremonies. If the Church of the apostolic age was the prototype of today's Mormon church, it must have had all these beliefs and practices. But why is there no evidence of them in the early centuries, before the alleged apostasy began?

Church History Is Catholic

The fact is that there is no historical or archaeological indication of any kind that the early Church was other than the Catholic Church. When dealing with Mormon missionaries, remember that all the evidence is in favor of the claims of the Catholic Church. If you want to watch their sails go slack quickly, ask the missionaries to produce any historical proof to support their claim that in the early centuries the Church was Mormon. They can't do it because there is no such evidence.

The *Book of Mormon* itself suffers the same fate when it comes to its own historical support. In short, it hasn't got any.

The *Book of Mormon* describes a vast pre-Columbian culture that supposedly existed for centuries in North and South America. It goes into amazingly specific detail describing the civilizations erected by the "Nephites" and "Lamanites," who were Jews who fled Palestine in three installments, built massive cities in the New World, farmed the land, produced works of art, and fought large-scale wars that culminated in the utter destruction of the Nephites in A.D. 421. The Latter-day Saints revere the *Book of Mormon* as the divinely inspired record of those people and of Christ's appearance to them shortly after his Crucifixion in Jerusalem.

The awkward part for the Mormon church is the total lack of historical and archaeological evidence to support the *Book of Mormon*. For example, after the cataclysmic last battle fought between the Nephites and Lamanites, there was no one left to clean up the mess. Hundreds of thousands of men and beasts allegedly perished in that battle, and the ground was strewn with weapons and armor.

Keep in mind that A.D. 421 is just yesterday in archaeological terms. It should be easy to locate and retrieve copious evidence of such a battle, and there hasn't been enough time for the weapons and armor to turn to dust. The Bible tells of similar battles that have been documented by archaeology, battles that took place long before A.D. 421.

The embarrassing truth—embarrassing for Mormons, that is—is that no scientist, Mormon or otherwise, has been able to find anything to substantiate that such a great battle took place.

"Lifting" from the King James Bible

There are other problems with the *Book of Mormon*. For example, critics of Mormonism have shown convincing proof that the *Book of Mormon* is a synthesis of earlier works (written by other men), the vivid imaginings of Joseph Smith, and simple plagiarisms of the King James Bible.

The only Bible that Joseph Smith relied on was the King James Version. This translation was based on a good but imperfect set of Greek and Hebrew manuscripts of the Bible.

Scholars now know that the *Textus Receptus* contains errors, which means the King James Version contains errors. The problem for Mormons is that these exact same errors show up in the *Book of Mormon*.

It seems reasonable to assume that since Smith was a prophet of God and was translating the *Book of Mormon* under divine inspiration, he would have known about the errors found in the King James Version and would have corrected them when passages from the King James Version appeared in the *Book of Mormon*. But the errors went in.

The "Fullness" of the Gospel?

According to a standard Mormon theological work, *Doctrines of Salvation*, one finds this definition: "By fullness of the gospel is meant all the ordinances and principles that pertain to the exaltation of the celestial kingdom" (vol. 1, p. 160). That's an official Mormon statement on the subject. But there's a problem.

If the *Book of Mormon* contains all the ordinances and principles that pertain to the gospel, why don't Mormonism's esoteric doctrines show up in it? The doctrine that God is nothing more than an "exalted man with a body of flesh and bones" appears nowhere in the *Book of Mormon*. Nor does the doctrine of Jesus Christ being the "spirit brother" of Lucifer. Nor do the doctrines that men can become gods and that God the Father has a god above him, who has a god above him, *ad infinitum*.

The Book of Mormon *Is Anti-Mormon*

These heterodox teachings, and many others like them, appear nowhere in the *Book of Mormon*. In fact, pivotal Mormon doctrines are flatly refuted by the *Book of Mormon*.

For instance, the most pointed refutation of the Mormon doctrine that the Father, Son, and Holy Ghost are actually three separate gods is found in Alma 11:28–31: "Now Zeezrom said: 'Is there more than one God?' and [Amulek] answered, 'No.' And Zeezrom said unto him again, 'How knowest thou these things?' And he said: 'An angel hath made them known unto me.'"

The Bottom Line

The *Book of Mormon* fails on three main counts. First, it utterly lacks historical or archaeological support, and there is an overwhelming body of empirical evidence that refutes it. Second, the

472   THE ESSENTIAL CATHOLIC SURVIVAL GUIDE

Book of Mormon contains none of the key Mormon doctrines. This is important to note because the Latter-day Saints make such a ballyhoo about it containing the "fullness of the everlasting gospel." (It would be more accurate to say it contains almost none of their "everlasting gospel" at all.) Third, the *Book of Mormon* abounds in textual errors, factual errors, and outright plagiarisms from other works.

If you're asked by Mormon missionaries to point out examples of such errors, here are two you can use:

We read that Jesus "shall be born of Mary at Jerusalem, which is in the land of our forefathers" (Alma 7:10). But Jesus was born in Bethlehem, not Jerusalem (cf. Matt. 2:1).

If you mention this to a Mormon missionary, he might say Jerusalem and Bethlehem are only a few miles apart and that Alma could have been referring to the general area around Jerusalem. But Bethany is even closer to Jerusalem than is Bethlehem, yet the Gospels make frequent reference to Bethany as a separate town.

Another problem: Scientists have demonstrated that honeybees were first brought to the New World by Spanish explorers in the fifteenth century, but the *Book of Mormon*, in Ether 2:3, claims they were introduced around 2000 B.C.

The problem was that Joseph Smith wasn't a naturalist; he didn't know anything about bees or where and when they might be found. He saw bees in America and threw them in the *Book of Mormon* as a little local color. He didn't realize he'd get stung by them.

Tell the Mormon missionaries: "Look, it is foolish to pray about things you know are not God's will. It would be wrong of me to pray about whether adultery is right when the Bible clearly says it is not. Similarly, it would be wrong of me to pray about the *Book of Mormon* when one can so easily demonstrate that it is not the word of God."

63

Mormonism's Baptism for the Dead

The first step toward being able to go to a Mormon temple is an interview with the "ward bishop" (roughly equivalent to a parish priest). During this interview a Mormon is questioned by the bishop to see if he has been faithful in his commitment to the teachings and ordinances of the Mormon church.

The questions cover a variety of subjects, including his tithing track record; use of alcohol, tobacco, or caffeine; sexual immorality; and any failures to adhere to church doctrines and disciplines. If the applicant has had difficulties in any of these areas, he will not receive a temple recommend. For the one who does not pass the interview, there is no trip to the temple.

It is interesting to note that the majority of Mormons do not have temple recommends. This is not to say that they fail their interviews with their bishops. Actually, for a variety of reasons, most Mormons never make the effort to obtain a temple recommend. But for the minority who do obtain one, their chief duties in the temple include baptism for the dead.

On any given day, in more than fifty Mormon temples around the world, thousands of faithful Mormons are baptized vicariously for the dead. Most non-Mormons are dimly aware that the Mormons are interested in genealogy, but they are not sure why. While there is nothing wrong with being interested in genealogy as a hobby, this is far from a hobby for Mormons.

They believe people who have died can be baptized by proxy, thus allowing them the opportunity to become Mormons after their deaths. The idea behind baptism for the dead is this: God wants each of us to be with him in glory. To effect this, he allows us to accept the Mormon gospel here on earth. If we do not, he

473

474 THE ESSENTIAL CATHOLIC SURVIVAL GUIDE

sends us to a "spirit prison" until the Mormon gospel has been preached to us there and we convert.

Mormons believe that their church has missionaries in the "spirit world" who are busy spreading the Mormon gospel to dead people who have not yet received it. Should any of these dead people want to convert to Mormonism, they are required to abide by all its rules, one of which is water baptism. Hence the need for proxies to receive the corporeal waters of baptism.

You might be surprised to learn that the Mormon church has teams of men and women microfilming records of Catholic and Protestant parishes, cemetery records, birth and death certificates —virtually any sort of record pertaining to past generations. Temple Mormons hope, in time, to have all of the dead of previous generations baptized posthumously into the Mormon church.

Baptism for the Dead vs. Baptism of Desire

One reason Mormons advance the practice of baptism for the dead is a sense of justice. Billions of people have died without ever hearing the gospel of Christ and without having the chance to be baptized into his Church. How could God consign such people to damnation without giving them the chance to be saved? Surely he would give them that chance. But if they never heard the gospel in this life, when else could they hear and respond to it except in the next life?

There are a number of problems with this line of reasoning. Scripture is very clear in stating that this life is the only chance we get. Once we die, our fate is sealed: "It is appointed for men to die once, and after that comes judgment" (Heb. 9:27). There are no "second chances" after death. Consequently, God judges individuals based on their actions in this life. Since he is a just judge, he does not hold people accountable for what they did not and could not have known. Thus, those who do not hear the gospel in this life will be judged based on the knowledge they *did* have in this life. God gives his light to all people (cf. John 1:9),

and the universe itself gives evidence of God (cf. Ps. 19:1–4)—
evidence that is sufficient to establish basic moral accountability
(cf. Rom. 1:18–21). For those who are ignorant by no fault of
their own, God will not hold their ignorance against them. But
it is wrong to assume that people have no light from God unless
they hear an oral proclamation of the gospel.

If they live up to the light that has been shown to them and
would have embraced Christ and the gospel had they known about
them, then they can be saved (cf. Rom. 2:15–16). Neither is their
lack of baptism an obstacle. Scripture reveals that sometimes the
graces that normally come through baptism are given early to those
who have not yet been baptized (Acts 10:44–48). Such people have
what the Church terms "baptism of desire" and are united to God
through their desire to do what he wants of them.

In the case of those who have not yet heard the gospel or learned
of God but nevertheless seek to follow the truth as they understand it, they have an *implicit* desire for God since they desire to
follow the truth. They simply do not know that God is the truth.
Consequently, they also can be saved through baptism of desire;
therefore, a proxy baptism is superfluous, either before death or
after it. They are already united to God, even if they are not fully
aware of it in this life (cf. *Catechism of the Catholic Church* 847–848,
1257–1260).

Thus the Mormon argument from fairness is not persuasive.
There are other ways for accounting for God's justice and mercy
in dealing with those who have not heard of God and the gospel.
It is not necessary to postulate another preaching of the gospel
and second chance of repentance in the afterlife—much less the
necessity of proxy baptism for the dead—on that basis. God can
simply let whomever he wants into heaven, whether they have
water baptism or not. God is not bound by the sacraments he
himself instituted (cf. CCC 1257).

The practice of baptism of the dead, then, must stand or fall
based on the direct evidence concerning it, and that is where the
Mormon position runs into fatal problems.

The Bible Doesn't Teach It

The doctrine of baptism for the dead was first given to the Mormon church by Joseph Smith in 1836 and is found in his *Doctrine and Covenants* (but not, as we'll see, in the *Book of Mormon*).

In Paul's first epistle to the Church in Corinth, he treats a number of subjects. This letter was written to counteract problems he saw developing in Corinth after he had established the Church there. Corinth had its share of pagan religions, but there were also quasi-Christian groups that practiced variations of orthodox Christian doctrines. Enter baptism for the dead.

Mormons cite a single biblical passage to support baptizing members on behalf of dead persons: "Otherwise, what do people mean by being baptized on behalf of the dead? If the dead are not raised at all, why are people baptized on their behalf?" (1 Cor. 15:29).

Mormons infer that in 1 Corinthians, Paul speaks approvingly of living Christians receiving baptism on behalf of dead non-Christians; however, the context and construction of the verse indicate otherwise. The Greek phrase rendered by the King James Version as "for the dead" is *huper tōn nekrōn*. This phrase is as ambiguous in Greek as it is in English. The preposition *huper* has a wide semantic range and can indicate "for the sake of," "on behalf of," "over," "beyond," or "more than." Like the English preposition *for*, it does not have a single meaning and does not require the Mormon idea of being baptized *in place of* the dead. Such a reading would be unlikely given the more plausible interpretations available, and even if *huper* were taken to mean "in the place of," it doesn't mean Paul endorses the practice.

First Corinthians 15 is a key chapter for Paul's teaching on the resurrection of the body. He makes no statement on baptism for dead persons except to note that some unnamed "they" practice it. While the rest of his teaching in chapter 15 refers to "we," his Christian followers, "they" are not further identified. Who this group was may not be known with certitude today, but there are some reasonable interpretations:

1. Some commentators assume this verse refers to the practice of giving newly baptized children the names of deceased non-Christian relatives, with the hope that the dead might somehow share in the Lord's mercy.

2. Another interpretation envisions the baptism of catechumens who have witnessed the persecution and martyrdom of their Christian predecessors. With their belief that the dead do rise, the Christian candidates come forward boldly and accept both the faith and its consequences.

3. A related view holds that the group consists of those baptized in connection with a dead Christian loved one. In the first century, many families were split religiously, as only one or two members may have converted to Christianity. When it came time for these new Christians to die, they no doubt exhorted their non-Christian family members to consider the Christian faith and embrace it so that they could be together in the next world. After the deaths of their Christian loved ones, many family members no doubt *did* investigate the Christian faith and were baptized so that they could be reunited with their loved ones in the afterlife. At the time, many pagans had at best an unclear idea of what the afterlife is like, and there were a large number of sects promising immortality to those who were willing to undergo their initiation rituals. A pagan husband mourning the death of his Christian wife might thus have an unclear idea of what her religion was all about but still have it fixed in his mind: "If I want to be with her again, I need to become a Christian, like she was, so I can go where Christians go in the afterlife." This, then, could prompt him to investigate Christianity, learn its teachings about the afterlife and the resurrection, and embrace faith in Christ, receiving Christian baptism for the sake of being united with his dead loved one. The same is true, by extension, for other family relations as well, such as parents and children, grandparents and grandchildren. Even today deathbed exhortations to live the Christian life are not uncommon. People still resolve to live as Christians in order to please dead loved ones, honor their memories, and be united with them in the next life. The difference is that, today, most of those being exhorted have already been baptized.

4. Others advance the possibility that Paul was referring to the practice of a heretical cult that existed in Corinth. On this theory, Paul was not endorsing the practice of the group but merely citing it to emphasize the importance of the resurrection. Rather, his point was: If even heterodox Christians have a practice that makes no sense if there is no resurrection of the dead, how much more, then, should we orthodox Catholics believe in and hope for the resurrection of the dead.

There is no other evidence in the Bible or in the early Church Fathers' writings of baptism being practiced on the living in place of the dead. Some Mormon writers assert that some Christian commentators have discussed the possibility of a kind of "baptism for the dead" among some in the Corinthian community in Paul's time. But these commentators do not suggest that the practice was accepted or mainstream. Given the silence of Scripture and Tradition, we conclude rightly when we see this behavior as another aberration within a community of believers already soundly scolded by Paul for its lack of charity, factionalism, immorality, abuse of the Eucharist, and other matters.

Although we have no way of knowing for sure who was engaging in this practice, it is certain that Paul was not referring to orthodox Christians baptizing the dead. Catholic and Protestant scholars agree on that.

A Flat-Out Contradiction

The case against baptism for the dead is also made by the Mormon scriptures themselves. The current Mormon doctrine on baptism for the dead is quite unlike what Joseph Smith first taught. As in other cases, the *Book of Mormon* becomes an important tool for the Christian apologist. It contradicts much Mormon theology, and baptism for the dead is no exception.

In Alma 34:35–36 we read: "For behold, if ye have procrastinated the day of your repentance even until death, behold ye have become subjected to the spirit of the devil, and he does seal you his. Therefore, the spirit of the Lord has withdrawn from you and hath no place in you; the power of the devil is over you, and this is the final state of the wicked."

In other words, those who die as non-Mormons go to hell, period. There's no suggestion of a later, vicarious admission into the Mormon church.

We also see present-day Mormon doctrine contradicted in 2 Nephi 9:15: "And it shall come to pass that when all men shall have passed from this first death unto life, insomuch as they have become immortal, they must appear before the judgment seat of the Holy One of Israel, and then cometh the judgment and then must they be judged according to the holy judgment of God. For the Lord God hath spoken it, and it is his eternal word, which cannot pass away, that they who are righteous shall be righteous still, and they who are filthy shall be filthy still; wherefore, they who are filthy . . . shall go away into everlasting fire, prepared for them; and their torment is as a lake of fire and brimstone, whose flame ascendeth up forever and ever and has no end."

It is unfortunate that Smith abandoned his own, earlier doctrine. It would not have made the Mormon scriptures any more authentic, but it would have prevented millions of futile Mormon proxy baptisms from being performed.

64

Mormon Stumpers

In your discussions with Mormons, they will most often wish to direct the topics presented into those areas where they feel most informed and comfortable. Whether they are the young missionaries at your door or friends or colleagues, they have all been taught several lines of approach and have been drilled in making their points.

We suggest that you take charge of such conversations. Besides acquainting yourself with the basics of Mormon teaching (in addition, of course, to the fundamentals of the Catholic faith), consider presenting the Mormon apologist with a few "stumpers."

"We don't bash your church. Why bash ours?"

Somehow, members of the Church of Jesus Christ of Latter-day Saints have been persuaded by their leaders that they have always been on the receiving end of uncharitable comments and unjust accusations. From the time Joseph Smith began his work in 1820, the Mormon church has gloried in the "fact" that it is a persecuted people. For them, this is a sure sign that it is the Lord's true church; all opposition comes ultimately from Satan. So, if you do offer a question or criticism, be prepared for this reaction.

Many Mormons, including their hierarchy, look upon any criticism—regardless of how honest and sincere—as perverseness inspired by the Evil One. But these same individuals ignore their own past (and present) attacks on Christian churches. You might like to point out a few of these to those Mormons who say their church "never attacks other churches."

1. "I was answered that I must join none of them [Christian churches], for they were all wrong. . . . Their creeds were an abomination in [God's] sight; that those professors were all corrupt" (Joseph Smith, *History* 1:19).

2. "Orthodox Christian views of God are pagan rather than Christian" (B. H. Roberts [General Authority], *Mormon Doctrine of Deity*, 116).

3. "Are Christians ignorant? Yes, as ignorant of the things of God as the brute beast" (John Taylor [third Mormon president], *Journal of Discourses*, 13:225).

4. "The Roman Catholic, Greek, and Protestant church, is the great corrupt, ecclesiastical power, represented by great Babylon" (Orson Pratt, *Writings of an Apostle*, n. 6, 84).

5. "All the priests who adhere to the sectarian [Christian] religions of the day with all their followers, without one exception, receive their portion with the devil and his angels" (Joseph Smith, ed. *The Elders Journal*, vol. 1, n. 4, 60).

6. [Under the heading "Church of the Devil," Apostle Bruce R. McConkie lists:] "The Roman Catholic Church specifically —singled out, set apart, described, and designated as being 'most abominable above all other churches' (I Ne. 13:5)" (*Mormon Doctrine* [1958], 129).

7. "Believers in the doctrines of modern Christendom will reap damnation to their souls (Morm. 8; Moro. 8)" (McConkie, *Mormon Doctrine* [1966], 177).

Some contemporary Mormons, embarrassed—at least publicly —by McConkie's ranting, will respond with "That's only his opinion." This is disingenuous at best. Keep in mind that McConkie, who died in 1985, was raised to the level of "apostle" in the Mormon church after he had written all these things. And still today, his *Mormon Doctrine* is published by a church-owned publishing company and remains one of the church's bestsellers.

"We have no revelation on abortion."

Didn't you assume Mormons were pro-life? That's certainly the image their church attempts to broadcast, and most Mormons, in fact, mistakenly believe their church opposes abortion and regards it as an objective evil. But not so.

Indeed, the Mormon church accepts abortion for a number of reasons. *The Church Handbook of Instructions*, approved in September 1998, states that abortion may be performed in the following circumstances: A pregnancy results from rape or incest, a competent physician says the life or health of the mother is in serious jeopardy, or a competent physician says that the "fetus" has severe defects that will not allow the "baby" to survive beyond birth. In any case, the people responsible must first consult with their church leader and receive God's approval in prayer (156).

This same *Handbook*—the official policies of the Mormon church to be followed by all local church leaders throughout the world— also claims: "It is a fact that a child has life before birth. However, there is no direct revelation on when the spirit enters the body" (156). Previous teachings by former Mormon prophets referred to the unborn child as "a child," "a baby," a "human being," and decried abortion as "killing," "a grievous sin," "a damnable practice." Spencer W. Kimball, the prophet who died in 1985, taught, "We have repeatedly affirmed the position of the church in unalterably opposing all abortions" (*Teachings of Spencer W. Kimball*, 189).

It appears that this "unalterable" position, constantly "affirmed," is just another in a series of doctrinal and moral teachings that Mormons have reworded, reworked, rescinded, or reneged—though never officially renounced. Such is the quality of the Mormon belief in "continuing revelation." Don't expect dogmatic or ethical consistency. Rather, look for expediency and conformity with "the times."

A further statement in the *Handbook* says: "The church has not favored or opposed legislative proposals or public demonstrations concerning abortion" (156) While the Mormon prophet claims to speak the mind and will of God, he can neither figure out when the unborn child becomes human or if it is God's desire that we protect the unborn unconditionally.

Your Mormon friend will offer the excuse that his church leaves many decisions to the free agency (free will) of its people and that abortion is one such concern. You might point out the irony in the fact that the Mormon church has no hesitation or uncertainty in making the following declarations:

1. "The church opposes gambling in any form" (including lotteries). Members are also urged to oppose legislation and government sponsorship of any form of gambling (*Handbook*, 150).

2. "The church also opposes [correctly, of course] pornography in any form" (158).

3. "Church members are to reject all efforts to legally authorize or support same-sex unions" (158).

There is no need for a member to pray for divine guidance or seek church approval for such activities, for there will be no divine or ecclesiastical finessing of morality to permit even an occasional bingo game. A prayerful game of poker, unrepented, will bar the member from the temple and ultimate salvation; a prayerful, by-the-book abortion, unrepented, won't.

Something's wrong here.

"Only Mormons teach the true nature of God."

Because they believe the Church established by Christ 2,000 years ago fell completely away from his teachings within a century

484 THE ESSENTIAL CATHOLIC SURVIVAL GUIDE

or so of his death, Mormons argue that only a thorough "restoration" (and not a simple "reformation") of the true Church and its holy doctrines would lead man to salvation. Joseph Smith organized this "restored church" in 1830. The Church of Jesus Christ of Latter-day Saints preaches a belief central to most religions: One must know the true nature of God. "It is the first principle of the gospel to know for a certainty the character of God" (*Teachings of Joseph Smith*, 345ff.).

No Christian disputes the absolute necessity of knowing the nature of God (to the extent our reason, aided by grace, can apprehend this great mystery). Indeed, the Catholic Church and other Christian denominations have been united in a constant belief in the supreme God as almighty, eternal, and unchanging. Mormons have not been favored by similar clarity from their self-described "prophets" who receive "direct revelation" from the gods.

You may wish to ask your Mormon acquaintance to consider the following authoritative statements by their earlier and present prophets.

1. In an early book of "Scripture" brought forth by Joseph Smith, the creation account consistently refers to the singular when speaking of God and creation: "I, God, caused. . . . I, God, created. . . . I, God, saw. . . . " The singular is used fifty times in the second and third chapters of the *Book of Moses* (1831).

2. In another of Smith's earlier works, the *Book of Mormon* (1830), there are no references to a plurality of gods. At best, there is a confusion, at times, between the Father and the Son, leading at times to the extreme of modalism (one divine Person who reveals himself sometimes as the Father, sometimes as the Son) or the other extreme of "binitarianism," belief in two Persons in God. The *Book of Mormon* also makes a strong point for God's spiritual and eternal unity (see Alma 11:44 and 22:10–11, which proclaims that God is the "Great Spirit").

3. Another early work of Smith is the *Lectures on Faith* (1834–1835). There is continual evidence that the first Mormon leader

taught a form of bitheism: the Father and the Son are separate gods. The Holy Spirit is merely the "mind" of the two.

4. At about the same time, we begin to see a doctrinal shift. Smith had acquired some mummies and Egyptian papyri, and he proclaimed the writings to be those of the patriarch Abraham, in his own hand, and set out to translate the text. His *Book of Abraham* records in chapters 4 and 5 that "the gods called," "the gods ordered," and "the gods prepared" some forty-five times. Smith thus introduces the notion of a plurality of gods.

5. The clearest exposition of this departure from traditional Christian doctrine is seen in Smith's tale of a "vision" he had as a boy of fourteen. Both the Father and the Son appeared to him, he wrote; they were two separate "personages." This story of two gods was not authorized and distributed by the church until 1838, after his *Book of Abraham* had paved the way for polytheism.

6. Readers will notice that the Father is said to have appeared, along with his resurrected Son. In his final doctrinal message, Smith showed how this was possible.

In the *King Follett Discourse* (a funeral talk he gave in 1844), Joseph Smith left his church with the clearest statement to date on the nature of God:

"God himself was once as we are now, and is an exalted man, and sits enthroned in yonder heavens[.] That is the great secret. If the veil were rent today, and the great God who holds this world in its orbit, and who upholds all worlds and all things by his power, was to make himself visible—I say, if you were to see him today, you would see him like a man in form—like yourselves in all the person, image, and very form as a man. The scriptures inform us that Jesus said, 'As the Father hath power to himself, even so hath the Son power'—to do what? Why, what the Father did. The answer is obvious—in a manner to lay down his body and take it up again. Jesus, what are you going to do? To lay down my life as my Father did, and take it up again. Do you believe it? If you do not believe it, you do not believe the Bible. The scriptures say it and I defy all the learning and wisdom and all the combined powers of earth and hell together to refute it."

As the Mormon church has taught since that time, God the Father was once a man who was created by his God, was born and
lived on another earth, learned and lived the "Mormon gospel,"
died, and was eventually resurrected and made God over this universe. As such, he retains forever his flesh-and-bones body.

7. Aside from some temporary detours (Orson Pratt said the
Holy Ghost was a spiritual fluid that filled the universe; Brigham
Young taught that Adam is the god of this world), the Mormon
church has constantly taught that God the Father is a perfected
man with a physical body and parts. Right-living Mormon men
may also progress, as did the Father, and eventually become gods
themselves. In fact, the fifth president, Lorenzo Snow, summed
up the Mormon teaching thus: "As man now is, God once was; as
God now is, man may be." Snow frequently claimed this summary
of the Mormon doctrine on God and man was revealed to him
by inspiration (see Stephen E. Robinson, *Are Mormons Christian?*,
60, note 1).

8. "Thou shalt not have strange gods before me." What is
stranger than a God who starts off as a single Spirit, eternal and
all-powerful; who then becomes, perhaps, two gods in one, and
then three; who never changes, yet was once born a man, lived,
sinned, repented, and died; who was made God the Father of this
world by his own God; and who will make his own children gods
someday of their own worlds?
    That all believing Christians are shocked and disturbed by this
blasphemy may—just may—be nudging the Mormon leadership
to soften their rhetoric (if not actually change their heresy). A case
in point is an interview with the current church prophet, Gordon B. Hinckley, published in the *San Francisco Chronicle* on April
13, 1997. When asked, "Don't Mormons believe that God was
once a man?" Hinckley demurred. "I wouldn't say that. There's
a little couplet coined, 'As man is, God once was. As God is, man
may become.' Now, that's more of a couplet than anything else.
That gets into some pretty deep theology that we don't know very
much about" (3/Z1).

A surprising admission, as Hinckley seems to disparage the constant teaching of all his prophetic predecessors.

Choose, if you like, any one of these three attacks: on Christians, on the sanctity of life, on God. Ask your Mormon listener to explain the contradictions of his church. Don't be satisfied with a personal, subjective, emotional "testimony." Demand clarification of confused and contradictory teachings.

When they aren't forthcoming, be prepared to offer the truth.

65

Iglesia ni Cristo

Iglesia ni Cristo (Tagalog for "Church of Christ") claims to be the true Church established by Christ. Felix Manalo, its founder, proclaimed himself God's prophet. Many tiny sects today claim to be the true Church, and many individuals claim to be God's prophet. What makes Iglesia ni Cristo different is that it is not as tiny as the others.

Since it was founded in the Philippines in 1914, it has grown to more than 200 congregations in sixty-seven countries outside the Philippines, including an expanding United States contingent. Iglesia keeps the exact number of members secret, but it is estimated to be between 3 million and 10 million worldwide. It is larger than the Jehovah's Witnesses, a better known sect (which also claims to be Christ's true Church). Iglesia is not better known, despite its numbers, because the majority of Iglesia's members are Filipino. Virtually the only exceptions are a few non-Filipinos who have married into Iglesia families.

The organization publishes two magazines, *Pasugo* and *God's Message*, which devote most of their energies toward condemning other Christian churches, especially the Catholic Church. The majority of Iglesia's members are ex-Catholics. The Philippines is the only dominantly Catholic nation in the Far East, with 84 percent of its population belonging to the Church. Since this is its largest potential source of converts, Iglesia relies on anti-Catholic scare tactics as support for its own doctrines, which cannot withstand biblical scrutiny. Iglesia tries to convince people of its doctrines not by proving they are right but by attempting to prove the Catholic Church's teachings are wrong.

Is Christ God?

The Catholic teaching that most draws Iglesia's fire is Christ's divinity. Like the Jehovah's Witnesses, Iglesia claims that Jesus Christ is not God but a created being.

Yet the Bible is clear: "In the beginning was the Word, and the Word was with God, and the Word was God" (John 1:1). We know Jesus is the Word because John 1:14 tells us, "And the Word became flesh and dwelt among us." God the Father was not made flesh; it was Jesus, as even Iglesia admits. Jesus is the Word, the Word is God, so therefore Jesus is God. Simple, yet Iglesia won't accept it.

In Deuteronomy 10:17 and 1 Timothy 6:15, God the Father is called the "Lord of lords," yet in other New Testament passages this divine title is applied directly to Jesus. In Revelation 17:14 we read, "They will make war on the Lamb, and the Lamb will conquer them, for he is Lord of lords and King of kings." And in Revelation 19:13–16, John sees Jesus "clad in a robe dipped in blood, and the name by which he is called is The Word of God. . . . On his thigh he has a name inscribed, King of kings and Lord of lords."

The fact that Jesus is God is indicated in numerous places in the New Testament. John 5:18 states that Jewish leaders sought to kill Jesus "because he not only broke the Sabbath but also called God his Father, making himself equal with God." Paul also states that Jesus was equal with God (Phil. 2:6). But if Jesus is equal with the Father, and the Father is God, then Jesus is God. Since there is only one God, Jesus and the Father must both be one God— one God in at least two Persons (the Holy Spirit, of course, is the third Person of the Trinity).

The same is shown in John 8:56–59, where Jesus directly claims to be Yahweh ("I Am"). " 'Your father Abraham rejoiced that he was to see my day; he saw it and was glad.' The Jews then said to him, 'You are not yet fifty years old, and you have seen Abraham?' Jesus said to them, 'Truly, truly, I say to you, before Abraham was, I am.' So they took up stones to throw at him; but Jesus hid himself, and went out of the temple." Jesus' audience understood *exactly* what he was claiming; that is why they picked up rocks to stone him. They considered him to be blaspheming God by claiming to be Yahweh.

The same truth is emphasized elsewhere. Paul stated that we are to live "awaiting our blessed hope, the appearing of the glory of our great God and Savior Jesus Christ" (Titus 2:13). And Peter addressed his second epistle to "those who have obtained a faith of equal standing with ours in the righteousness of our God and Savior Jesus Christ" (2 Pet. 1:1).

Jesus is shown to be God most dramatically when Thomas, finally convinced that Jesus has risen, falls down and exclaims, "My Lord and my God!" (John 20:28)—an event many in Iglesia have difficulty dealing with. When confronted with this passage in a debate with Catholic Answers founder Karl Keating, Iglesia apologist Jose Ventilacion replied with a straight face, "Thomas was wrong."

God's Messenger?

A litmus test for any religious group is the credibility of its founder in making his claims. Felix Manalo's credibility and, consequently, his claims, are impossible to take seriously. He claimed to be "God's messenger," divinely chosen to re-establish the true Church, which, according to Manalo, disappeared in the first century due to apostasy. It was his role to restore numerous doctrines that the Church had abandoned. A quick look at Manalo's background shows where these doctrines came from: Manalo stole them from other quasi-Christian religious sects.

Manalo was baptized a Catholic, but he left the Church as a teen. He became a Protestant, going through five different denominations, including the Seventh-day Adventists. Finally, Manalo started his own church in 1914. In 1919, he left the Philippines because he wanted to learn more about religion. He came to America to study with Protestants, whom Iglesia would later declare to be apostates, just like Catholics. Why, five years after being called by God to be his "last messenger," did Manalo go to the U.S. to learn from apostates? What could God's messenger learn from a group that, according to Iglesia, had departed from the true faith?

The explanation is that, contrary to his later claims, Manalo did not believe himself to be God's final messenger in 1914. He didn't use the last messenger doctrine until 1922. He appears to have adopted the messenger doctrine in response to a schism in the Iglesia movement. The schism was led by Teogilo Ora, one of its early ministers. Manalo appears to have developed the messenger doctrine to accumulate power and re-assert his leadership in the church.

This poses a problem for Iglesia, because if Manalo had been the new messenger called by God in 1914, why didn't he tell anybody prior to 1922? Because he didn't think of it until 1922. His situation in this respect parallels that of Mormonism's founder Joseph Smith, who claimed that when he was a boy, God appeared to him in a vision and told him that all existing churches were corrupt and he was not to join them, that he would lead a movement to restore God's true Church. But historical records show that Smith did join an inquirer's class at an established Protestant church *after* his supposed vision from God. It was only in later years that Smith came up with *his* version of the "true messenger" doctrine, proving as much of an embarrassment for the Mormon church as Manalo's similar doctrine does for Iglesia.

Iglesia Prophesied?

A pillar of Iglesia belief is that its emergence in the Philippines was prophesied in the Bible. This idea is supposedly found in Isaiah 43:5–6, which states, "Fear not, for I am with you; I will bring your offspring from the east, and from the west I will gather you; I will say to the north, Give up, and the south, Do not withhold;

bring my sons from afar and my daughters from the end of the earth."

Iglesia argues that in this verse, Isaiah is referring to the Far East and that this is the place where the "Church of Christ" will emerge in the last days. This point is constantly repeated in Iglesia literature: "The prophecy stated that God's children shall come from the far east" (*Pasugo*, March 1975, 6).

But the phrase "far east" is not in the text. In fact, in the Tagalog (Filipino) translation, as well as in the original Hebrew, the words *far* and *east* are not even found in the same verse, yet Iglesia recklessly combines the two verses to translate "far east." Using this fallacious technique, Iglesia claims that the Far East refers to the Philippines.

Iglesia is so determined to convince its followers of this "fact" that it quotes Isaiah 43:5 from an inexact paraphrase by Protestant Bible scholar James Moffatt that reads, "From the far east will I bring your offspring." Citing this mistranslation, one Iglesia work states, "Is it not clear that you can read the words 'far east'? Clear! Why does not the Tagalog Bible show them? That is not our fault, but that of those who translated the Tagalog Bible from English —the Catholics and Protestants" (*Isang Pagbubunyag Sa Iglesia ni Cristo*, 1964:131). Iglesia accuses everyone else of mistranslating the Bible, when it is Iglesia that is taking liberties with the original language.

The Name Game

Iglesia points to its name as proof it is the true Church. They argue, "What is the name of Christ's Church, as given in the Bible? It is the 'Church of Christ.' Our church is called the 'Church of Christ.' Therefore, ours is the Church Christ founded."

Whether or not the exact phrase "Church of Christ" appears in the Bible is irrelevant, but since Iglesia makes it an issue, it is important to note that the phrase "Church of Christ" never once appears in the Bible.

The verse Iglesia most often quotes on this issue is Romans

16:16: "Greet one another with a holy kiss. All the churches of Christ greet you" (*Pasugo*, November 1973, 6). But the phrase in this verse is "*churches* of Christ." And it's not a technical name. Paul is referring to a collection of local churches, not giving an organizational name.

To get further "proof" of its name, Iglesia cites Acts 20:28: "Take heed therefore . . . to feed the church of Christ which he has purchased with his blood" (Lamsa translation; cited in *Pasugo* [April 1978]). But the Lamsa translation is not based on the original Greek, the language in which the book of Acts was written. In Greek, the phrase is "the church of God" (*tān ekklāsian tou Theou*), not "the church of Christ" (*tān ekklāsian tou Christou*). Iglesia knows this, yet it continues to mislead its members.

Even if the phrase "church of Christ" did appear in the Bible, it would not help Iglesia's case. Before Manalo started his church, there were already groups calling themselves "the Church of Christ." There are several Protestant denominations that call themselves "Church of Christ" and use exactly the same argument. Of course, they aren't the true Church for the same reason Iglesia isn't—they were not founded by Christ.

Did Christ's Church Apostatize?

The doctrines upon which all Iglesia's other doctrines depend is its teaching that Christ's Church apostatized in the early centuries. Like Mormonism, the Jehovah's Witnesses, and other fringe groups, Iglesia asserts that the early Christian Church suffered a total apostasy. It believes in "the complete disappearance of the first-century Church of Christ and the emergence of the Catholic Church" (*Pasugo*, July-August 1979, 8).

But Jesus promised that his Church would *never* apostatize. He told Peter, "And I tell you, you are Peter, and on this rock I will build my Church, and the powers of death *shall not prevail* against it" (Matt. 16:18). If his Church had apostatized, then the gates of hell would have prevailed against it, making Christ a liar.

In other passages, Christ teaches the same truth. In Matthew 28:20 he said, "I am with you always, to the close of the age." And in John 14:16–18 he said, "And I will pray the Father, and he will give you another Counselor, to be with you *for ever*. . . . I will not leave you desolate."

If Iglesia members accept the apostasy doctrine, they make Christ a liar. Since they believe Jesus Christ is not a liar, they are ignoring what Christ promised, and their doctrine contradicts Scripture.

They are, however, fulfilling Scripture. While Jesus taught that his Church would never apostatize, the Bible does teach that there will be a great apostasy, or falling away from the Church. Paul prophesies: "[Do not be] quickly shaken in mind or excited . . . to the effect that the day of the Lord has come. Let no one deceive you in any way; for that day will not come, unless the rebellion [Greek: *apostasia*] comes first" (2 Thess. 2:2–3); "now the Spirit expressly says that in later times some will depart from the faith by giving heed to deceitful spirits and doctrines of demons" (1 Tim. 4:1); and "for the time is coming when people will not endure sound teaching, but having itching ears they will accumulate for themselves teachers to suit their own liking, and will turn away from listening to the truth and wander into myths" (2 Tim. 4:3–4). By falling away from the Church, members of Iglesia are committing precisely the kind of apostasy of which they accuse the Catholic Church.

The Bible tells us in 1 John 4:1: "Do not believe every spirit, but test the spirits to see whether they are of God; for many false prophets have gone out into the world." Was Felix Manalo a true prophet? Is his church the "true Church?" If we test the claims of Iglesia ni Cristo, the answer is apparent. His total apostasy doctrine is in flat contradiction to Christ's teaching. There is no way that Iglesia ni Cristo can be the true Church of Christ.

66

The Lost Tribes of Israel

Around 926 B.C., the kingdom of Israel split in two. Up to that point, all twelve tribes of Israel (plus the priestly tribe of Levi) had been united under the monarchies of Saul, David, and Solomon. But when Solomon's son Rehoboam ascended to the throne, the ten northern tribes rebelled and seceded from the union. This left only two tribes—Judah and Benjamin (plus much of Levi)—under the control of the king in Jerusalem. From that time on, the tribes were divided into two nations, which came to be called the House of Israel (the northern ten tribes) and the House of Judah (the southern two tribes).

This situation continued until around 723 B.C., when the Assyrians conquered the northern kingdom. To keep conquered nations in subjection, it was Assyrian policy to break them up by deporting their native populations to other areas and resettling the land with newcomers. When the House of Israel was conquered, most people belonging to the ten northern tribes were deported and settled elsewhere in the Assyrian kingdom, including places near Nineveh, Haran, and on what is now the Iran-Iraq border. They were replaced by settlers from locations in or near Babylon and Syria.

These settlers intermarried, together with the remaining Israelites, and became the Samaritans mentioned in the New Testament (a few hundred of whom still survive today). The Israelites who had been deported also intermarried with the peoples of the places where they had been resettled. They eventually lost their distinct identity, disappeared, and their culture was lost to history. Some refer to them as "the lost tribes of Israel."

A movement called "British Israelism" claims to have found the ten "lost tribes," however, and in some very unlikely places.

For many years, one of the leaders in the British Israelism movement was Herbert W. Armstrong, founder of the self-proclaimed "Worldwide Church of God." Especially for Americans, Armstrong was just about the only person they ever heard advocating British Israelism. With his own paid television program, Armstrong regularly advertised his book *The United States and Britain in Prophecy*, which advocated the view.

British Israelism was not Armstrong's only eccentric view. Among other things, he believed in Saturday rather than Sunday worship and, most seriously, he rejected the doctrine of the Trinity and claimed that individual humans could be added to the Godhead.

After Armstrong's death, the Worldwide Church of God did a serious review of the doctrines it had taught up to that point and moved to a more biblically and theologically orthodox position. Today, the organization is basically another Evangelical Protestant church (they have even been admitted to the National Association of Evangelicals), though with a few distinctive practices. Many of their congregations still worship on Saturdays, for example, but they no longer regard keeping the Jewish Sabbath and feasts as points of doctrine. They have embraced the doctrine of the Trinity, denied that created beings can become part of the Godhead, and acknowledged that other churches contain true Christians. They have also rejected the distinctive idea behind British Israelism—the claim that the lost tribes of Israel are to be specially identified with the Anglo-Saxons.

Unfortunately, there are still advocates of British Israelism out there (including some groups that split off from the Worldwide Church of God when it underwent its doctrinal renewal), and, though the book is out of print, Armstrong's *The United States and Britain in Prophecy* continues to circulate.

The United States and Britain in Prophecy teaches the notion that the lost tribes of Israel are really the descendants of Anglo-Saxons, which is to say the British and Americans of British extraction.

This exotic doctrine had been around for decades before Herbert W. Armstrong founded his church in 1933, and it appeals, nat-

THE LOST TRIBES OF ISRAEL

urally enough, to those of British heritage. After all, who wouldn't want to be a member of the "chosen race" (assuming there is one)? And according to Armstrong, that's precisely what the Anglo-Saxons are—God's chosen race, where can be found the direct descendants of King David and, even today, the true "heirs" to King David's throne.

The United States and Britain in Prophecy opens with this epigraph: "The prophecies of the Bible have been grievously misunderstood. And no wonder! For the vital key, needed to unlock prophetic doors to understanding, had become lost. That key is a definite knowledge of the true identity of the American and British peoples in biblical prophecy." Only the first sentence of this epigraph is strictly correct, and a good share of the "grievous misunderstanding" is by people who put faith in the writings of Armstrong.

The Argument Begins

"We know Bible prophecies definitely refer to Russia, Italy, Ethiopia, Libya, and Egypt of today. Could they then ignore modern nations like Britain and America? Is it reasonable?" This is how the argument begins, and notice what kind of argument it is. If these "lesser" countries are mentioned in Scripture, would it be fair for God to ignore *us*, important as we are? (We won't examine here the highly dubious premise that Russia is mentioned in Scripture.) You might call this an "appeal to pride."

Never fear, says Armstrong. "The fact is, [the British and Americans] are mentioned more often than any other race [*sic*]. Yet their prophetic identity has remained hidden to the many." Why is that? Because the Bible refers to them not by their modern names but by an ancient name. And what is that name? None other than Israel.

"Hold it!" you say. The people who came from Israel are Jews. Britons and Americans, for the most part, aren't Jewish. How can one claim otherwise? Easily. Armstrong assures us that "the house of Israel is not Jewish! Those who constitute it are not Jews, and

never were! That fact we shall now see conclusively, beyond refute."

Actually, there is something of a point here. The term *Jew* originated as a way of referring to the people of the southern kingdom
of Judah, whether their own tribe was Judah, Benjamin, or Levi.
The term appears late in Israel's history—after the division into
northern and southern kingdoms—and it can be fairly claimed
that the term does not apply to the members of the ten northern
tribes, who are properly known as "Israelites" since they belonged
to the House of Israel rather than the House of Judah.

"Certainly this proves that the Jews are a different nation altogether from the House of Israel," claims Armstrong. "The Jews
of today are Judah! They call their nation 'Israel' today because
they, too, descend from the patriarch Israel or Jacob. But remember that the 'House of Israel'—the ten tribes that separated from
Judah—does not mean Jew! Whoever the lost ten tribes of Israel
are today, they are not Jews!

"By the year 721 B.C., the House of Israel was conquered and
its people were soon driven out of their own land—out of their
homes and cities—and carried captives to Assyria, near the southern shores of the Caspian Sea!" So it was in 721 B.C. that the lost
tribes got "lost."

The Year Nothing Happened

Had the tribes remained faithful to God, Armstrong explains, all
would have been well. "But, if they refused and rebelled, they
were to be punished seven times—a duration of 2,520 years—
in slavery, servitude, and want." They did rebel, and Armstrong
theorizes that their punishment extended from 721 B.C. to A.D.
1800.

And what remarkable thing happened in 1800? Well, if we don't
count the election of Thomas Jefferson to the presidency of the
United States, not a whole lot. In fact, 1800 was a pretty dull
year for history. But Armstrong disagrees, saying that from that

date, Britain and America became world powers; the former (at that time) politically, and the latter economically (and later, also politically).

According to Armstrong's scheme, the figure of "2,520 years of punishment" is arrived at by multiplying the "seven years of punishment" by 360—the number of days in the year as it was reckoned by the ancients—on the principle that each "day" of punishment really stood for a whole year of punishment. If you think this is convoluted reasoning, just wait until you read the remainder of the argument in *The United States and Britain in Prophecy*. It's enough to note here that Armstrong determines from Scripture that the lost tribes ended up on islands in the sea, and these islands are northwest of Palestine.

We're told, for example, that the forty-ninth chapter of Isaiah begins with "Listen, O isles, unto me." Do you see how this suggests the British Isles? Armstrong says, "Take a map of Europe. Lay a line due northwest of Jerusalem across the continent of Europe, until you come to the sea, and then to the islands in the sea! This line takes you direct to the British Isles!"

The skeptic might note that the line first comes to the Aegean islands, which are also in the sea—the Mediterranean Sea—but this would mean the Greeks are the lost tribes, so the theory would not play into the desires of some British or Americans to identify themselves with the lost tribes.

Linguistic Legerdemain

You want more proof? Armstrong has it. "The House of Israel," he explains, "is the 'covenant people.' The Hebrew word for 'covenant' is brit [*b'rith*]. And the word for 'covenant man,' or 'covenant people,' would therefore sound, in English word order, Brit-ish (the word *ish* means 'man' in Hebrew, and it is also an English suffix on nouns and adjectives). And so, is it mere coincidence that the true covenant people today are called the 'British'? And they reside in the 'British Isles'!"

This reasoning may impress some, but no linguist would take this seriously. The word *British* is not derived from Hebrew but from the Celtic word *Brettas*. It's significant that the Celtic *Brettas* referred to the Britons, who were inhabitants of England before the arrival of the Anglo-Saxons, whom Armstrong claims were Israelites. One possible reason for Armstrong's linguistic confusions may be that in *Webster's Dictionary* (for example, in the 3,200-page unabridged edition published in 1932—an edition Armstrong may have had access to) the entry for *b'rith* (Hebrew: "covenant") appears sandwiched between the entries for *Britannic* and *Briticism*. Perhaps he simply didn't read carefully enough and assumed, wrongly, that *b'rith* must somehow be etymologically connected with the other words before and after pertaining to things British. Neither does the common English suffix *-ish* derive from the Hebrew word for man. Instead, it derives from the Greek diminutive suffix *-iskos*.

It was bad enough to suggest that the word *British* is Hebrew, but he also made another claim: If you take the name Isaac, you see it's easy for someone to drop the *I* when speaking quickly and end up with "Saac" as the name of the patriarch. He had descendants, of course, and these may be called "Saac's sons," from which we get the word *Saxons*.

"Is it only coincidence," asks Armstrong, "that 'Saxons' sounds the same as 'Saac's sons'—sons of Isaac?" This doesn't even qualify as a coincidence, since Armstrong had to make up the nickname of "Saac" in order for the "coincidence" to exist. In reality, the term *Saxon* is derived from the Anglo-Saxon word *seax*, which means "knife" or "dagger," not the Hebrew word *Isaac* (*Yitskhaq*), which means "laughter" (cf. Gen. 17:15–19; 18:9–15).

Another Remarkable Coincidence?

Armstrong found other coincidences. When the lost tribes were scattered, he says, they "brought with them certain remarkable things, including a harp and a wonderful stone called *lia-fail*, or stone of destiny. A peculiar coincidence is that Hebrew reads from right to left, while English reads from left to right. Read this name either way—and it still is *lia-fail*. Another strange coincidence—or is it just coincidence?—is that many kings in the history of Ireland, Scotland, and England have been coronated sitting over a remarkable stone—including the present queen. The stone rests today in Westminster Abbey in London, and the coronation chair is built over and around it. A sign once beside it labeled it 'Jacob's pillar-stone.' "

Here Armstrong's argument becomes even weaker. After all, one could note that Hebrew and English are not the only languages that, when contrasted, are read in different directions. For example, Arabic is read right to left, while Gaelic is read left to right. What does that prove? Nothing! Just as Armstrong's muddled reasoning proves nothing at all about a connection between Hebrew and English. If it did, one could just as easily "prove" that the lost tribes were also responsible for bringing the Blarney Stone with them. And that's just plain blarney.

Armstrongism's Appeal

What makes Armstrong's notion so attractive to some folks? First, it appeals to their nationalistic vanity: "I'm of English descent, and now I see that I'm right in the thick of things, biblically speaking. Having English blood in my veins makes me special. It puts me above the rest of the crowd." It also perpetuates ethnic prejudice: "Thank God I'm not Italian! I never liked Italians anyway, and now I see they aren't descended from the lost tribes and so are only secondary players in the divine drama—something I always suspected."

At first glance, Armstrong's argument seems to be based on a sophisticated understanding of Scripture: "Armstrong provides lots of citations, and I can't find fault with his argument. It's so convoluted and technical it *must* be right." But, still, it's wrong, no matter how satisfying it seems to some.

67

Starting Out As an Apologist

People often ask, "How should I begin to train myself to defend my faith? How do I prepare for the inevitable knock on the door? I don't want to have to stand there open-mouthed." The best place to start your homework is the Bible. Almost every American home has one. It's either a well-worn, well-used book (if that's how it is in your home, you may skip the next several paragraphs), or it's the book with the thickest layer of dust.

Step 1. Blow off the dust.

Step 2. Open the Bible to the Gospels. Here is where you should start. St. Jerome, that wise, old Doctor of the Church, noted that a Catholic who isn't immersed in the Gospels doesn't know Christ (*Comm. in Is.*, prol.). Knowing propositions about Christ is one thing, and it's needed, but reading his words and understanding the settings is crucial. It doesn't matter in what order you take the Gospels. The easiest way is to follow the order in the text: Matthew, Mark, Luke, and John. The first three, known as the Synoptics, are much alike; they follow the same general order in the way that they present the material about Christ's life and teachings. The fourth Gospel, John's, is distinct. Beginning with Matthew, set aside a fixed amount of time each day until you get all four Gospels read. Plan to read slowly, but not too slowly. Some people take only one verse at a sitting. That's fine, if you've already gone through the Gospels a dozen times. If you're on your first reading or your fifth, you'll want to read either straight through or at least in long stretches. That way you'll get more of an overview. Later you can do the detail work. The Gospels aren't long. The New Testament itself isn't long. The Gospels comprise close to a third of the New Testament, and in most printings they run about thirty pages each—just about right for a leisurely evening. So make that your goal: one Gospel a night. In four nights you'll have them done. Then re-read them before doing anything else.

After the Gospels

Next? Try Acts, which is about the same length as each of the Gospels. Then go to the epistles: Romans, 1 Corinthians, Ephesians. Work in the other epistles gradually, and be in no rush to get to Revelation. Take it last. You can get through everything within two weeks, reading no more than thirty pages an evening. Each evening's work is about equal to a thorough reading of the daily paper, which you may be in the habit of doing anyway.

So now you're ready to do battle, right? Wrong. You've just begun. But you have begun, and that's the important thing. You've situated yourself and obtained an overview, but there's much homework to do.

Read the Catechism

Next you should read a systematic presentation of the Catholic faith. Virtually all of the Church's teachings are present, either explicitly or implicitly, in the pages of the New Testament, but they aren't organized in an easy-to-remember manner. Now that you have read the New Testament and begun to absorb its material, you need to know how to organize and interpret that material. This is something we cannot do on our own. Many sects start precisely because someone reads the Bible and interprets a particular passage in an unusual way, then makes this normative for how they read everything else in Scripture. Rather than reading the passage in the context of the whole of Scripture's teachings, they lock on to a particular passage and give it a strange interpretation. They may be unaware of the rest of what Scripture has to say on the same subject, or if they are aware of it, they may twist the rest of what Scripture says to fit their interpretation of this passage.

504   THE ESSENTIAL CATHOLIC SURVIVAL GUIDE

The apostle Peter was very concerned about this problem and addressed it in his letters. In 2 Peter 1:20–21, we find our first rule of Bible interpretation: "First of all you must understand this, that no prophecy of scripture is a matter of one's own interpretation, because no prophecy ever came by the impulse of man, but men moved by the Holy Spirit spoke from God." By *prophecy*, he simply means anything that Scripture teaches (prophecy does not always mean predicting the future). For this reason, we must avoid the temptation to evaluate passages by simply asking, "What do I think this verse means?" Christ gave the Church teachers, and he did so for a very specific reason: to assist people in how to understand Scripture and its teachings. Therefore, rather than simply looking to private interpretations, we must look to the public interpretation of Scripture, which is what the Church has. We must read Scripture in the context of what the Church has historically understood it to mean, for it was the Church that Christ established as "the pillar and bulwark of the truth" (1 Tim. 3:15).

There are significant dangers if we do not do this. The letter of Peter spoke highly of what his fellow apostle Paul had written, but he cautioned that Paul's letters can be difficult: "There are some things in them hard to understand, which the ignorant and unstable twist to their own destruction, as they do the other scriptures" (2 Pet. 3:16). So ignorant people (those who have not been taught the true interpretation of Scripture) and unstable people (those who do not adhere to the true interpretation that they have been taught) can twist Scripture to their own destruction. Strong words, indeed! Yet Scripture includes them so we would know that we must not approach Scripture as an ignorant or unstable person would do, ignoring the context of how the Church has always understood it.

This makes it important to have a thorough grasp of the Catholic faith as you read Scripture. The best way to get an overview of what the Church teaches is to read a catechism. You may already have read one while growing up, but even if you have, it never hurts to review what the Church teaches. The *Catechism of the Catholic Church* is the first universal catechism the Church has issued in four hundred years. Reading it requires some commitment, since it is seven hundred pages long, but it is well worth the effort. For those who are not able to invest that much time at once, there are many excellent shorter catechisms available too. (Contact Catholic Answers if you would like recommendations.)

Learn the Objections

Next you need to learn what kinds of objections are made against the Catholic faith. Sit down and read the right stuff. Get samples of anti-Catholic literature, by ordering it from anti-Catholic groups if necessary.

After you learn what the charges are, you need to learn the responses. Don't presume that mastering the Bible will be sufficient. It's trickier than that.

True, you'll have to make much use of the Bible in your talks with non-Catholics. (Don't swallow the argument that discussing interpretations is worthless; it can be immensely worthwhile for everyone concerned.) But, as a rule, you'll find it difficult to know just where to look for the most appropriate verse unless you've studied arguments by other Catholics, which means turning to books other than the Bible. We recommend Karl Keating's *Catholicism and Fundamentalism*, which is a full-length treatment of the disputes between Catholics and "Bible Christians."

All the major issues are discussed, and the positions of "professional anti-Catholics" are given in their own words, so you know exactly what they say to their own people. The Catholic position on each issue is proved from the Bible, early Christian writings, and plain, old common sense. Other practical books, by authors such as lay apologist Frank Sheed and Scripture scholar Fr. William Most, are also distributed by Catholic Answers.

There are also publications available to help you learn how to tackle anti-Catholic arguments. One of the best is *This Rock*. (Contact Catholic Answers to subscribe.)

After Your Homework Is Done

Let's flip a few pages on the calendar. You've read the New Testament any number of times. You've dipped into the Old Testament. You've read a catechism and learned its teachings thoroughly. You sent away for anti-Catholic literature. You have gone through Catholic books, such as *Catholicism and Fundamentalism*, with yellow marker. You "know it all," or at least you think you know enough. This is a good start to your preparation as an apologist. More study will certainly be necessary, but now the fun begins.

Today's Catchword: Divisive

If you engage in apologetics, the branch of theology that deals with how to defend the faith, sooner or later you will be brought up short by someone who says disagreeing with others about religion is "divisive." (*Divisive* seems to be the "in" word nowadays.) If you acquiesce—that is, if you give up ever mentioning differences of opinion and speak only platitudes—the result is that no mental progress is made, either for you or for others.

C. S. Lewis wrote about what he called "mere Christianity," more or less those positions on which nearly all Christians could agree. But "mere Christianity" is also incomplete Christianity, and it can be at best a way station, not a final destination, as Lewis pointed out in his book on the subject. He compared staying with "mere Christianity," with only those doctrines all Christians accept, as living perpetually in the hallway of a house rather than entering into one of its rooms, where the living is meant to be done. Even though we may have to go through a hallway to get to a room, it is the room that is our destination, not the corridor. Thus Lewis rightly declared that we have the responsibility to accept and embrace that set of particular doctrines that we find to be true upon investigation. We cannot stay in the incomplete (if ecumenically comfortable) no-man's-land of "mere Christianity."

And if that is true of "mere Christianity," it is all the truer of the "religion" upon which all people—Christians, agnostics, what have you—can agree, which, if it ever existed, would be a religion no one would be willing to die for.

The Ways to Handle Differences

Some have proposed the analogy of the world's religions being as different roads winding up a tall mountain, with God in a cloud at the top awaiting our arrival. The paths are supposedly all man-made conventions reaching to heaven, so no one religion is really any better than the others. However, this misconception overlooks one enormous truth. One religion's path was paved not by man from the bottom to the top but by God down the mountain to man. That road is Christianity, and it is arrogant to prefer a man's path to the one blazed for our sake by God himself.

The fact is that not all religions lead to God. Christianity teaches that there is one God, we have one life, and human destiny lies either in an eternal heaven or an eternal hell. Buddhism, by contrast, teaches that there is no God and that human destiny lies in reincarnating to suffer until we use the Eightfold Path to kill our individual identity. Two more different religions can scarcely be imagined. The first step in true ecumenism is to understand others as they really are, their beliefs as they really are. There are differences between the Catholic and Protestant faiths. To pretend there are not isn't ecumenical—it's just ignorant. What is true on a grand scale in inter-religious dialogue is also true in ecumenical dialogue between Christians. There are real differences that divide people, and it's vitally important that those differences be clearly understood. After all, solutions cannot be found unless the problem is clear. What is truly ecumenical is to get around the squabbles and finger pointing, which so often obscured discussions in the past, to see what commonality there is and cooperate based on that commonality, to the extent one's own principles aren't compromised. Let's admit it: There's much room for cooperation

—not infinite room, since the real differences preclude that, but still much room. This cooperation can be all the more fruitful if we have a real appreciation of one another's positions. Cooperation becomes almost impossible if we ignore differences. Fear of differences result in paralysis, not increased cooperation. This means, in the long run, that abject avoidance of "divisiveness" actually promotes present divisions, while honest and good-natured discussion of differences (and yes, of similarities) makes for fewer, not greater, divisions. The road to unity is paved with good sense, not merely good intentions.

68

The Apologist's Bookshelf

Aspiring defenders of the faith frequently contact Catholic Answers to find out which apologetical works they should read and keep as reference materials. This chapter will serve as a guide to some of the most essential books for each apologist to have on his bookshelf. The most useful, "must have" works are designated by an asterisk (*).

Many of these works are available on the Internet, but you may find it more convenient to contact the publishers directly. Any library will have a recent edition of *Books in Print*, which includes a volume on publishers, complete with addresses and telephone numbers for placing orders.

General Apologetics

Chesterton, G. K. *Everlasting Man*. San Francisco: Ignatius, 1993.

* Kreeft, Peter, and Ronald K. Tacelli. *Handbook of Christian Apologetics*. Downers Grove, Ill.: InterVarsity, 1994.

Kreeft, Peter. *Socrates Meets Jesus*. Downers Grove, Ill.: InterVarsity, 1987.

Lewis, C. S. *Miracles*. New York: Simon and Schuster Trade, 1996.

Catholic Apologetics

Butler, Scott, Norman Dahlgren, and David Hess, *Jesus, Peter, and the Keys*. Santa Barbara, Calif.: Queenship, 1996.

Drummey, James J. *Catholic Replies*. Norwood, Mass.: C. R. Publications, 1995.

Kreeft, Peter. *Fundamentals of the Faith*. San Francisco: Ignatius, 1997.

Mirus, Jeffrey, ed. *Reasons for Hope*. Front Royal, Va.: Christendom Press, 1982.

Ray, Stephen K. *Upon This Rock*. San Francisco: Ignatius, 1999.

Rumble, Leslie, and Charles M. Carty. *Radio Replies*. Rockford, Ill.: TAN, 1979.

Conversions

St. Augustine. *The Confessions*. Indianapolis, Ind.: Hackett Publishing Company, 1993.

Currie, David B. *Born Fundamentalist, Born Again Catholic*. San Francisco: Ignatius, 1996.

Madrid, Patrick, ed. *Surprised by Truth*. San Diego, Calif.: Basilica, 1995.

Ray, Stephen K. *Crossing the Tiber: Evangelical Protestants Discover the Historical Church*. San Francisco: Ignatius, 1997.

Scripture

Blomberg, Craig. *The Historical Reliability of the Gospels*. Downers Grove, Ill.: InterVarsity, 1987.

de Vaux, Roland. *Ancient Israel: Its Life and Institutions*. Grand Rapids, Mich.: W. B. Eerdmans; Livonia, Mich.: Dove Booksellers, 1997.

Fuentes, Antonio. *A Guide to the Bible*. Houston, Tex.: Lumen Christi Press, 1987.

Graham, Henry. *Where We Got the Bible: Our Debt to the Catholic Church*. San Diego, Calif.: Catholic Answers, 1997.

* *Ignatius Bible*. Revised Standard Version: Catholic Edition. San Francisco: Ignatius, 1994.

Most, William. *Free from All Error*. Libertyville, Ill.: Franciscan Marytown Press, 1985.

Shea, Mark P. *By What Authority? An Evangelical Discovers Catholic Tradition*. Huntington, Ind.: Our Sunday Visitor, 1996.

Stravinskas, Peter. *The Catholic Church and the Bible*. San Francisco: Ignatius, 1996.

Strong, James ed. *Strong's Exhaustive Concordance of the Bible*. Lake Wylie, S.C.: Christian Heritage Publishing, 1988.

Church Fathers

Aquilina, Mike. *The Fathers of the Church*. Huntington, Ind.: Our Sunday Visitor, 1999.

Eusebius. *The History of the Church*. New York: Penguin, 1989

Jurgens, William A., ed. *Faith of the Early Fathers*. Collegeville, Minn.: Liturgical Press, 1970.

* Staniforth, Maxwell, ed. *Early Christian Writings*. Harmondsworth, England: Penguin, 1968.

Church Documents

* *Catechism of the Catholic Church*. Liguori, Mo.: Liguori Publications, 1994.

Code of Canon Law. Washington, D.C.: Canon Law Society, 1983.

Flannery, Austin P., ed. *Vatican II: Conciliar and Postconciliar Documents*. Collegeville, Minn.: Liturgical Press, 1998.

Neuner, J. and J. Dupuis. *The Christian Faith in the Doctrinal Documents of the Catholic Church*. London, England: HarperCollins Religious, 1992.

Church History

* Bunson, Matthew. *Encyclopedia of Catholic History*. Huntington, Ind.: Our Sunday Visitor, 1995.

Carroll, Warren H. *A History of Christendom*. Front Royal, Va.: Christendom Press, 1987.

Vol. I: *The Founding of Christendom*. to 324 A.D..
Vol. II: *The Building of Christendom*. 324–1100.
Vol. III: *The Glory of Christendom*. 1100–1517.
Vol. IV: *The Cleaving of Christendom*. 1517–1661.

Chesterton, G. K. *Orthodoxy*. San Francisco: Ignatius, 1996.

Peters, Edward. *Inquisition*. New York: Free Press, 1988.

Wiltgen, Ralph M. *Rhine Flows into the Tiber: A History of Vatican II*. Rockford, Ill.: TAN, 1991.

Theology

Adam, Karl. *The Spirit of Catholicism*. Steubenville, Ohio: Franciscan University Press, 1996.

Keating, Karl. *What Catholics Really Believe*. San Francisco: Ignatius, 1995.

* Ott, Ludwig. *Fundamentals of Catholic Dogma*. Rockford, Ill.: TAN, 1992.

Sheed, Frank. *Theology and Sanity*. San Francisco: Ignatius, 1993.

————. *Theology for Beginners*. Ann Arbor, Mich.: Servant, 1981.

Jesus

Guardini, Romano. *The Lord*. Washington, D.C.: Regnery, 1996.

Kempis, Thomas à. *Imitation of Christ*. New York: Random House, 1998.

Sheed, Frank J. *To Know Christ Jesus*. San Francisco: Ignatius, 1997.

* Sheen, Fulton J. *Life of Christ*. New York: Doubleday, 1977.

―――. *The Seven Last Words of Christ*. New York: Alba House, 1996.

Mary and the Saints

* Father Mateo. *Refuting the Attack on Mary*. San Diego, Calif.: Catholic Answers, 1999.

Groeschel, Benedict J. *A Still Small Voice: A Practical Guide on Reported Revelations*. San Francisco: Ignatius, 1993.

Madrid, Patrick. *Any Friend of God's Is a Friend of Mine*. San Diego, Calif.: Basilica, 1996.

Newman, John Henry. *Mary, the Second Eve*. Rockford, Ill.: TAN, 1991.

―――. *Mystical Rose*. Princeton, N.J.: Scepter, 1996.

Thurston, H. and D. Attwater, eds. *Butler's Lives of the Saints*, 4 vols.. Allen, Tex.: Christian Chorus, 1996. Also available in a single abridged volume.

The Sacraments

* Akin, Jimmy. *Mass Confusion: The Do's and Don'ts of Catholic Worship*. San Diego, Calif.: Catholic Answers, 1998.

Ball, Ann. *A Handbook of Catholic Sacramentals*. Huntington, Ind.: Our Sunday Visitor, 1991.

Halligan, Nicholas. *The Sacraments and Their Celebration*. New York: Alba House, 1986.

O'Connor, James T. *The Hidden Manna: A Theology of the Eucharist*. San Francisco: Ignatius, 1998.

Peters, Edward. *100 Answers to Your Questions about Annulments*. Needham Heights, Mass.: Simon and Schuster, 1997.

Shea, Mark P. *This Is My Body: An Evangelical Discovers the Real Presence*. Front Royal, Va.: Christendom Press, 1993.

Dissenters

Clowes, Brian. *Call to Action or Call to Apostasy?*. Front Royal, Va.: Human Life International, 1997.

Hauke, Manfred. *Women in the Priesthood*. San Francisco: Ignatius Press, 1988.

Steichen, Donna. *Ungodly Rage: The Hidden Face of Catholic Feminism*. San Francisco: Ignatius, 1991.

von Hildebrand, Alice, and Peter Kreeft. *Women and the Priesthood*. Steubenville, Ohio: Franciscan University Press, 1994.

Radical Traditionalism

* Likoudis, James, and Kenneth D. Whitehead. *The Pope, the Council, and the Mass*. W. Hanover, Mass.: Christopher Publishing House, 1981.

Fundamentalism

Akin, Jimmy. *The Salvation Controversy.* San Diego, Calif.: Catholic Answers, 2001.

Howard, Thomas. *Evangelical Is Not Enough.* San Francisco: Ignatius, 1984.

* Keating, Karl. *Catholicism and Fundamentalism: The Attack on "Romanism" by "Bible Christians."* San Francisco: Ignatius, 1988.

Other Christians

Likoudis, James. *Ending the Byzantine-Greek Schism.* New Rochelle, N.Y.: Catholics United for the Faith, 1992.

* Mead, Frank. *Handbook of Denominations.* New York: Abingdon Press, 1990.

Mormonism and Jehovah's Witnesses

Bennett, Isaiah. *Inside Mormonism: What Mormons Really Believe.* San Diego, Calif.: Catholic Answers, 1999.

―――――. *When Mormons Call: Answering Mormon Missionaries at Your Door.* San Diego, Calif.: Catholic Answers, 1999.

Evert, Jason. *Answering Jehovah's Witnesses.* San Diego, Calif.: Catholic Answers, 2001.

The New Age Movement

Pacwa, Mitch. *Catholics and the New Age.* Ann Arbor, Mich.: Servant, 1992.

Robillard, Edmond. *Reincarnation: Illusion or Reality?* New York: Alba House, 1982.

World Religions

Campbell, William. *The Quran and the Bible in the Light of History and Science*. Upper Darby, Pa.: Middle Eastern Resources, 1992.

Geisler, Norman, and Abdul Saleeb. *Answering Islam*. Grand Rapids, Mich: Baker Books, 1993.

Islam: A Catholic Perspective. San Diego, Calif.: Catholic Answers, 2001.

Moral Issues

Harvey, John. *The Truth about Homosexuality*. San Francisco: Ignatius, 1996.

John Paul II, *The Gospel of Life*. New York: Times Books, 1995.

Kreeft, Peter. *The Unaborted Socrates*. Downers Grove, Ill.: Inter-Varsity, 1983.

Smith, Janet, ed. *Why* Humanae Vitae *Was Right: A Reader*. San Francisco: Ignatius, 1993.

Science

Behe, Michael. *Darwin's Black Box*. New York: Free Press, 1996.

Jaki, Stanley. *Apes, Angels, and Men*. Peru, Ill.: Sugden Sherwood and Company, 1983.

*Jaki, Stanley. *God and the Cosmologists*. Washington, D.C.: Regnery Gateway Press, 1989.

⸻. *The Savior of Science*. Washington, D.C.: Regnery Gateway Press, 1988.

⸻. *Universe and Creed*. Milwaukee, Wisc.: Marquette University Press, 1992.

Ratzinger, Joseph. *In the Beginning*. Huntington, Ind.: Our Sunday Visitor, 1990.

Spirituality

Chautard, Dom Jean-Baptiste. *The Soul of the Apostolate*. Garden City, N.Y.; Image Books, 1961.

Guardini, Romano. *The Art of Praying*. Manchester, N.H.: Sophia, 1994.

Sheen, Fulton J. *Peace of Soul*. Liguori, Mo.: Liguori Publications, 1996.

Reference

* *Catechism of the Catholic Church*. New York: Image Books, 1995.

Catholic Almanac (Huntington, Ind.: Our Sunday Visitor, 1998) (published annually).

Companion to the Catechism of the Catholic Church. San Francisco: Ignatius, 1994.

Hardon, John A. *Pocket Catholic Dictionary*. New York: Doubleday, 1985.

69

Common Catholic Prayers

Prayer, the lifting of the mind and heart to God, plays an essential role in the life of a devout Catholic. Without a life of prayer, we risk losing the life of grace in our souls, grace that comes to us first in baptism and later chiefly through the other sacraments and through prayer itself (cf. *Catechism of the Catholic Church*, 2565). Through prayer we enter into the presence of the Godhead dwelling in us. It is prayer that allows us to adore God by acknowledging his almighty power; it is prayer that allows us to bring our thanks, petitions, and sorrow for sin before our Lord and God.

While prayer is not a practice unique to Catholics, those prayers that are called "Catholic" are generally formulaic in nature. That is, the teaching Church sets before us how we ought to pray. Drawing from the words of Christ, the writings of Scripture and the saints, and the guidance of the Holy Spirit, it supplies us with prayers that are grounded in Christian Tradition. Further, our informal, spontaneous prayers, both vocal and meditative, are informed and shaped by those prayers taught by the Church, prayers that are the wellspring for the prayer life of all Catholics. Without the Holy Spirit speaking through the Church and the saints, we would not know how to pray as we ought (cf. CCC 2650).

As the prayers themselves witness, the Church teaches us that we should pray not only directly to God but also to those who are close to God, those who have the power to intercede upon our behalf. Indeed, we pray to the angels to help and watch over us; we pray to the saints in heaven to ask their intercession and assistance; we pray to the Blessed Mother to enlist her aid, to ask her to beg her Son to hear our prayers. Further, we pray not only on our own behalf but also on the behalf of those souls in purgatory and those brothers on earth who are in need. Prayer unites us to God; in doing so, we are united to the other members of the mystical body.

This communal aspect of prayer is reflected not only in the nature of Catholic prayers but also in the very words of the prayers themselves. In reading many of the basic formulaic prayers, it will become apparent that, for the Catholic, prayer is often meant to be prayed in the company of others. Christ himself encouraged us to pray together: "For where two or three are gathered in my name, there am I in the midst of them" (Matt. 18:20).

Keeping in mind the aforementioned characteristics of Catholic prayer will enable you to appreciate and to understand the prayers listed below. While this list is certainly not an exhaustive one, it will illustrate the different kinds of Catholic prayers that help to form the treasury of prayers in the Church.

Fundamental Catholic Prayers

SIGN OF THE CROSS

In the name of the Father, and of the Son, and of the Holy Spirit. Amen.

OUR FATHER

Our Father, who art in heaven, hallowed be thy name; thy kingdom come, thy will be done, on earth as it is in heaven. Give us this day our daily bread and forgive us our trespasses, as we forgive those who trespass against us, and lead us not into temptation but deliver us from evil. Amen.

HAIL MARY

Hail Mary, full of grace, the Lord is with thee. Blessed art thou among women, and blessed is the fruit of thy womb, Jesus. Holy Mary, Mother of God, pray for us sinners now and at the hour of our death. Amen.

GLORY BE

Glory be to the Father, and to the Son, and to the Holy Spirit, as it was in the beginning, is now, and ever shall be, world without end. Amen.

APOSTLES' CREED

I believe in God, the Father almighty, creator of heaven and earth, and in Jesus Christ, his only Son, our Lord, who was conceived by the Holy Spirit, born of the Virgin Mary, suffered under Pontius Pilate, was crucified, died, and was buried. He descended into hell; on the third day he rose again from the dead; he ascended into heaven and is seated at the right hand of the Father; from thence he shall come to judge the living and the dead. I believe in the Holy Spirit, the holy Catholic Church, the communion of saints, the forgiveness of sins, the resurrection of the body, and life everlasting. Amen.

Prayers to Our Lady

THE ROSARY

The six fundamental prayers listed above are also part of the Catholic rosary, a devotion dedicated to the Blessed Virgin, the Mother of God (cf. CCC 971). The rosary consists of fifteen decades. Each decade focuses upon a particular mystery in the life of Christ and his Blessed Mother. It is customary to say five decades at a time, while meditating upon one set of mysteries.

Joyful Mysteries

   I. The Annunciation
  II. The Visitation
 III. The Birth of Our Lord
  IV. The Presentation of Our Lord
   V. The Finding of Our Lord in the Temple

Sorrowful Mysteries

I. The Agony in the Garden
II. The Scourging at the Pillar
III. The Crowning with Thorns
IV. The Carrying of the Cross
V. The Crucifixion and Death of Our Lord

Glorious Mysteries

I. The Resurrection
II. The Ascension
III. The Descent of the Holy Spirit
IV. The Assumption of Our Blessed Mother into Heaven
V. The Coronation of Mary As Queen of Heaven and Earth

HAIL HOLY QUEEN

Hail, Holy Queen, Mother of mercy, our light, our sweetness, and our hope. To thee do we cry, poor banished children of Eve. To thee do we send up our sighs, mourning, and weeping in this vale of tears. Turn then, most gracious advocate, thine eyes of mercy toward us, and after this, our exile, show unto us the blessed fruit of thy womb, Jesus. O clement, O loving, O sweet Virgin Mary.

V. Pray for us, O holy Mother of God.

R. That we may be made worthy of the promises of Christ.

MEMORARE

Remember, O most gracious Virgin Mary, that never was it known that anyone who fled to thy protection, implored thy help, or sought thy intercession was left unaided. Inspired with this confidence, we turn to thee, O Virgin of virgins, our Mother. To thee we come, before thee we stand, sinful and sorrowful. O Mother of the Word Incarnate, do not despise our petitions, but in thy mercy hear and answer us. Amen.

THE ANGELUS

V. The angel of the Lord declared unto Mary.

R. And she conceived by the Holy Spirit. (Hail Mary . . .)

V. Behold the handmaid of the Lord.

R. Be it done unto me according to thy word. (Hail Mary . . .)

V. And the Word was made flesh.

R. And dwelt among us. (Hail Mary . . .)

V. Pray for us, O holy Mother of God.

R. That we may be made worthy of the promises of Christ.

Let us pray: Pour forth, we beseech thee, O Lord, thy grace into our hearts, that, we to whom the Incarnation of Christ, thy Son, was made known by the message of an angel, may, by his Passion and cross, be brought to the glory of his Resurrection, through the same Christ our Lord. Amen.

Daily Prayers

PRAYER BEFORE MEALS

Bless us O Lord, and these thy gifts, which we are about to receive, from thy bounty, through Christ, our Lord. Amen.

PRAYER TO OUR GUARDIAN ANGEL

Angel of God, my guardian dear, to whom God's love commits me here, ever this day be at my side to light and guard, to rule and guide. Amen.

MORNING OFFERING

O Jesus, through the Immaculate Heart of Mary, I offer you my prayers, works, joys, and sufferings of this day in union with the holy sacrifice of the Mass throughout the world. I offer them for all the intentions of your sacred heart: the salvation of souls, reparation for sin, the reunion of all Christians. I offer them for the intentions of our bishops and all the apostles of prayer, and in particular for those recommended by our Holy Father this month.

EVENING PRAYER

O my God, at the end of this day I thank you most heartily for all the graces I have received from you. I am sorry that I have not made a better use of them. I am sorry for all the sins I have committed against you. Forgive me, O my God, and graciously protect me this night. Blessed Virgin Mary, my dear heavenly Mother, take me under your protection. St. Joseph, my dear guardian angel, and all you saints of God, pray for me. Sweet Jesus, have pity on all poor sinners, and save them from hell. Have mercy on the suffering souls in purgatory.

Generally, this evening prayer is followed by an act of contrition, which is usually said in conjunction with an examination of conscience. A daily examination of conscience consists of a brief recounting of our actions during the day. What sins did we commit? Where did we fail? In what areas of our lives can we strive to make virtuous progress? Having determined our failures and sins, we make an act of contrition.

ACT OF CONTRITION

O my God, I am heartily sorry for having offended thee, and I detest all my sins, because I dread the loss of heaven and the pains of hell, but most of all because they offend thee, my God, who are all good and deserving of all my love. I firmly resolve, with the help of thy grace, to confess my sins, do penance, and amend my life.

Prayer after Mass

ANIMA CHRISTI

Soul of Christ, make me holy. Body of Christ, save me. Blood of Christ, fill me with love. Water from Christ's side, wash me. Passion of Christ, strengthen me. Good Jesus, hear me. Within your wounds, hide me. Never let me be parted from you. From the evil enemy, protect me. At the hour of my death, call me, and tell me to come to you that with your saints I may praise you through all eternity. Amen.

Prayers to the Holy Spirit

PRAYER TO THE HOLY SPIRIT

Breathe into me, Holy Spirit, that all my thoughts may be holy. Move in me, Holy Spirit, that my work, too, may be holy. Attract my heart, Holy Spirit, that I may love only what is holy. Strengthen me, Holy Spirit, that I may defend all that is holy. Protect me, Holy Spirit, that I always may be holy.

COME, HOLY SPIRIT

Come, O Holy Spirit, fill the hearts of your faithful and enkindle in them the fire of your love. Send forth your Spirit, and they shall be created. And you shall renew the face of the earth.

Let Us Pray: O God, who has taught the hearts of the faithful by the light of the Holy Spirit, grant that by the gift of the same Spirit we may be always truly wise and ever rejoice in his consolation, through Christ our Lord. Amen.

Prayers to the Angels and Saints

PRAYER TO ST. JOSEPH

O glorious St. Joseph, you were chosen by God to be the foster father of Jesus, the most pure spouse of Mary, ever virgin, and the head of the Holy Family. You have been chosen by Christ's vicar as the heavenly patron and protector of the Church founded by Christ.

Protect the Holy Father, our sovereign pontiff, and all bishops and priests united with him. Be the protector of all who labor for souls amid the trials and tribulations of this life, and grant that all peoples of the world may follow Christ and the Church he founded.

Dear St. Joseph, accept the offering I make to you. Be my father, protector, and guide in the way of salvation. Obtain for me purity of heart and a love for the spiritual life. After your example, let all my actions be directed to the greater glory of God, in union with the Sacred Heart of Jesus, the Immaculate Heart of Mary, and your own paternal heart. Finally, pray for me that I may share in the peace and joy of your holy death. Amen.

PRAYER TO ST. MICHAEL THE ARCHANGEL

St. Michael the Archangel, defend us in battle; be our defense against the wickedness and snares of the devil. May God rebuke him, we humbly pray, and do thou, O prince of the heavenly host, by the power of God, thrust into hell Satan and all the other evil spirits who prowl about the world seeking the ruin of souls. Amen.

70

Scriptural Reference Guide

The Catholic Church bases her teaching upon one source: The word of God. This divine revelation is transmitted in two ways: through Scripture and apostolic Tradition. Many assume that only the writings of the apostles are the word of God. However, their oral transmission of the faith is also considered the word of God (cf. 1 Thess. 2:13). Few Protestant groups today accept the validity, let alone the authority, of Tradition. In fact, many believe that Scripture is the only definitive source of divine truth. For this reason, they are critical of certain doctrines of the Catholic Church that, according to them, have no basis in Scripture. In fact, those who embrace the theory of *sola scriptura* attempt to use the Bible to contradict, to prove baseless, certain Church teachings, such as the Real Presence and the existence of purgatory. However, these teachings *are* reflected in Scripture, as the passages we will look at illustrate.

Our purpose here is not to dissect the opposition. Rather, our purpose is to provide scriptural evidence for these doctrines. Under each Catholic doctrine in the list that follows are passages from Scripture that witness to the doctrine's divine origin. For the Catholic, what follows will make clear the harmony of Scripture and Tradition: truth cannot contradict truth. Whether God speaks to us through the Bible or through the voice of Tradition, the word spoken is always a true and steadfast guide.

Please note that all scriptural citations are taken from the Revised Standard Version: Catholic Edition of the Holy Bible.

Scripture and Tradition

"I commend you because you remember me in everything and maintain the traditions even as I have delivered them to you" (1 Cor. 11:2).

"Follow the pattern of the sound words which you have heard from me, in the faith and love which are in Christ Jesus; guard the truth that has been entrusted to you by the Holy Spirit who dwells within us" (2 Tim. 1:13–14).

"So then, brethren, stand firm and hold to the traditions which you were taught by us, either by word of mouth or by letter" (2 Thess. 2:15).

"You, then, my son, be strong in the grace that is in Christ Jesus, and what you have heard from me before many witnesses entrust to faithful men who will be able to teach others also" (2 Tim. 2:1–2).

"First of all you must understand this, that no prophecy of Scripture is a matter of one's own interpretation, because no prophecy ever came by the impulse of man, but men moved by the Holy Spirit spoke from God" (2 Pet. 1:20–21).

"Though I have much to write to you, I would rather not use paper and ink, but I hope to come to see you and talk with you face to face, so that our joy may be complete" (2 John 12).

Faith and Works

"Not everyone who says to me, 'Lord, Lord,' shall enter the kingdom of heaven, but he who does the will of my Father who is in heaven" (Matt. 7:21).

"Why do you call me 'Lord, Lord,' and not do what I tell you?" (Luke 6:46).

"For he will render every man according to his works" (Rom. 2:6–8).

"For it is not the hearers of the law who are righteous before God, but the doers of the law who will be justified" (Rom. 2:13).

"For if we sin deliberately after receiving the knowledge of the truth, there no longer remains a sacrifice for sins, but a fearful prospect of judgments" (Heb. 10:26–27).

"What does it profit, my brethren, if a man says he has faith but has not works? Can his faith save him?" (Jas. 2:14).

"So faith by itself, if it has no works, is dead" (Jas. 2:17).

"But some one will say, 'You have faith and I have works.' Show me your faith apart from your works, and I by my works will show you my faith. . . . Do you want to be shown, you foolish fellow, that faith apart from works is barren?" (Jas. 2:18–20).

"You see that a man is justified by works and not by faith alone" (Jas. 2:24).

The Trinity

"Then God said, 'Let us make man in our image, after our likeness'" (Gen. 1:26).

"Go therefore and make disciples of all nations, baptizing them in the name of the Father and of the Son and of the Holy Spirit" (Matt. 28:19).

"In the beginning was the Word, and the Word was with God, and the Word was God" (John 1:1).

"But Peter said, 'Ananias, why has Satan filled your heart to lie to the Holy Spirit and to keep back part of the proceeds of the land? While it remained unsold, did it not remain your own? And after it was sold, was it not at your disposal? How is it that you have contrived this deed in your heart? You have not lied to men but to God'" (Acts 5:3–4).

"The grace of the Lord Jesus Christ and the love of God and the fellowship of the Holy Spirit be with you all" (2 Cor. 13:14).

Christ's Divinity

"For to us a child is born, to us a son is given; and the government will be upon his shoulder, and his name will be called 'Wonderful Counselor, Mighty God, Everlasting Father, Prince of Peace'" (Is. 9:6).

"Simon Peter replied, 'You are the Christ, the Son of the living God.' And Jesus answered him, 'Blessed are you, Simon Bar-Jona! For flesh and blood has not revealed this to you, but my Father who is in heaven'" (Matt. 16:16–17).

"In the beginning was the Word, and the Word was with God, and the Word was God" (John 1:1).

"Jesus said to them, 'Truly, truly, I say to you, before Abraham was, I am'" (John 8:58).

"I and the Father are one" (John 10:30).

"For in him [Christ] the whole fulness of deity dwells bodily" (Col. 2:9).

"In many and various ways God spoke of old to our fathers by the prophets; but in these last days he has spoken to us by a Son, whom he appointed the heir of all things, through whom also he created the world. He reflects the glory of God and bears the very stamp of his nature, upholding the universe by his word of power" (Heb. 1:1–3).

"But of the Son he says, 'Thy throne, O God, is for ever and ever, the righteous scepter is the scepter of thy kingdom.' . . . And, 'Thou, Lord, didst found the earth in the beginning, and the heavens are the work of thy hands' " (Heb. 1:8, 10).

Real Presence in the Eucharist

" 'Truly, truly, I say to you, he who believes has eternal life. I am the bread of life. Your fathers ate the manna in the wilderness, and they died. This is bread which comes down from heaven, that a man may eat of it and not die. I am the living bread which came down from heaven; if any one eats of this bread, he will live for ever; and the bread which I shall give for the life of the world is my flesh.' The Jews then disputed among themselves, saying, 'How can this man give us his flesh to eat?' So Jesus said to them, 'Truly truly, I say to you, unless you eat the flesh of the Son of man and drink his blood, you have no life in you; he who eats my flesh and drinks my blood has eternal life, and I will raise him up at the last day. For my flesh is food indeed, and my blood is drink indeed' " (John 6:47–55).

"For I received from the Lord what I also delivered to you, that the Lord Jesus on the night when he was betrayed took bread, and when he had given thanks, he broke it, and said, 'This is my body which is for you. Do this in remembrance of me.' In the same way also the cup, after supper, saying, 'This cup is the new covenant of my blood. Do this, as often as you drink it, in remembrance of me.' For as often as you eat this bread and drink the cup, you proclaim the Lord's death until he comes" (1 Cor. 11:23–26).

"Whoever, therefore, eats the bread or drinks the cup of the Lord in an unworthy manner will be guilty of profaning the body and blood of the Lord" (1 Cor. 11:27).

The Papacy

"And he called to him his twelve disciples and gave them authority over unclean spirits, to cast them out, and to heal every disease and every infirmity. The names of the twelve apostles are these: first, Simon, who is called Peter" (Matt. 10:1–2).

"And I tell you, you are Peter, and on this rock I will build my Church, and the powers of death shall not prevail against it. I will give you the keys of the kingdom of heaven, and whatever you bind on earth shall be bound in heaven, and whatever you loose on earth shall be loosed in heaven" (Matt. 16:18–19).

"Simon, Simon, behold Satan has demanded to have you, that he might sift you like wheat, but I have prayed for you that your faith may not fail; and when you have turned again, strengthen your brethren" (Luke 22:31–32).

"He brought him to Jesus. Jesus looked at him, and said, 'So you are Simon the son of John? You shall be called Cephas' (which means Peter)" (John 1:42).

"When they had finished breakfast, Jesus said to Simon Peter, 'Simon, son of John, do you love me more than these?' He said to him, 'Yes, Lord; you know that I love you.' He said to him, 'Feed my lambs.' A second time he said to him, 'Simon, son of John, do you love me?' He said to him, 'Yes, Lord; you know that I love you.' He said to him, 'Tend my sheep.' He said to him the third time, 'Simon, son of John, do you love me?' Peter was grieved because he said to him the third time, 'Do you love me?'

And he said to him, 'Lord, you know that I love you.' Jesus said to him, 'Feed my sheep' " (John 21:15–17).

Purgatory

"For if he were not expecting that those who had fallen would rise again, it would have been superfluous and foolish to pray for the dead. But if he was looking to the splendid reward that is laid up for those who fall asleep in godliness, it was a holy and pious thought. Therefore he made atonement for the dead, that they might be delivered from their sin" (2 Macc. 12:44–45).

"Make friends quickly with your accuser, while you are going with him to court, lest your accuser hand you over to the judge, and the judge to the guard, and you be put in prison; truly, I say to you, you will never get out till you have paid the last penny" (Matt. 5:25–26).

"Each man's work will become manifest; for the Day will disclose it, because it will be revealed with fire, and the fire will test what sort of work each one has done. If the work which any man has built on the foundation survives, he will receive a reward. If any man's work is burned up, he will suffer loss, though he himself will be saved, but only as through fire" (1 Cor. 3:13–15).

"For Christ also died for sins once for all, the righteous for the unrighteous, that he might bring us to God, being put to death in the flesh but made alive in the spirit; in which he went and preached to the spirits in prison, who formerly did not obey" (1 Pet. 3:18–20).

"But nothing unclean shall enter it [heaven]" (Rev. 21:27).

Honor Due to the Virgin Mary

"And when Elizabeth heard the greeting of Mary, the babe leaped in her womb, and Elizabeth was filled with the Holy Spirit and she exclaimed with a loud cry, 'Blessed are you among women and blessed is the fruit of your womb! And why is this granted me, that the mother of my Lord should come to me?'" (Luke 1:41–43).

"And Mary said, 'My soul magnifies the Lord, and my spirit rejoices in God my Savior, for he has regarded the low estate of his handmaiden. For behold, henceforth all generations will call me blessed; for he who is mighty has done great things for me, and holy is his name'" (Luke 1:46–49).

"If one member suffers, all suffer together; if one member is honored, all rejoice together" (1 Cor. 12:26).

Praying to the Saints

"And as for the dead being raised, have you not read in the book of Moses, in the passage about the bush, how God said to him, 'I am the God of Abraham, and the God of Isaac, and the God of Jacob'? He is not God of the dead, but of the living" (Mark 12:26–27)   .

"Therefore, since we are surrounded by so great a cloud of witnesses, let us also lay aside every weight, and sin which clings so closely" (Heb. 12:1).

"And when he had taken the scroll, the four living creatures and the twenty-four elders fell down before the Lamb, each holding a harp, and with golden bowls full of incense, which are the prayers of the saints" (Rev. 5:8).